I0419040

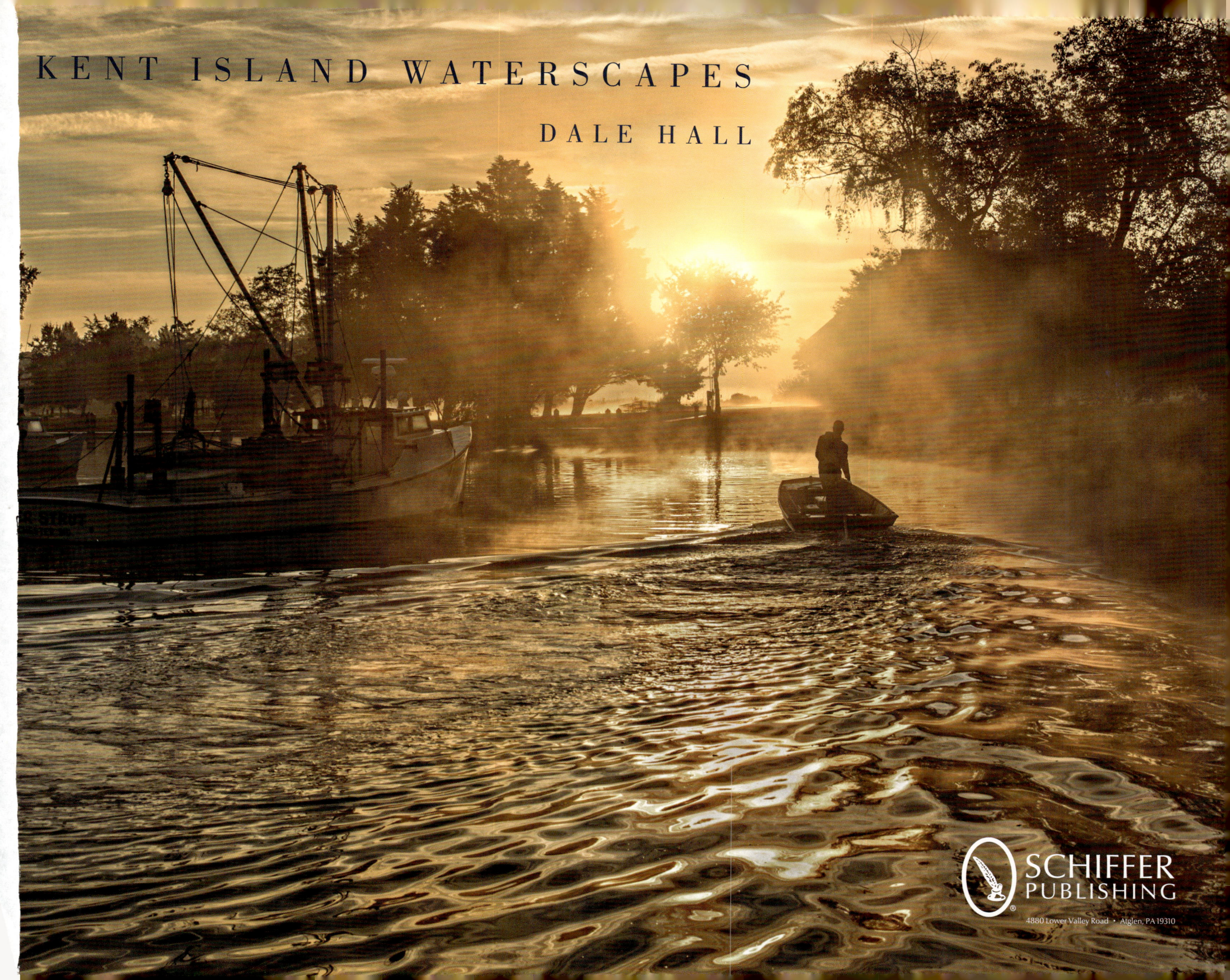

KENT ISLAND WATERSCAPES

DALE HALL

SCHIFFER PUBLISHING

4880 Lower Valley Road • Atglen, PA 19310

Other Schiffer Books on Related Subjects:

The Best of Times on the Chesapeake Bay: An Account of a Rock Hall Waterman, Robert L. Rich Jr., 978-0-7643-4277-6

Bodine's Chesapeake Bay Country, A. Aubrey Bodine, edited by Jennifer Bodine, 978-0-8703-3562-4

Copyright © 2023 by Dale Hall

Library of Congress Control Number: 2023931192

All rights reserved. No part of this work may be reproduced or used in any form or by any means—graphic, electronic, or mechanical, including photocopying or information storage and retrieval systems—without written permission from the publisher.

The scanning, uploading, and distribution of this book or any part thereof via the Internet or any other means without the permission of the publisher is illegal and punishable by law. Please purchase only authorized editions and do not participate in or encourage the electronic piracy of copyrighted materials.

"Schiffer," "Schiffer Publishing, Ltd.," and the pen and inkwell logo are registered trademarks of Schiffer Publishing, Ltd.

Cover design by Christopher Bower
Chart on p. 6 by Alan James Robinson (TheMapGuy.com)
Type set in Bodoni/Fira Sans/Helvetica

ISBN: 978-0-7643-6688-8
Printed in China

Published by Schiffer Publishing, Ltd.
4880 Lower Valley Road
Atglen, PA 19310
Phone: (610) 593-1777; Fax: (610) 593-2002
Email: info@schifferbooks.com
Web: www.schifferbooks.com

For our complete selection of fine books on this and related subjects, please visit our website at www.schifferbooks.com. You may also write for a free catalog.

Schiffer Publishing's titles are available at special discounts for bulk purchases for sales promotions or premiums. Special editions, including personalized covers, corporate imprints, and excerpts, can be created in large quantities for special needs. For more information, contact the publisher.

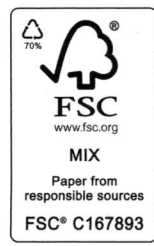

FSC
www.fsc.org
MIX
Paper from
responsible sources
FSC® C167893

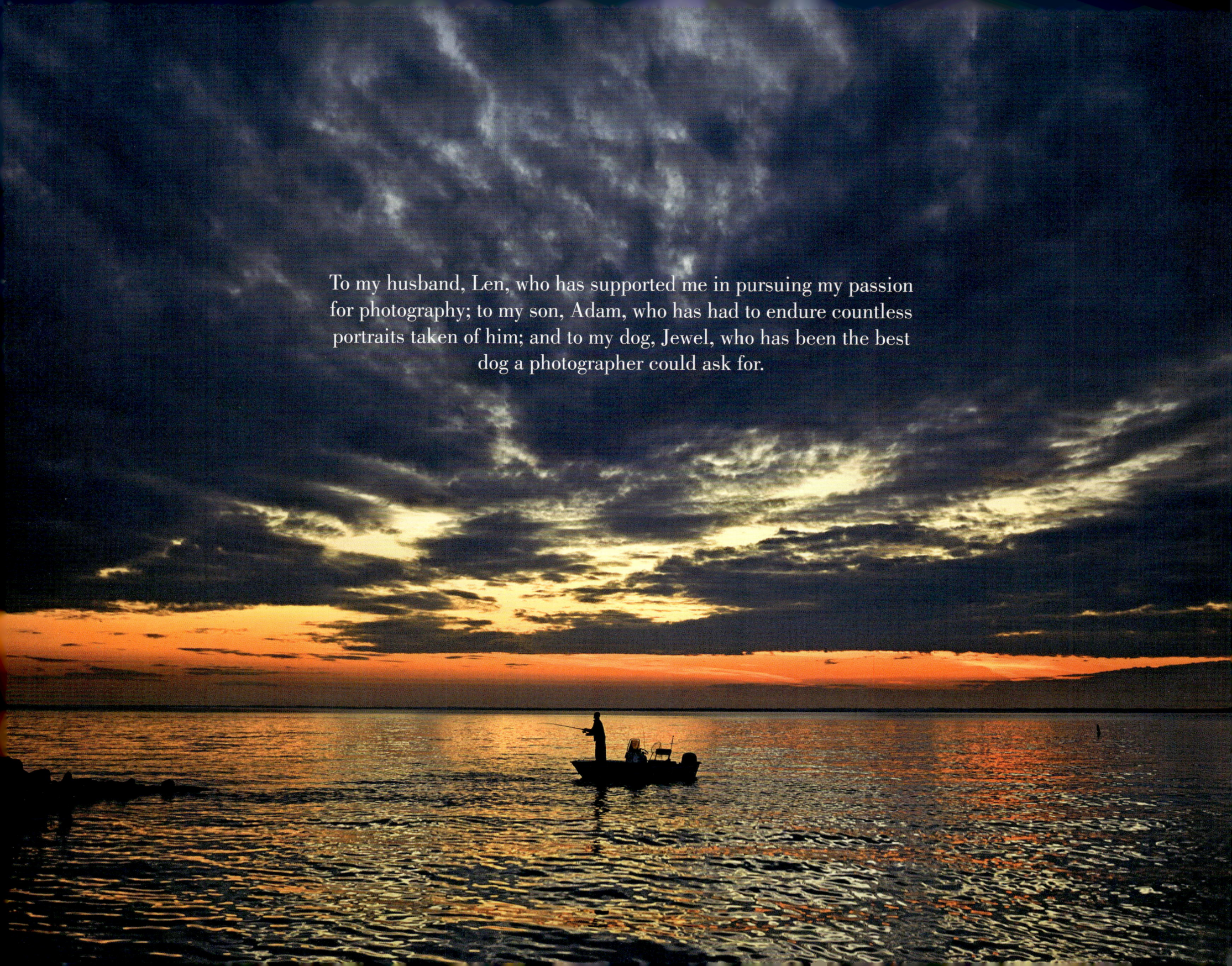

To my husband, Len, who has supported me in pursuing my passion for photography; to my son, Adam, who has had to endure countless portraits taken of him; and to my dog, Jewel, who has been the best dog a photographer could ask for.

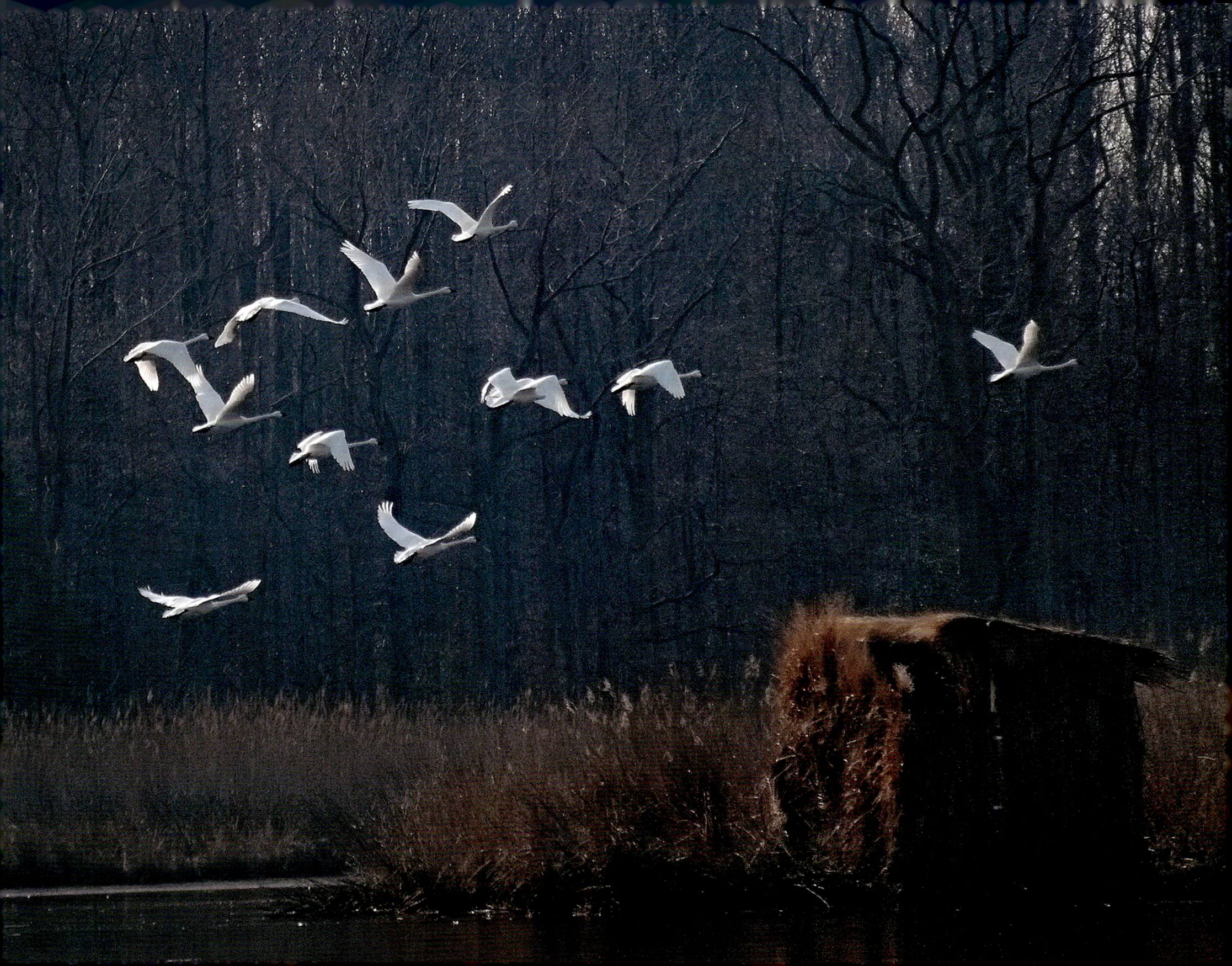

TABLE OF CONTENTS

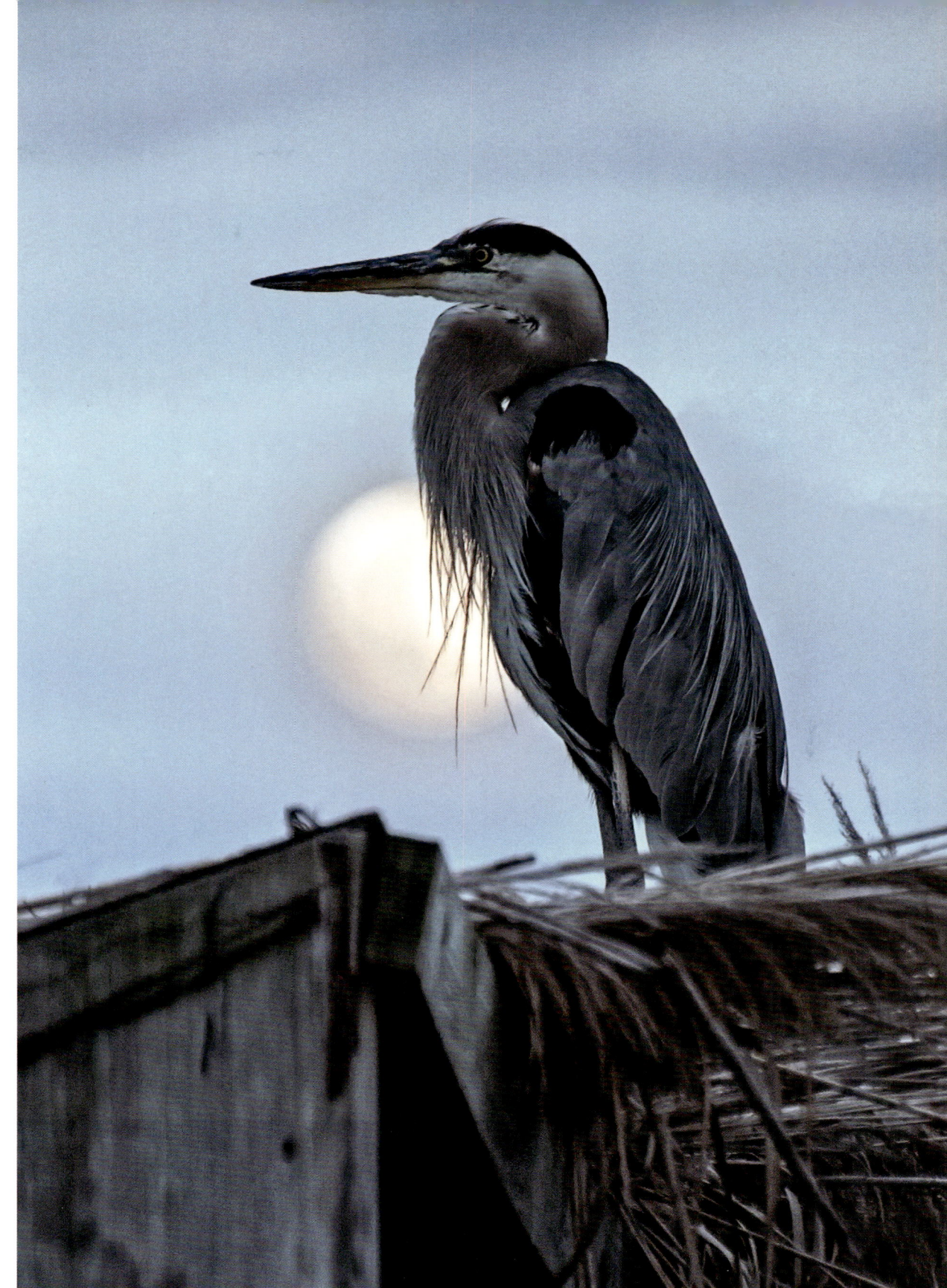

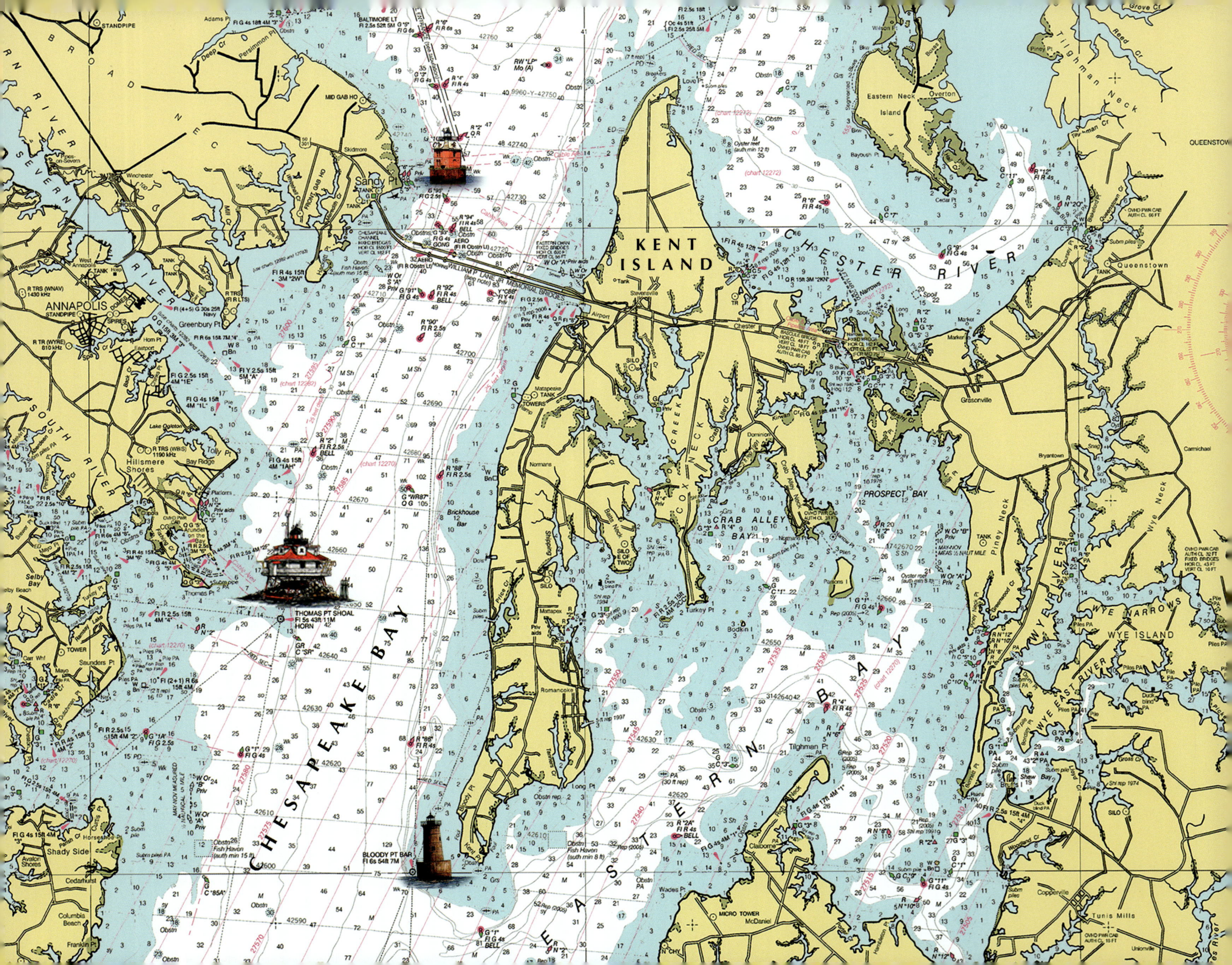

FOREWORD

Kent Island can be a magical place! Captain John Smith's famous quote about the Chesapeake Bay country, written in 1608, still rings true today: "Heaven and earth never agreed better to frame a place for man's habitation . . ." Captain William Claiborne of Jamestown agreed and thought this island was the best of the best when he decided to establish his permanent settlement here about two decades later, in 1631. He named it after his home country in England, "the Isle of Kent." That magic that Claiborne saw and felt when he and his colleagues stepped off their ships at Kent Point still exists.

The Indigenous people had shared the awe and the bounty of this special place for at least ten thousand years before that. Lord Baltimore would later claim it as part of his new Maryland Colony. The island would grow as the beginning of the new Eastern Shore, with a rich human heritage spanning nearly four centuries of human change. There were new towns, plantations, and farms connected by boats, ships, and railroads. Then there was the Bay Bridge, with all the changes that it has ushered in. But Kent Island still continues to show glimpses of that life from a time long gone. Much of that natural heritage still persists, and Dale Hall has captured it in everyday life on Kent Island. And you don't have to go very far off the Route 50 highway to see it.

Dale has an artist's eye and an uncanny sense of timing. Her photos capture the colors, the light, and the living creatures and their natural setting with a true sense of magic that is still very much a part of the island. Kent Island is blessed with a vivid change of seasons. Each season brings a new sense of wonder with its changing sky, light, weather, and wildlife—especially the birds— and the human life out on the water. Dale shares her special thoughts and her stunning images that highlight each of our changing seasons.

Most of us have had that special "Wow!" moment out in nature, that sunrise or sunset across the creek, that moonrise across the marsh, that cloud formation with that eerie light, that circling eagle with diving osprey and a flock of geese pitching in, the much-celebrated heron. Dale has filled this book with her own reflections and her own "Wow!" moments. They sure have touched my heart. Dale's photos just may spark your own next "Wow!" moment of Kent Island's timeless natural heritage.

—Jack Broderick, president, Kent Island Heritage Society

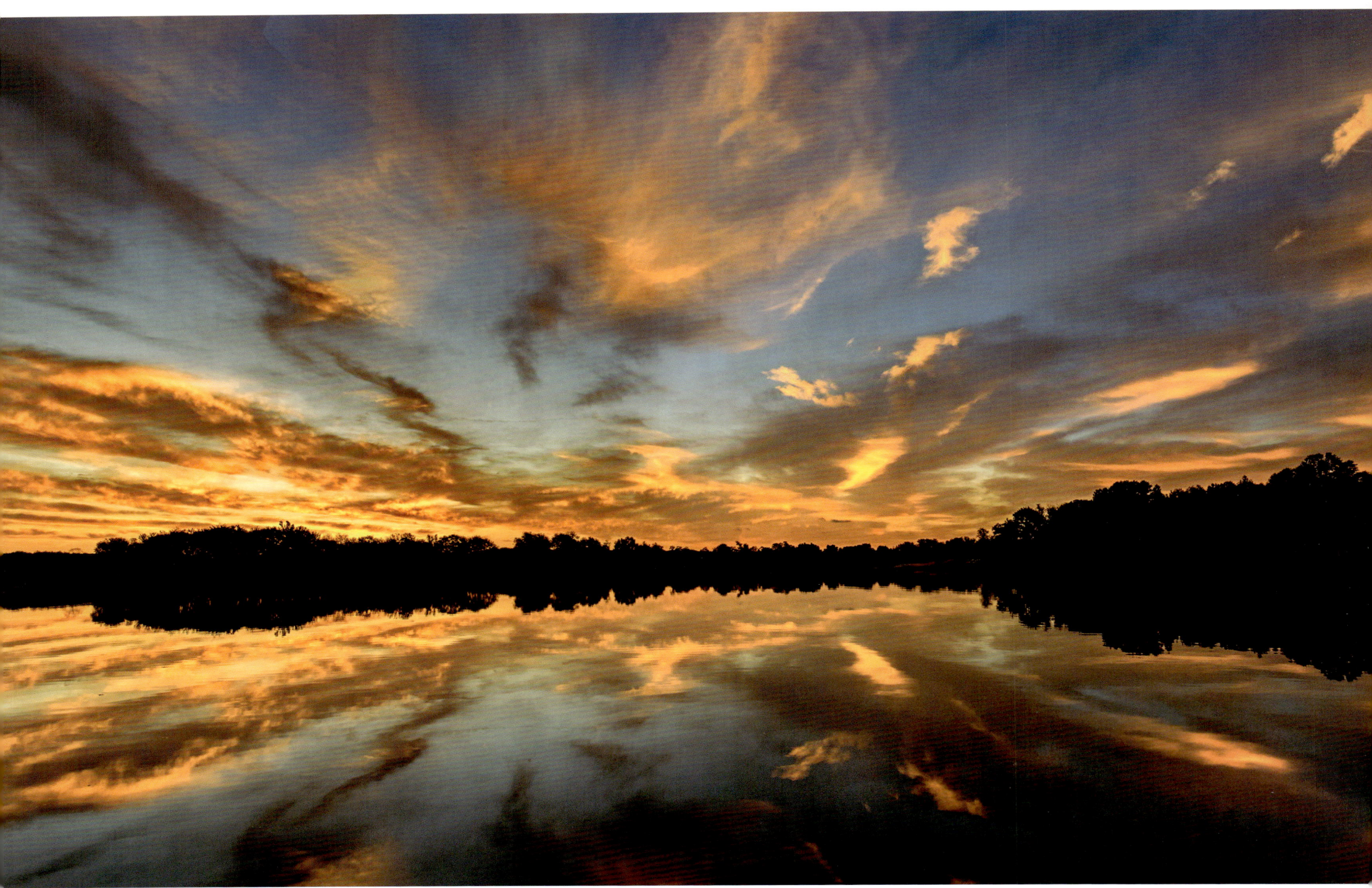

PREFACE

I fell in love with photography in my early teens and got my first single-lens reflex camera at age fifteen. The Severn River in Severna Park, Maryland, where I grew up, inspired my love of nature photography.

This book is a collection of fine-art photographs that I have captured over the past few decades, with a few editorial tidbits thrown in. My family moved to Kent Island thirty years ago, but it was not until we moved onto Price Creek a little over a decade ago that I became immersed in photographing all that Mother Nature has to offer in all four seasons. Living in such close proximity to the natural world kept me "hopping" due to all the abundant wildlife, nautical imagery, and beautiful coastal scenery. I am drawn to photographing waterscapes because being around the water feeds the soul and gives one a sense of calmness. I love trying to capture everything encompassed by life on the waterways, and I never take for granted seeing the sunrise over glassy water, with colorful clouds reflecting on the creek to create a perfect mirror image. Or when swans fly in or a cormorant pops up out of nowhere. It is almost mind-boggling to witness such things against such a beautiful "backdrop." The picturesque boats coming and going in the marinas seem to tell a story of Kent Island life carrying on as it had begun, way back when. When a waterman happens to be on his way out when I'm trying to capture the scenery, the thrill of being at the right place at the right time is like icing on the cake.

I hope you enjoy what I have been able to capture. This book has been in my head for many years, but it really started to jell about five years ago when I attended a book signing at the Kent Island Federation of Arts for Mark Hendricks's book, *Natural Wonders of Assateague Island*. I knew I had to get that book on Kent Island done. Whether you live on Kent Island or are just passing through and don't get out on the water, I hope this book will enlighten you as to what living on the shores of Kent Island truly is— besides traffic backups on the Bay Bridge.

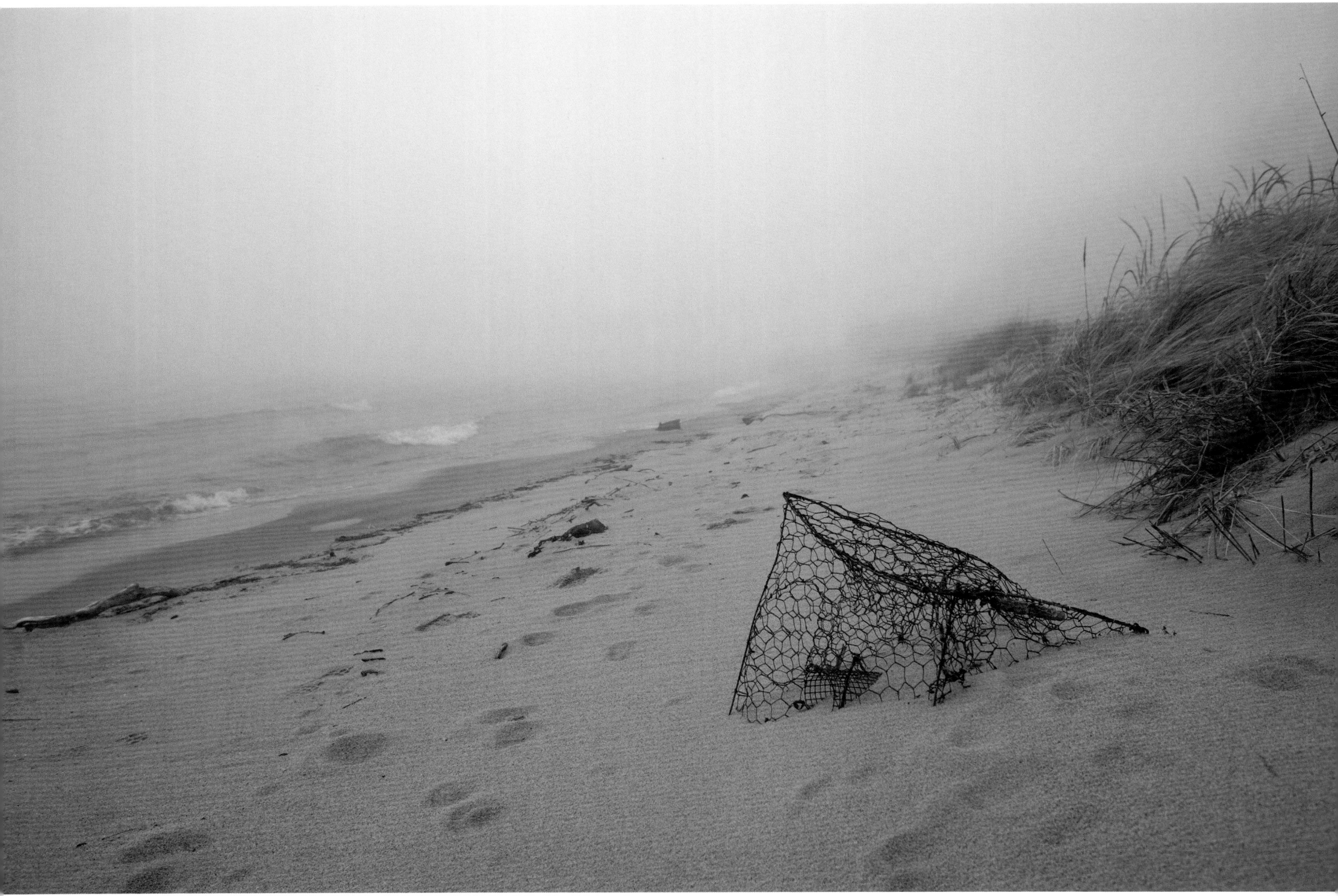

CHAPTER 1

WINTER

Winter on Kent Island can give one a sense of stillness. The Chesapeake Bay and the connecting waterways are void of the pleasure boats, so as to let one's eyes skim the vast horizon bathed in coastal light without interruption.

Working on the water in the winter can be daunting at times, but when there is little wind and golden light is reflecting off the water, the feeling can be almost ethereal. Then there are times when it seems unconscionable to even think about getting out on the bay—but work must go on . . . there are oysters to be harvested and fish to be caught. Watermen cannot be given enough praise for their hard work in all kinds of weather, diligently striving to bring in the bounty of the bay. Not only is the work needed for the watermen to support their families, but it is also vital to the local economy as well as local tourism.

Many different kinds of ducks can be seen bobbing and diving around the shores of the bay and in the creeks. Canadian geese that returned in the fall are still around. Tundra swans can be seen as it gets colder. Swans are increasing in numbers year after year. Seeing all the different kinds of birds return makes the cold weather a little more bearable.

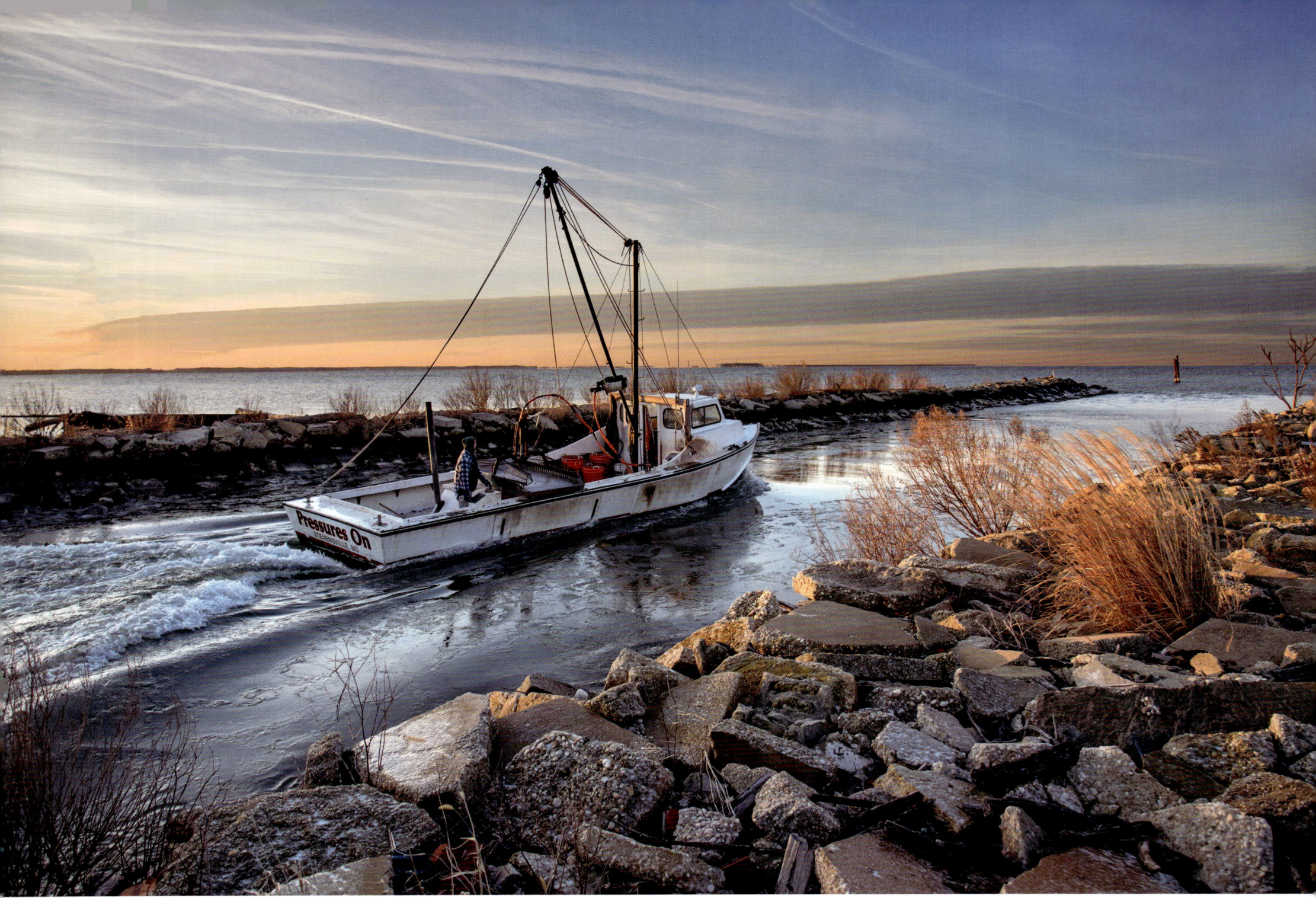

Pressure's On plows through a thin layer of ice on the inlet of Kent Point Marina, located on the southern end of Kent Island. With temperatures in the 20s inland, no doubt this day was challenging.

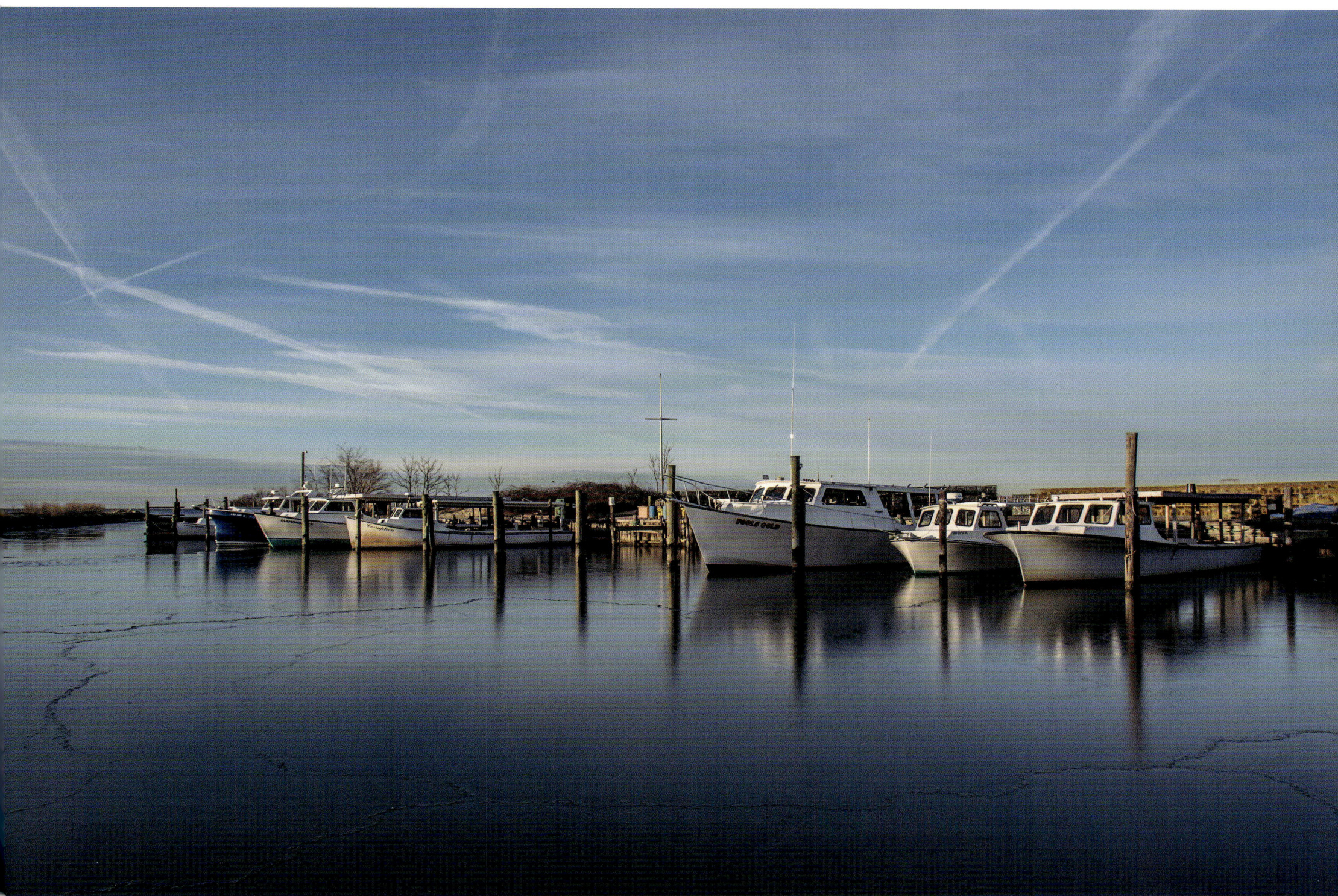

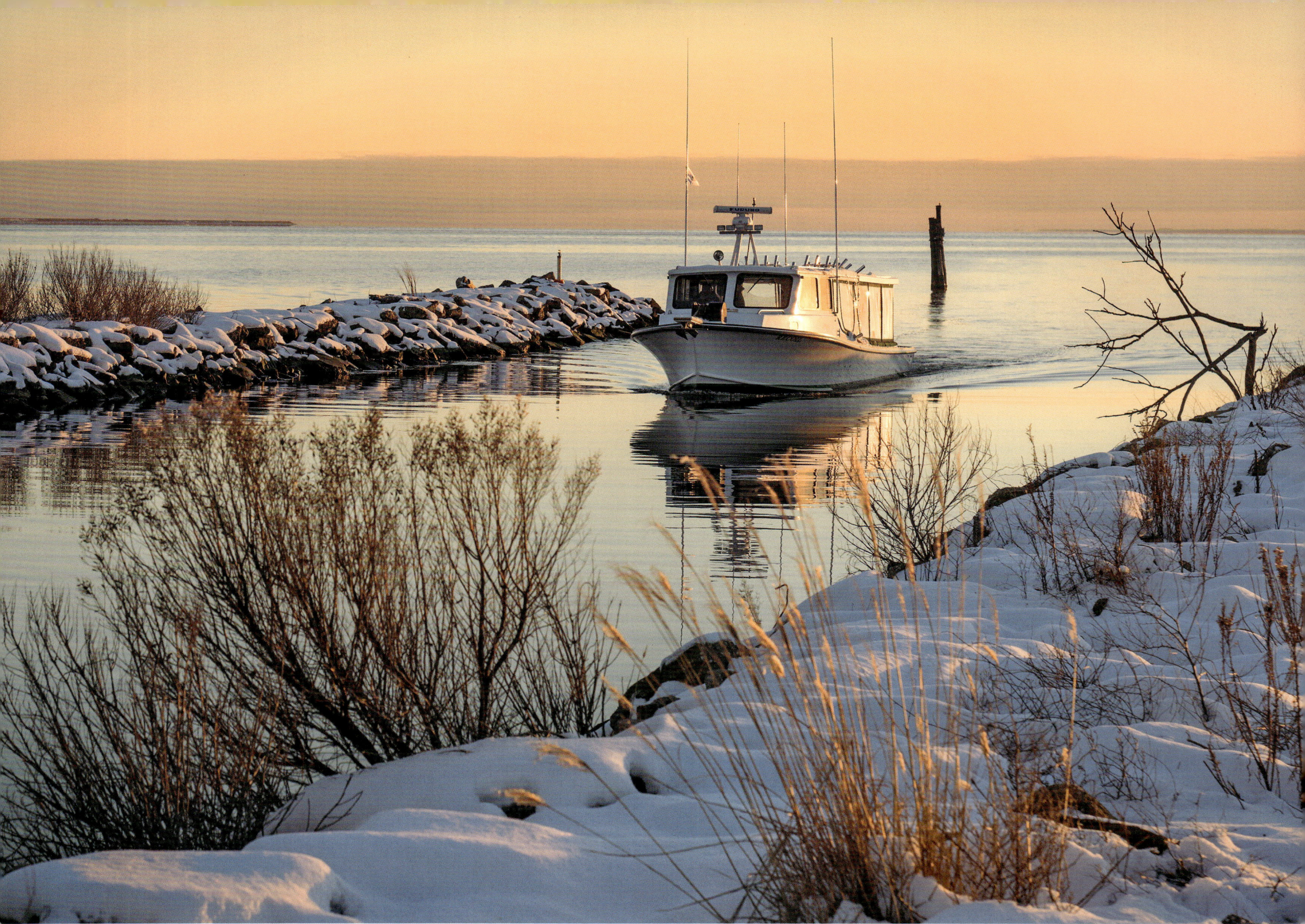

Recoil returns to Kent Point Marina after a day of gill net fishing.

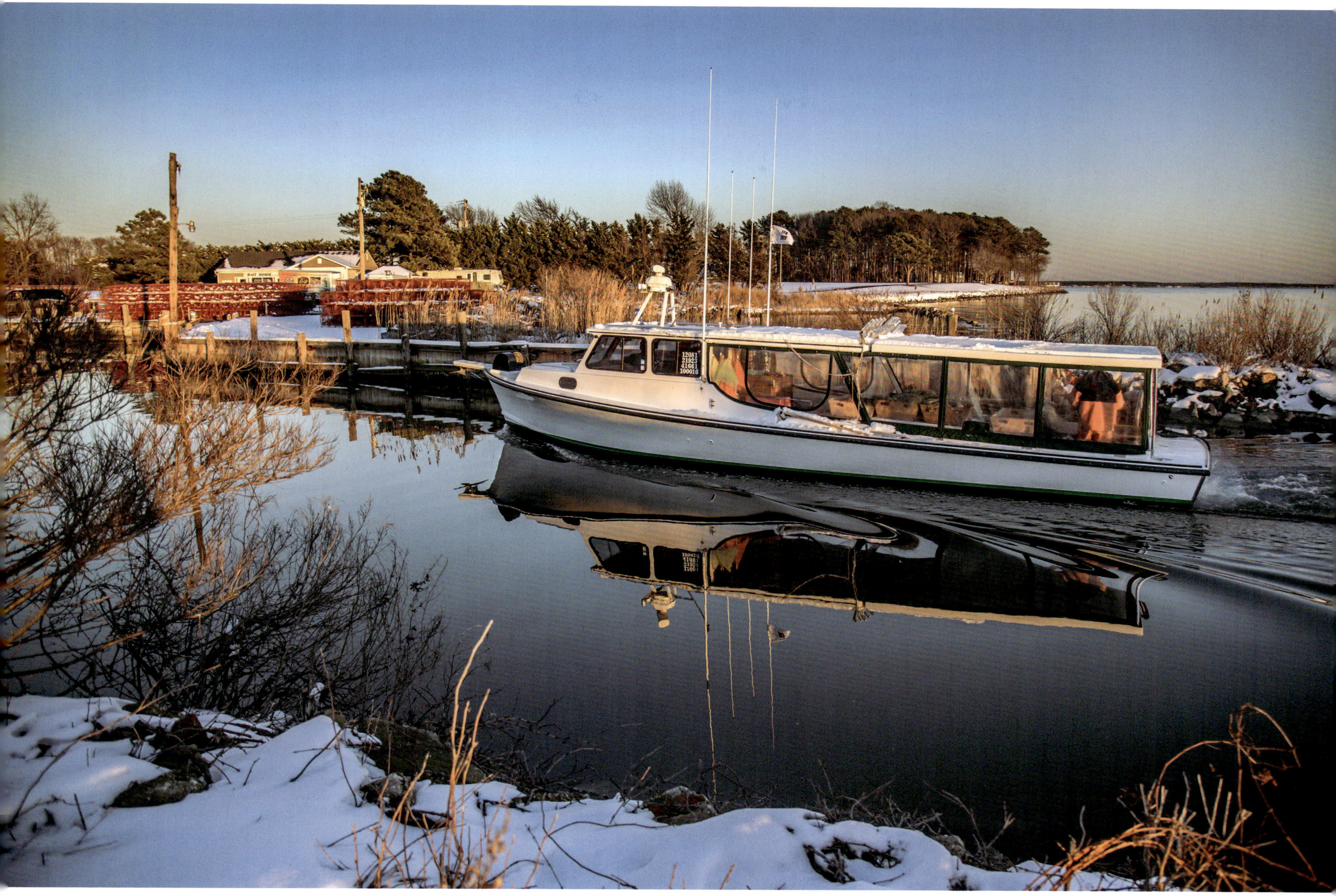

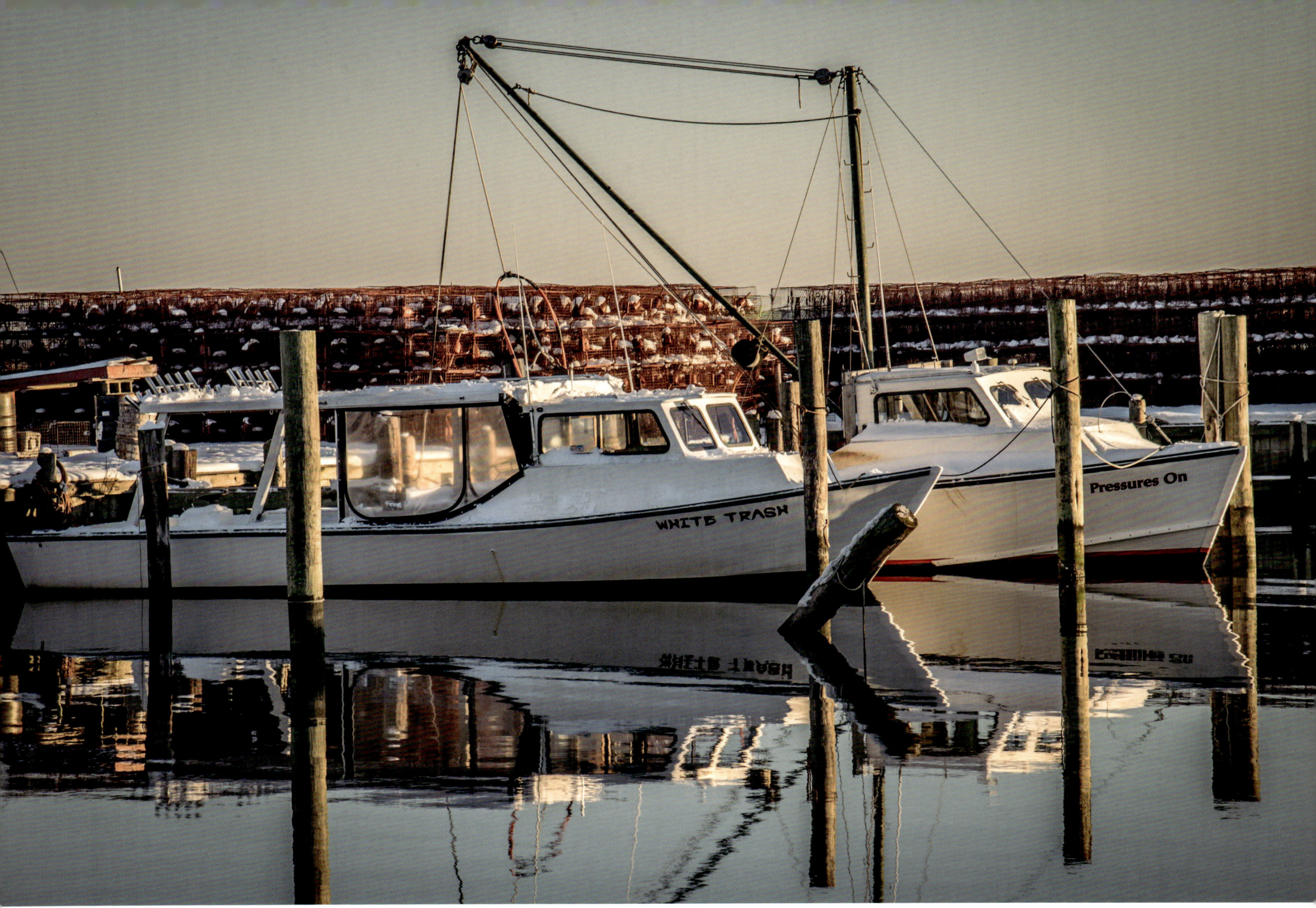

Crab pots stacked up high and snow-covered workboats mirrored in the glassy water on
a late afternoon make for a pretty winter scene.

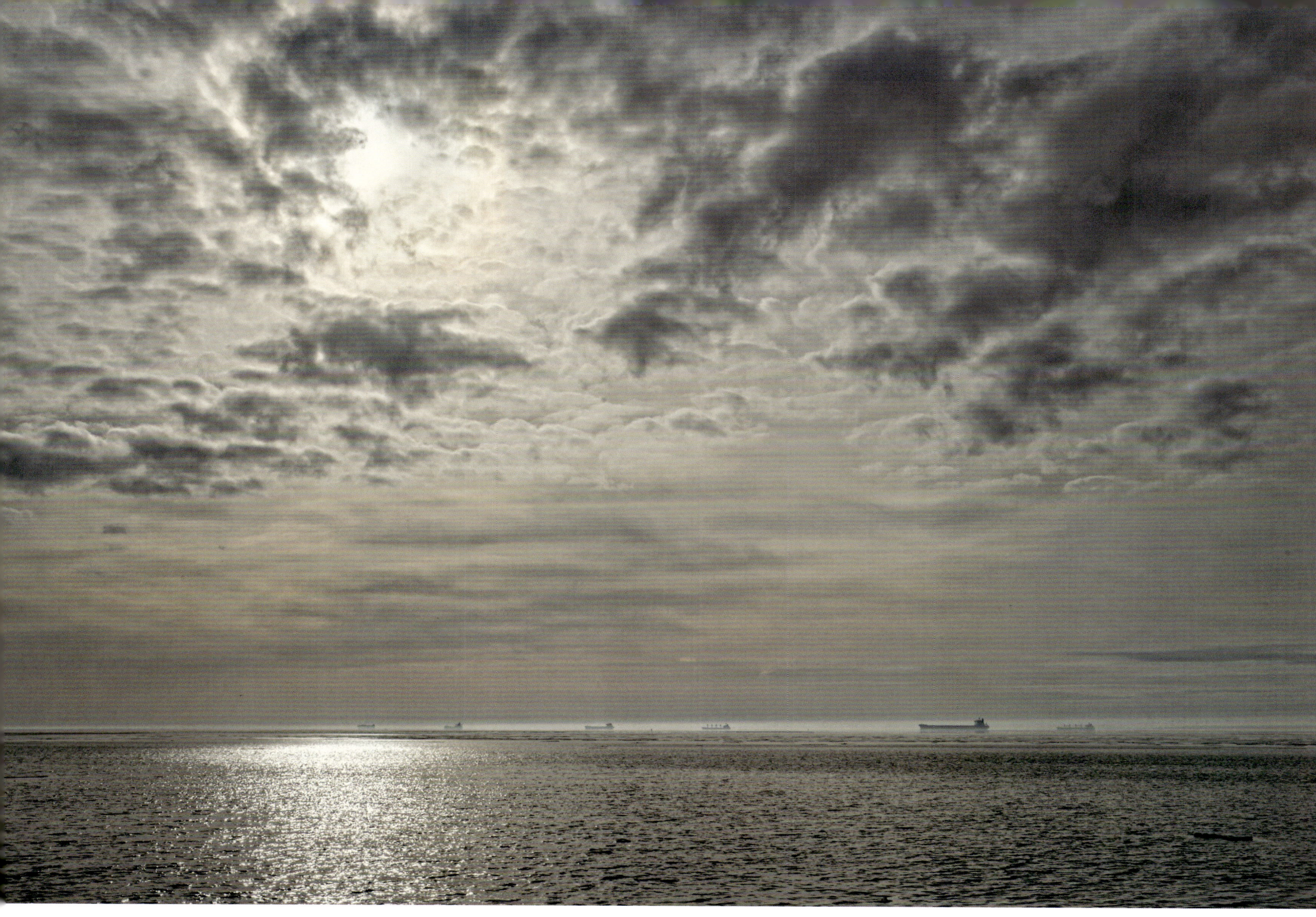

Tankers looking like ghosts in the fog—this shot from 2018 shows them lying in wait due
to the thick ice on the bay, not yet seen by icebreakers.

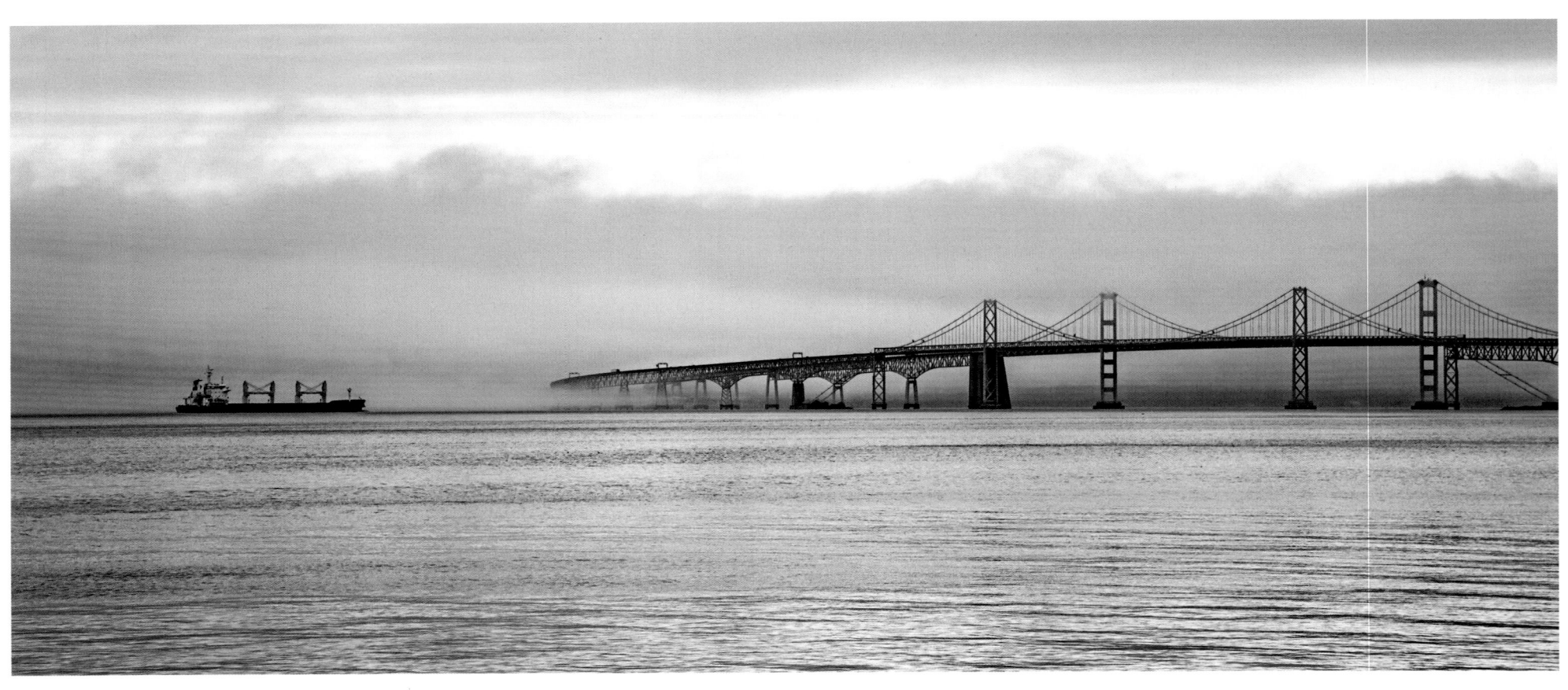

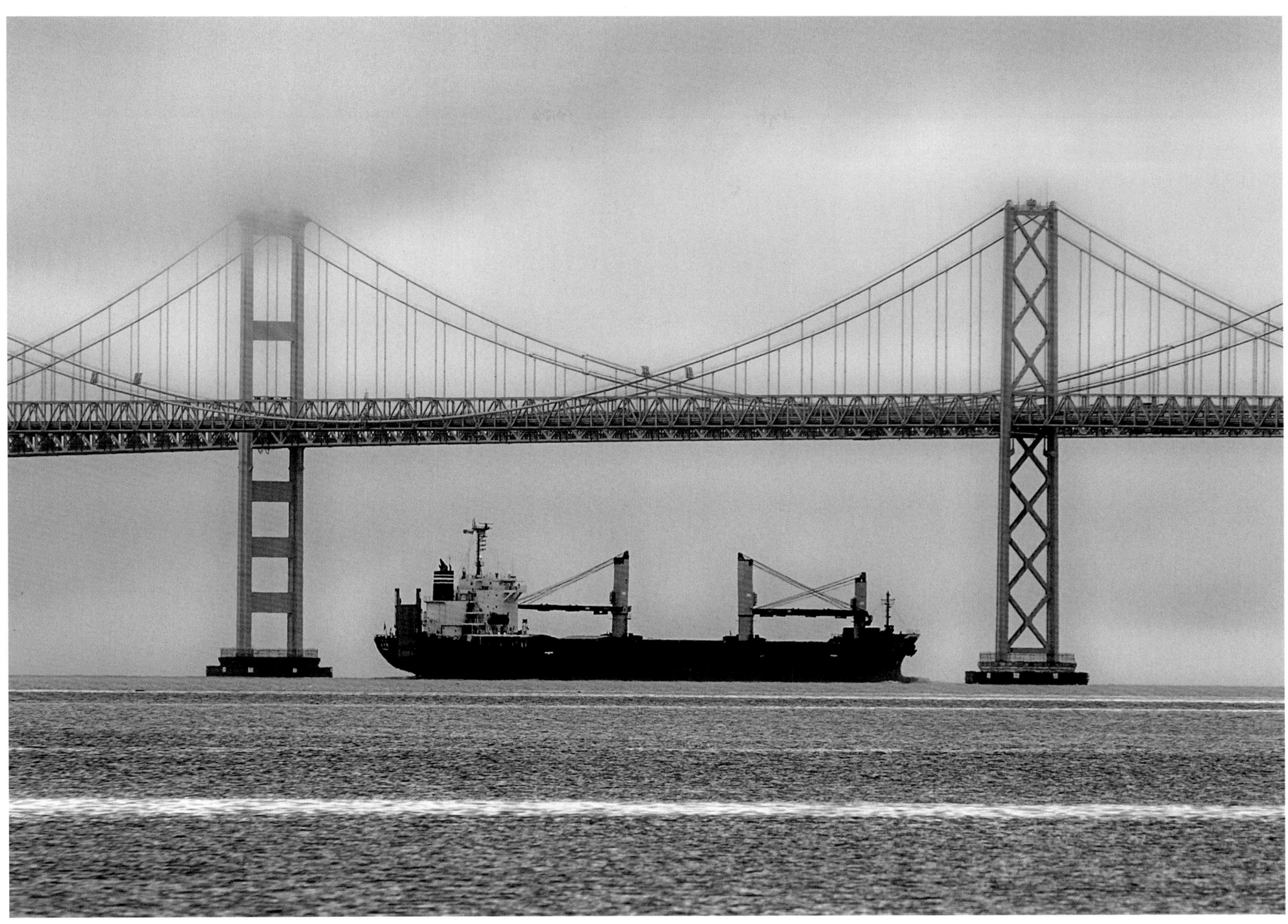

A timely capture of a vessel headed through the Chesapeake Bay Bridge
amid the hovering fog

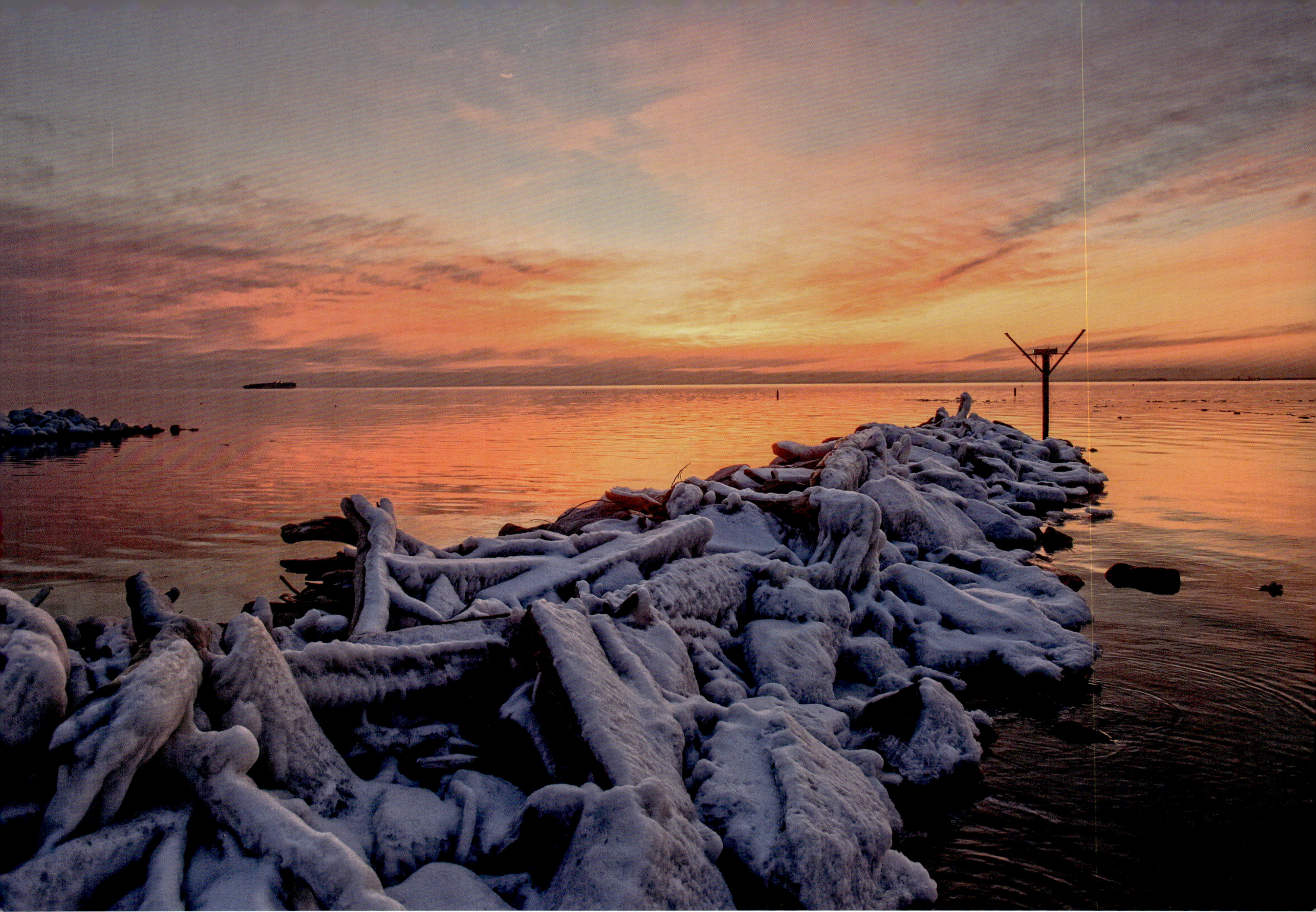

This shot makes the rocks and driftwood look as if they are coated with icing amid a tangerine-colored sky.

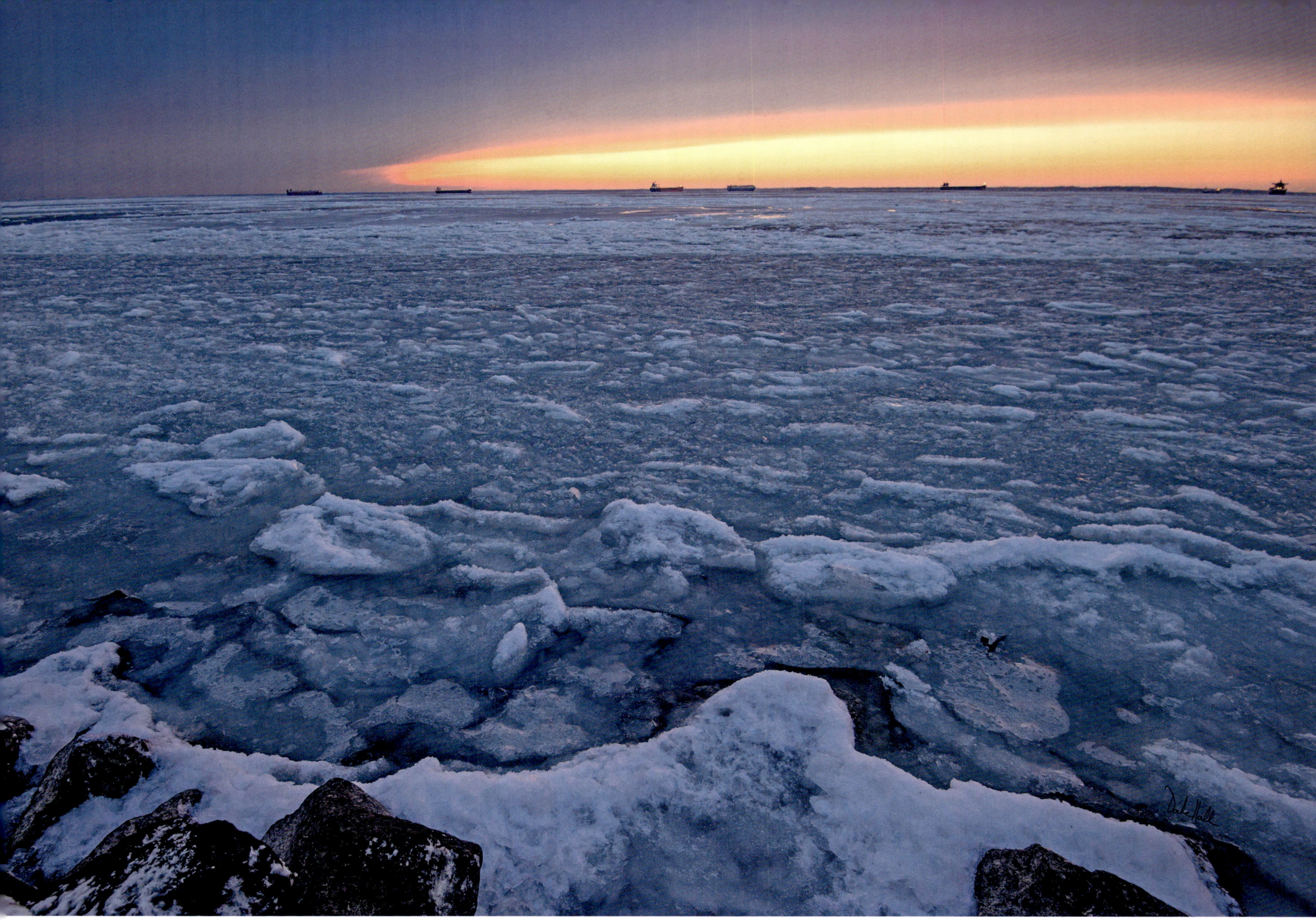

After a dreary day of clouds over the icy craters on the bay, a pop of color emerged just as the sun hit the horizon. The title of this shot is *Pop of Color on Ice*.

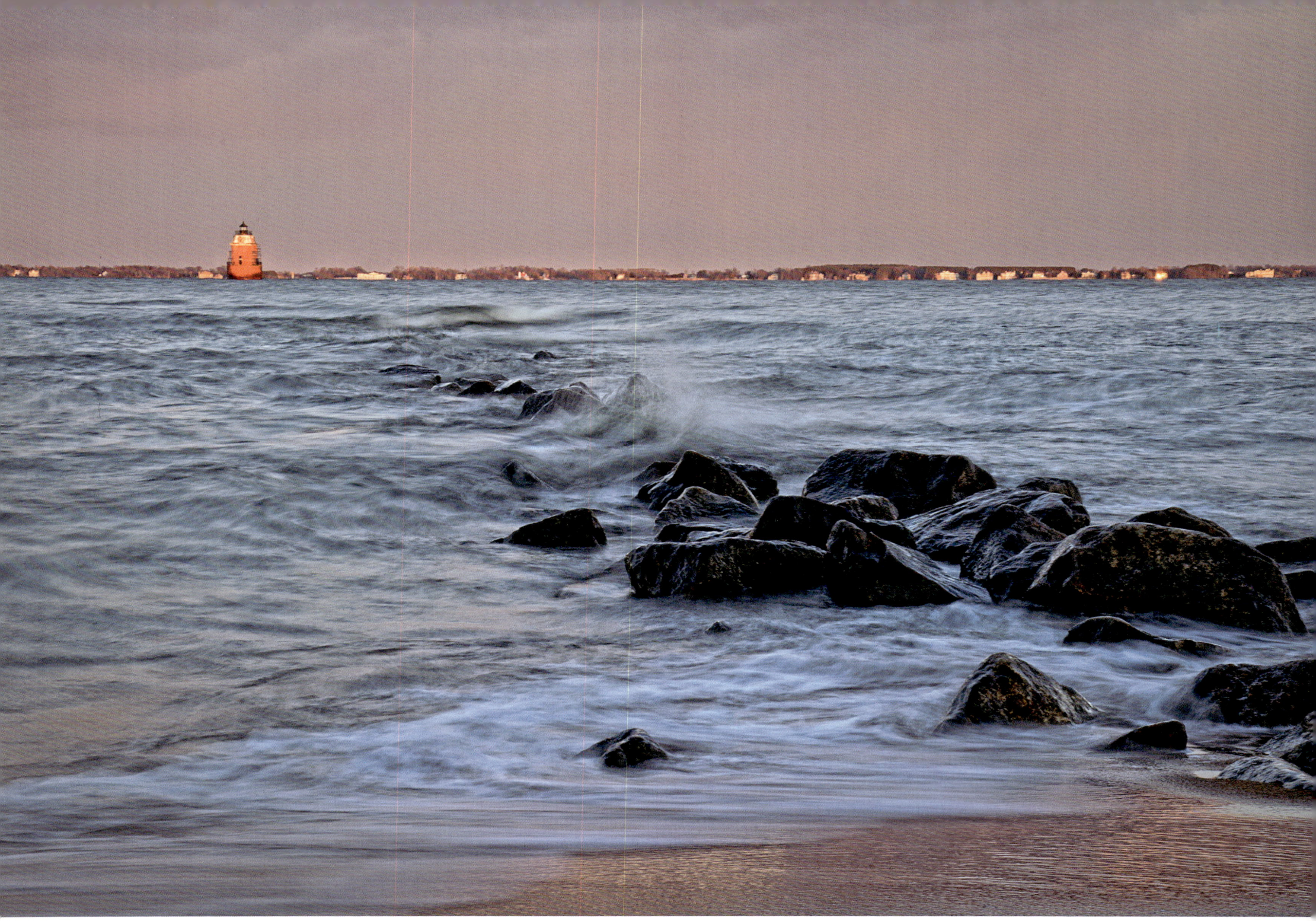

The Sandy Point Shoal Lighthouse, facing the northern end of Kent Island, was lit up in
the pink hues of the setting sun on this frigid late afternoon in January.

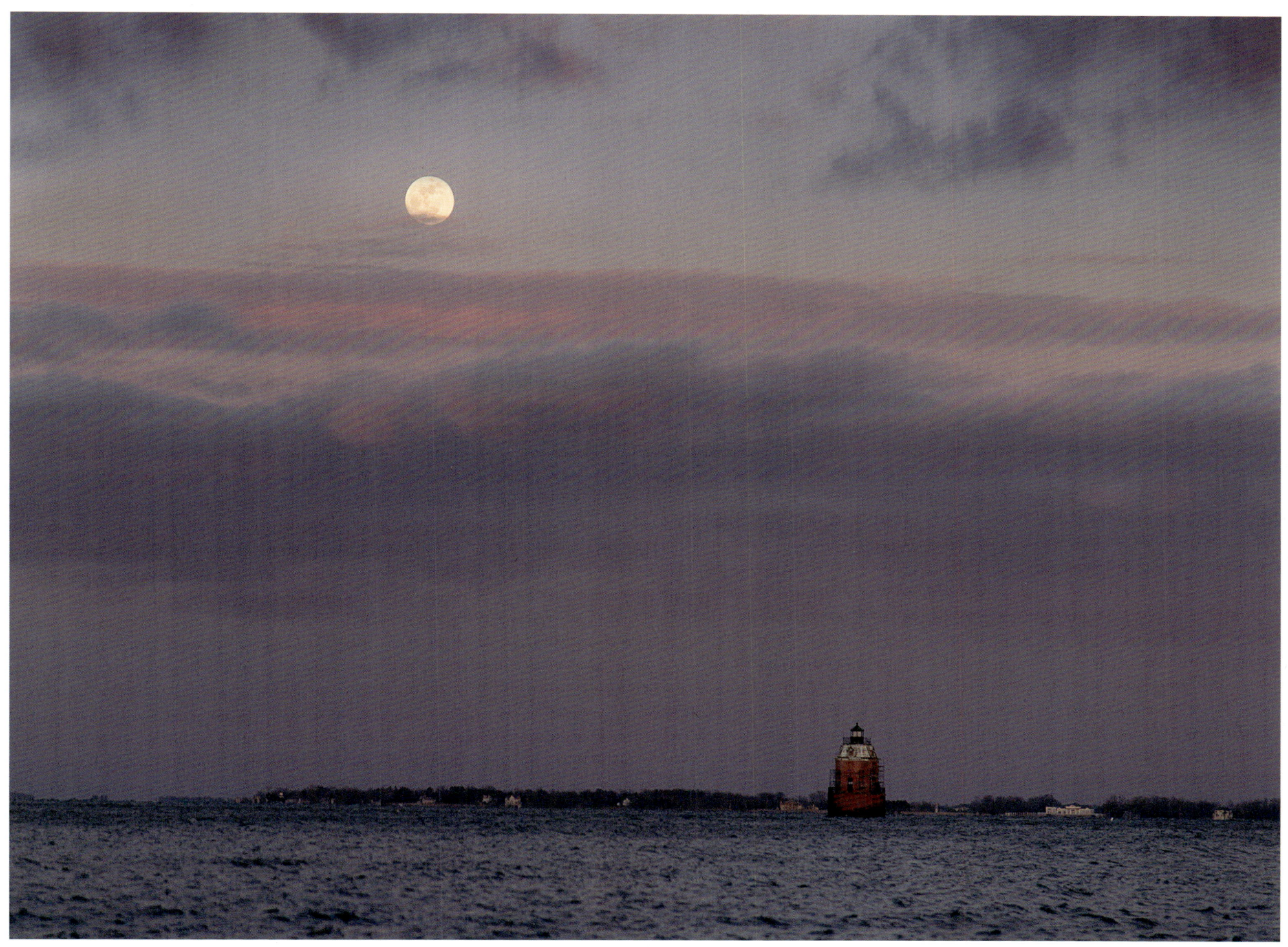

Super blue blood moon, January 2018

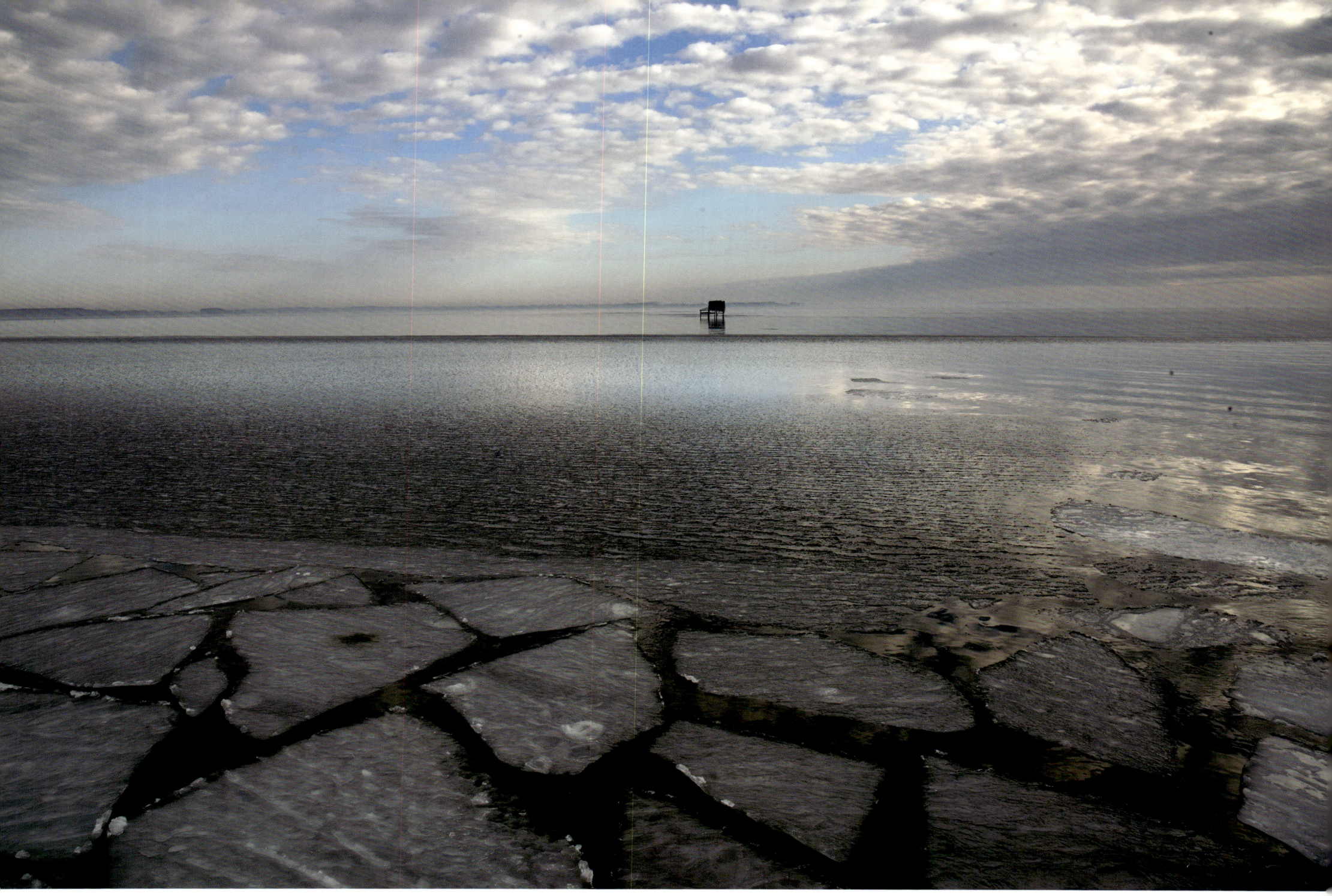

Eastern Bay from Romancoke

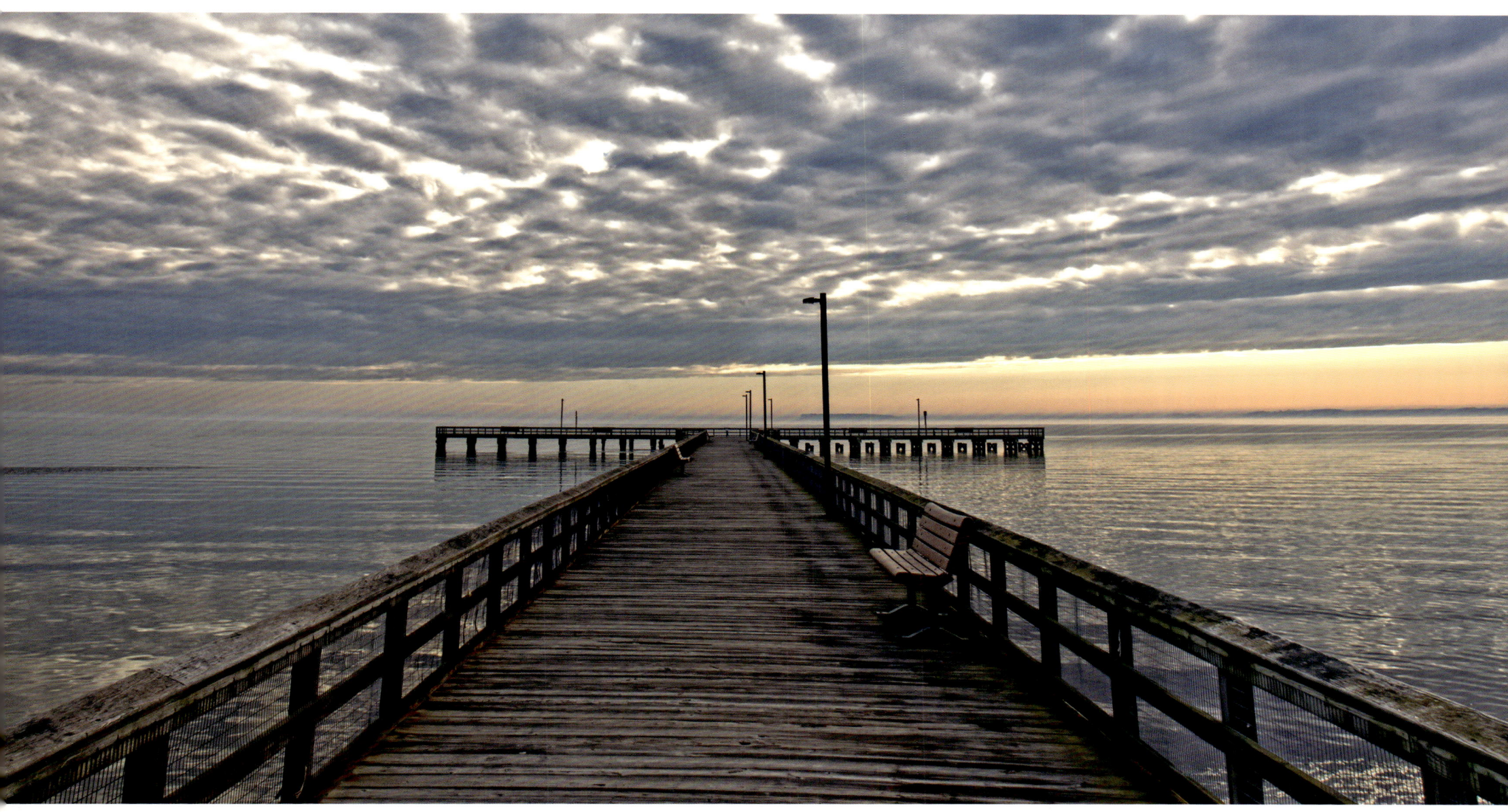

Romancoke Pier

As I was moseying along the dock looking at all the beautiful nautical imagery enveloped by a veil of fog, I came upon a great blue heron standing stoically on this piling. I was awestruck by this scene and knew I had to be as still as I could be, so I held my breath and slowly raised my camera to my eye. Then this happened.

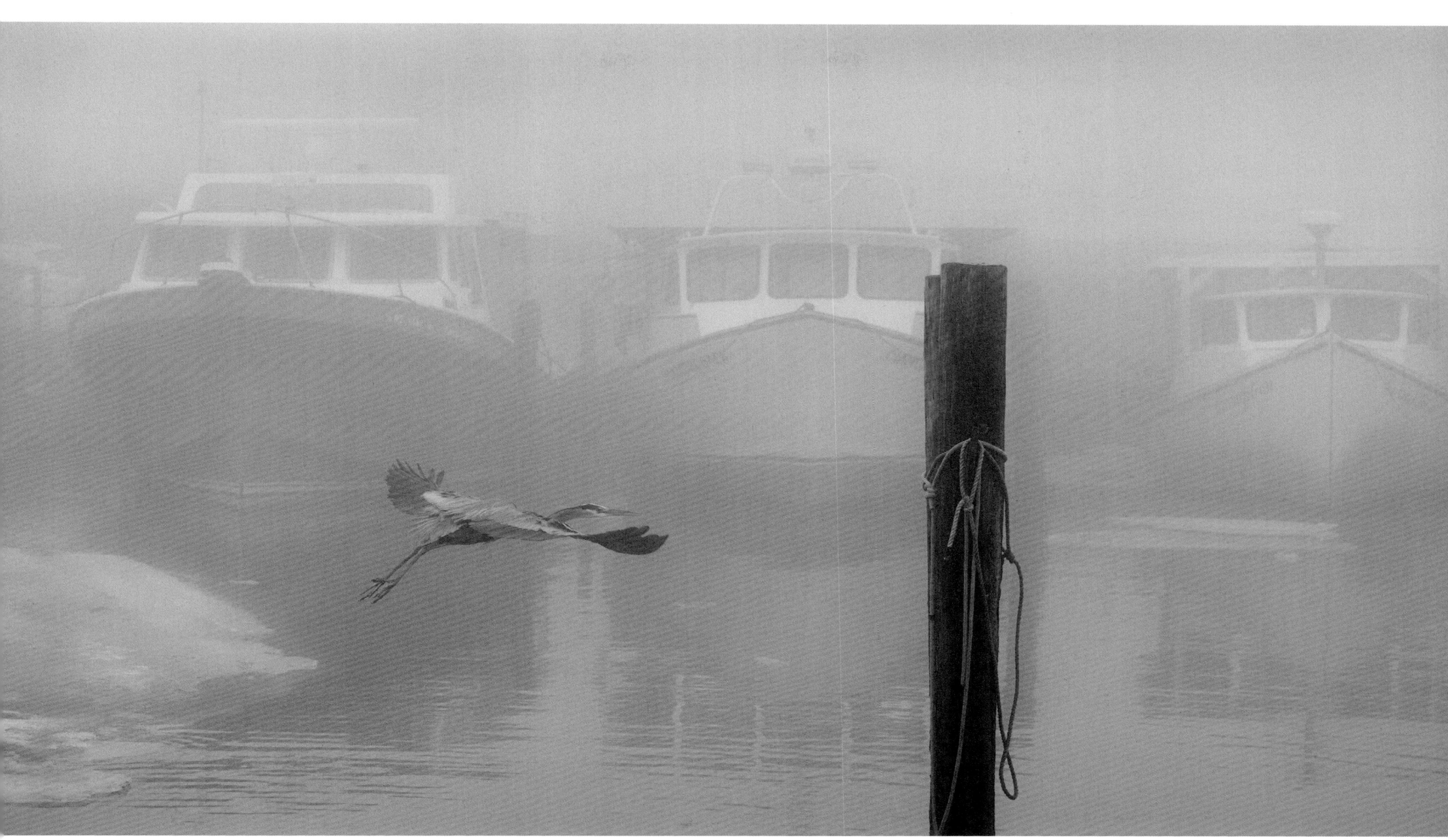

Foggy flight

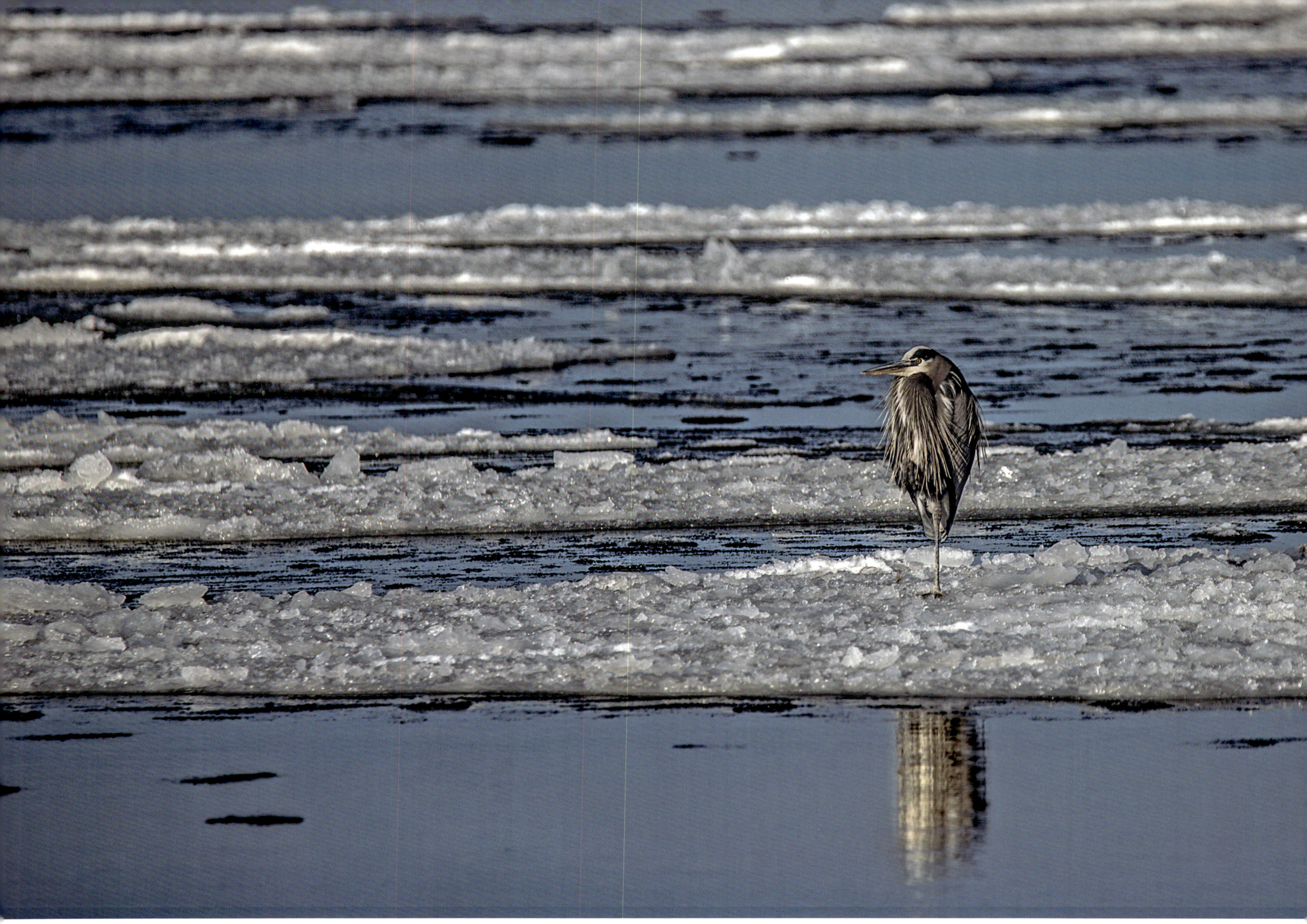

Ice statue

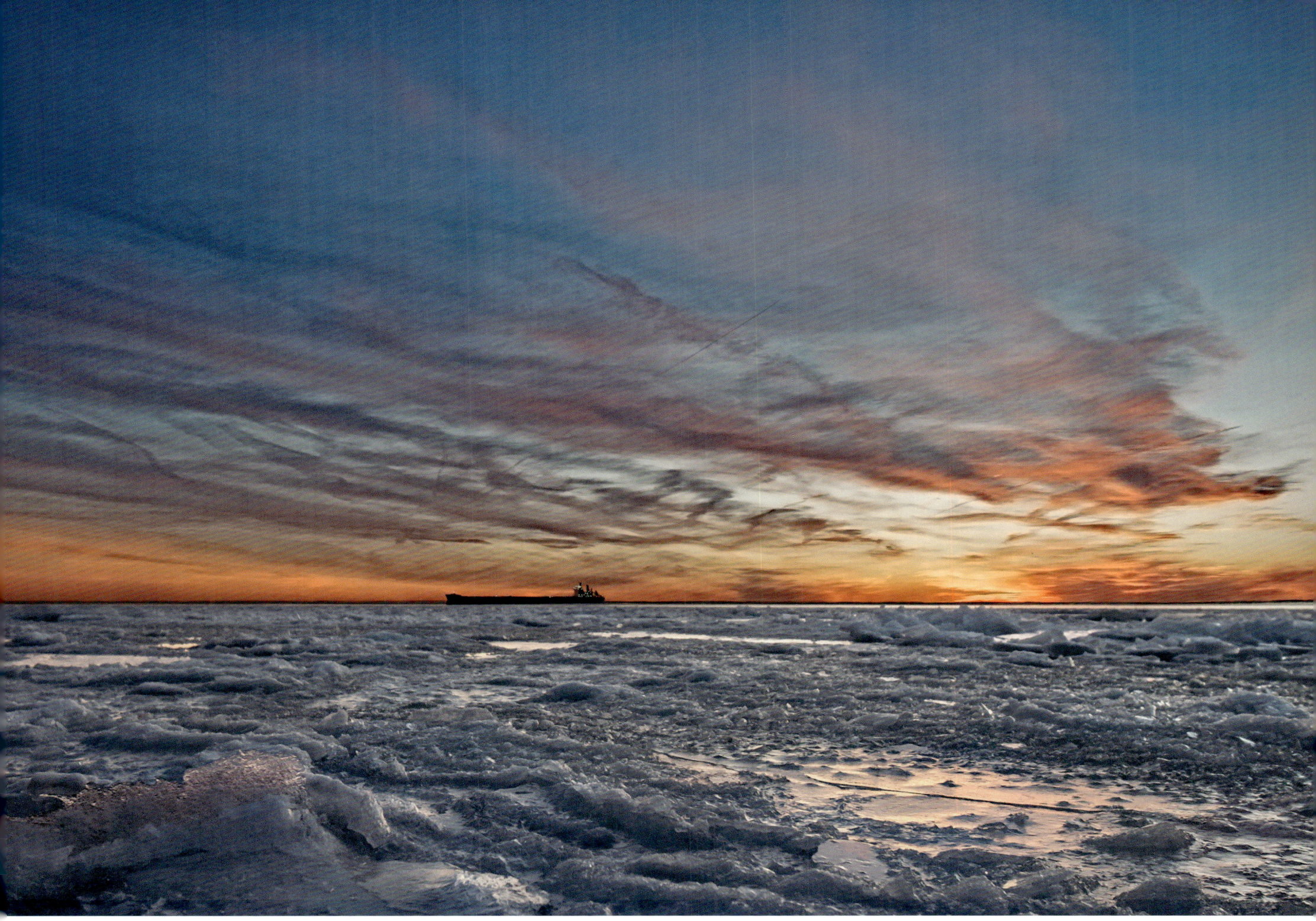

Fire and ice

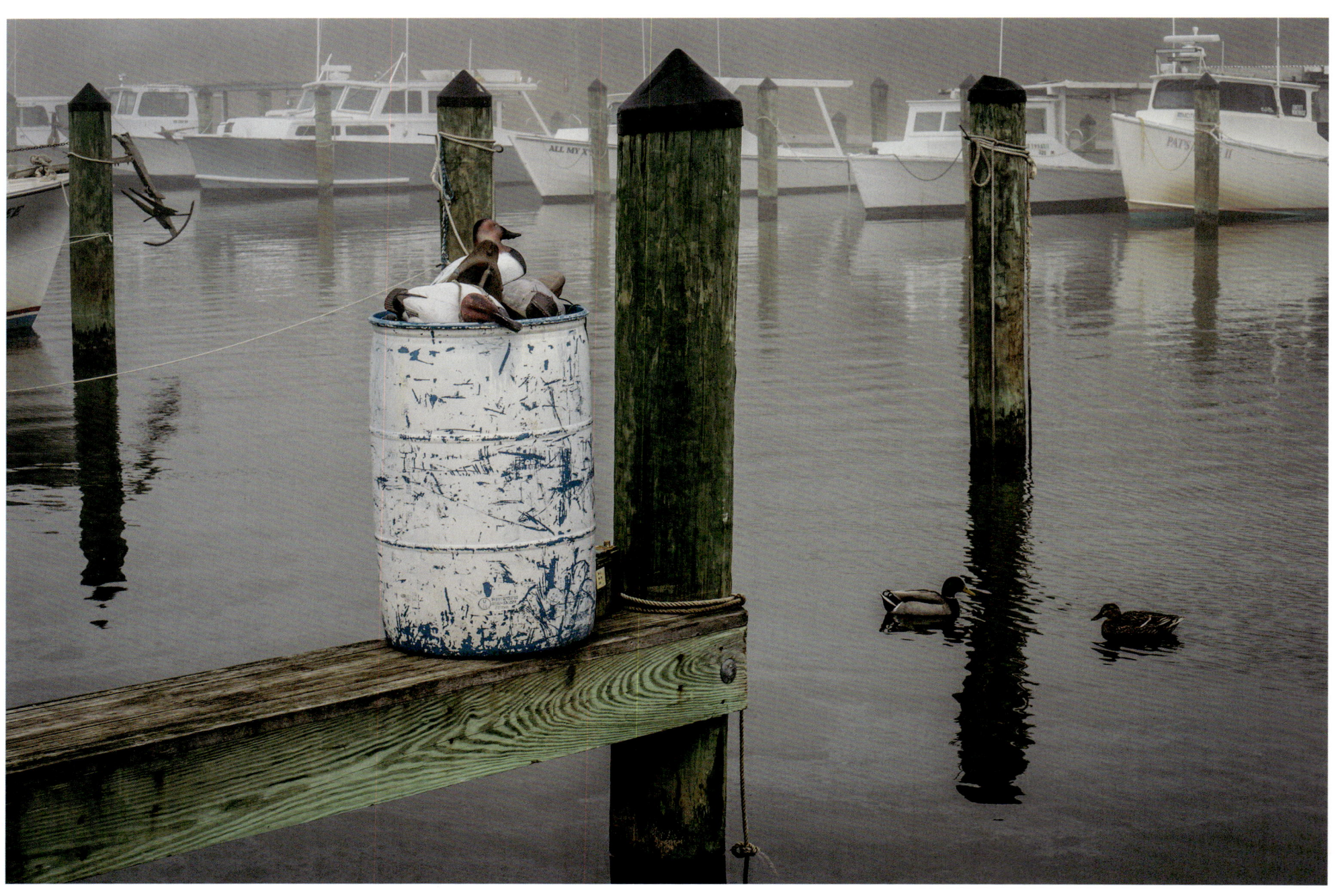

Waterman's Boat Basin remains busy in winter with commercial fishermen and hunting charters coming and going.

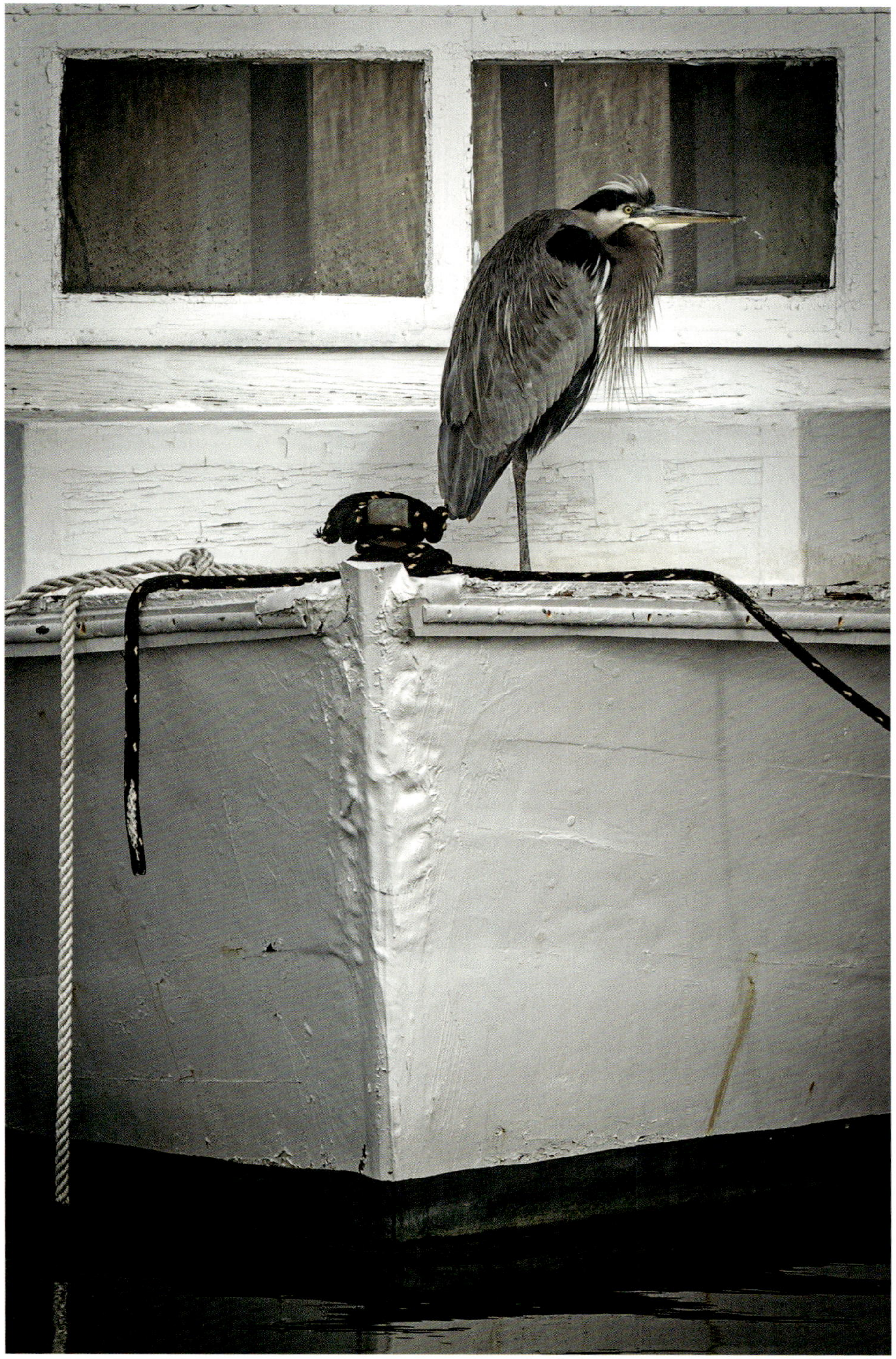

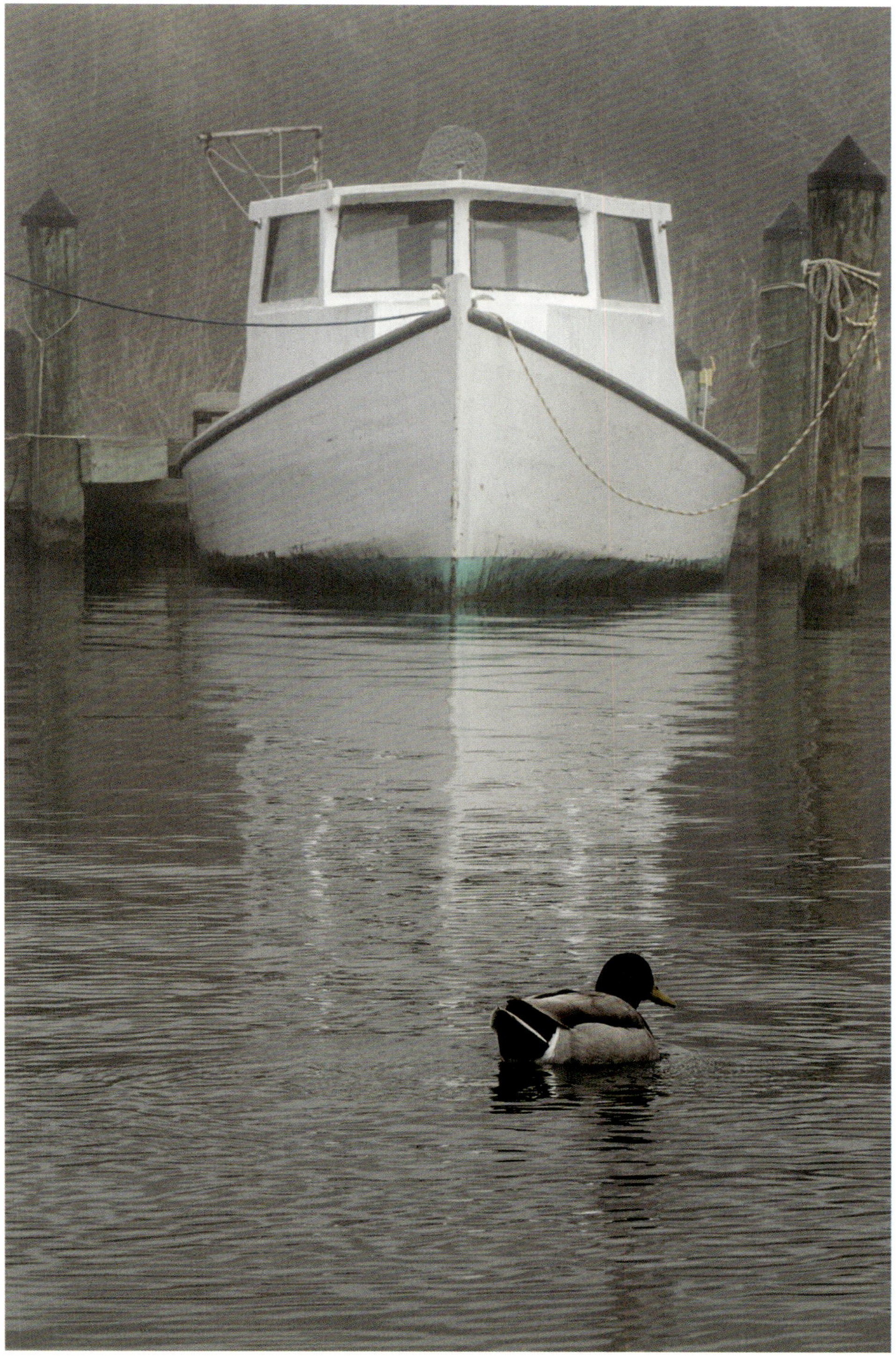

No one goes hungry when watermen return with their catch and toss unwanted scraps overboard during cleanup.

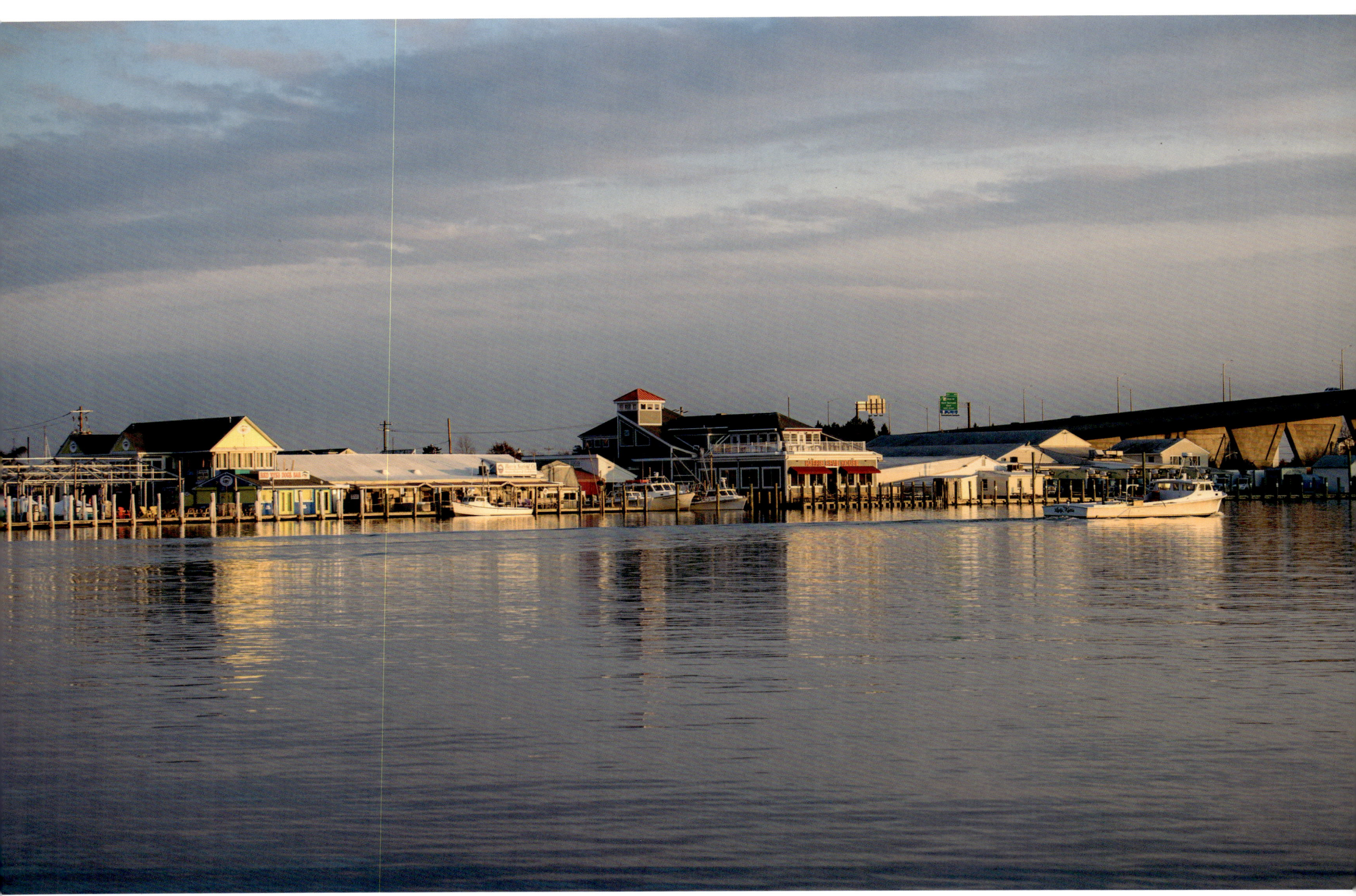

A beautiful calm winter day on the Narrows

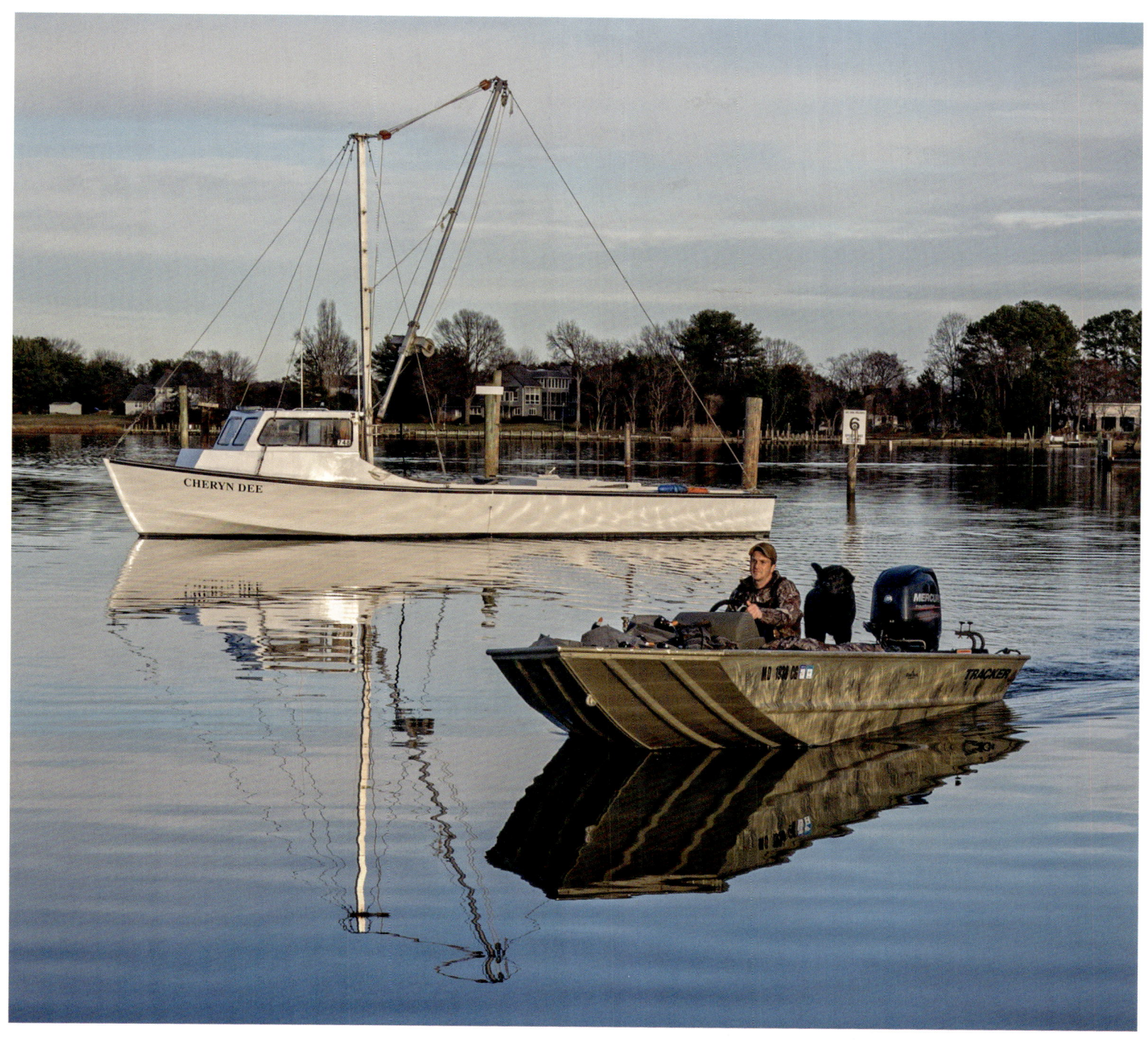

Returning after a day of duck hunting with Keeper, the Labrador retriever

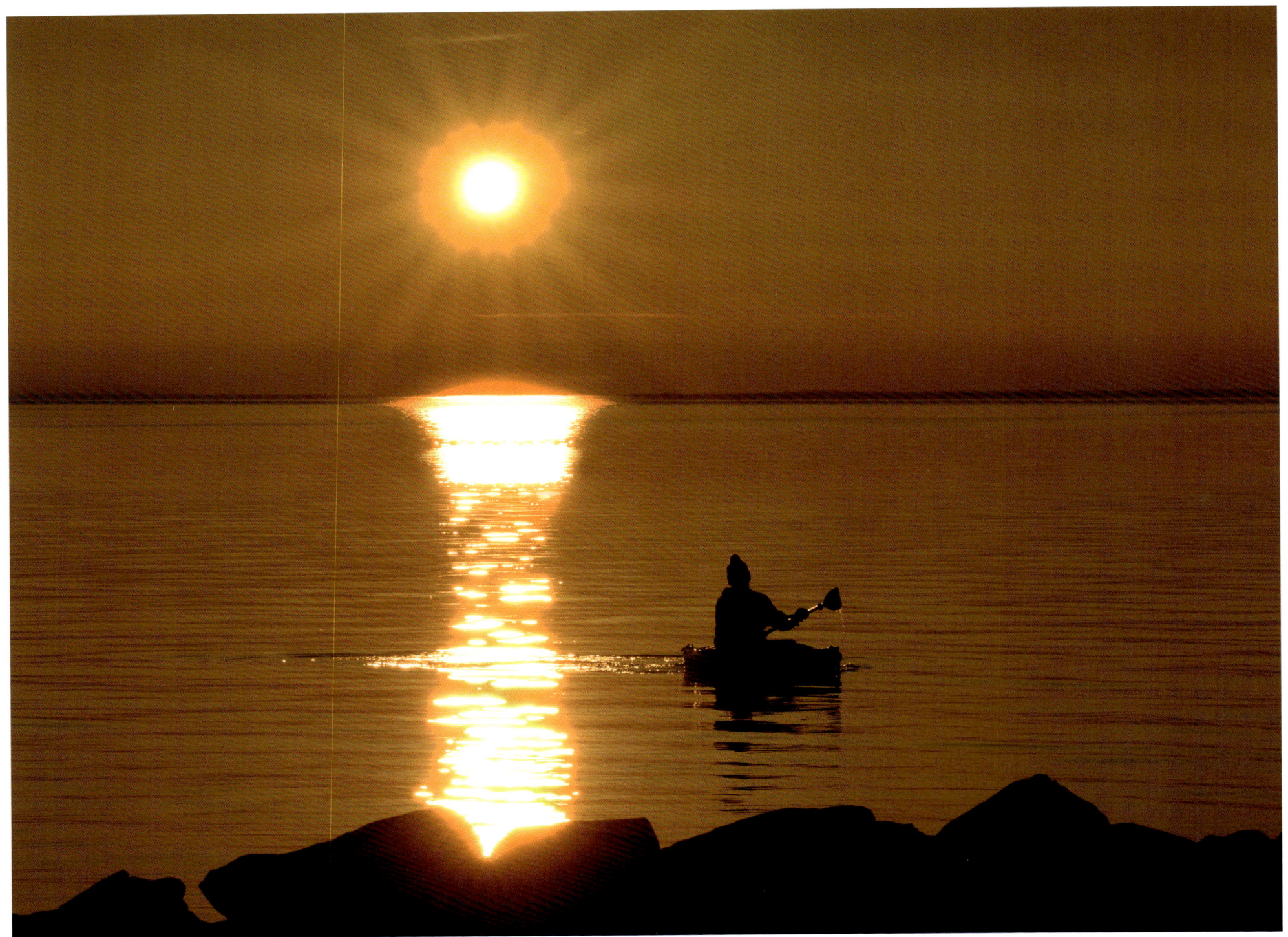

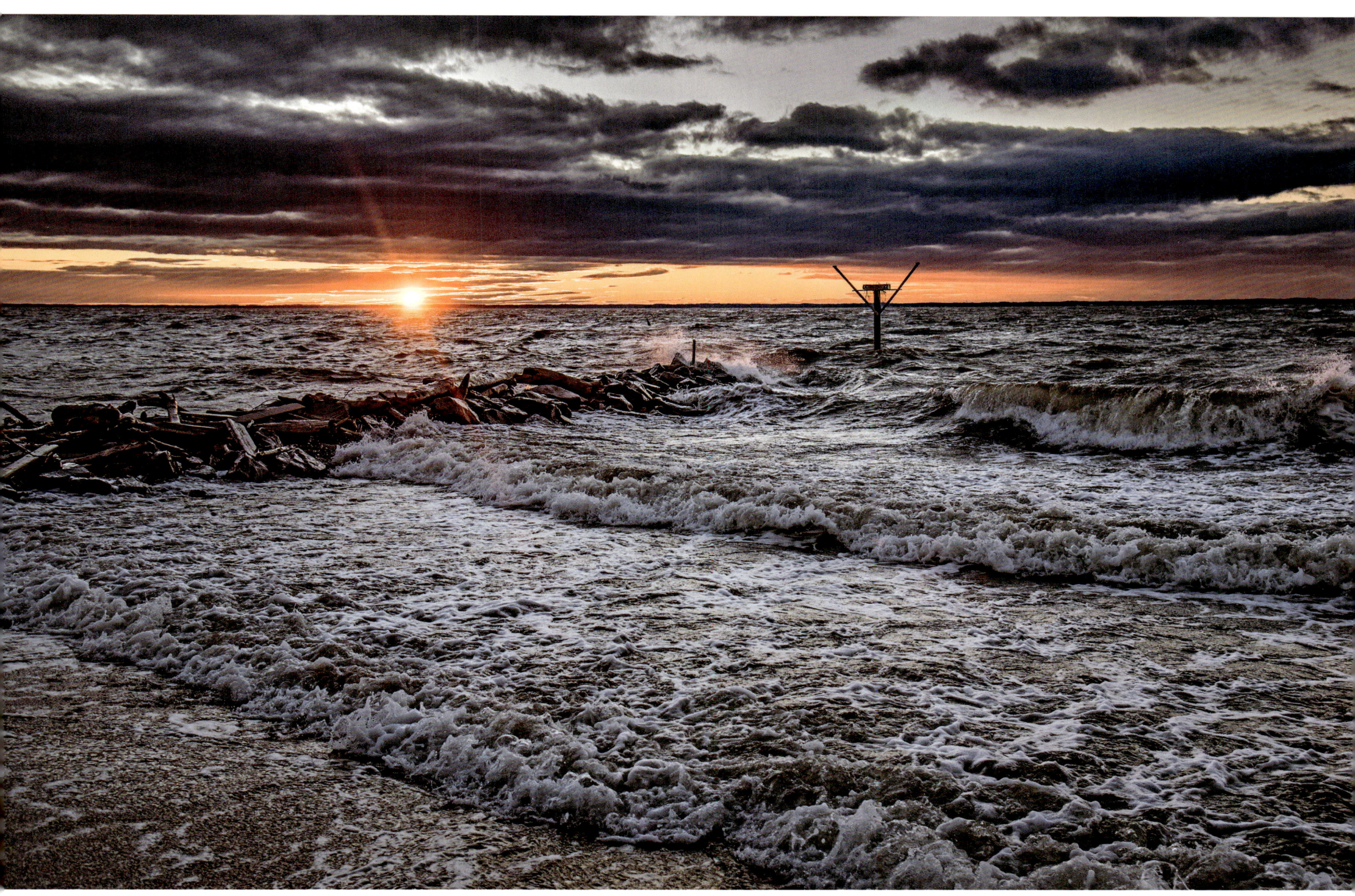

Same place, different kind of day. Both of these pictures were taken at Queen Anne Marina Inlet.

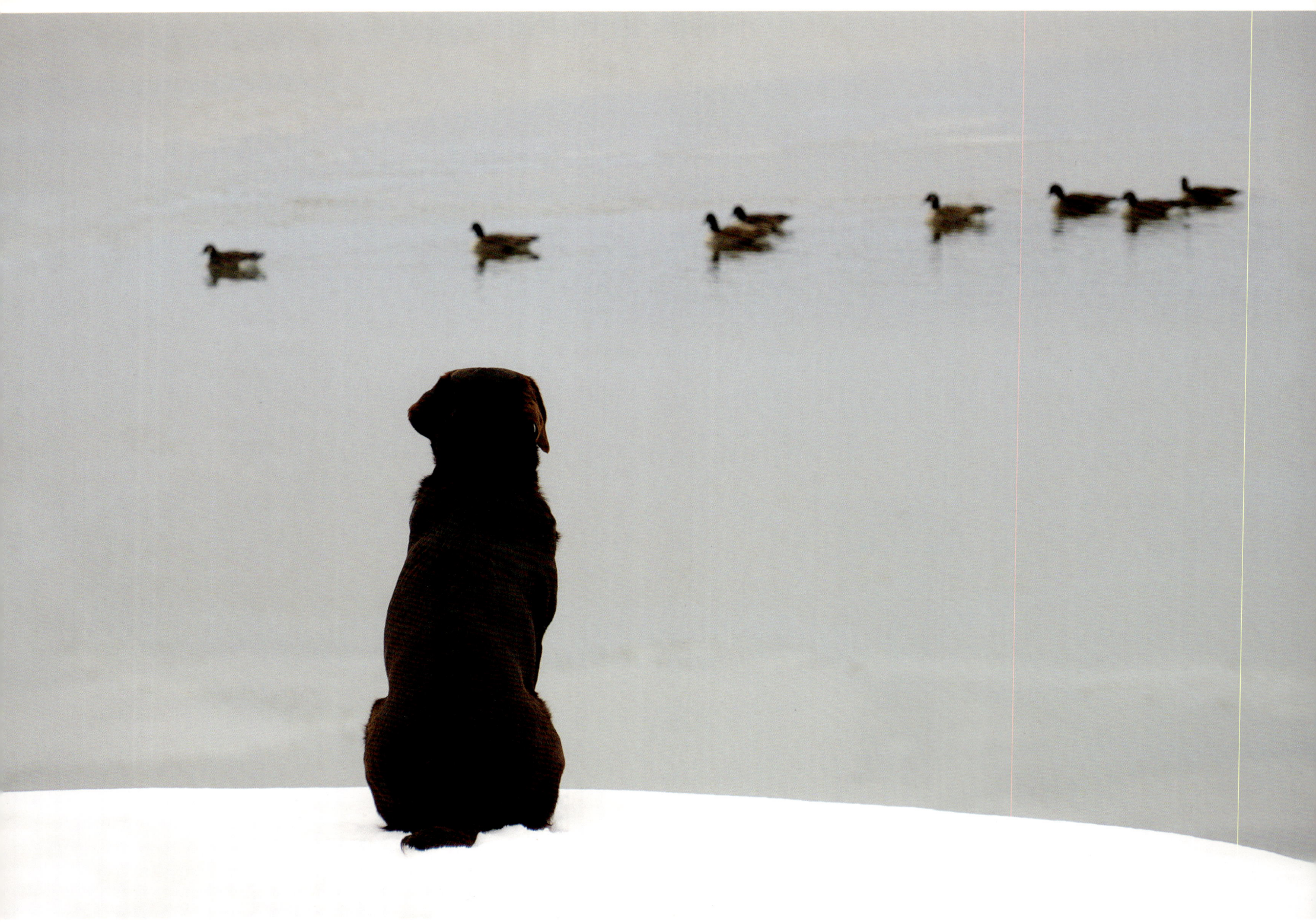

Penny for her thoughts. Thank goodness for the electric fence.

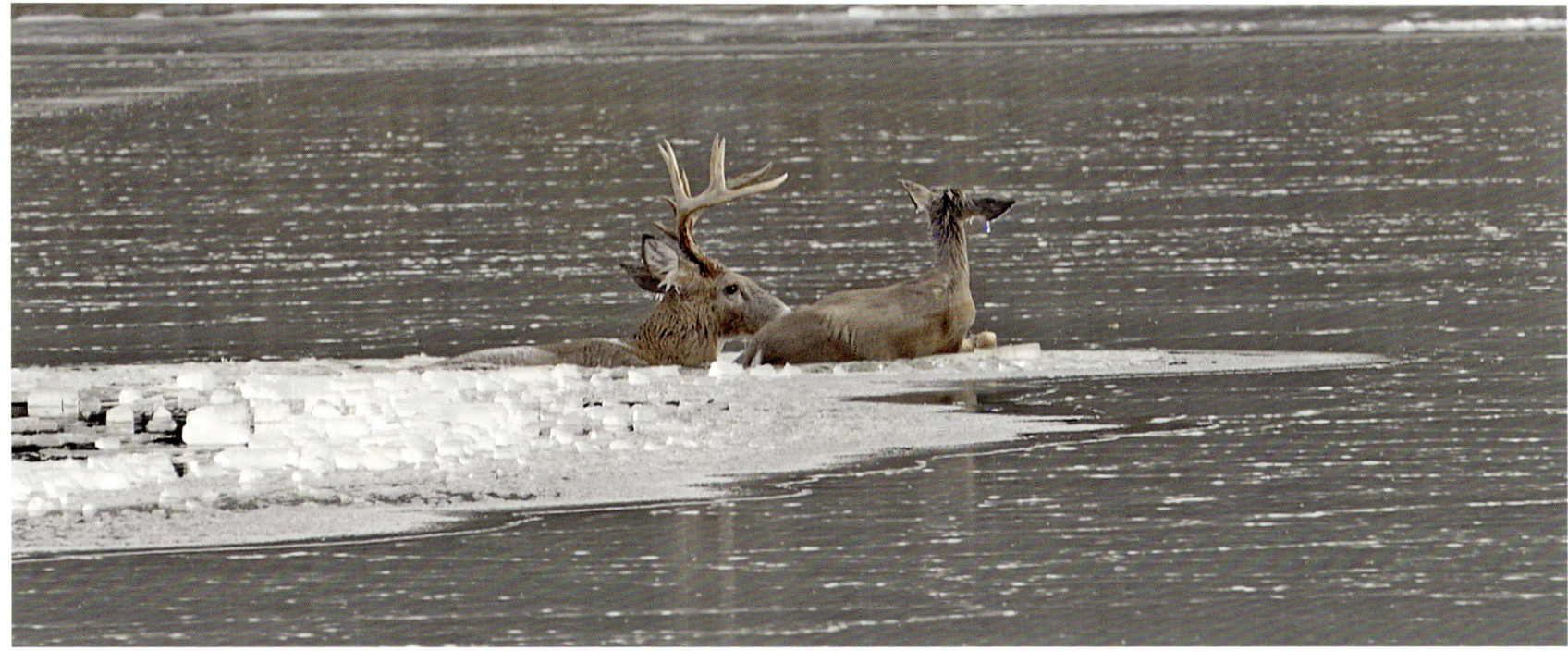

In these shots taken with my telephoto lens and then cropped tightly, a buck guides its doe across the ice to get to less inhabited land. The doe made it across, but, sadly, the buck stayed in the icy waters all night and froze to death. It was a horrific event for the residents on Price Creek. A hunter came the next day and made good use of the meat.

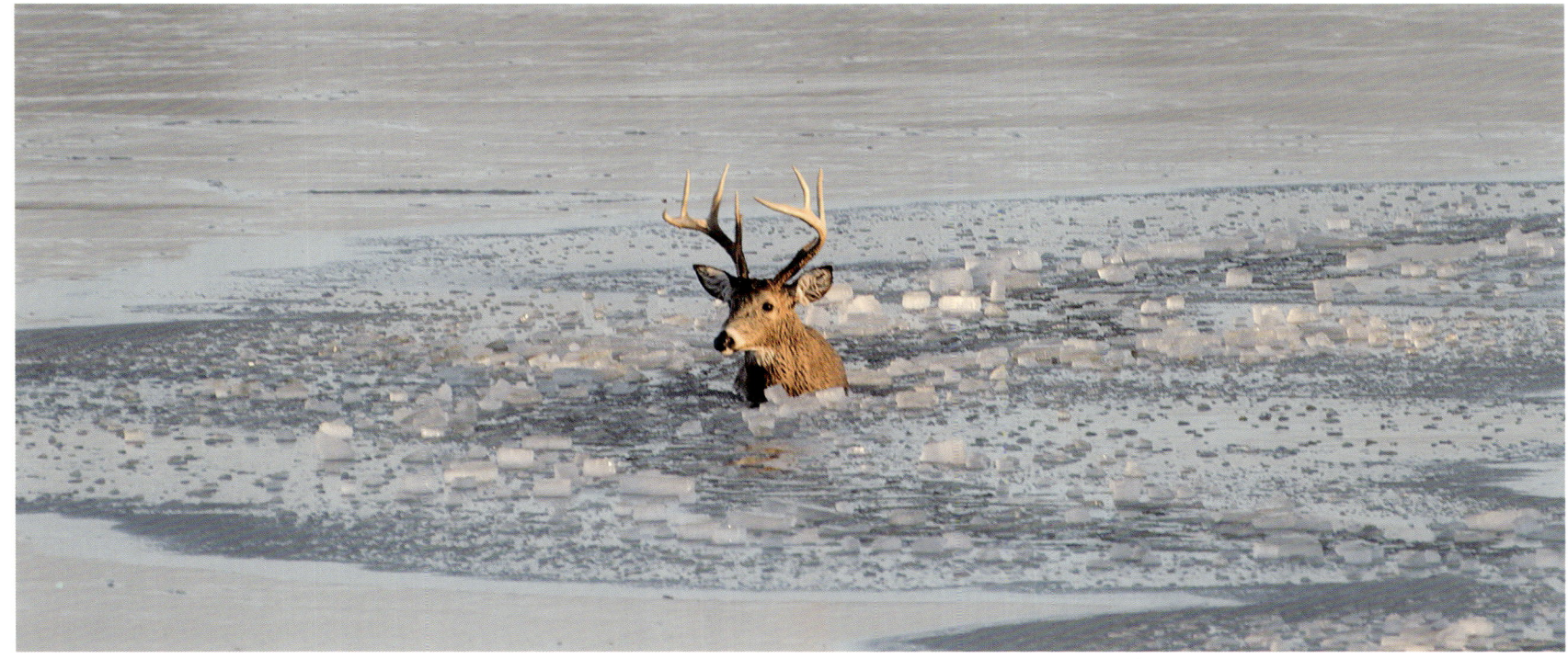

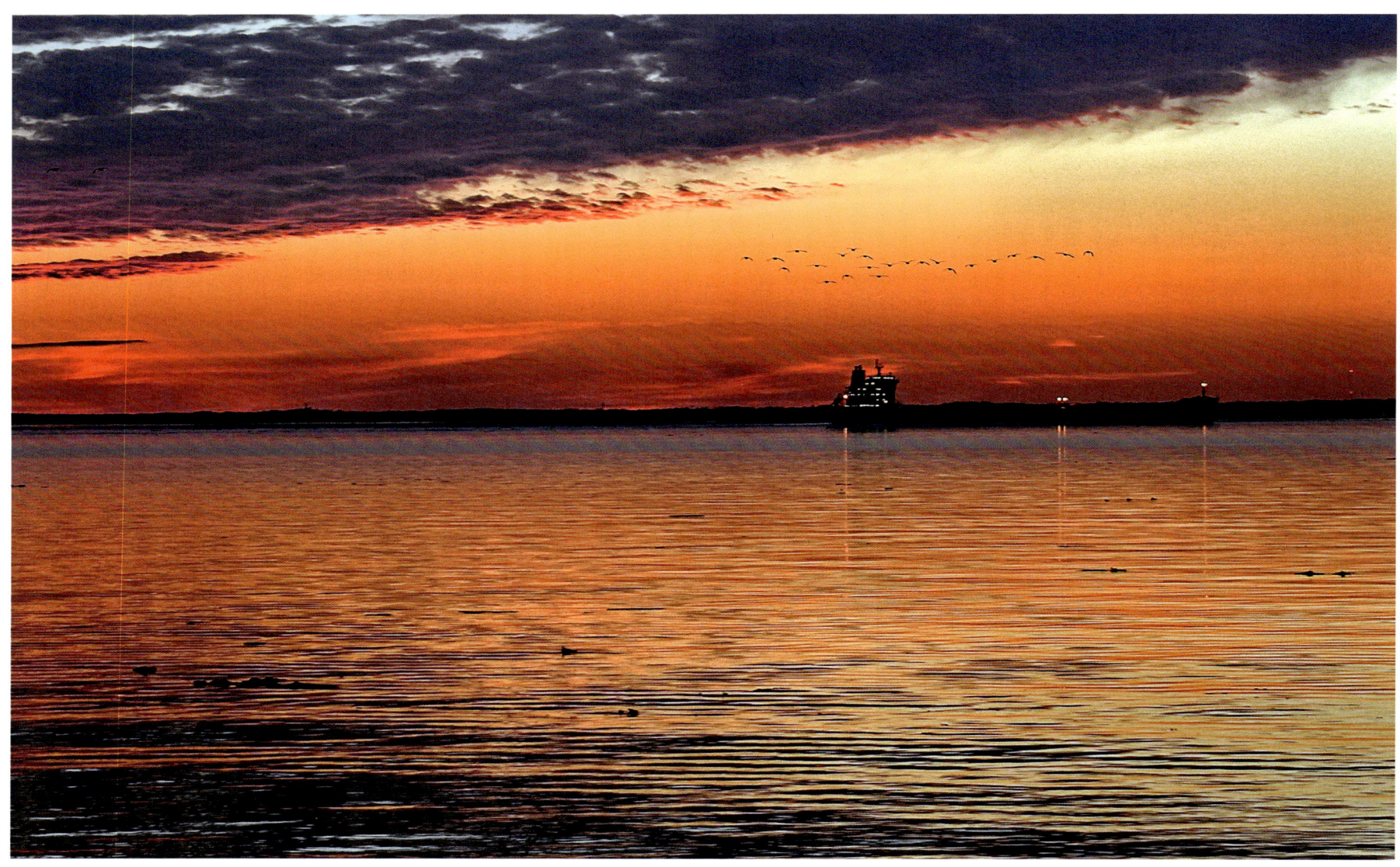

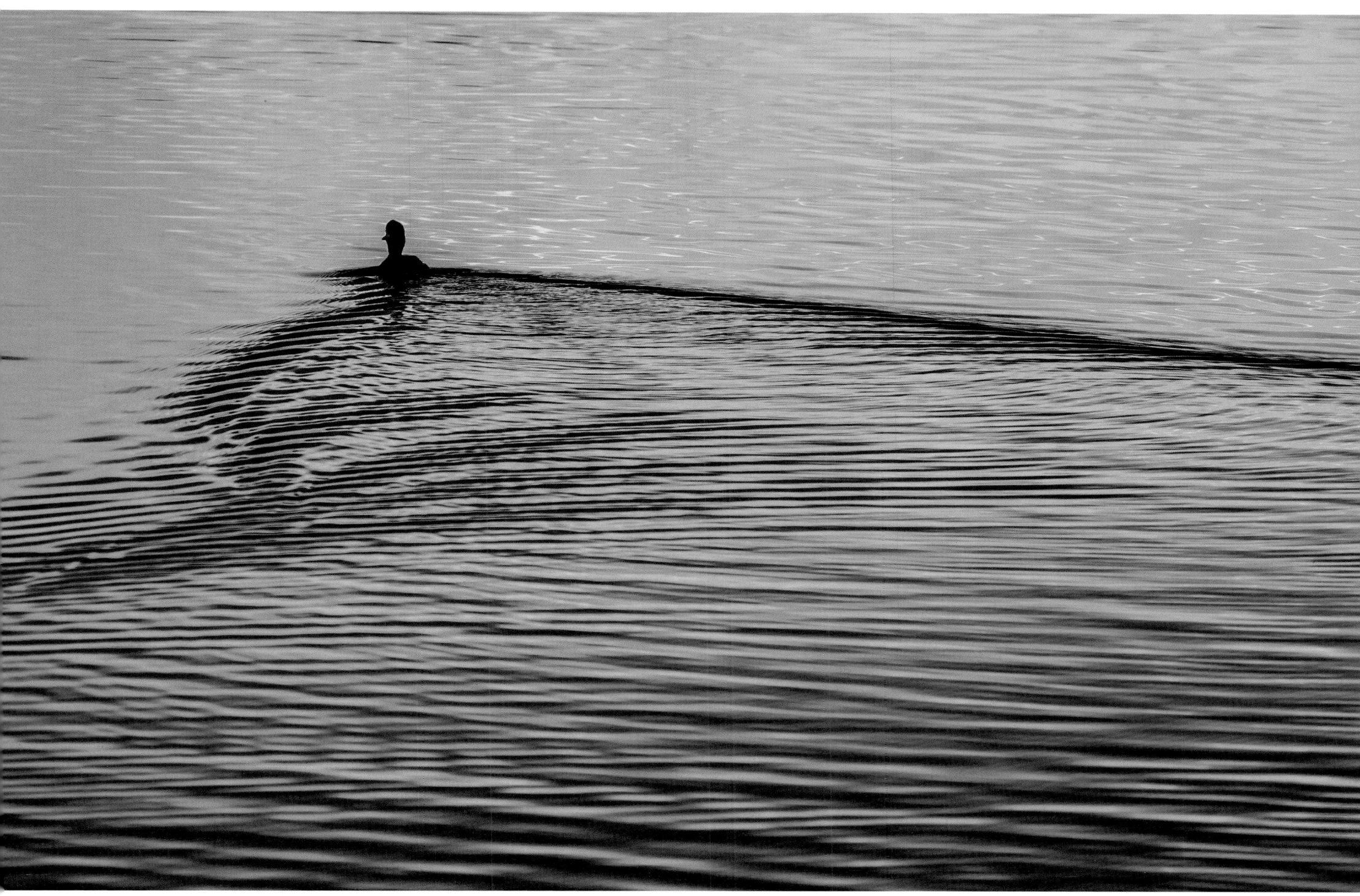

A bufflehead's graceful gliding leaves beautiful ripples in the water.

Snow moon o'er Price Creek

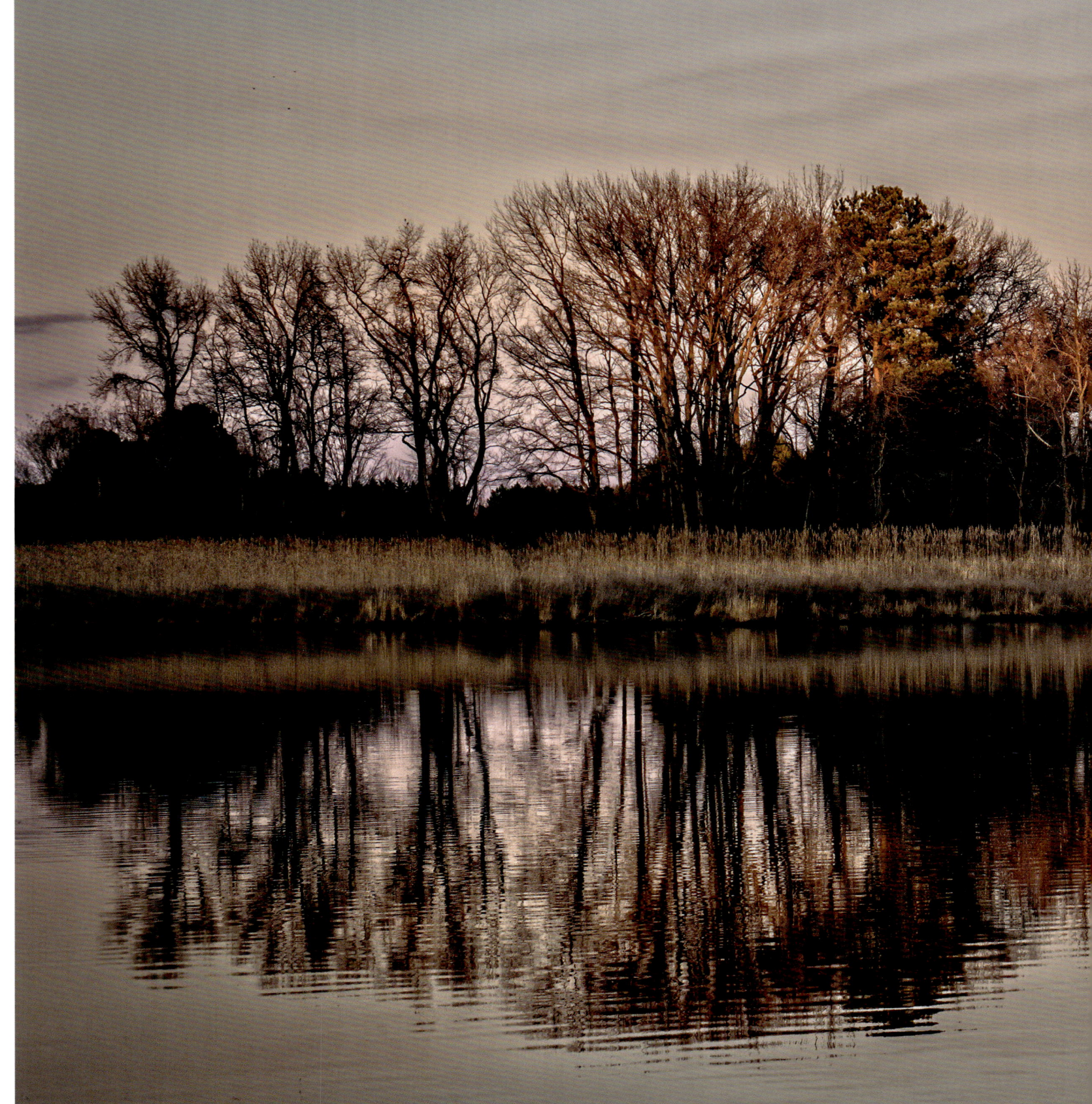

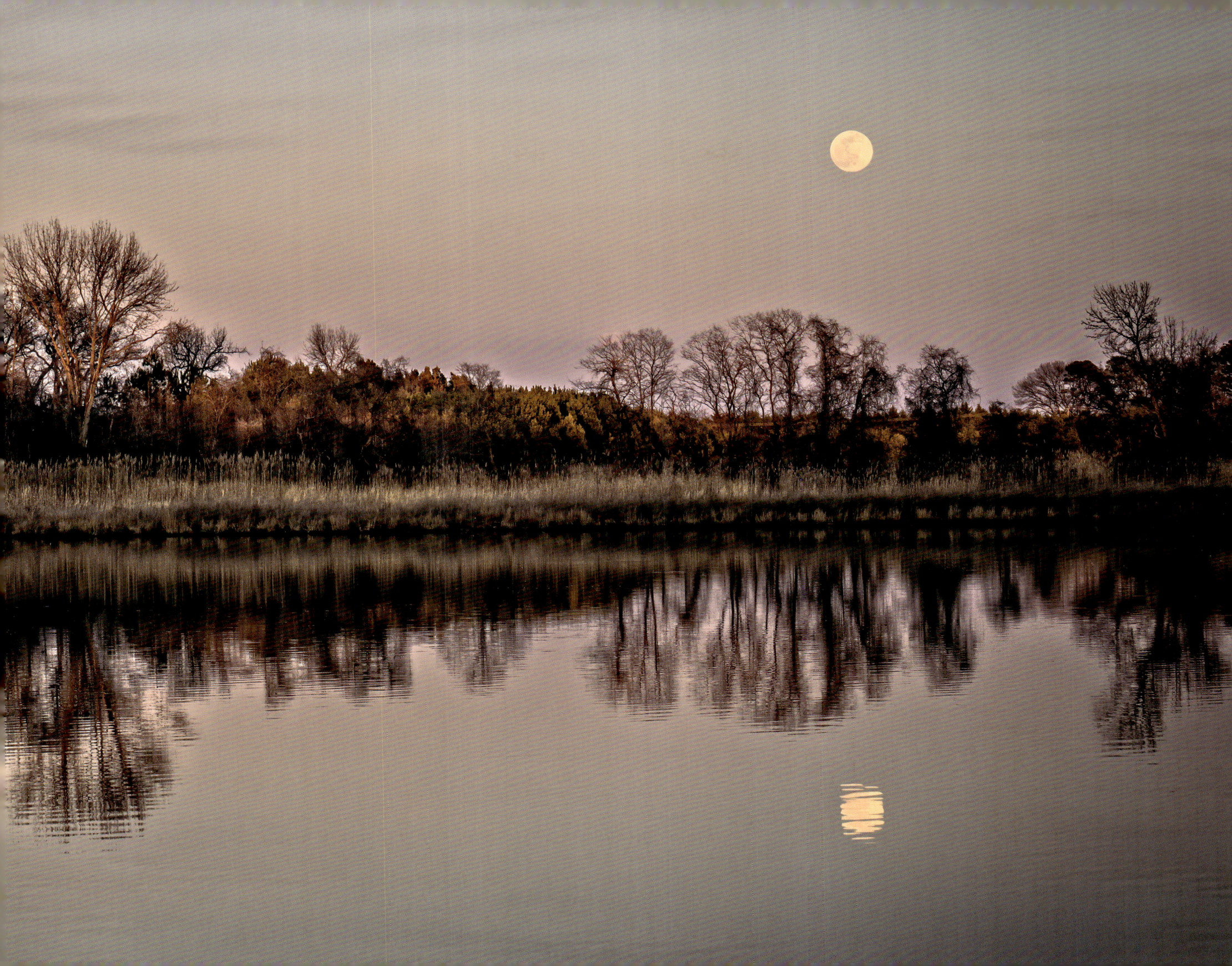

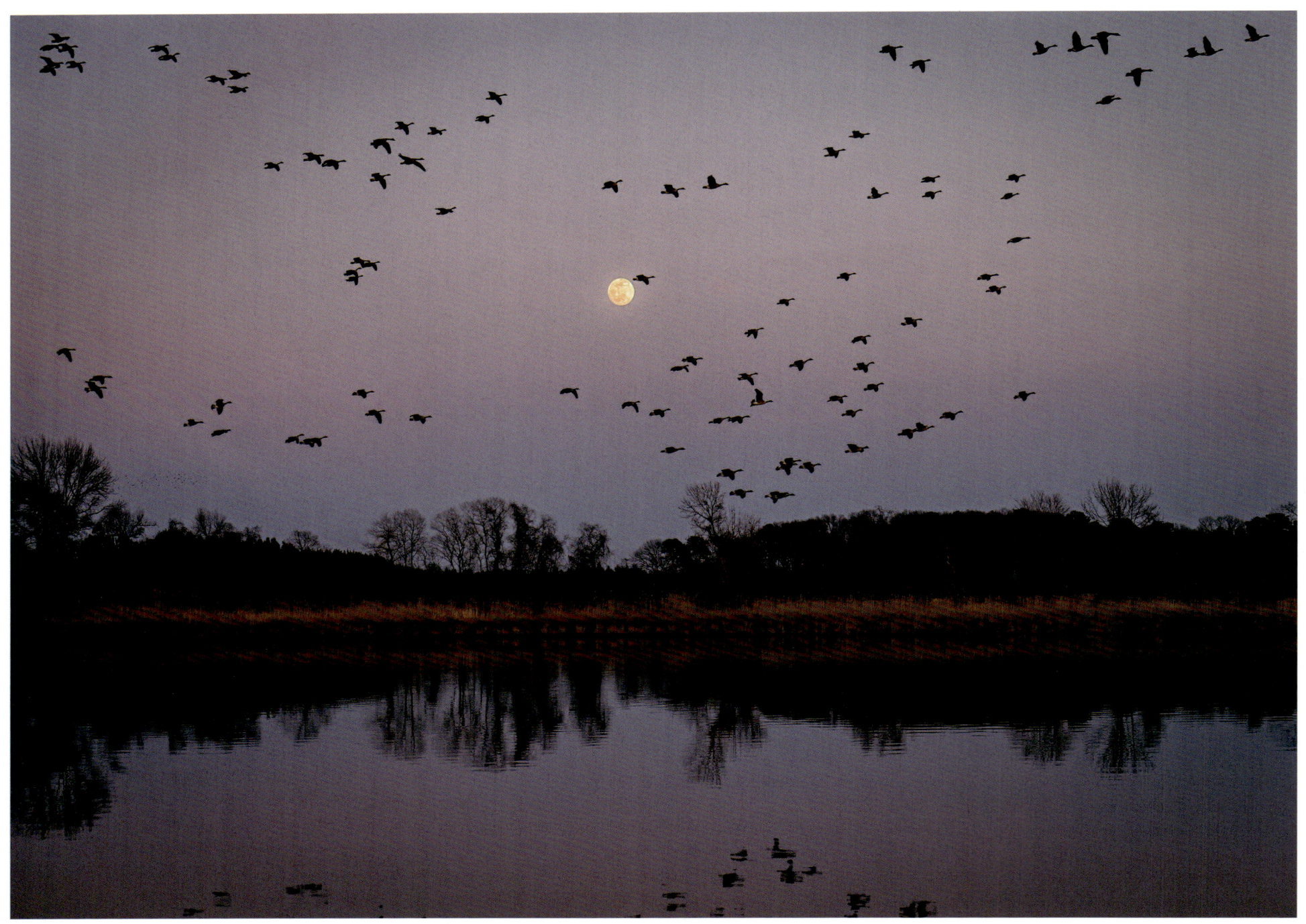

This was definitely one of those "Wow!" moments, having the geese fly in while I was capturing the full snow moon.

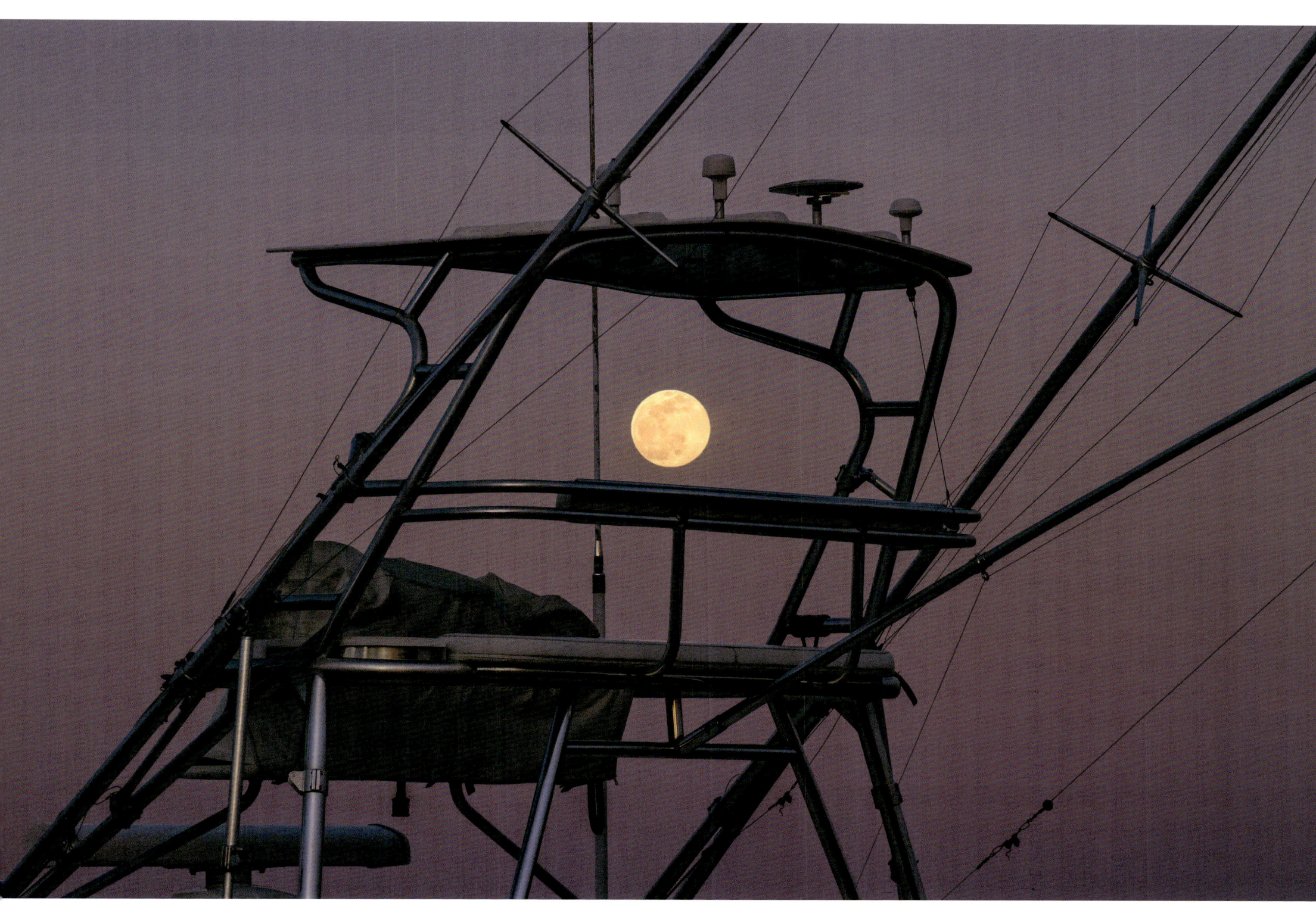

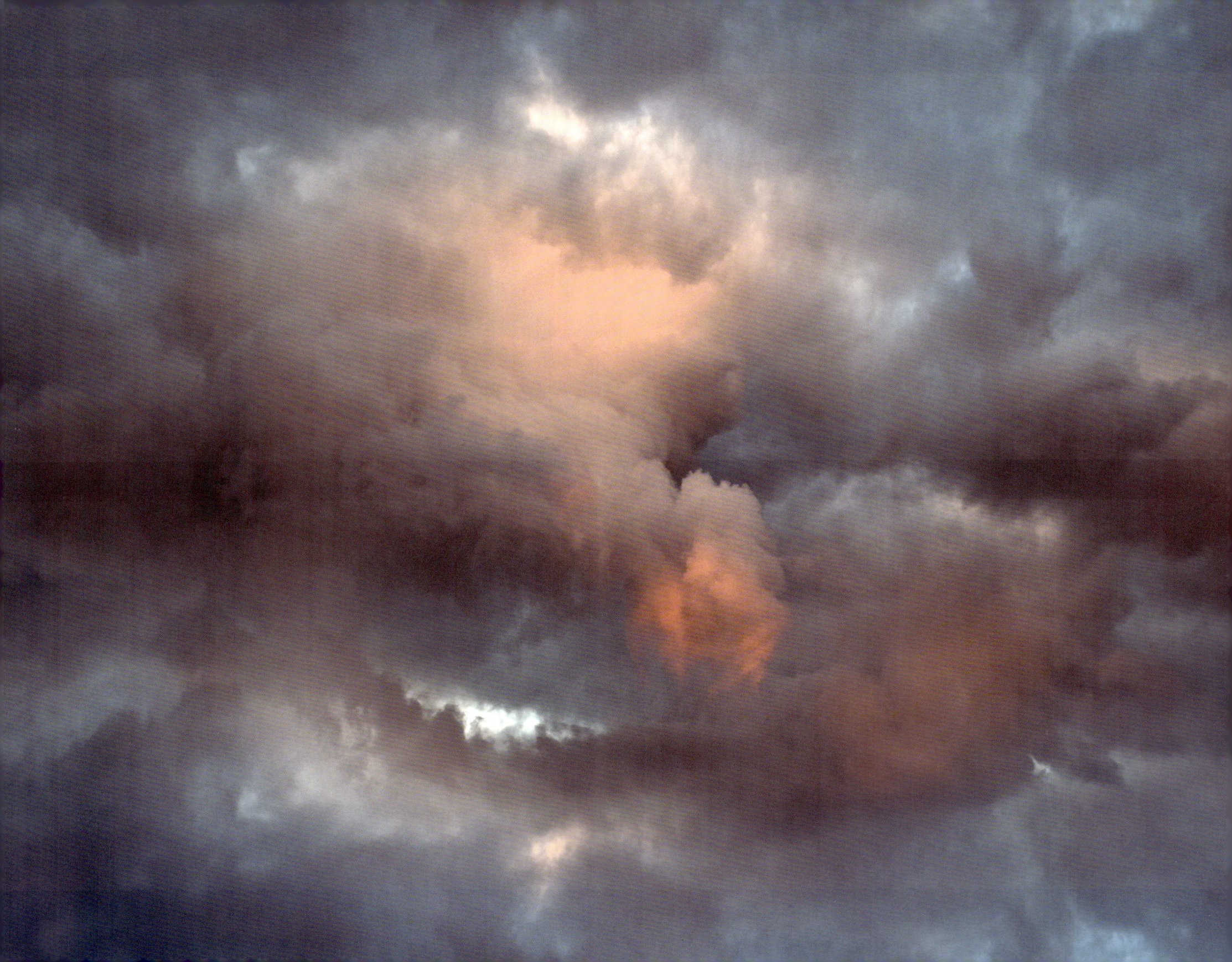

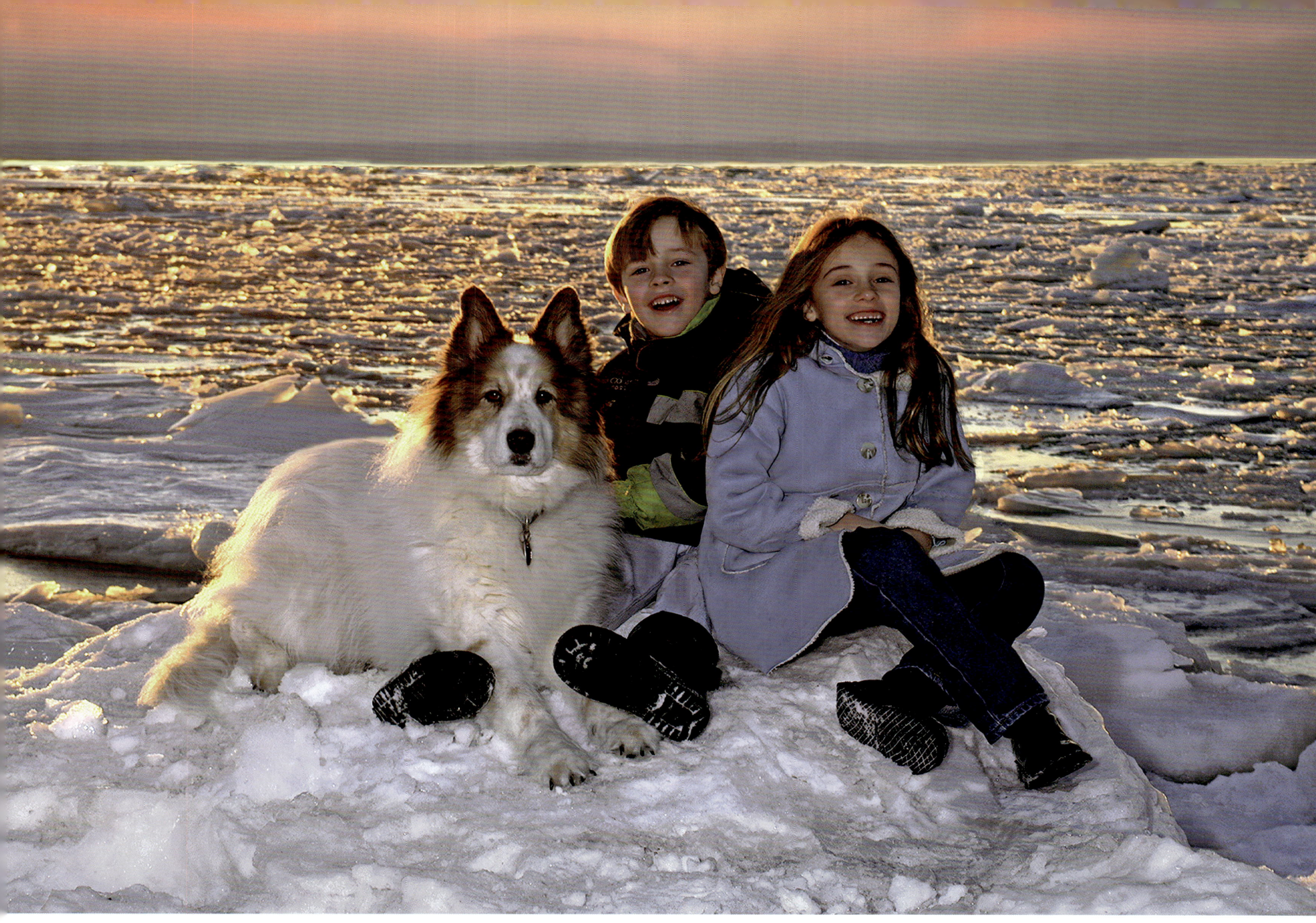

The frozen bay made for such an awesome sight. These kids enjoyed having this amazing "backdrop" for their photo op.

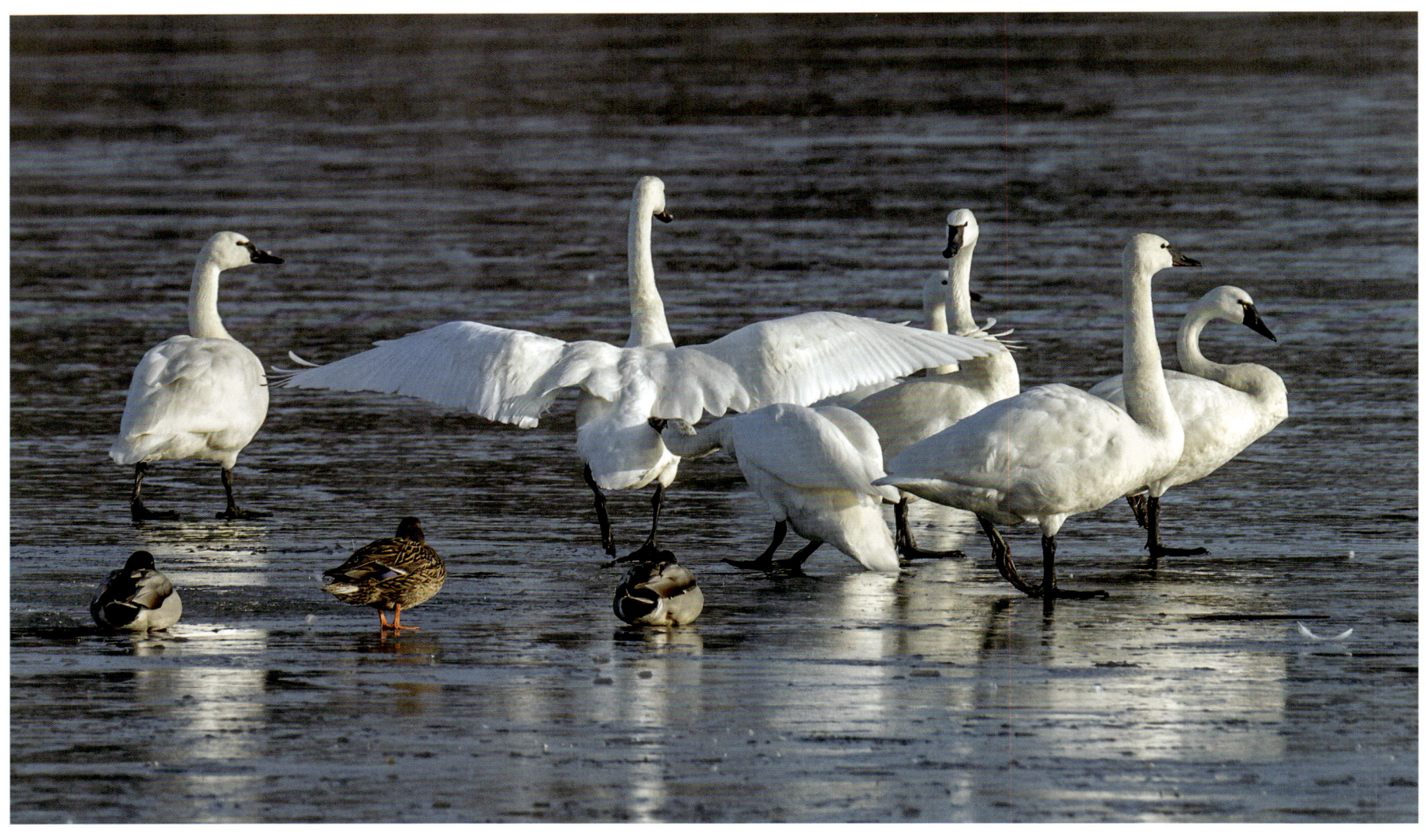

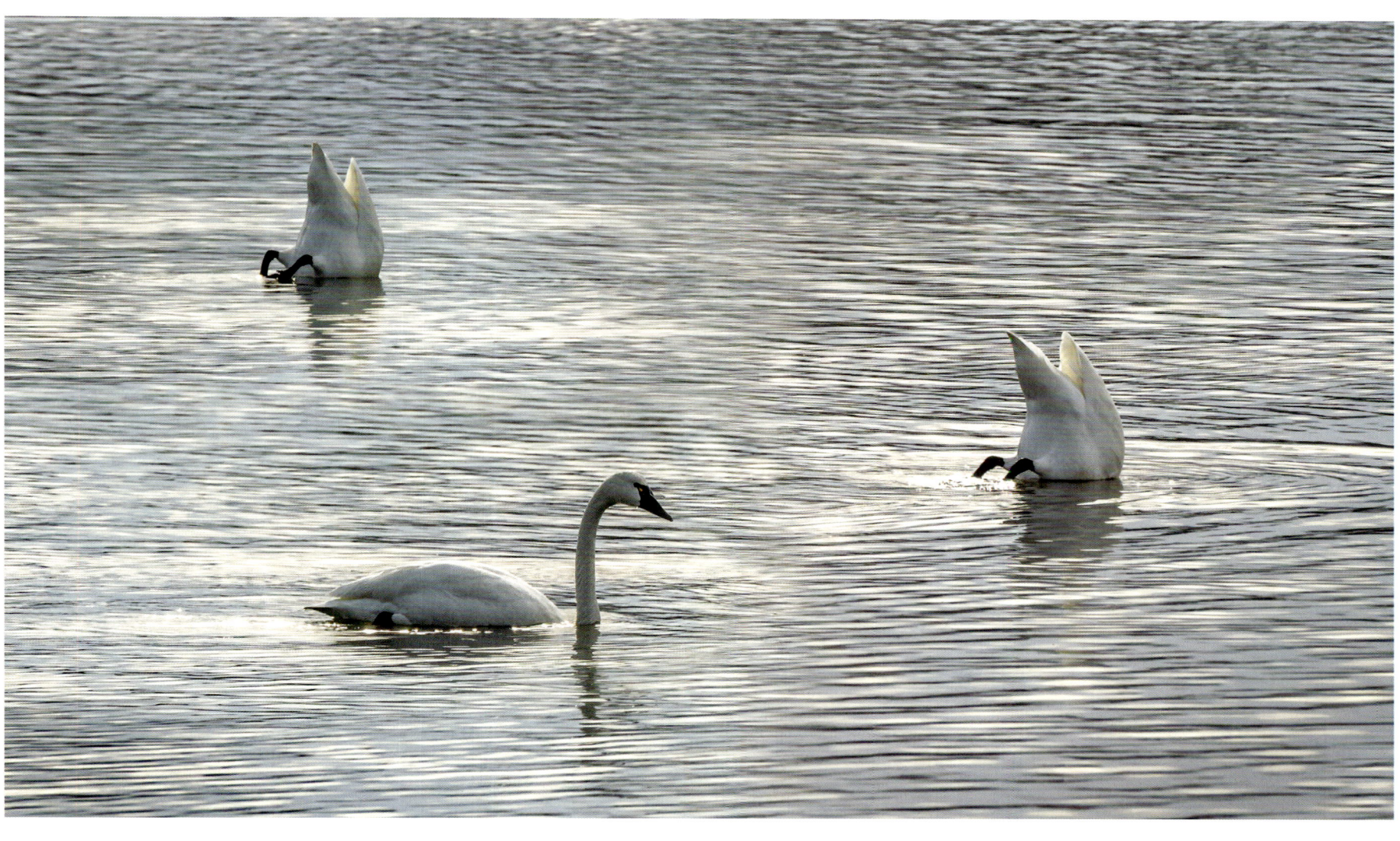

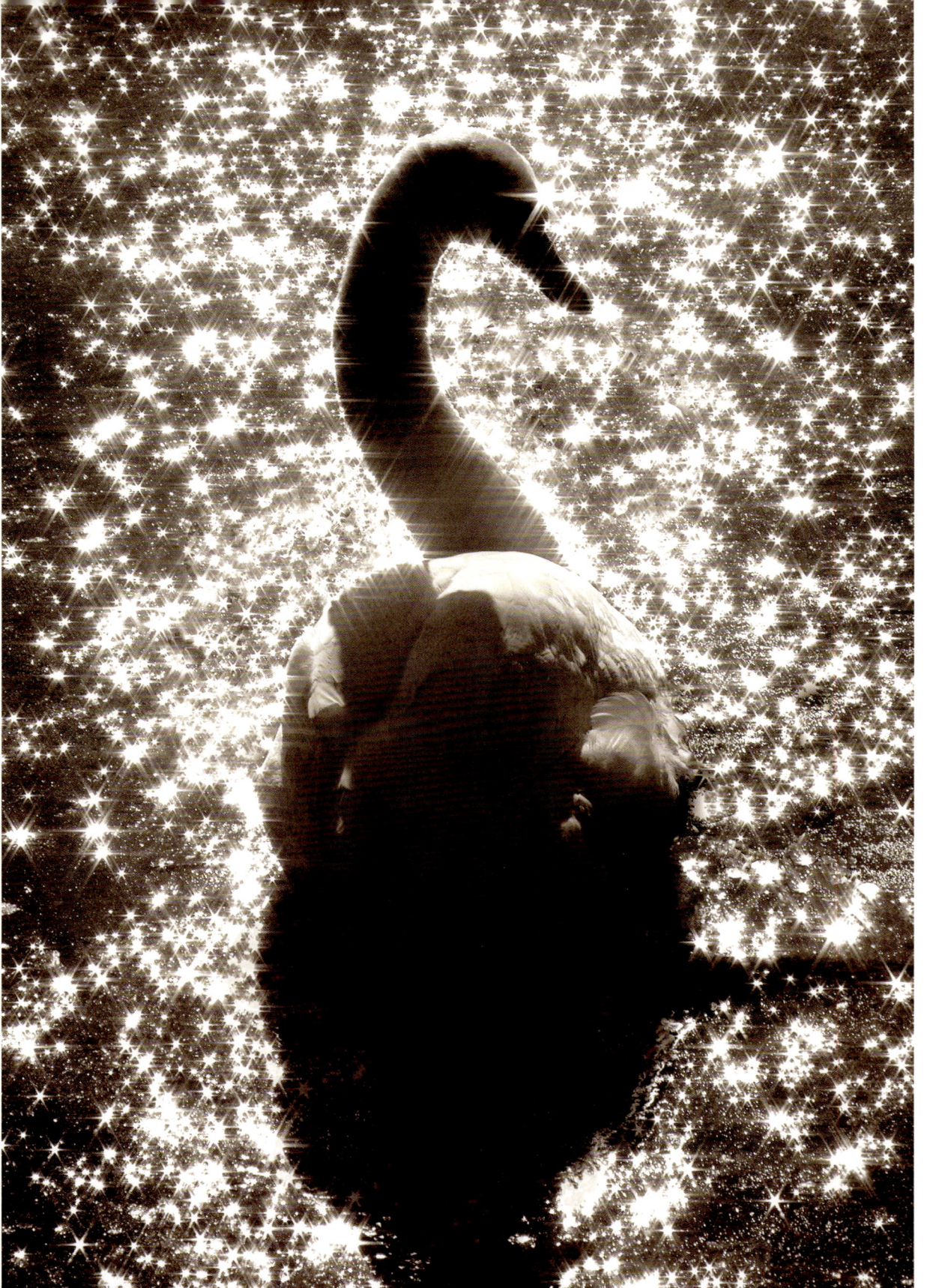

Icy sparkling swan

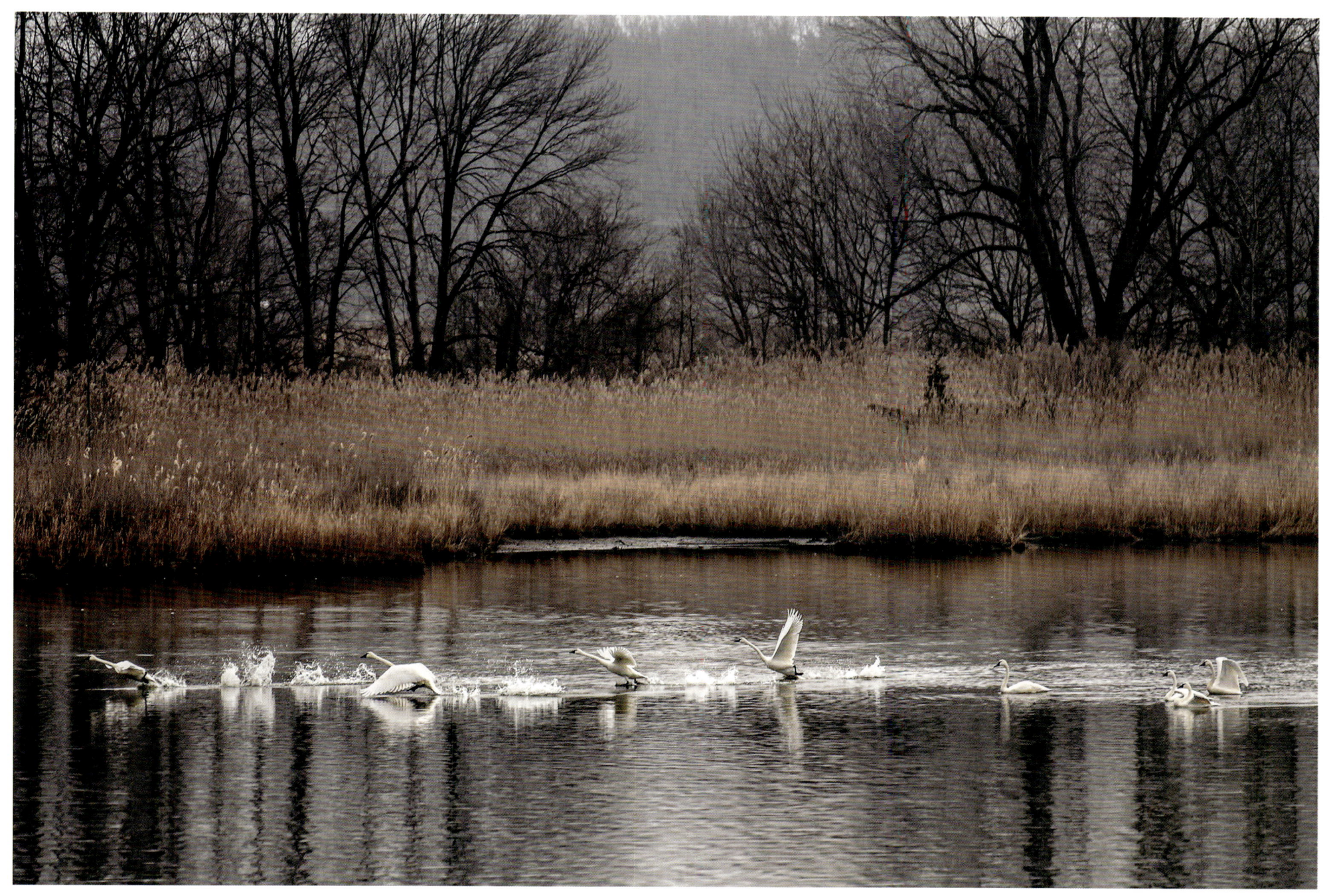

It's a mystery as to who decides it's time to take off.

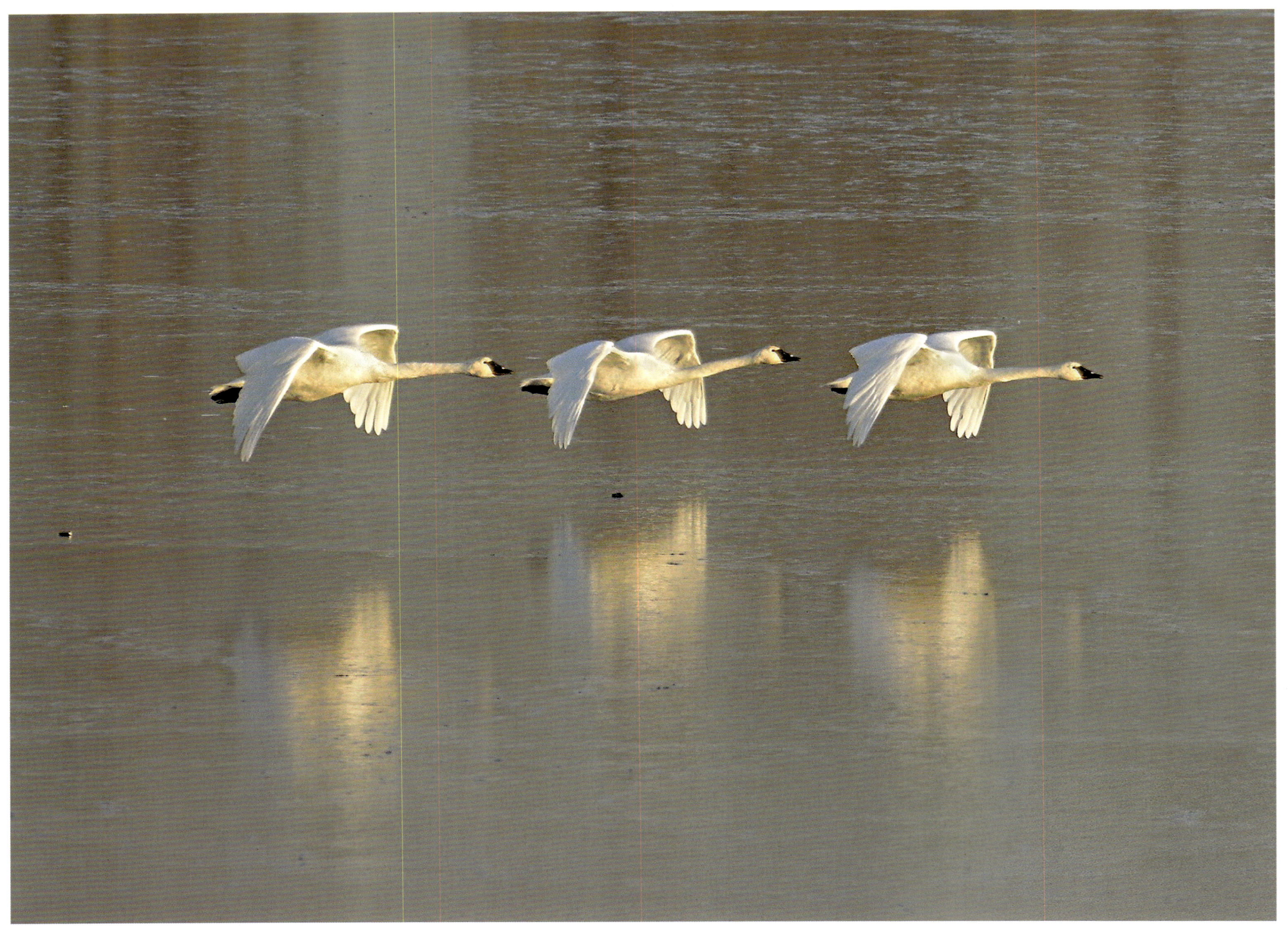

In sync

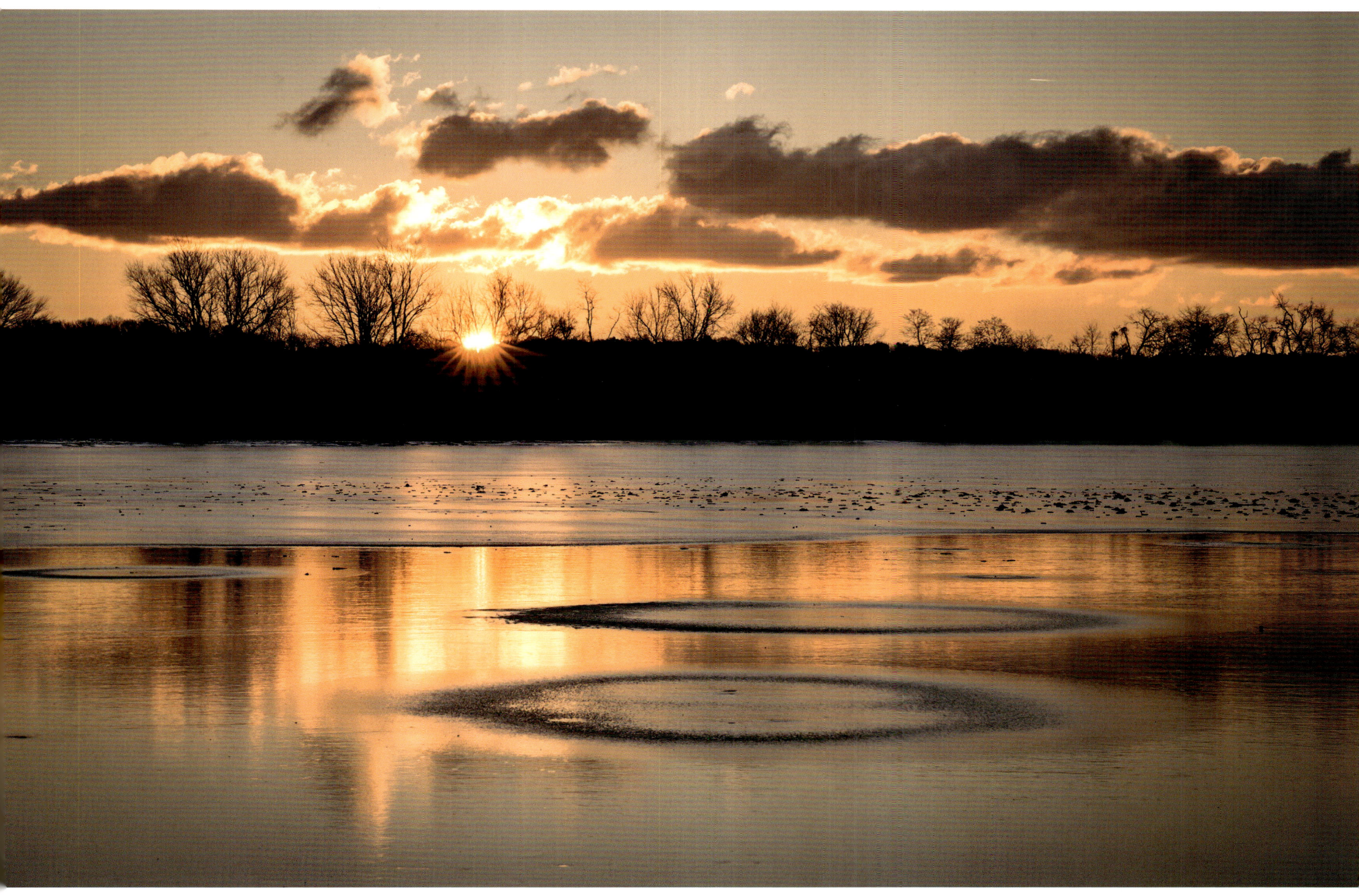

New Year's Day sunrise

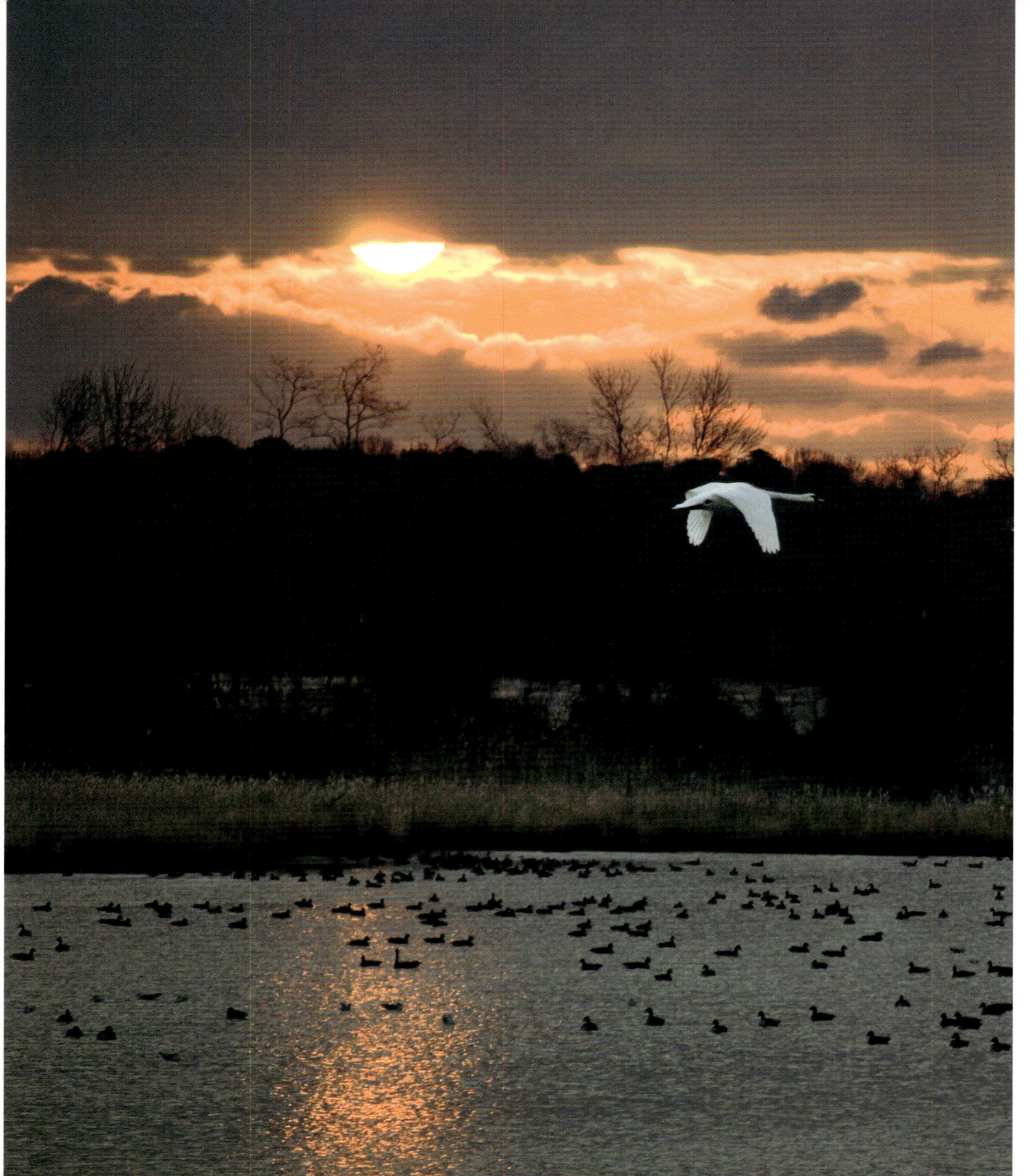

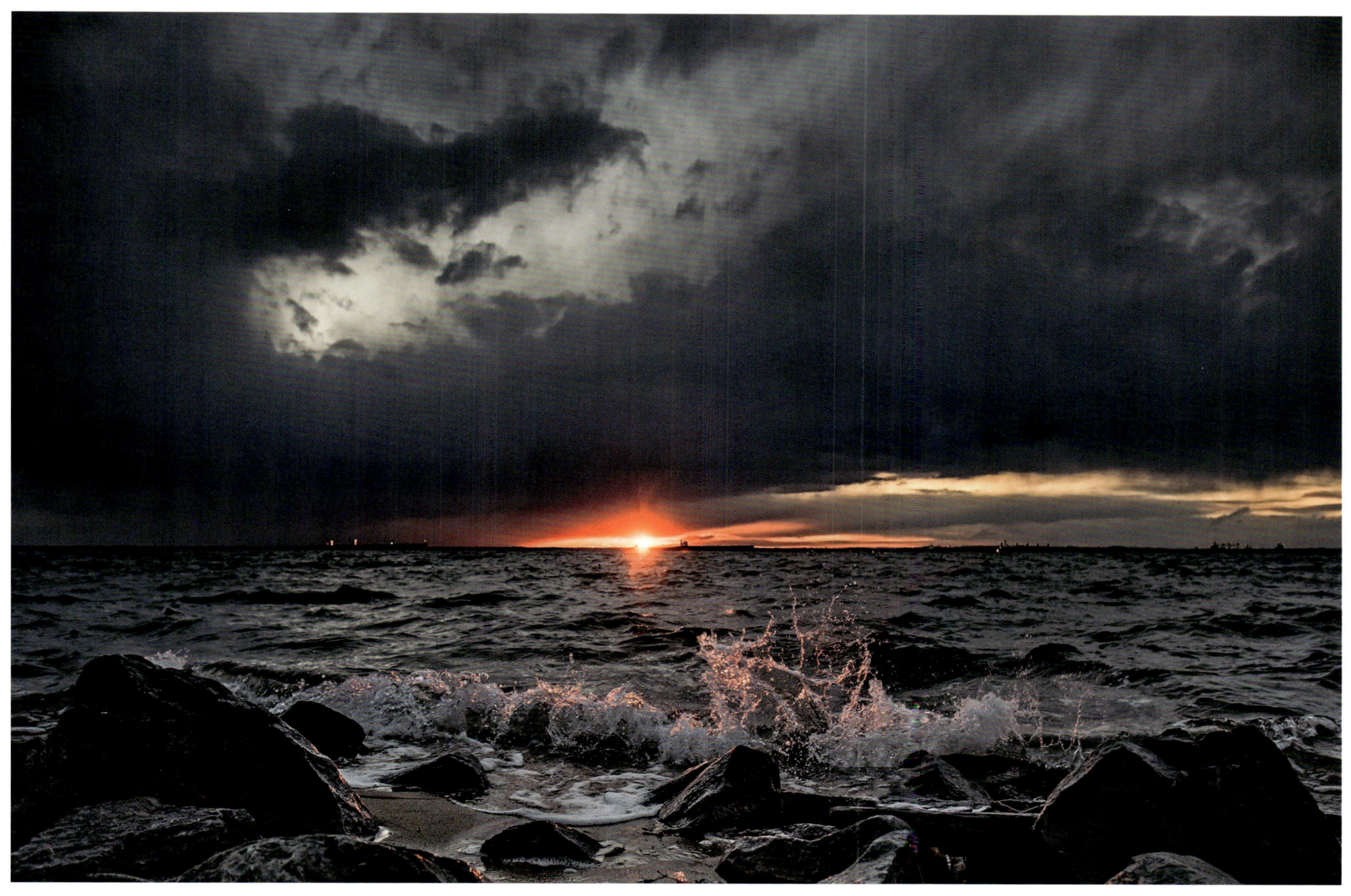

Another "Wow!" moment—the sun popped out under this dark cloud in rich hues and, in turn, created colorful splashes of water upon the shore.

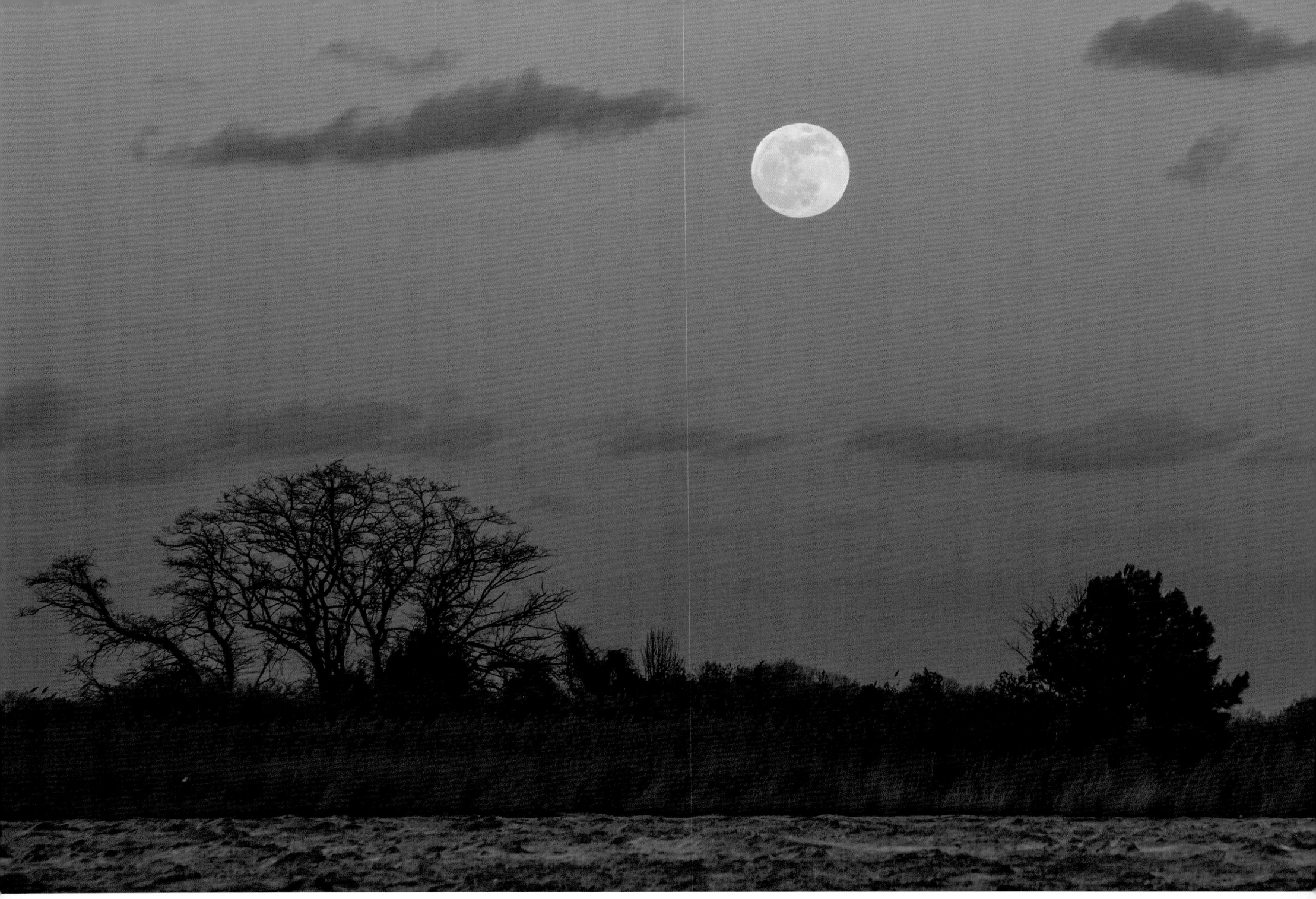

Super blood wolf moon o'er the Narrows

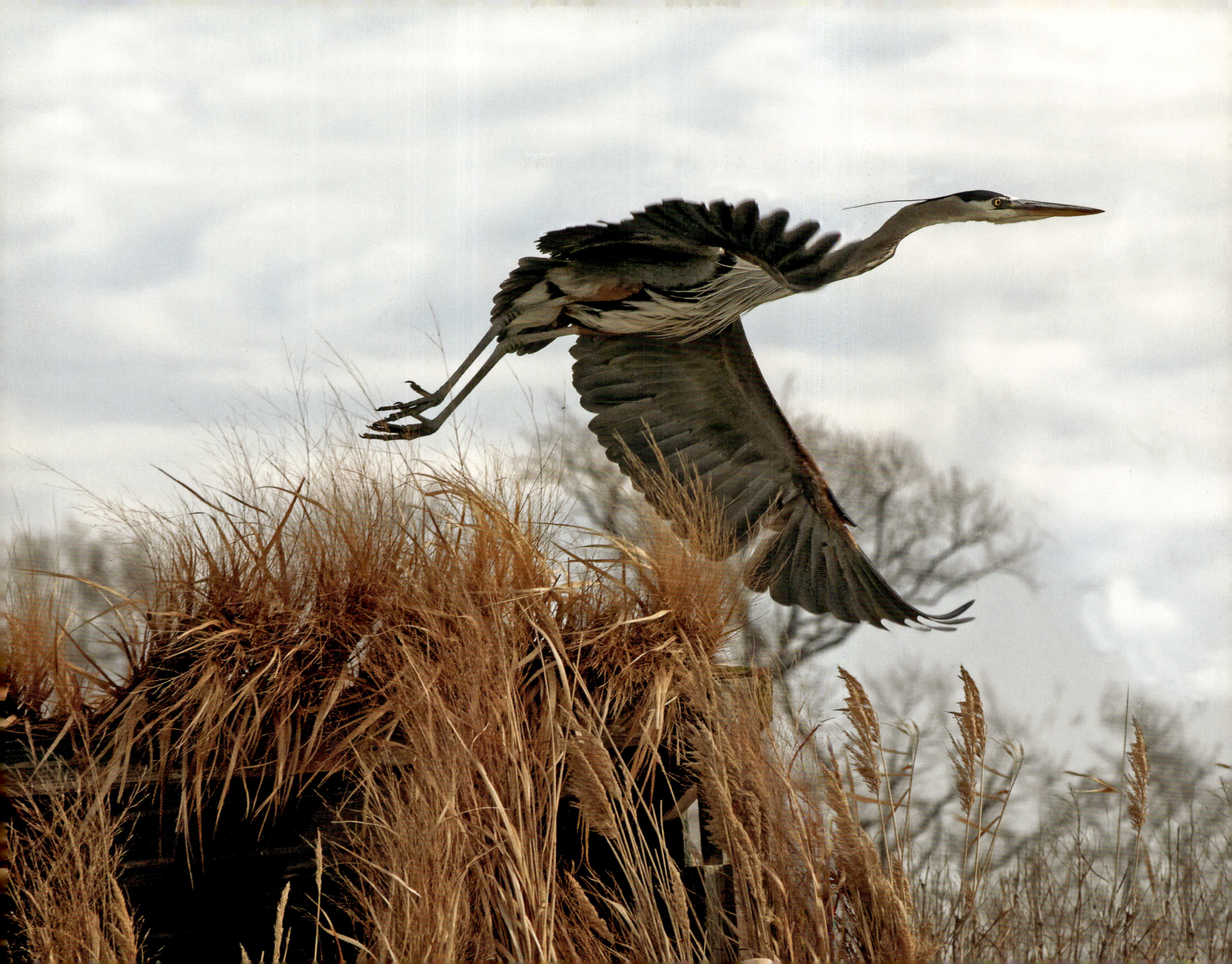

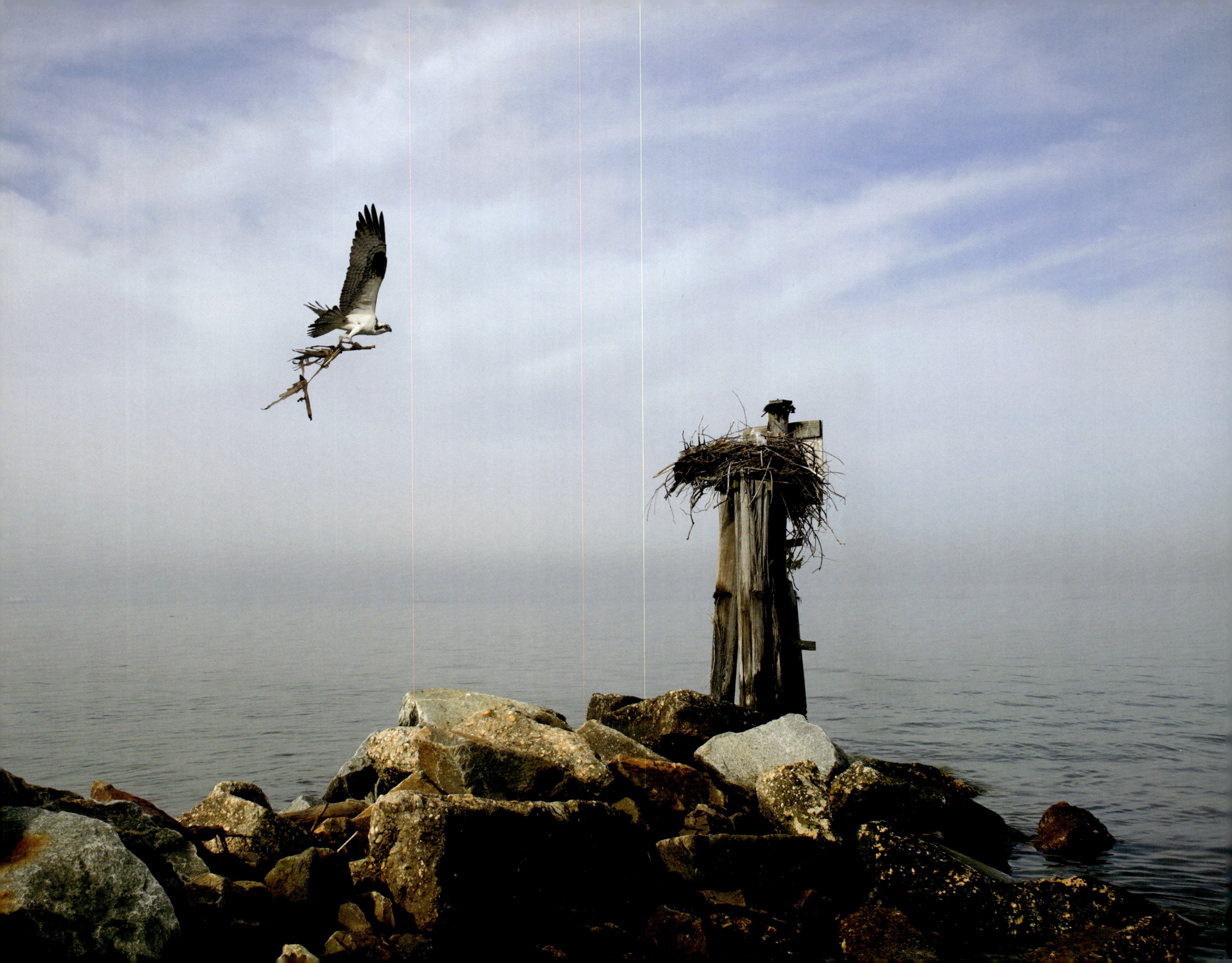

CHAPTER 2

SPRING

Spring weather can sometimes seem to take forever to arrive, due to the amount of rainfall the island typically gets in March and April as well as fluctuating temperatures. The birds that have migrated here from the North head back, while other birds that had taken flight for warmer climates return—usually to the very same nesting spots year after year.

Hearing the osprey peeps is a sure sign that spring has sprung. The osprey have multiplied in significant numbers after dwindling in the 1960s due to pesticide use around the bay area. You will see their nests on pilings around the water, which makes the search for their meals easy. You can also see nests in surprising areas, such as on some kind of structure next to a highway or on a boat. Bird enthusiasts have lent a hand by building nesting platforms that include one or two perches for the parents to keep watch of their young and to ensure stability so that all the hard work and preparation for the arrival of new chicks does not blow away with the wind.

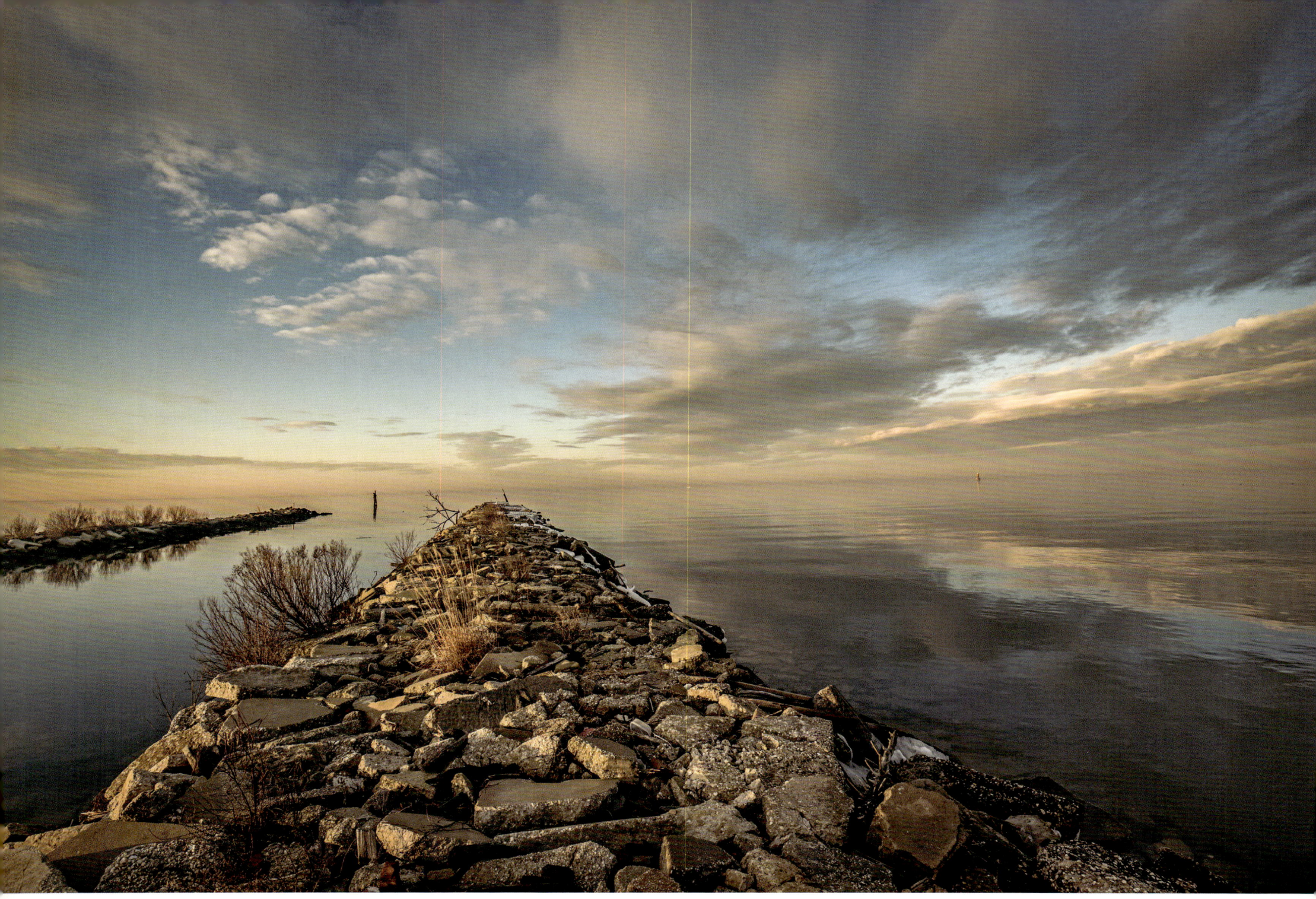

It almost looks like the water is flowing right into the sky in this photo.

In this photo, it looks like the Blood Point Bar Lighthouse had its light on, but that was not the case. It was a split second in time when the sun was shining so brightly early in the morning that it reflected off the metal in the light fixture—which in turn made a reflection on the water.

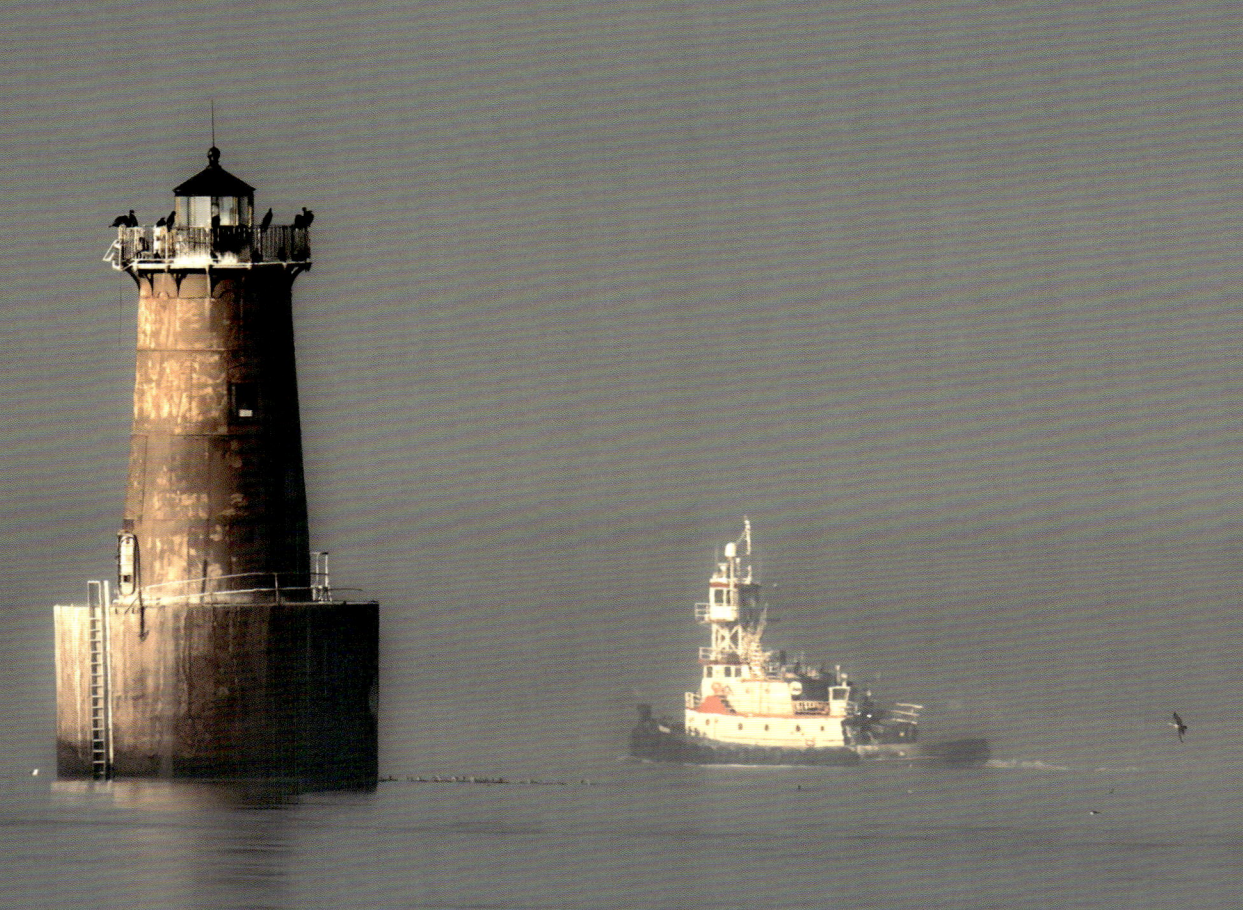

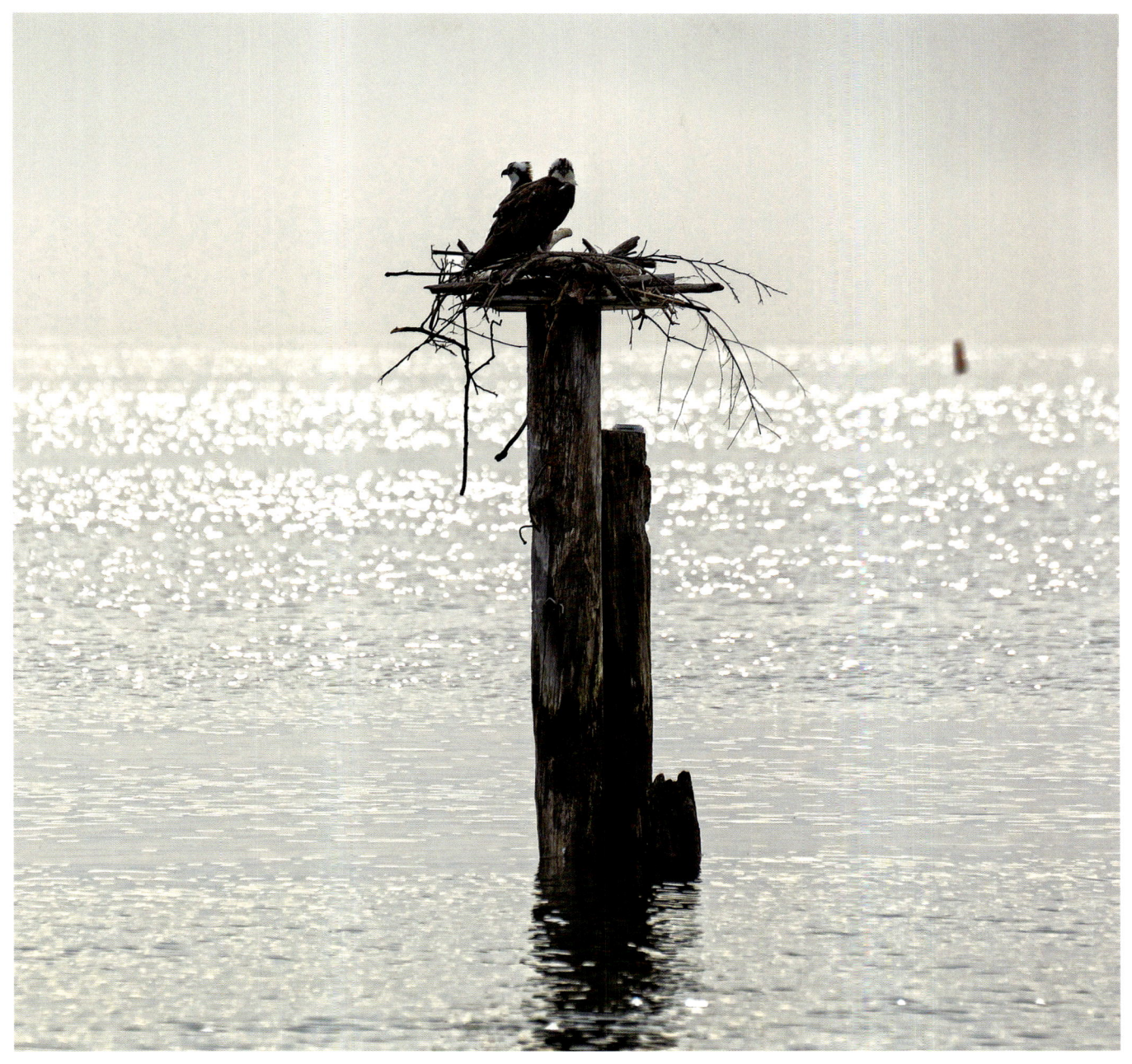

THE KENT NARROWS

BY JENNIFER GAYMAN RUFFNER

The Kent Narrows is the strait that separates Kent Island from the mainland of Queen Anne's County and the Eastern Shore. Known as the "Wading Place" in colonial times, this waterway was once quite shallow, with marshland on either side. A ferry once carried passengers across.

In 1826 an earthen causeway, or raised road across the marshland or water, was built, and it closed the Narrows to all boat traffic. In 1876, the causeway was removed and a new, deeper channel was dredged. Also, a series of bridges have connected Kent Island to the mainland, including drawbridges and several railroad bridges. Today, two bridges—the lower drawbridge and the higher Route 50/301 bridge—cross the Narrows.

The Narrows was once the heart of the seafood industry, with twelve packing houses in operation along its waters. In its heyday in the latter half of the twentieth century, hundreds of boats arrived daily to deliver their catch to the seafood houses. Only two packing houses remain today, but the Narrows still boasts numerous seafood restaurants. The waterway is regularly dredged to prevent it from silting closed.

Excerpt from kentislandheritagesociety.org

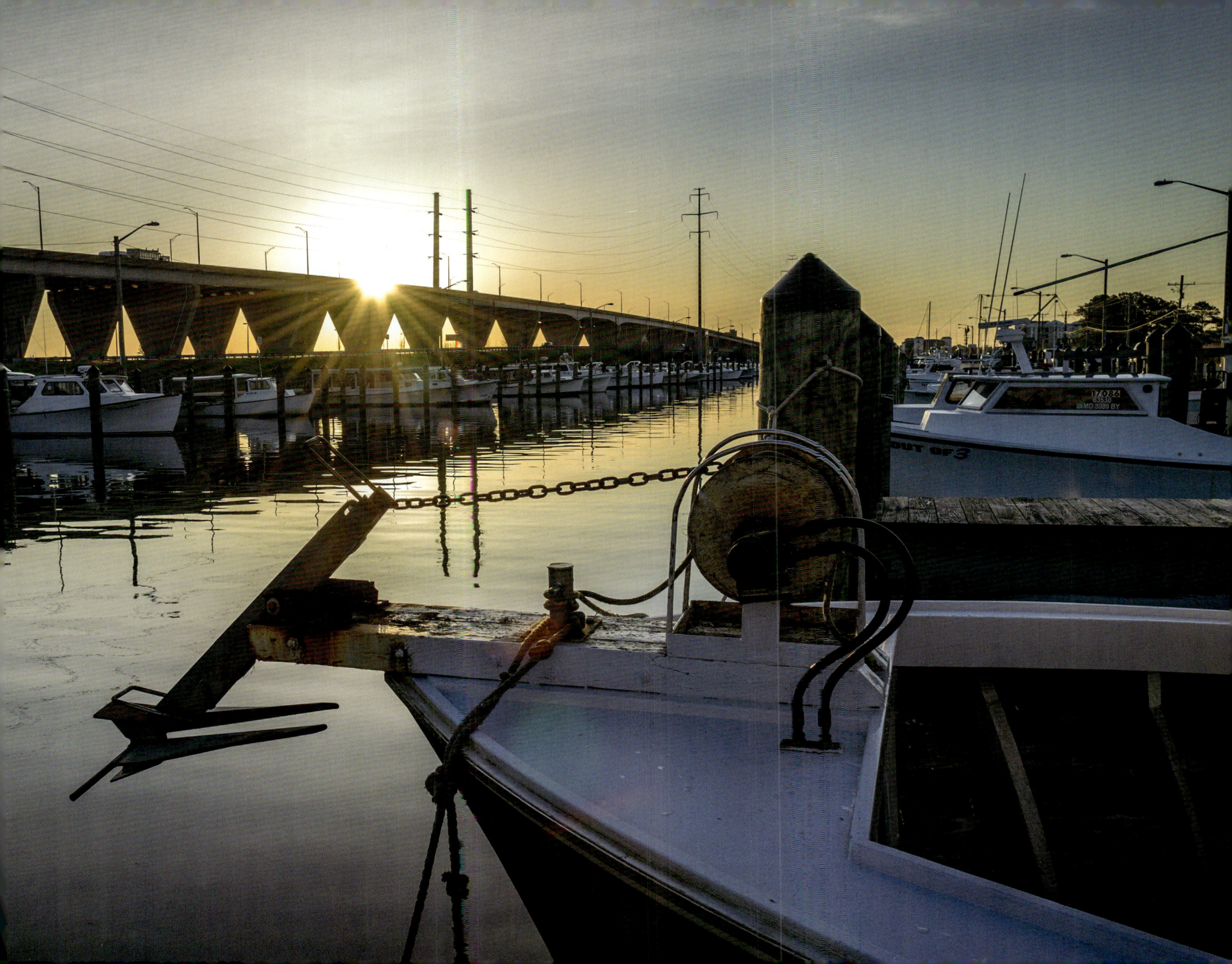

One pretty spring morning a few years ago, I decided to head over to Watermen's Boat Basin at Kent Narrows to see what interesting shots I might get. The late Captain Warren Butler was there having his morning coffee while leaning against his vehicle, which was parked in front of his boat, *Angel Lynn*. We said our pleasantries and became engaged in a long conversation. He began telling me his life story, which was quite impressive to say the least. Before we parted, I made a point to ask him if he would mind if I got a shot of him next to his boat. He seemed to enjoy having his picture taken. After we parted ways, I just knew I had met someone special.

Shortly after Captain Butler's passing a few years later, I learned more about just how special he was in a *Bay Times* article by Doug Bishop. Captain Butler had many accomplishments during his time working on the water, not to mention a long list of lifetime achievements during his career in the US Army and as a correctional officer. He also served on a number of boards of directors, including serving as president of the Queen Anne's County Watermen's Protective Association. He was also the first African American president of the Queen Anne's County Board of Education.

Butler's calling as a waterman was sparked at a young age when he worked alongside his father and brothers to support his family. During the span of his lifetime, he owned seventeen commercial boats that he used for carrying fishing and sightseeing parties out on the Chesapeake Bay and the surrounding waterways of Kent Narrows.

Butler was featured in the documentary *Black Captains of the Chesapeake Bay*, and information about his life is included in exhibits at the Kennard African American Cultural Heritage Center in Centreville, Maryland, and the Chesapeake Heritage & Visitor Center located at Kent Narrows in Chester, Maryland.

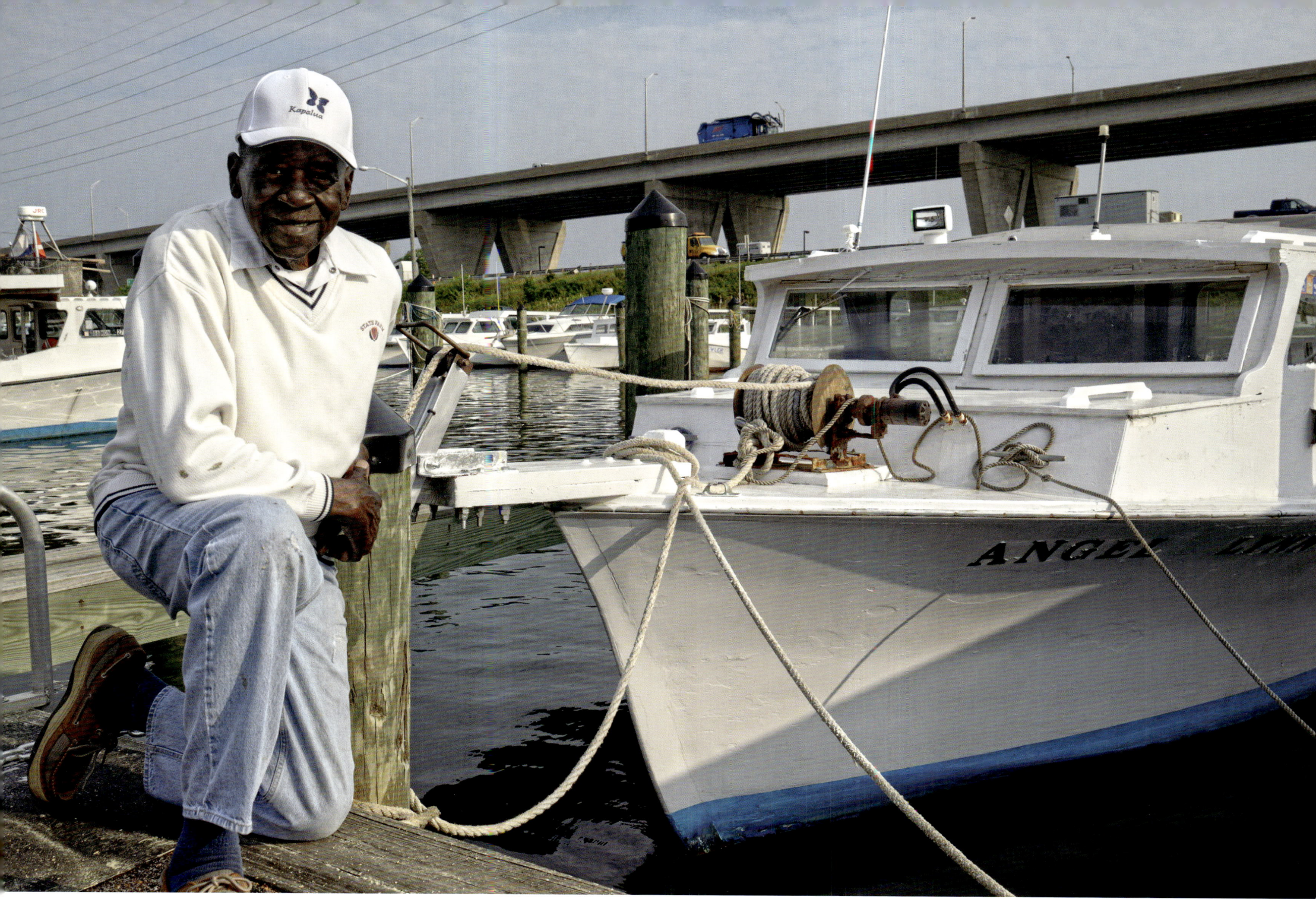

The late Captain Butler with his boat

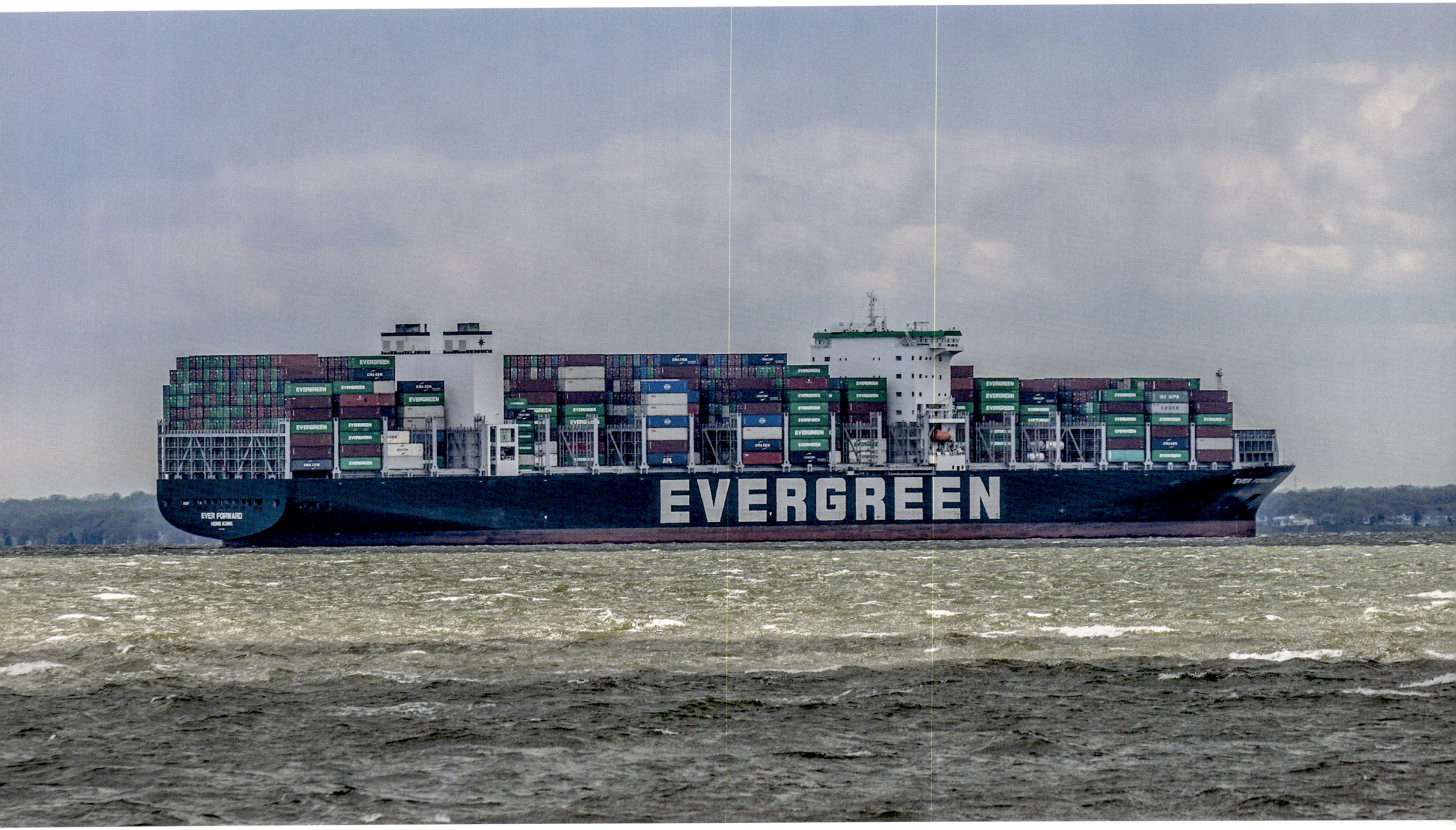

The container ship *Ever Forward* was moved to Annapolis Anchorage, adjacent to Kent Island, for inspection after running aground on the Craighill Channel just north of the Chesapeake Bay Bridge on March 13, 2022. It had been stuck for five weeks, and after several unsuccessful attempts to free it up by dredging around it, it became clear that the load would have to be lightened. So five hundred containers weighing a total of 15 million pounds or more were taken off, which freed up enough weight to get it to move. Two barges and six tugboats pulled the 1,100-foot vessel off and into the channel. It was truly a historic event, because that operation had never before been accomplished on a vessel that size, and it made international news.

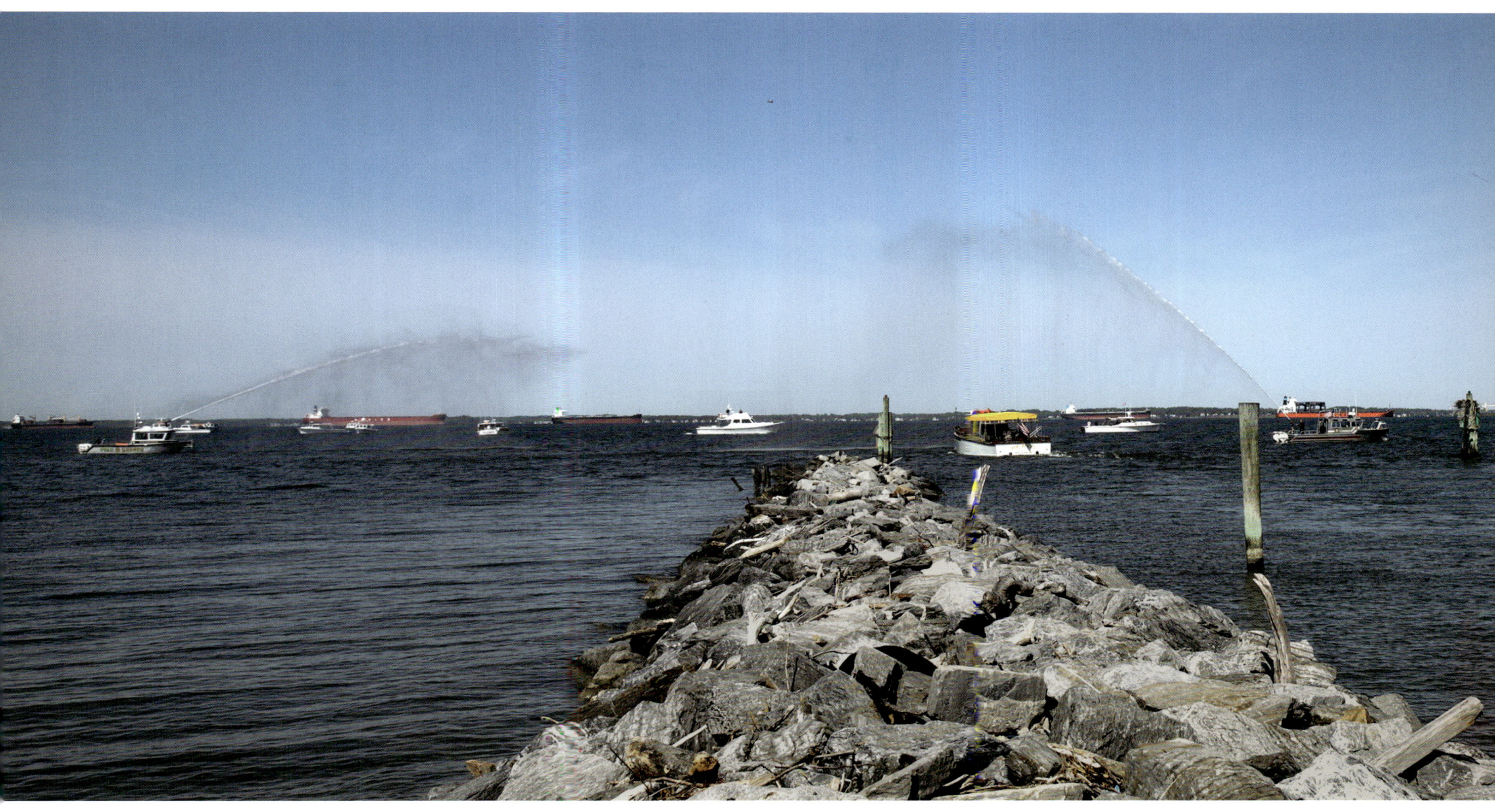

During Kentmorr Marina's inaugural Blessing of the Fleet, after each boat had had its blessing announced and had proceeded through the fireboat spray, the boats headed back into the marina inlet.

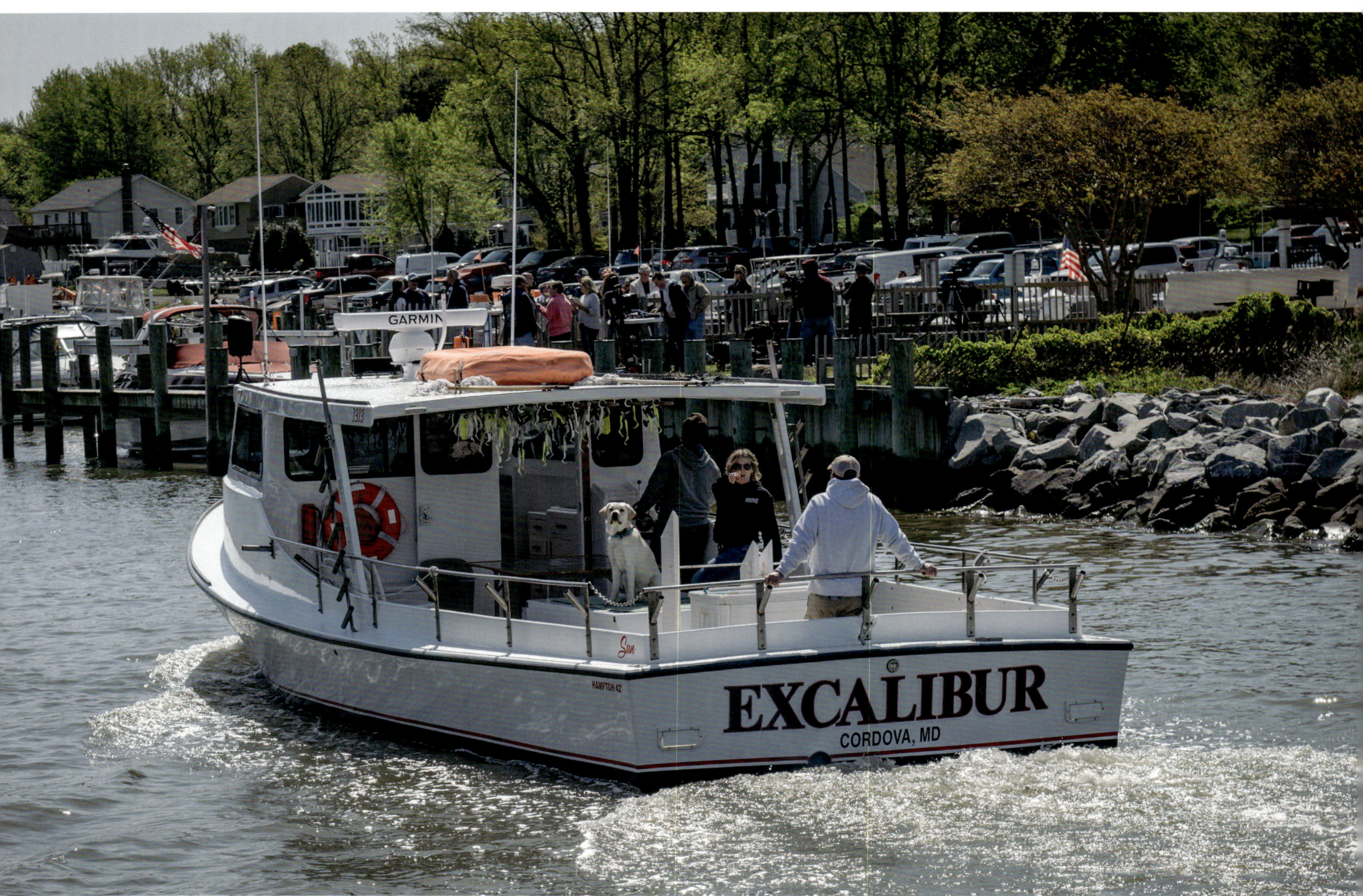

Labrador retriever Billy is instructed to look at the camera for a photo op.

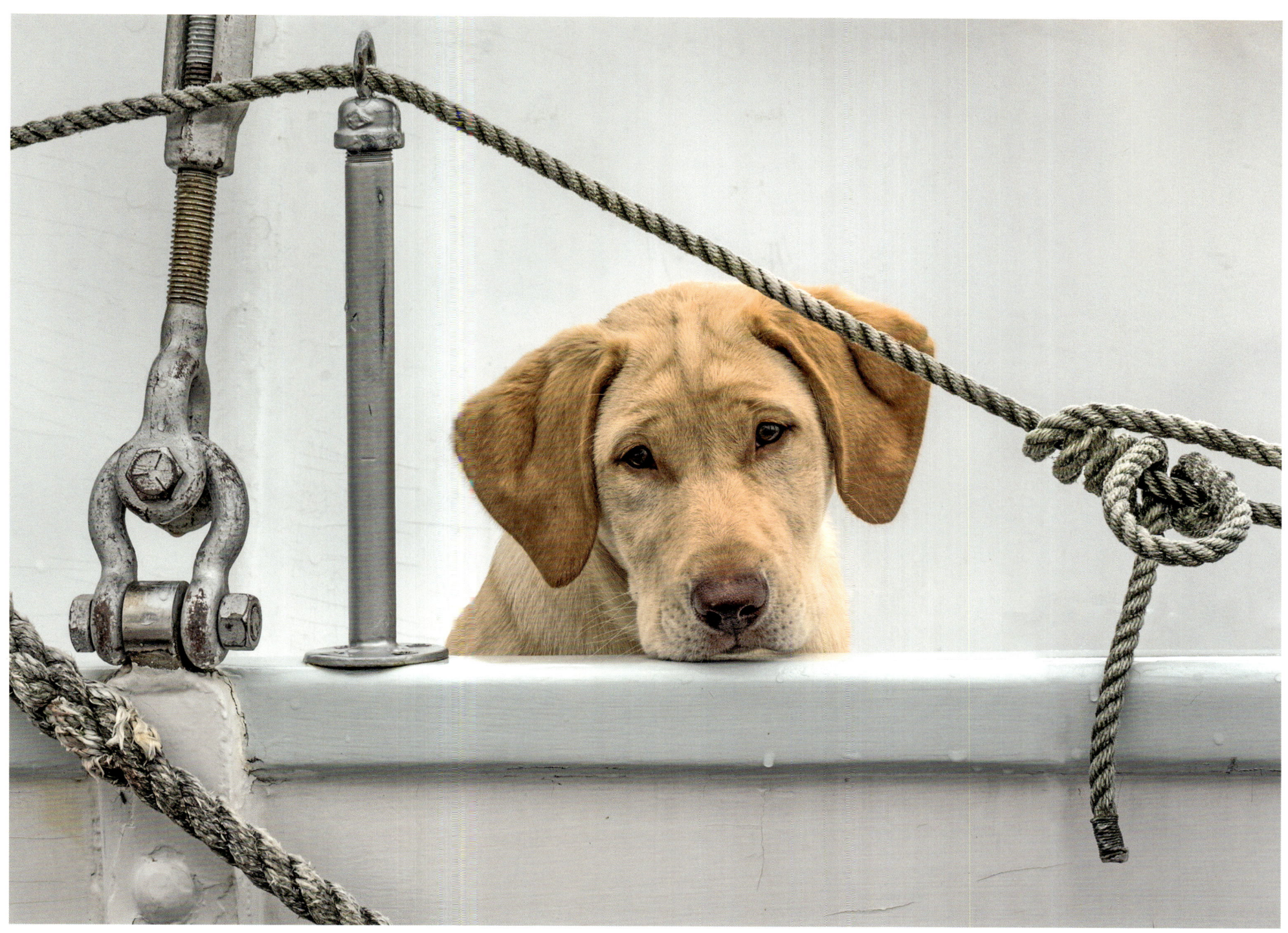

Roxy Sunshine waits patiently for a sail on skipjack *Lady Helen,*
docked at Queen Anne Marina.

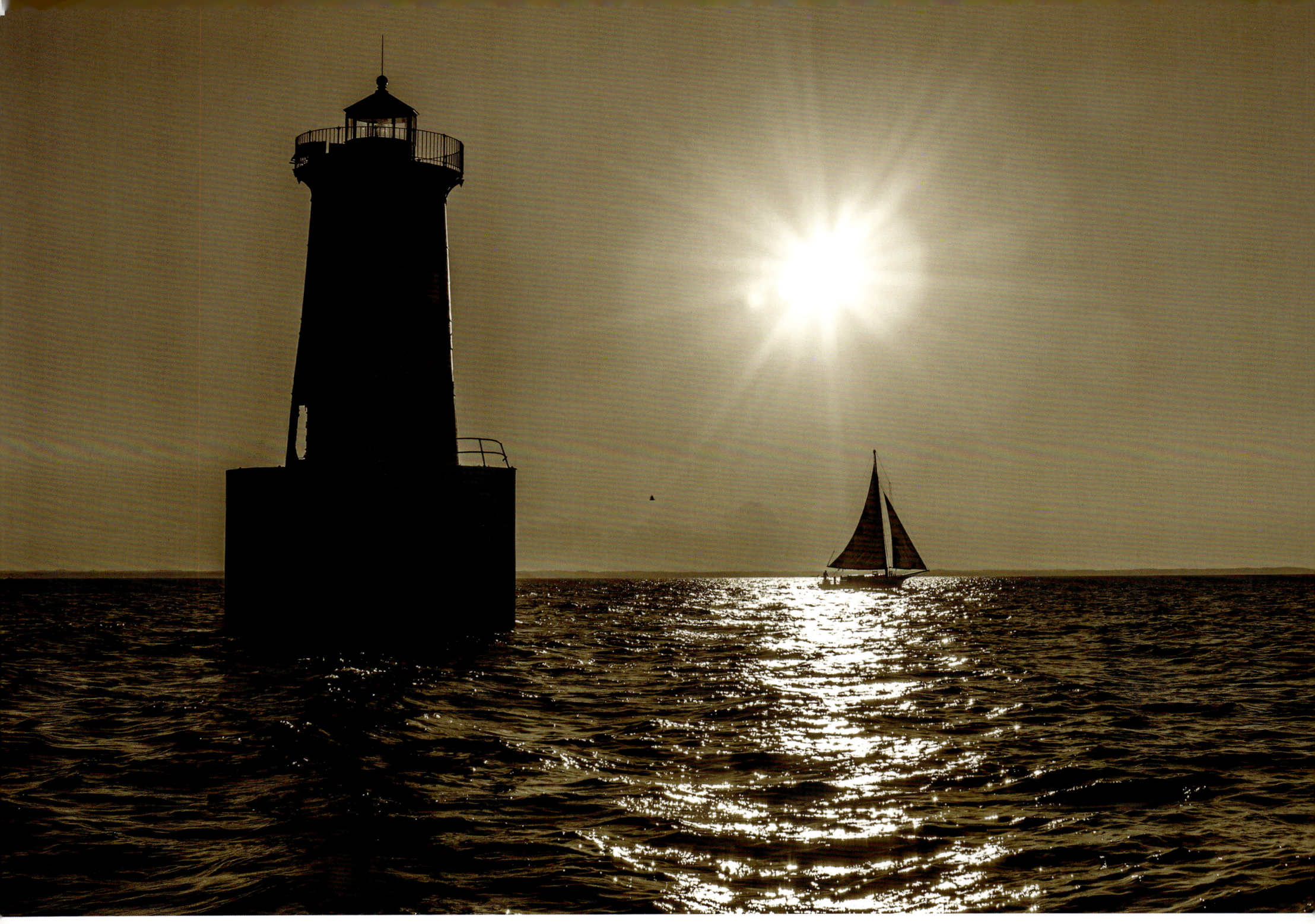

Pictured here and on the next page is skipjack *Lady Helen*,
chartered out of Queen Anne Marina.

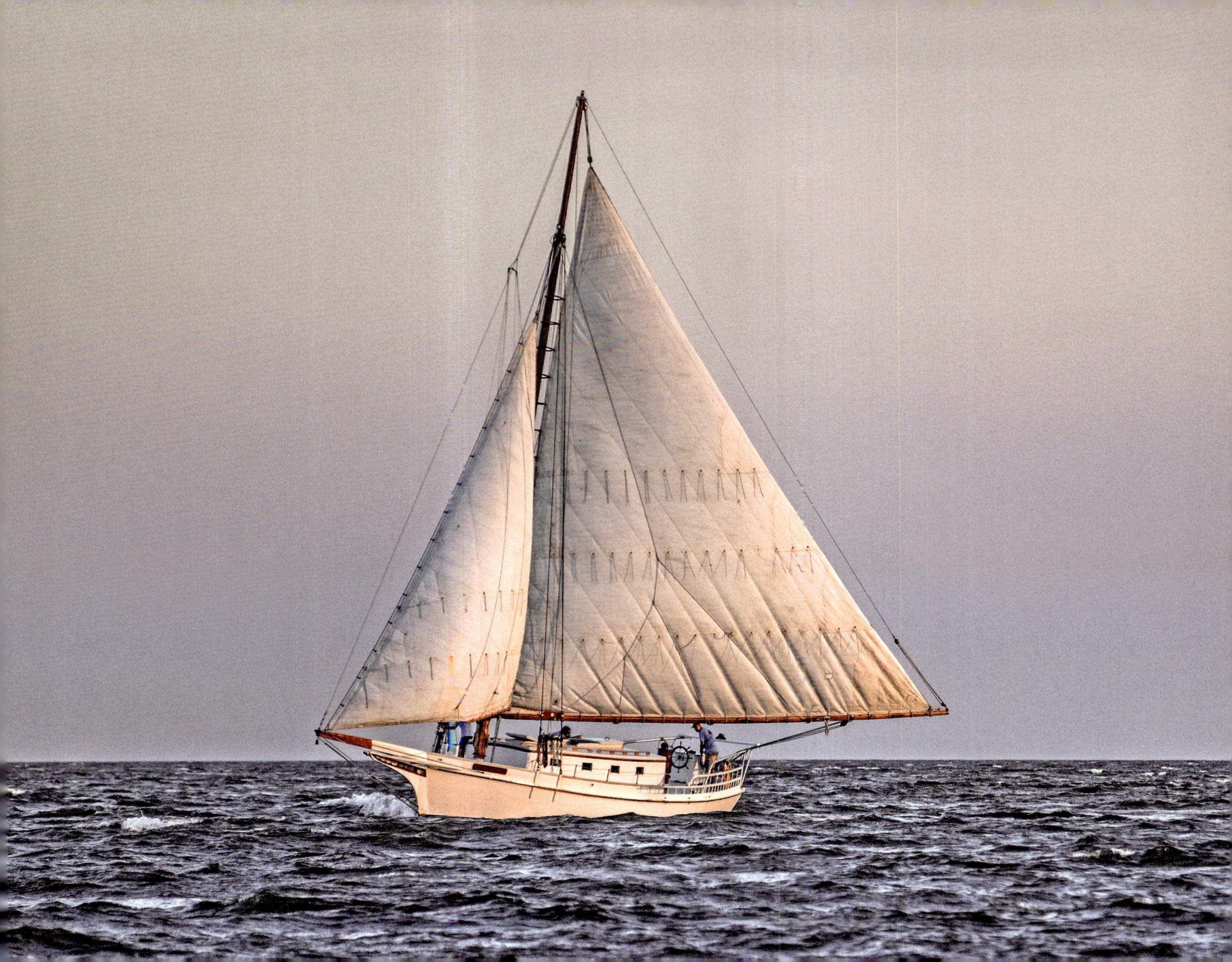

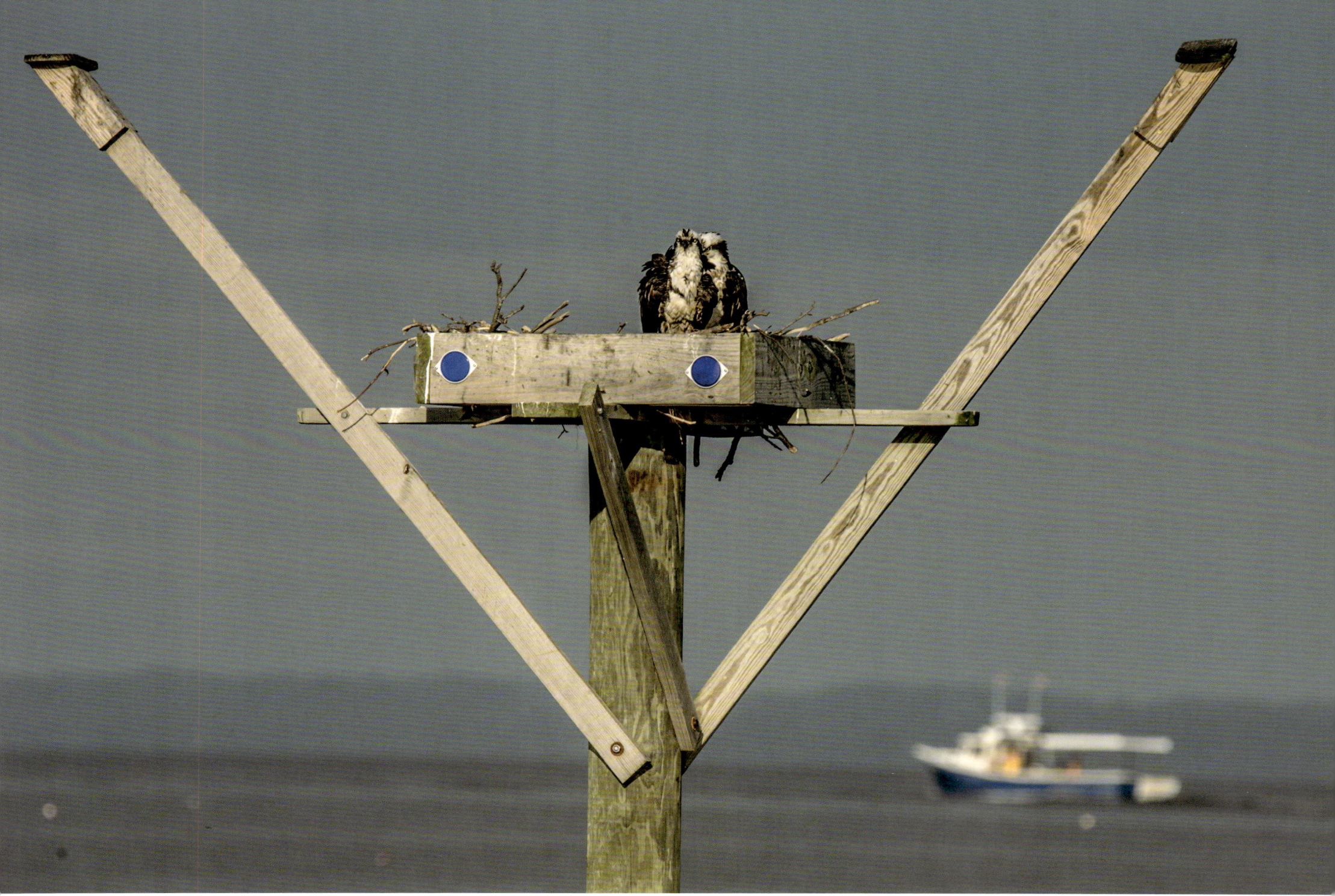

This photo shows a couple of osprey that seem to delight in each other's company.
Osprey are monogamous but not always lovey-dovey when it comes to squabbling over a catch.

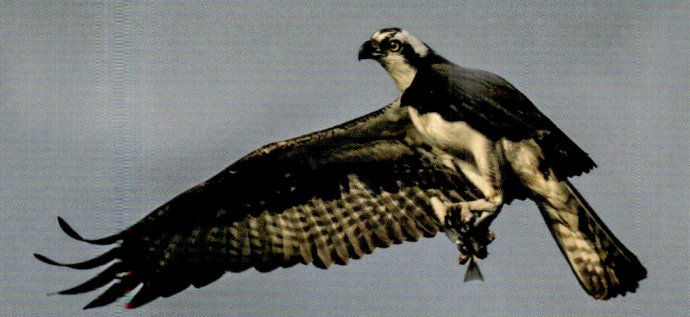
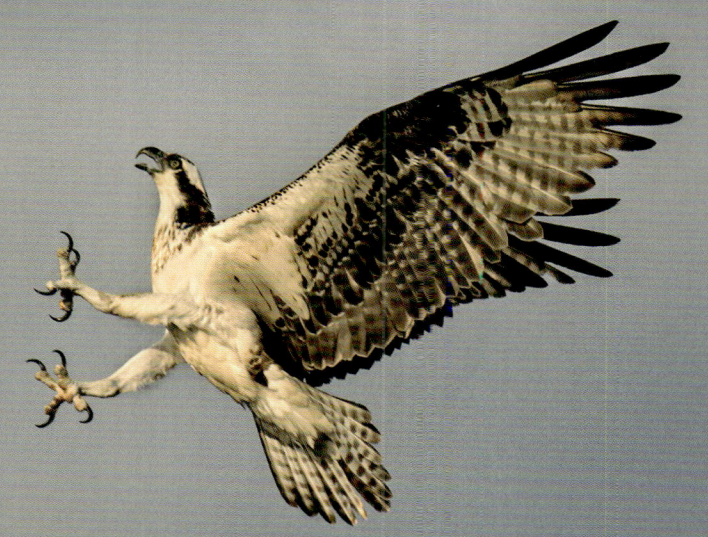

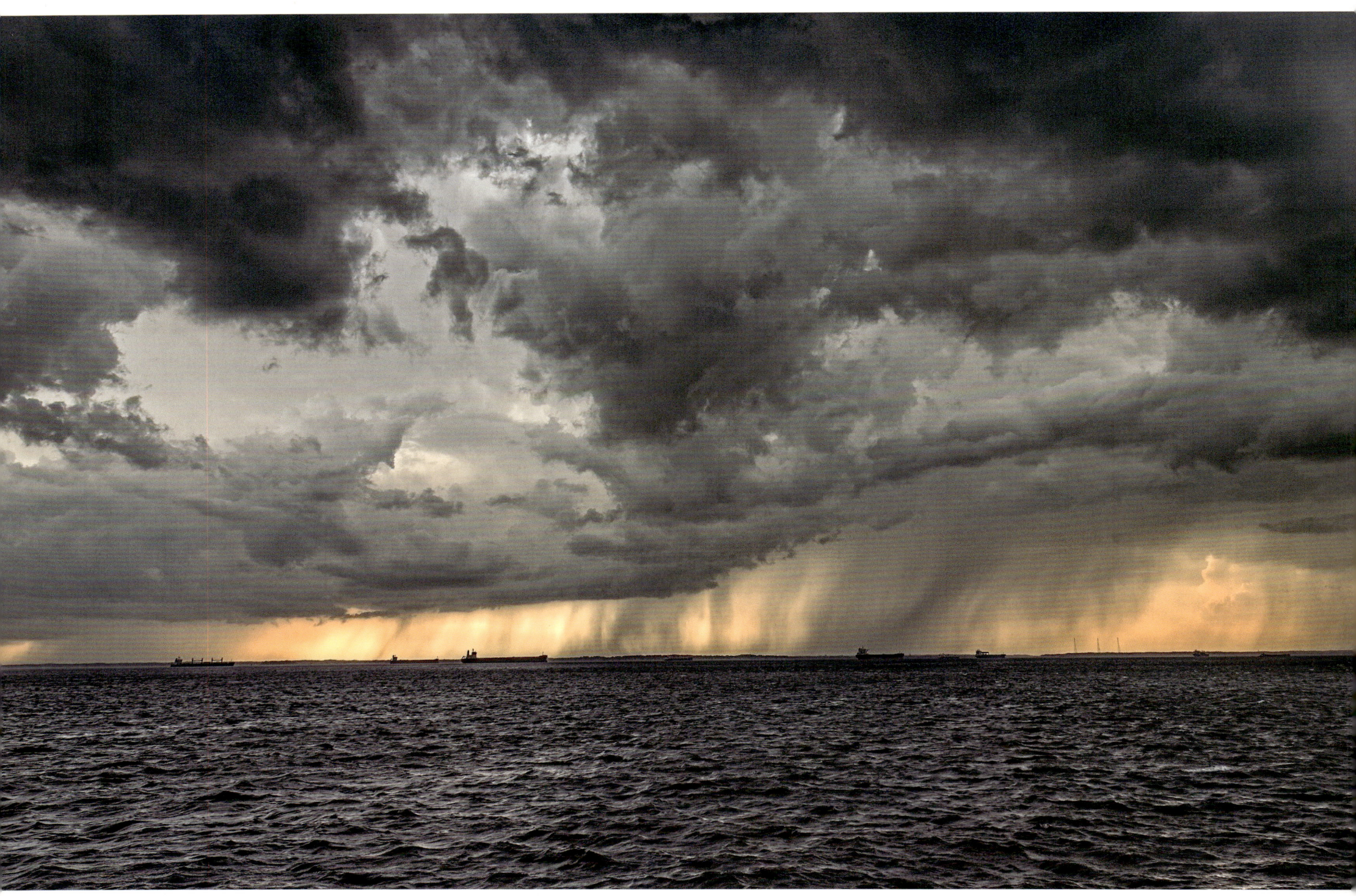

A storm brewin' may be an awesome sight, but it's not a welcome one for boaters.

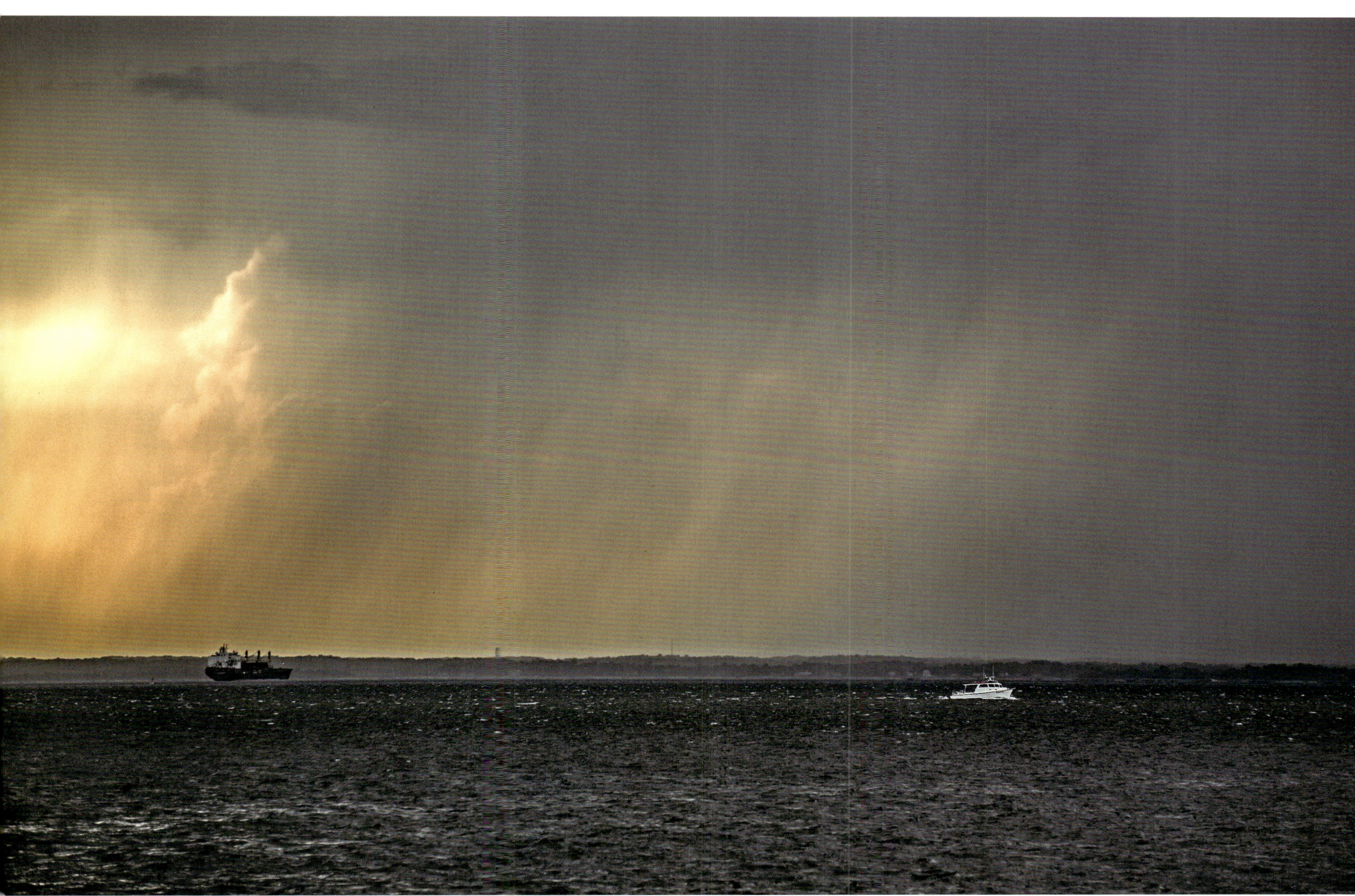

Charter boat *Marylander* races the storm.

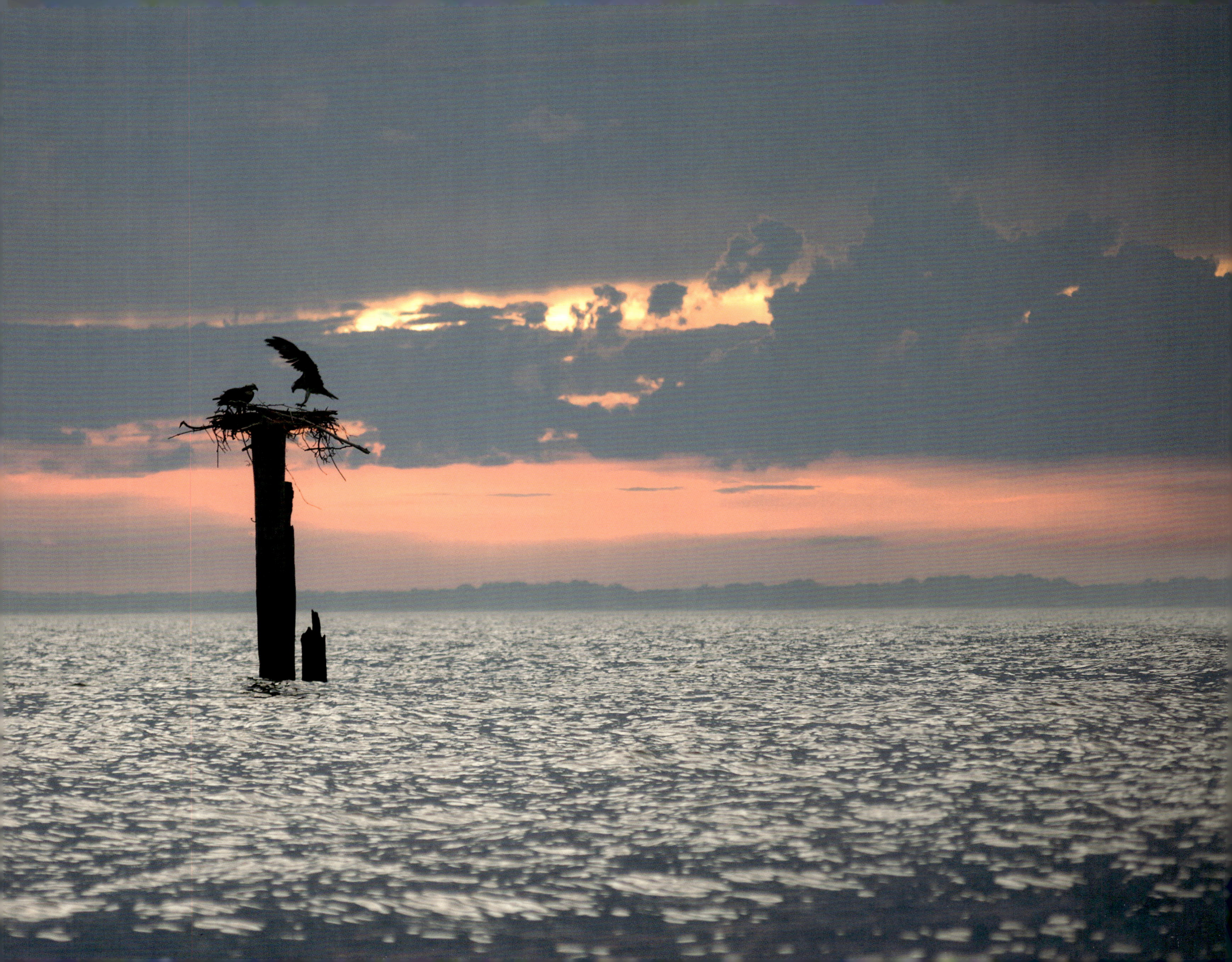

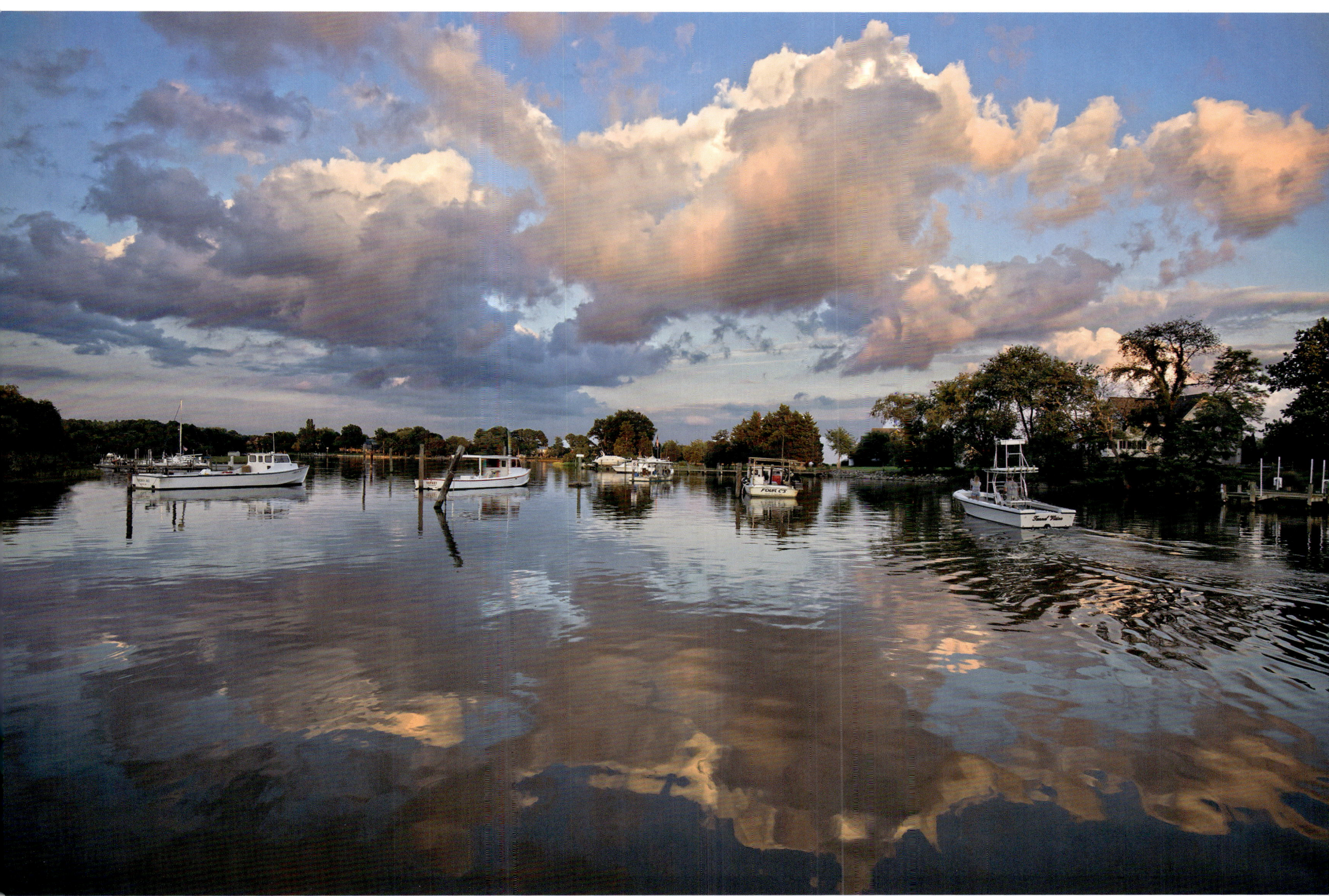

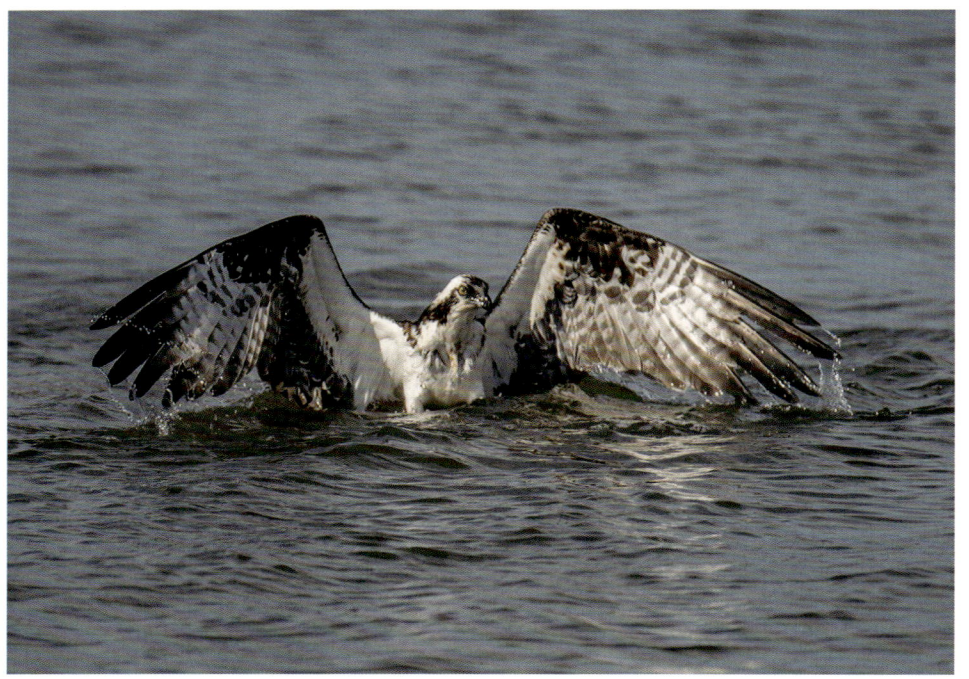 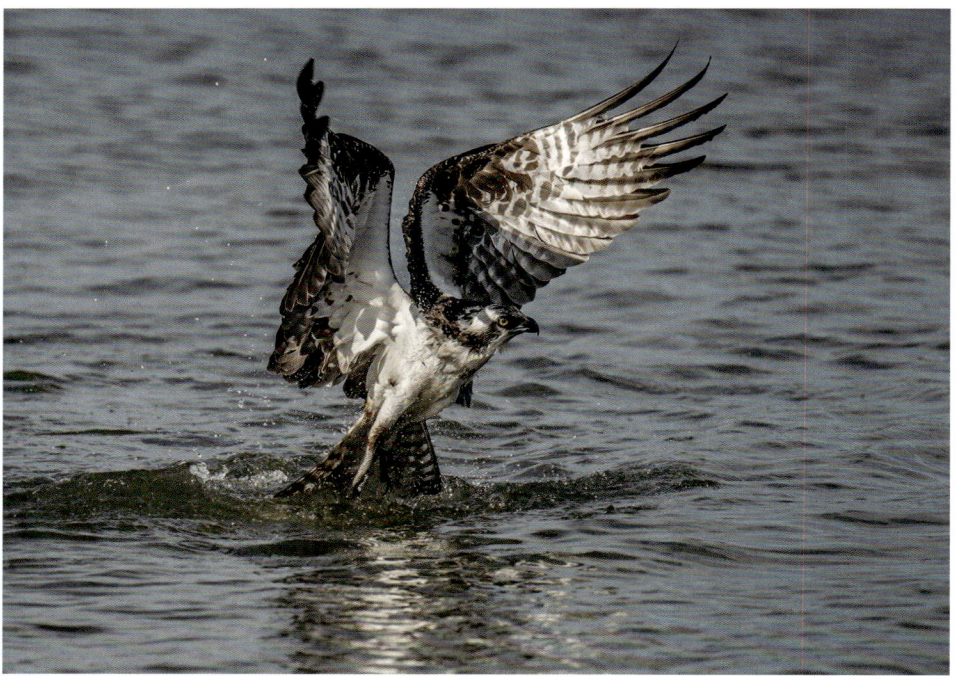

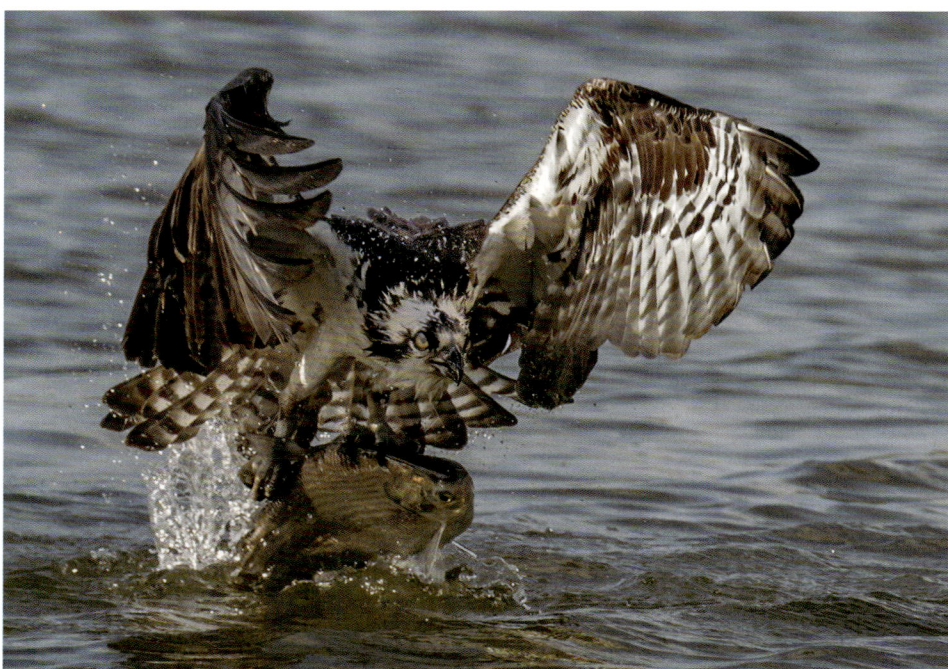 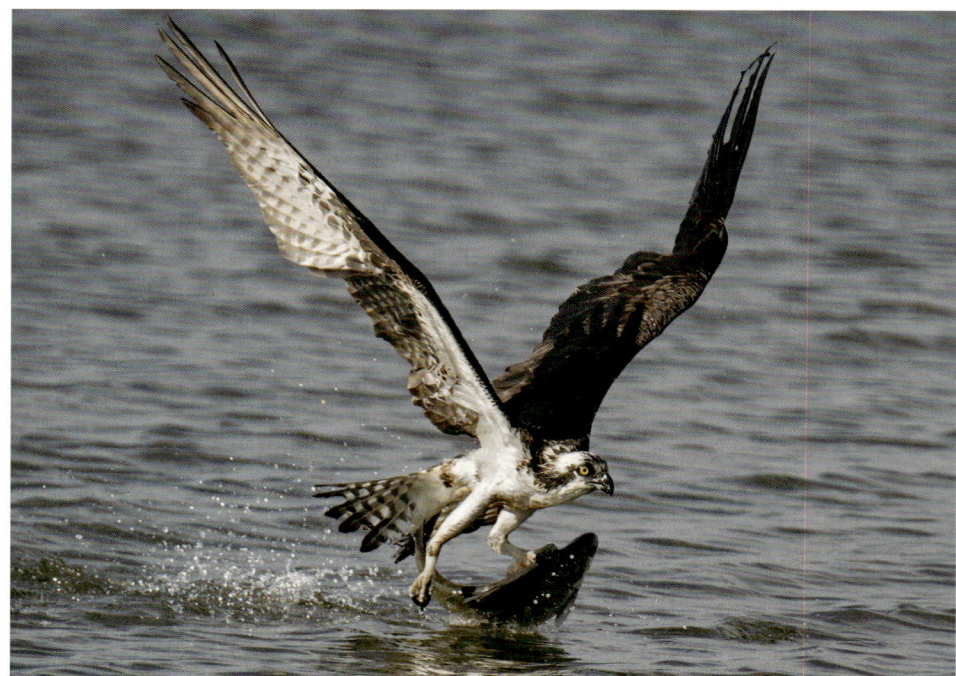

Witnessing an osprey diving straight down with such speed and then seeing it pop up
with a fish makes for such an extraordinary moment.

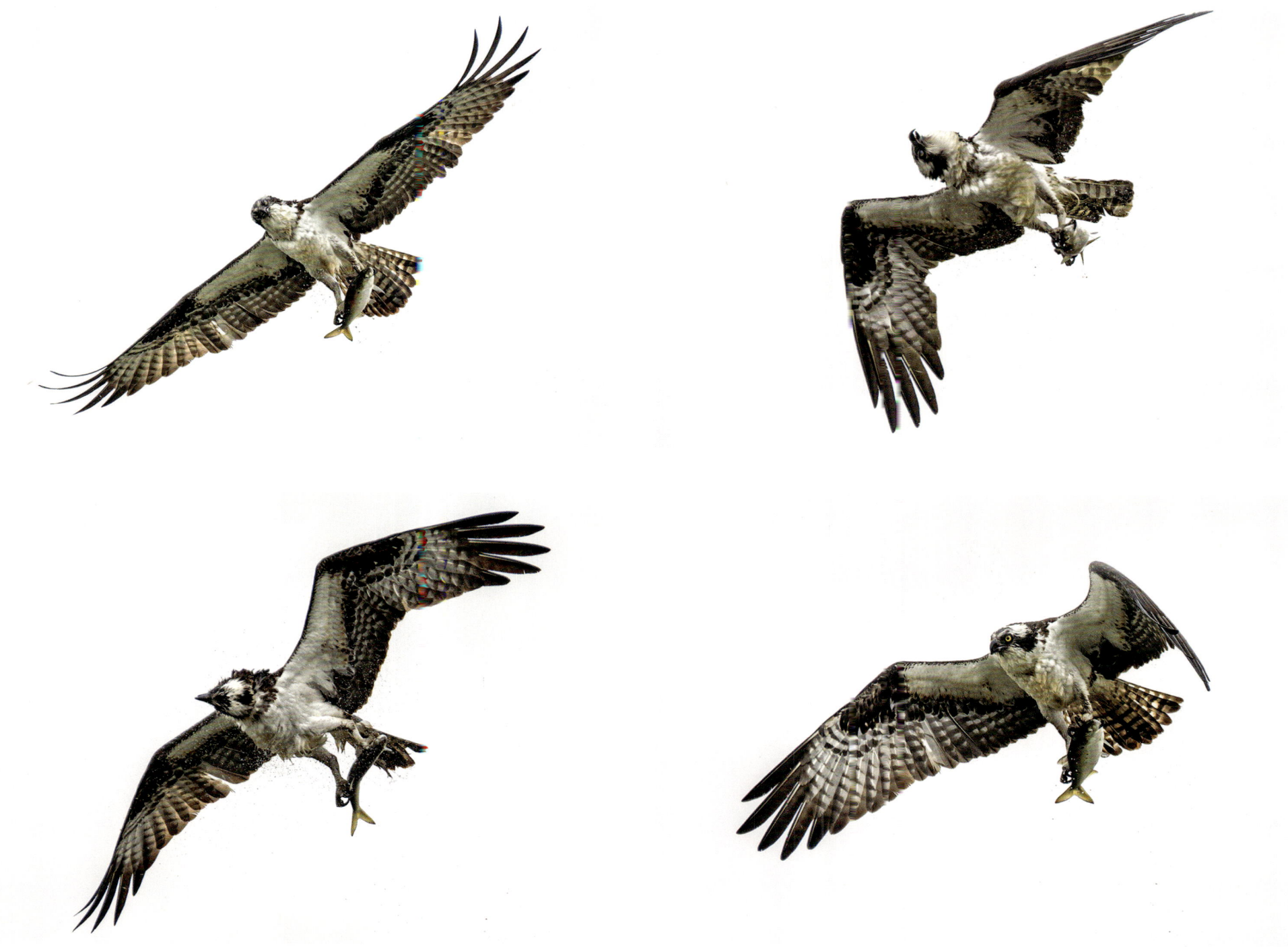

Osprey go through a series of movements to shake off the water, which can weigh them down in their flight back to hungry chicks.

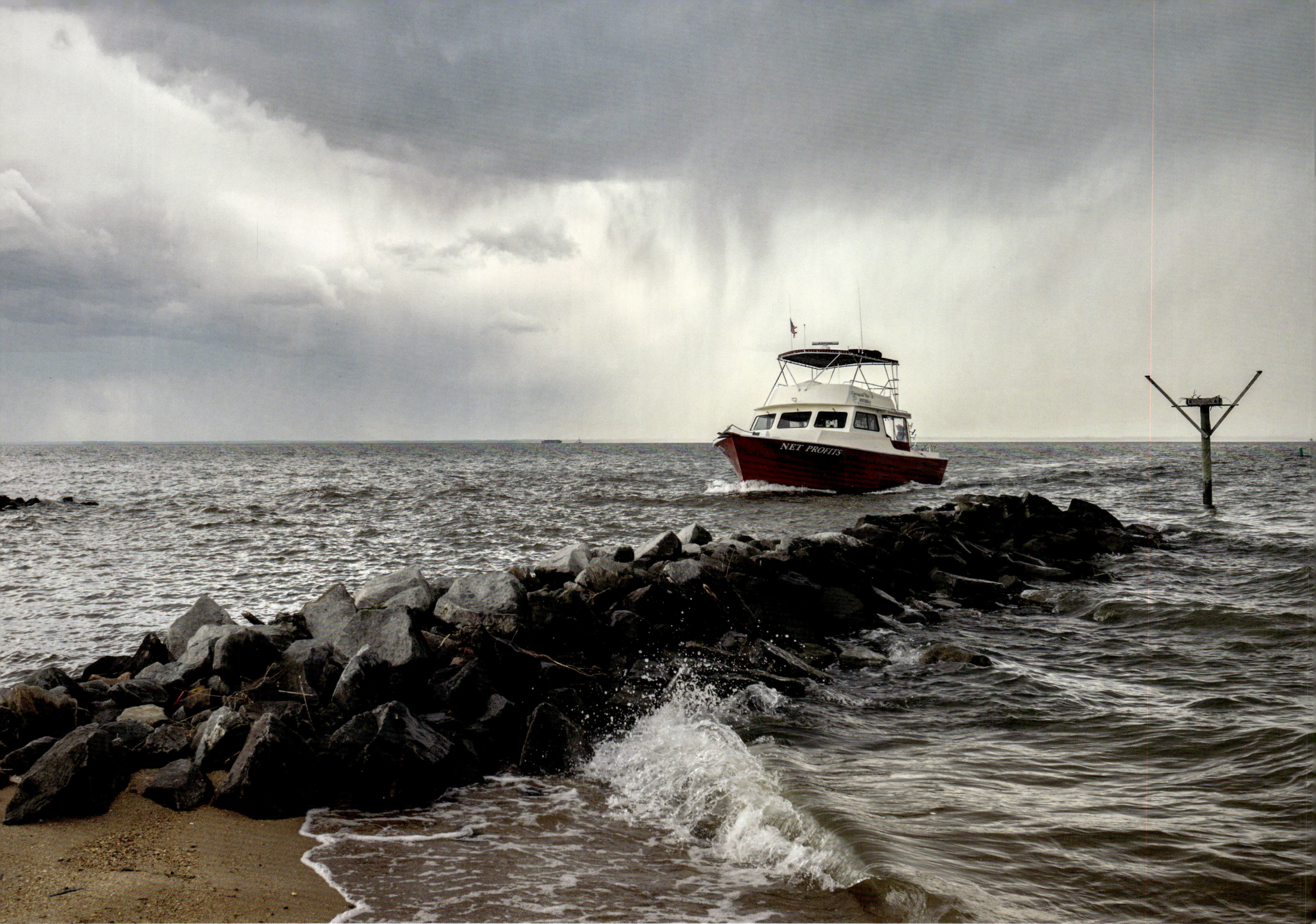

Net Profits heads in before the storm.

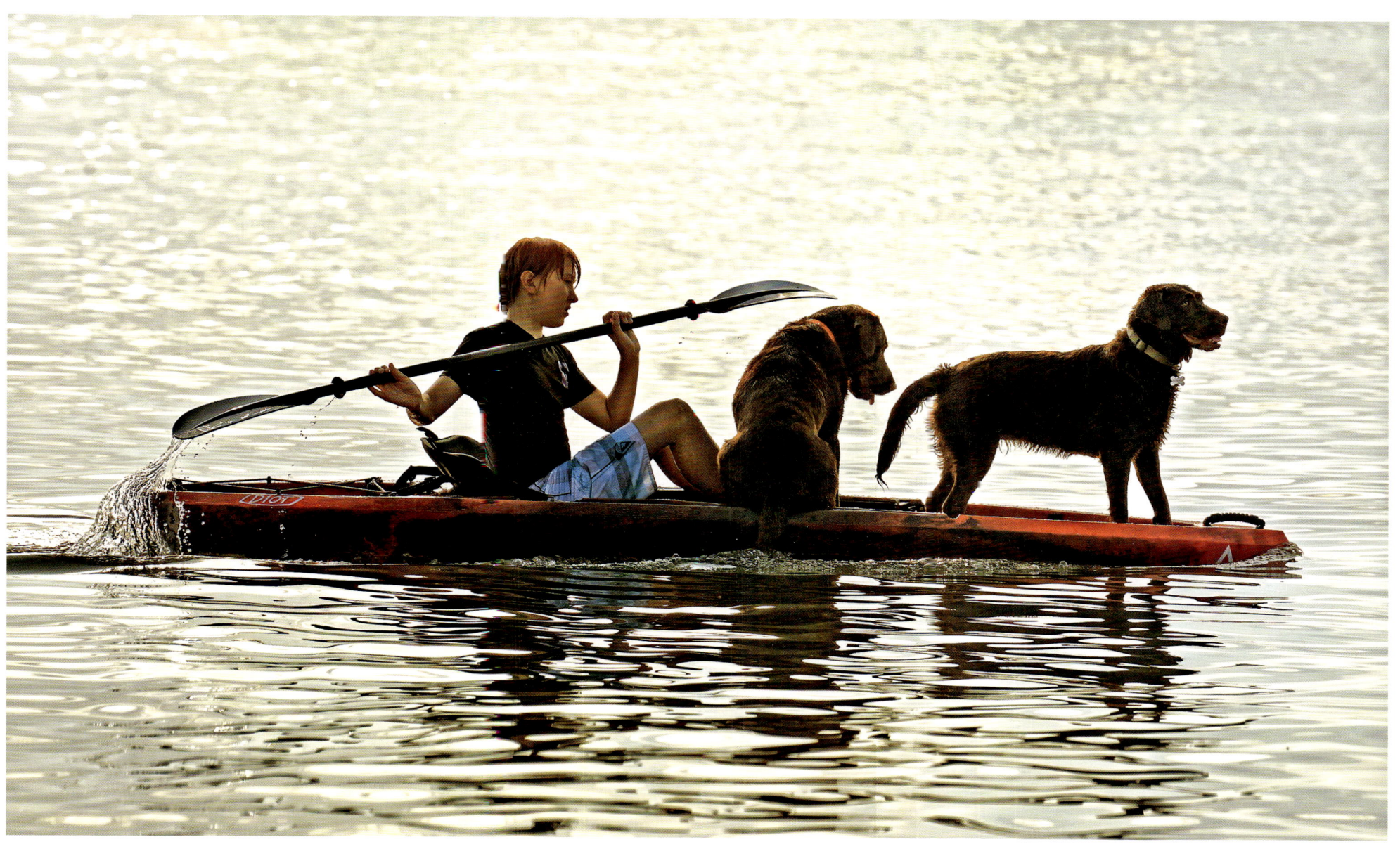

Hitchin' a ride

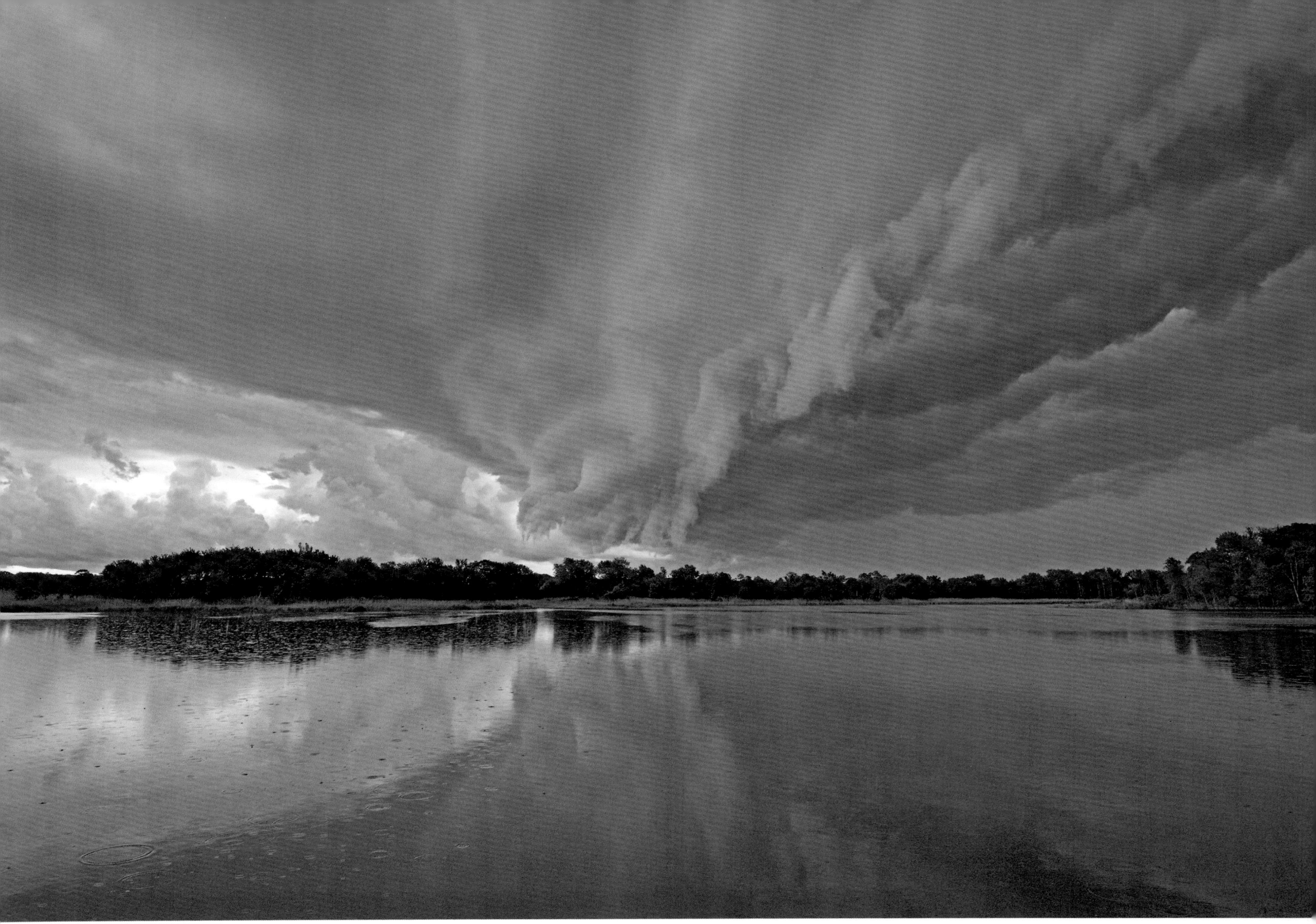
Another "Wow!" moment while shooting on a small dock on Price Creek

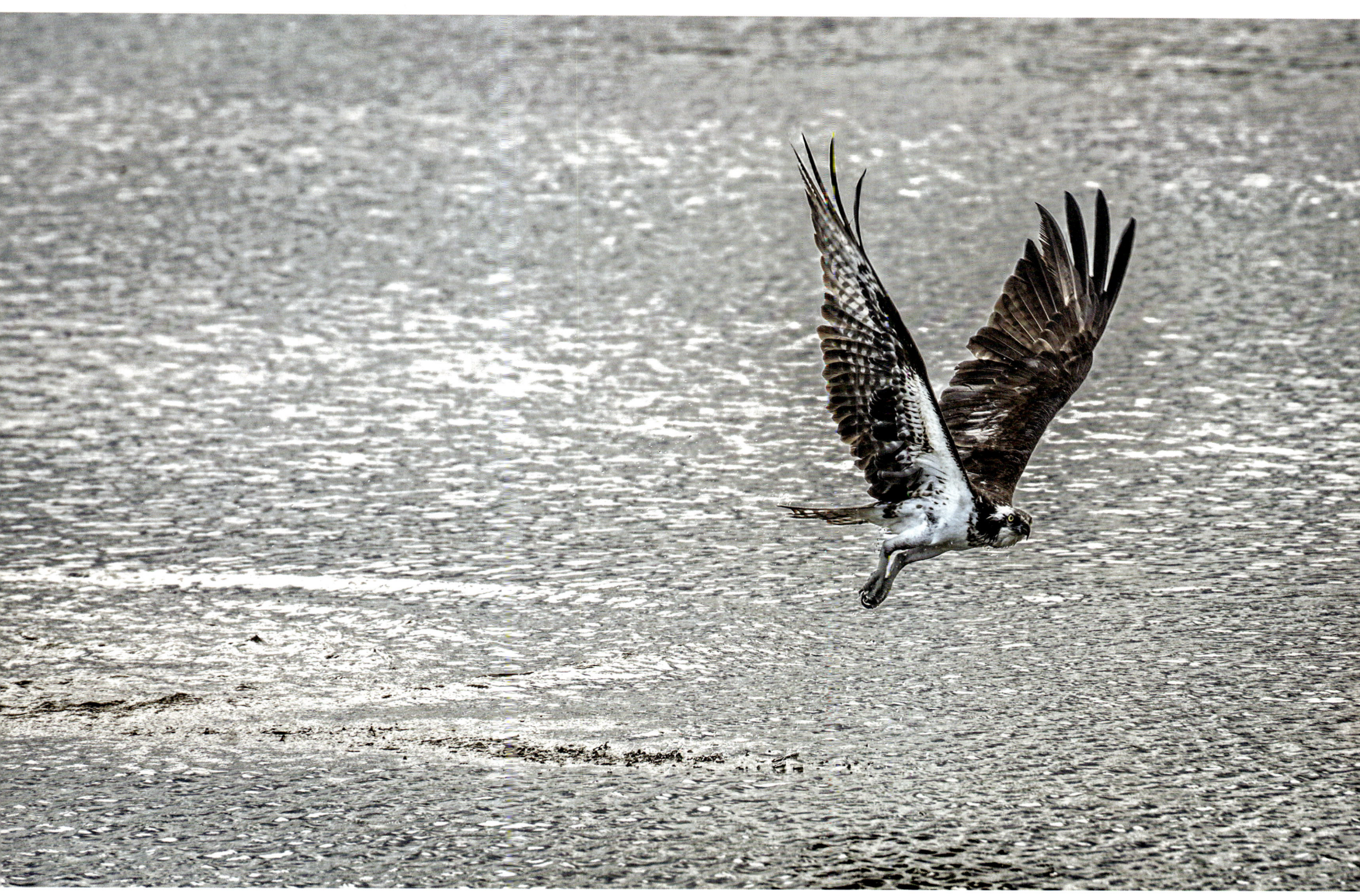

When an osprey looks at you, it's as if its eyes are boring right through you.

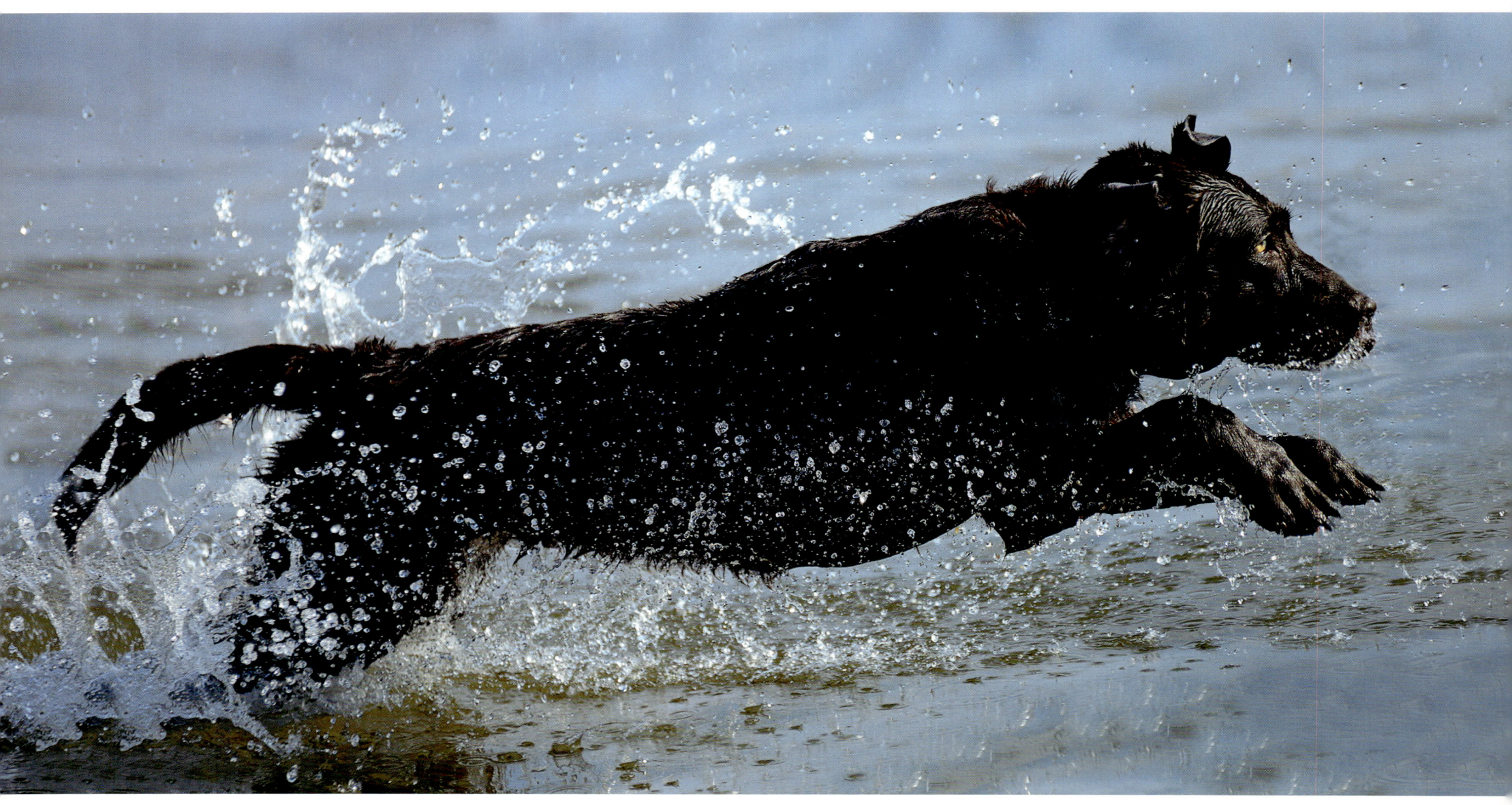

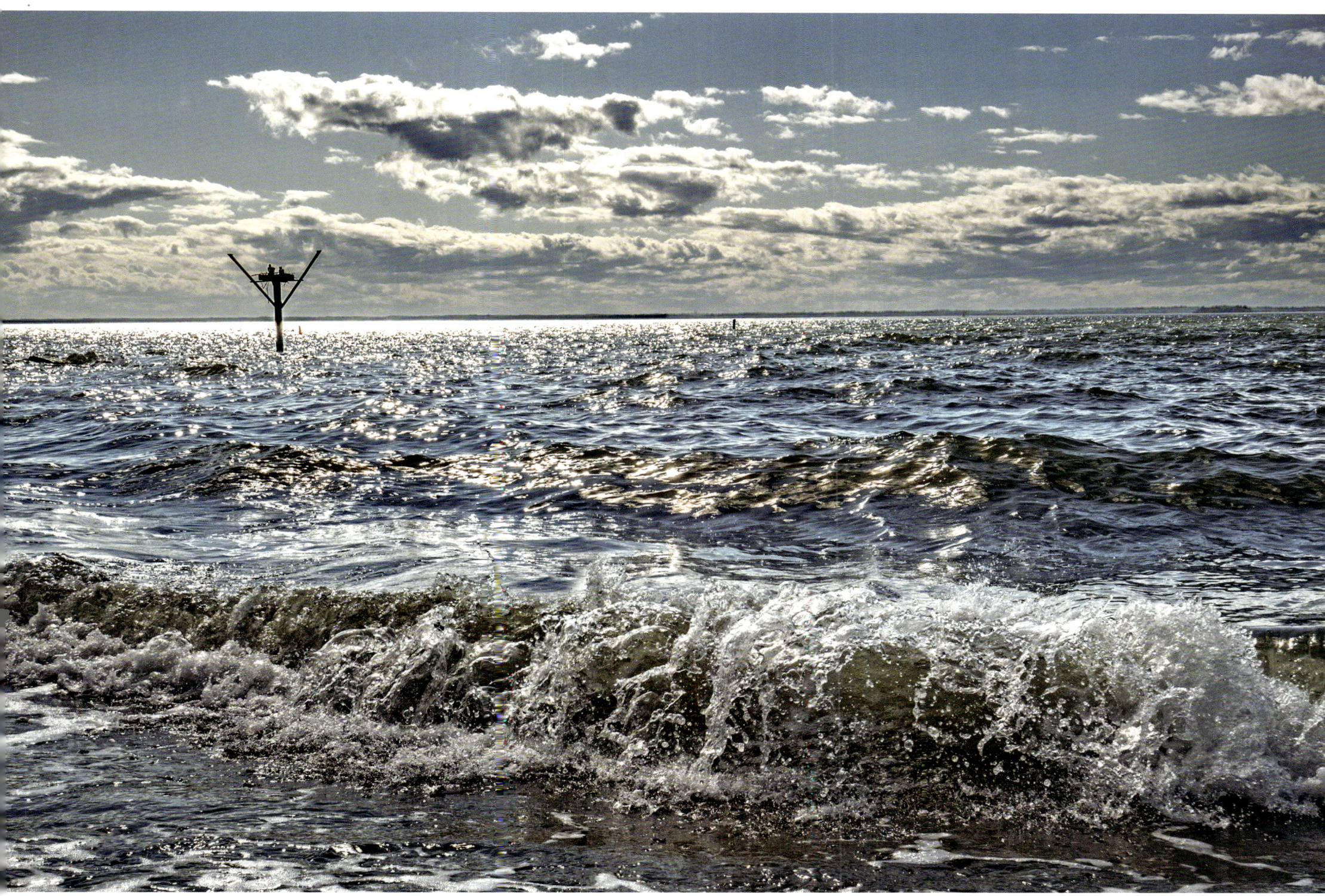

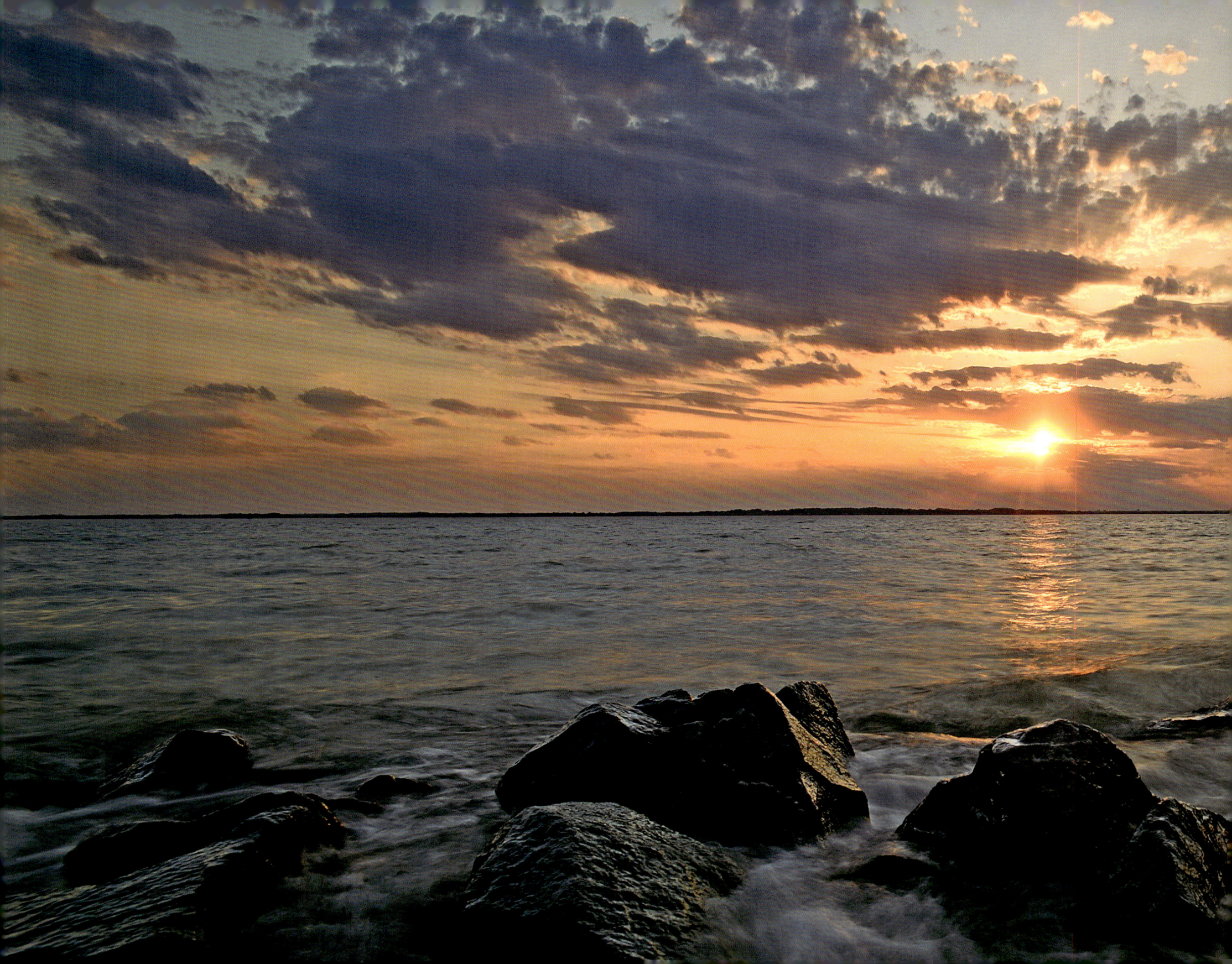

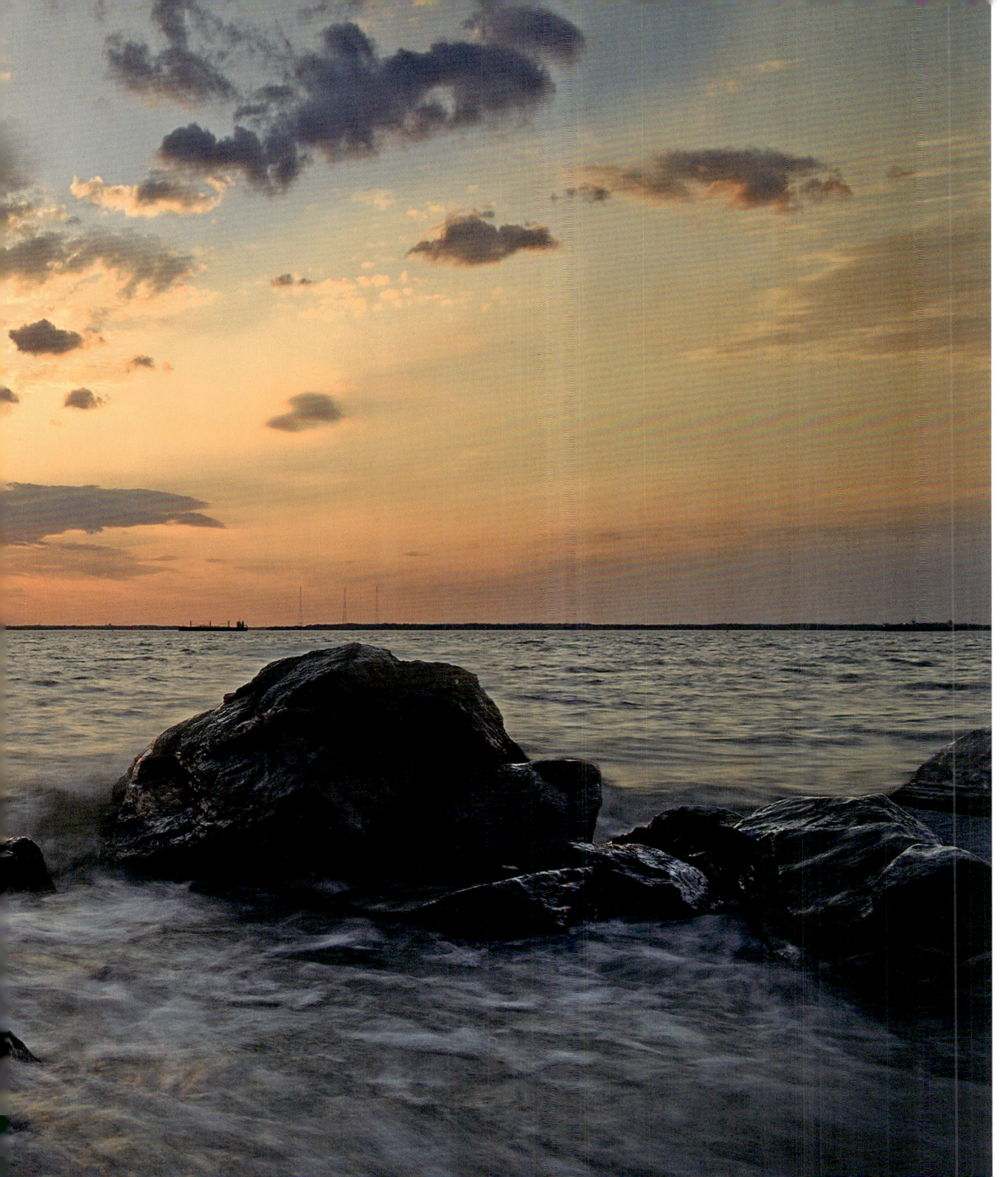

Mother's Day sunset

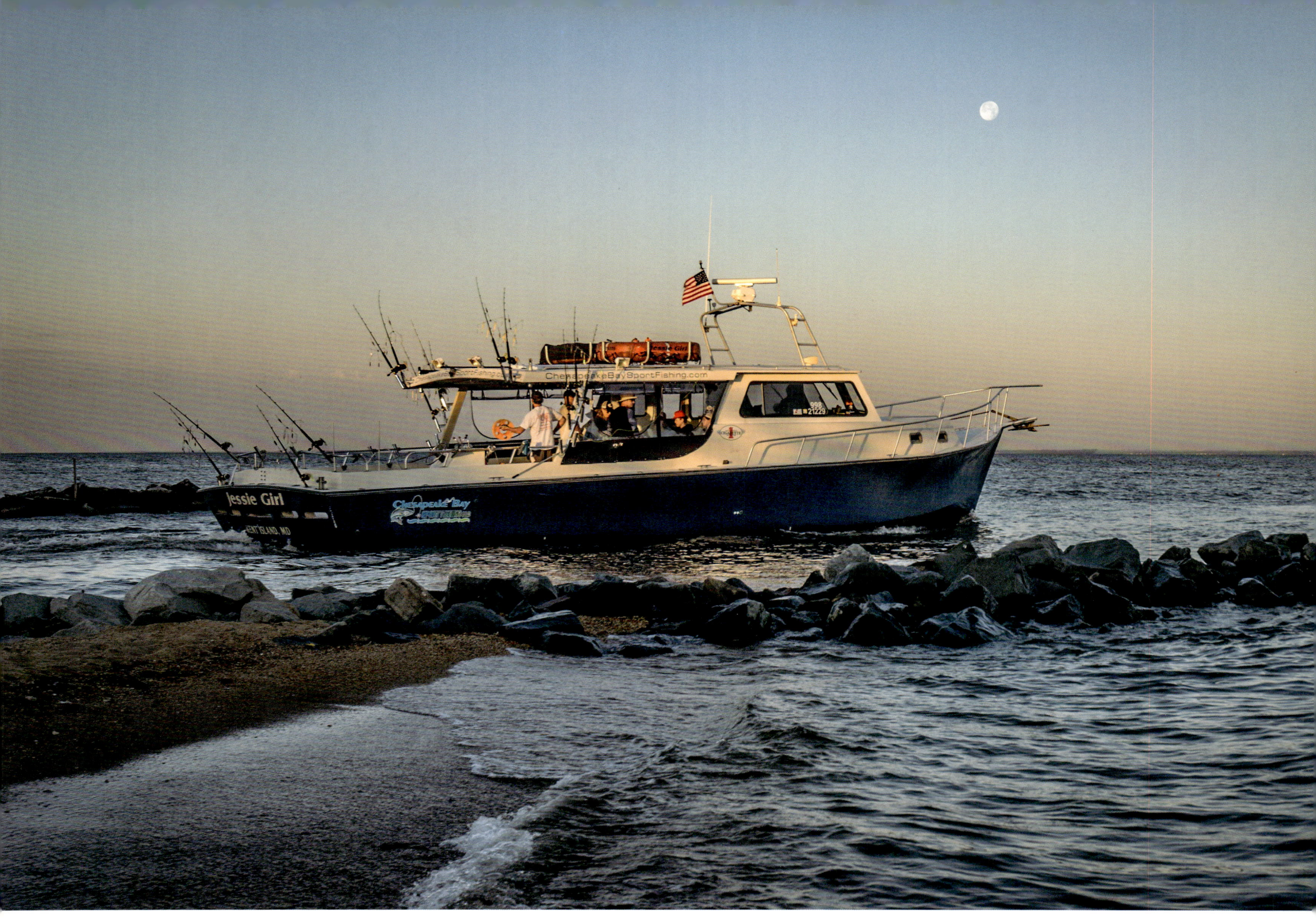

Jessie Girl emerges out of the Queen Anne Marina with the first rays of the sun as the
Strawberry Moon descends on the horizon.

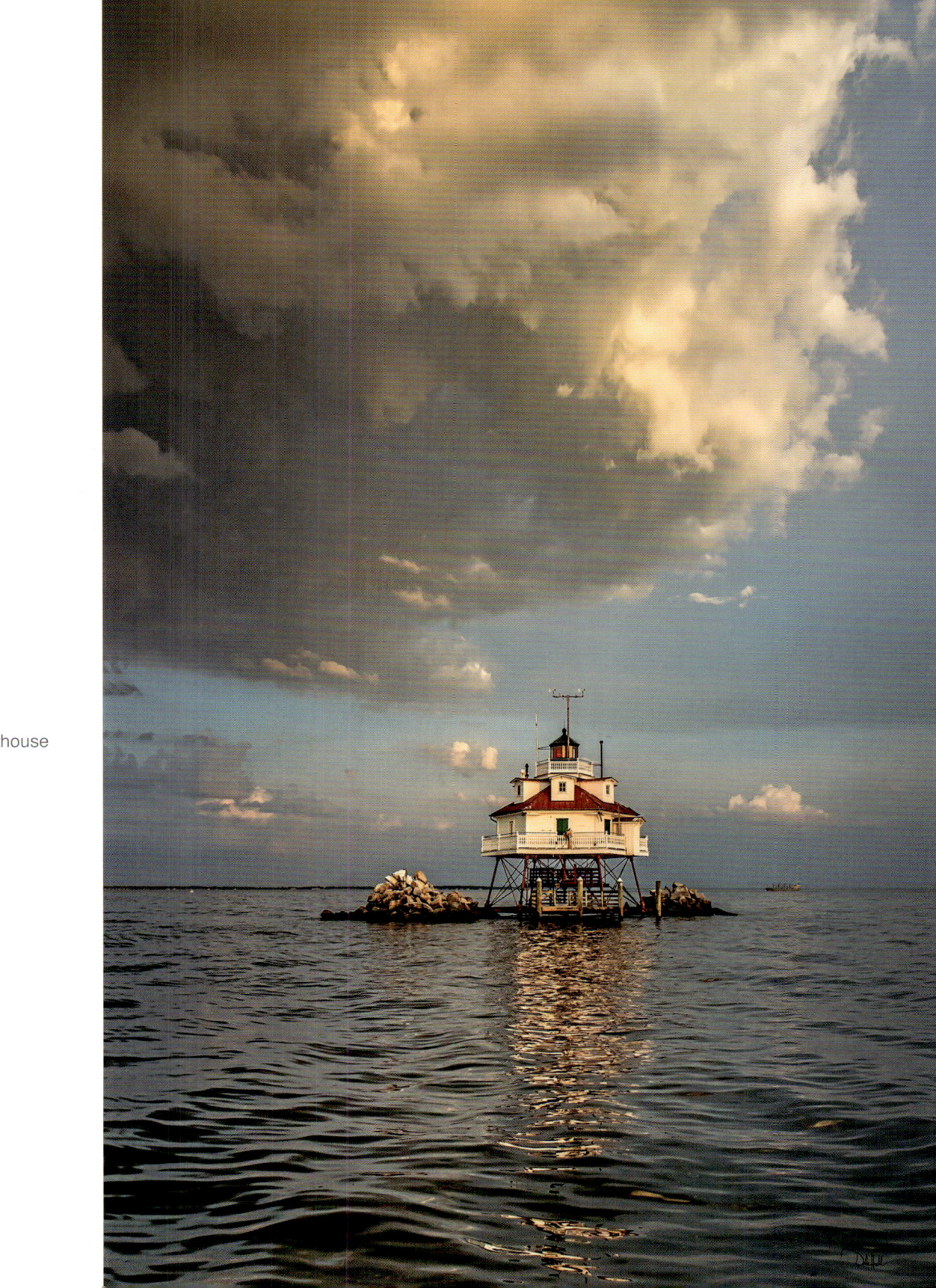

Ominous clouds o'er Thomas Point Shoal Lighthouse

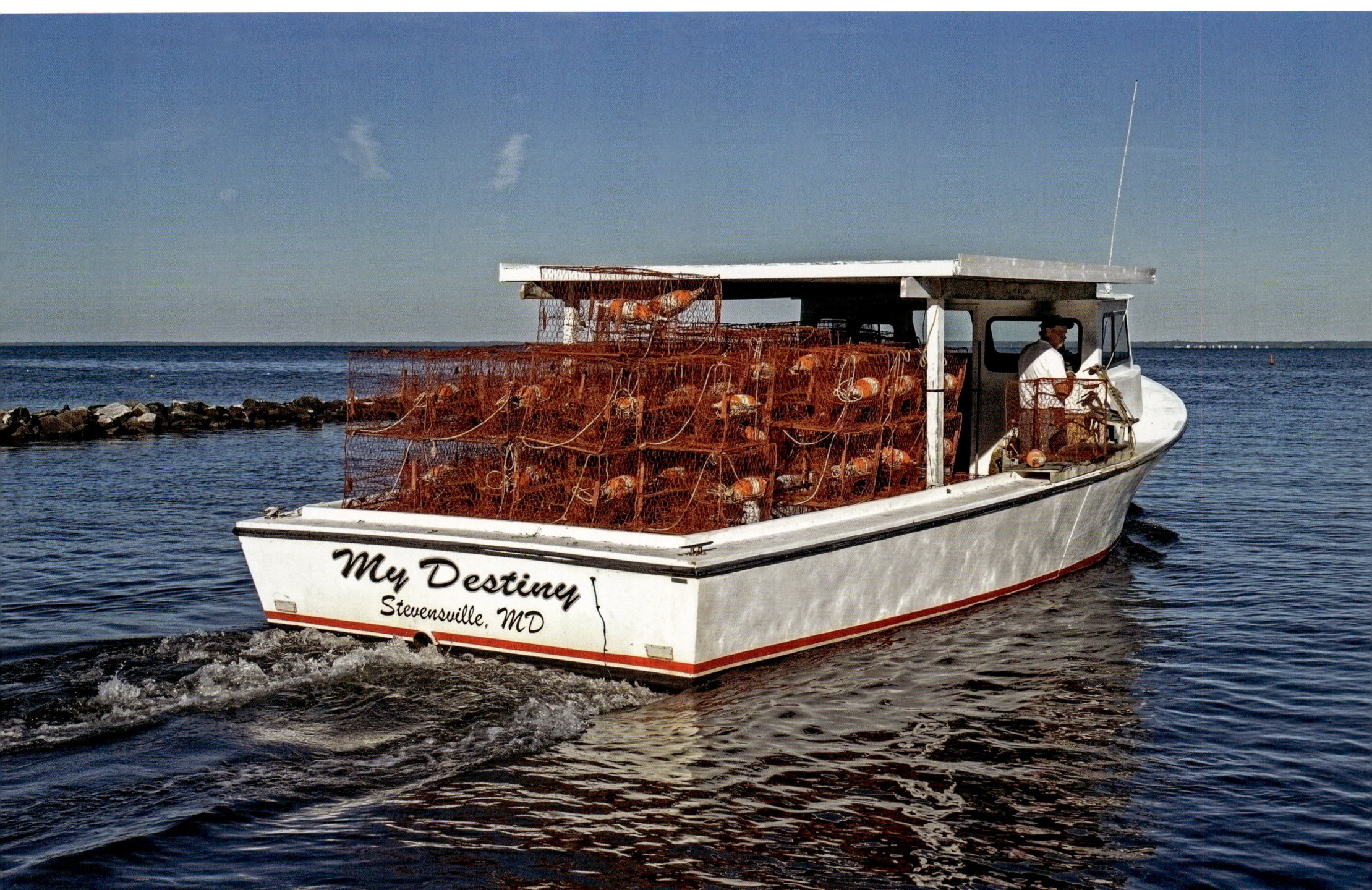

At it again for the forty-fourth year

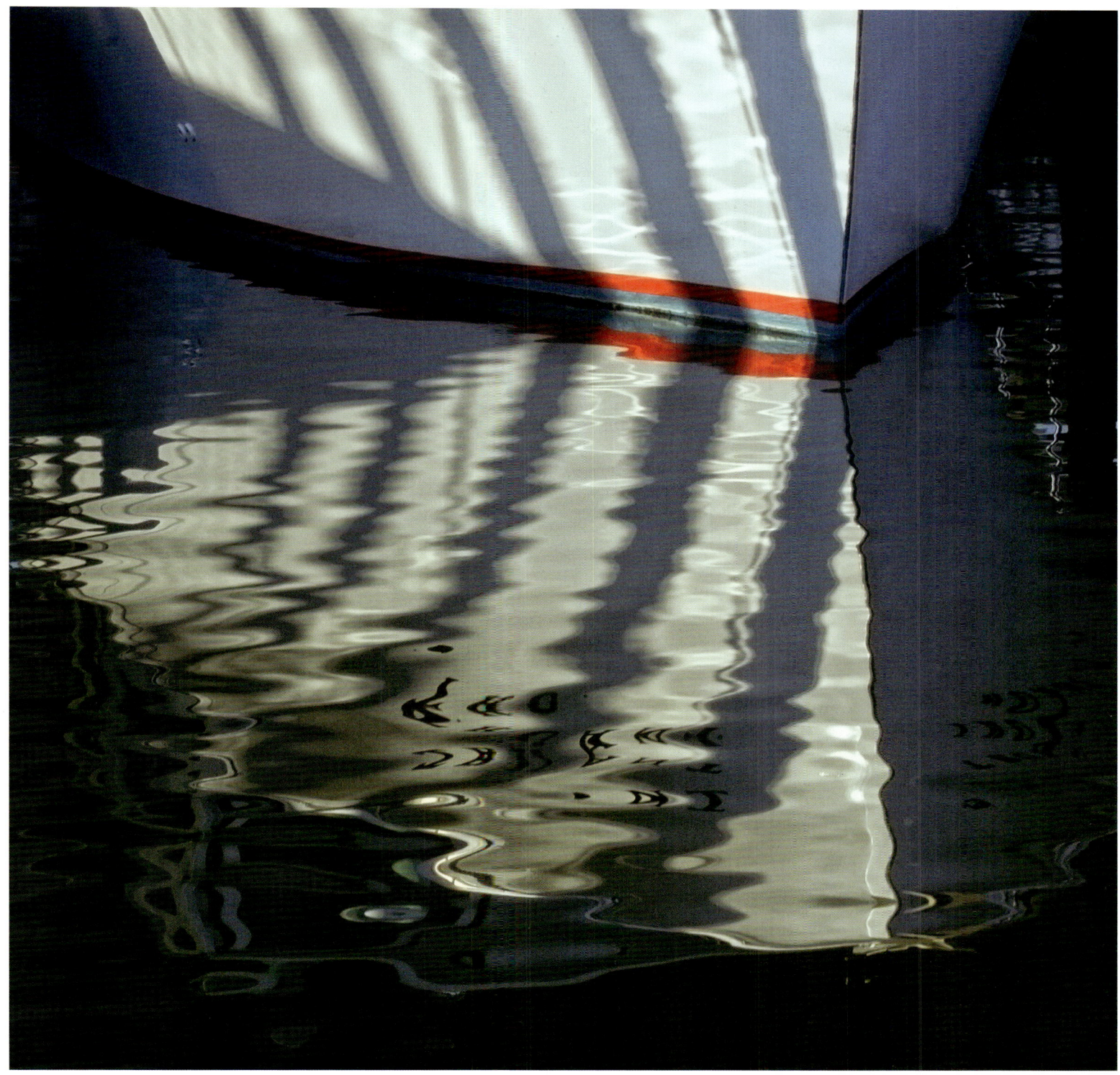

Truant is reflected in the calm waters of Kentmorr Marina, creating a mirror of abstract lines of light.

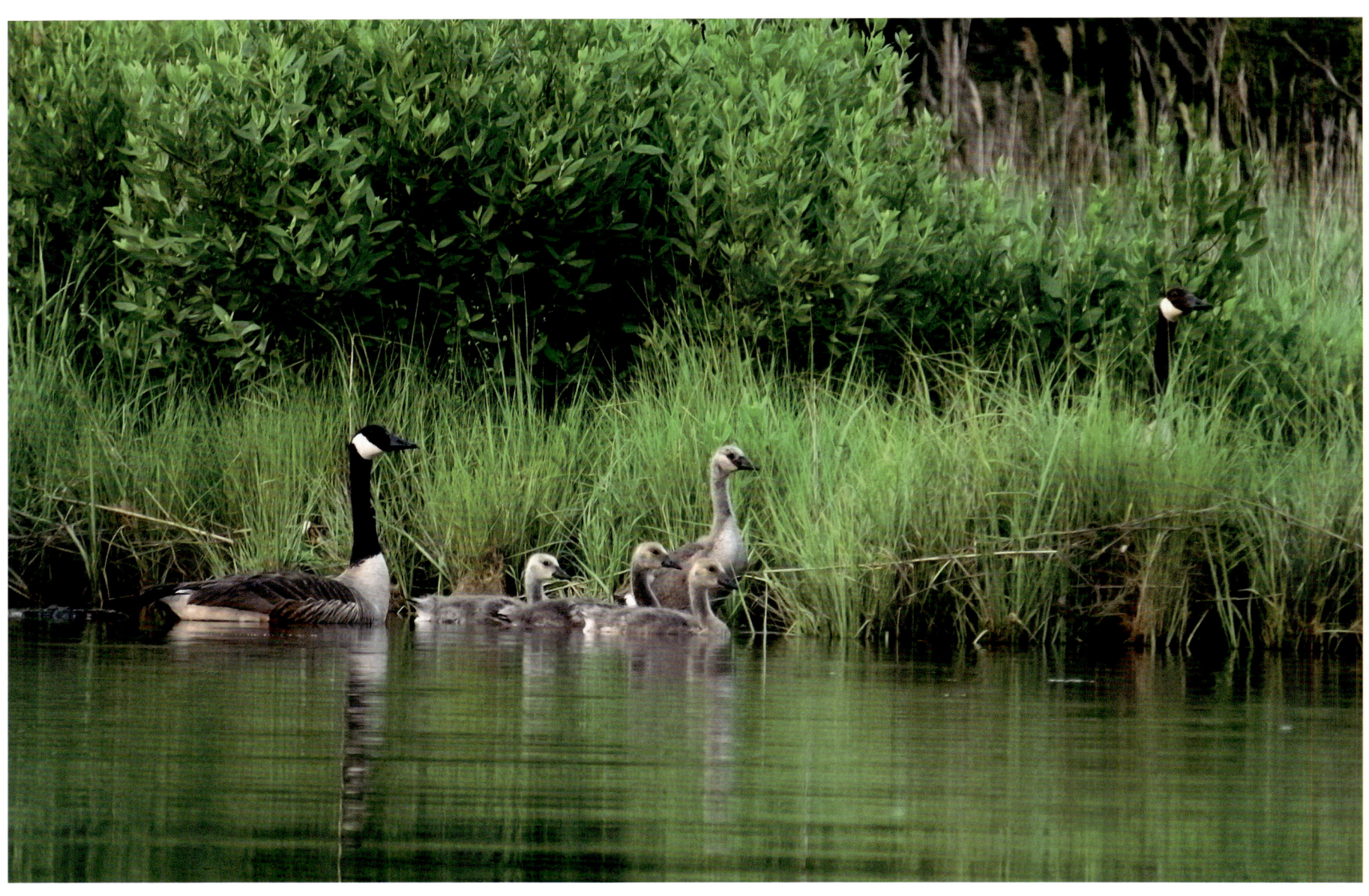

Mom is always seen hovering right next to her babies. Dad may not be readily seen, but
he is always nearby keeping a good eye on his family.

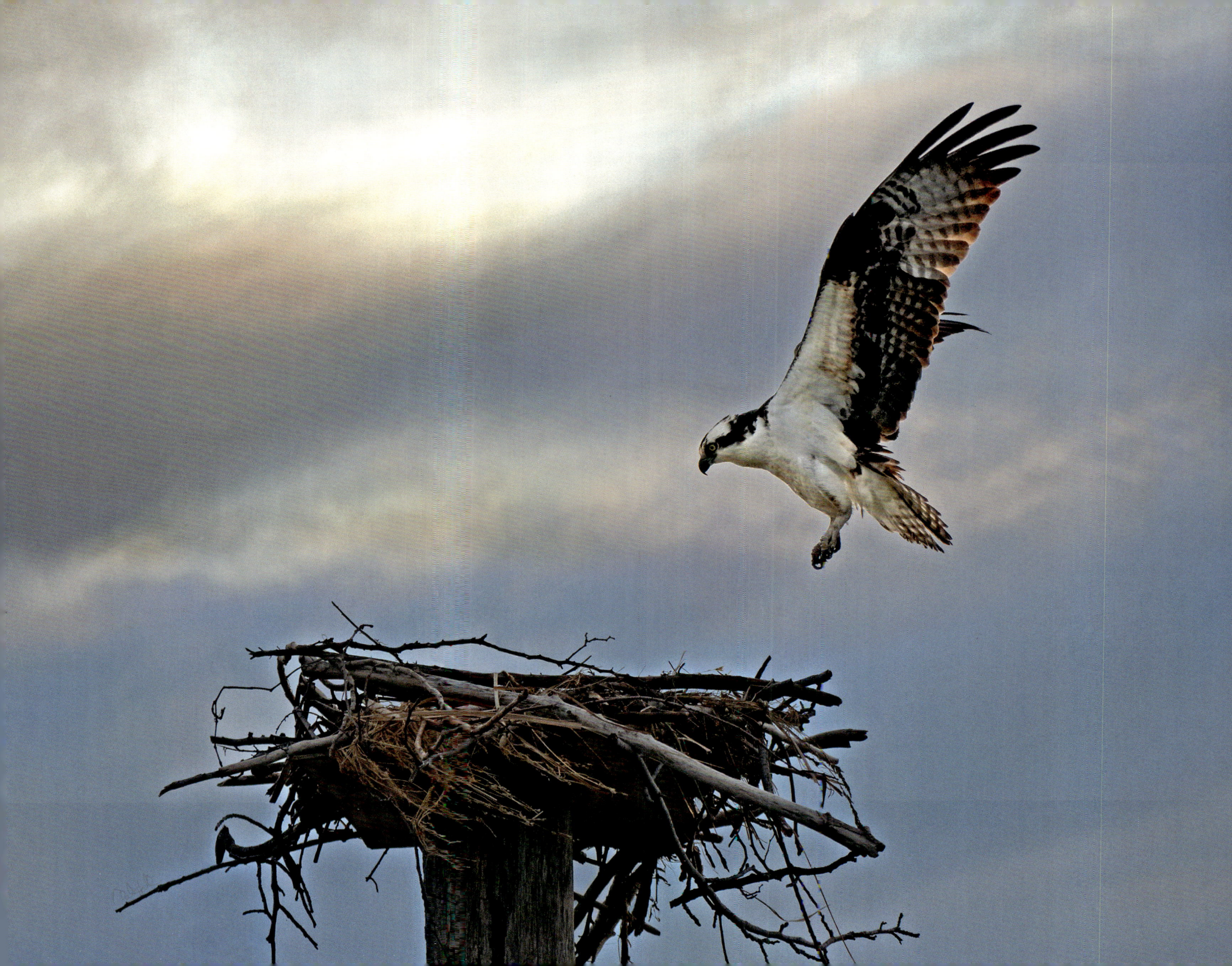

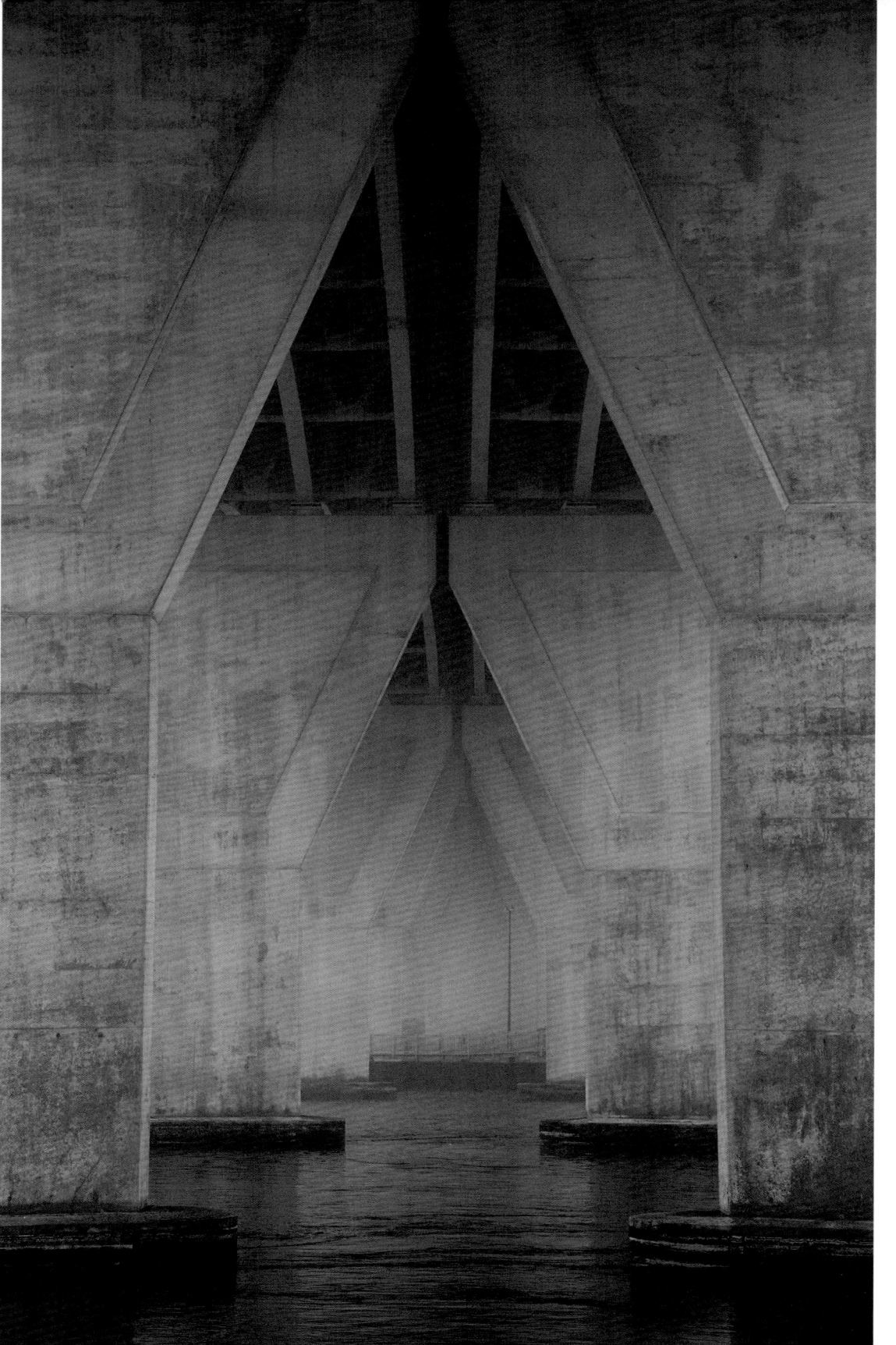

The geometric patterns and lines of symmetry under the Kent Narrows Bridge peering through a veil of fog create an interesting composition.

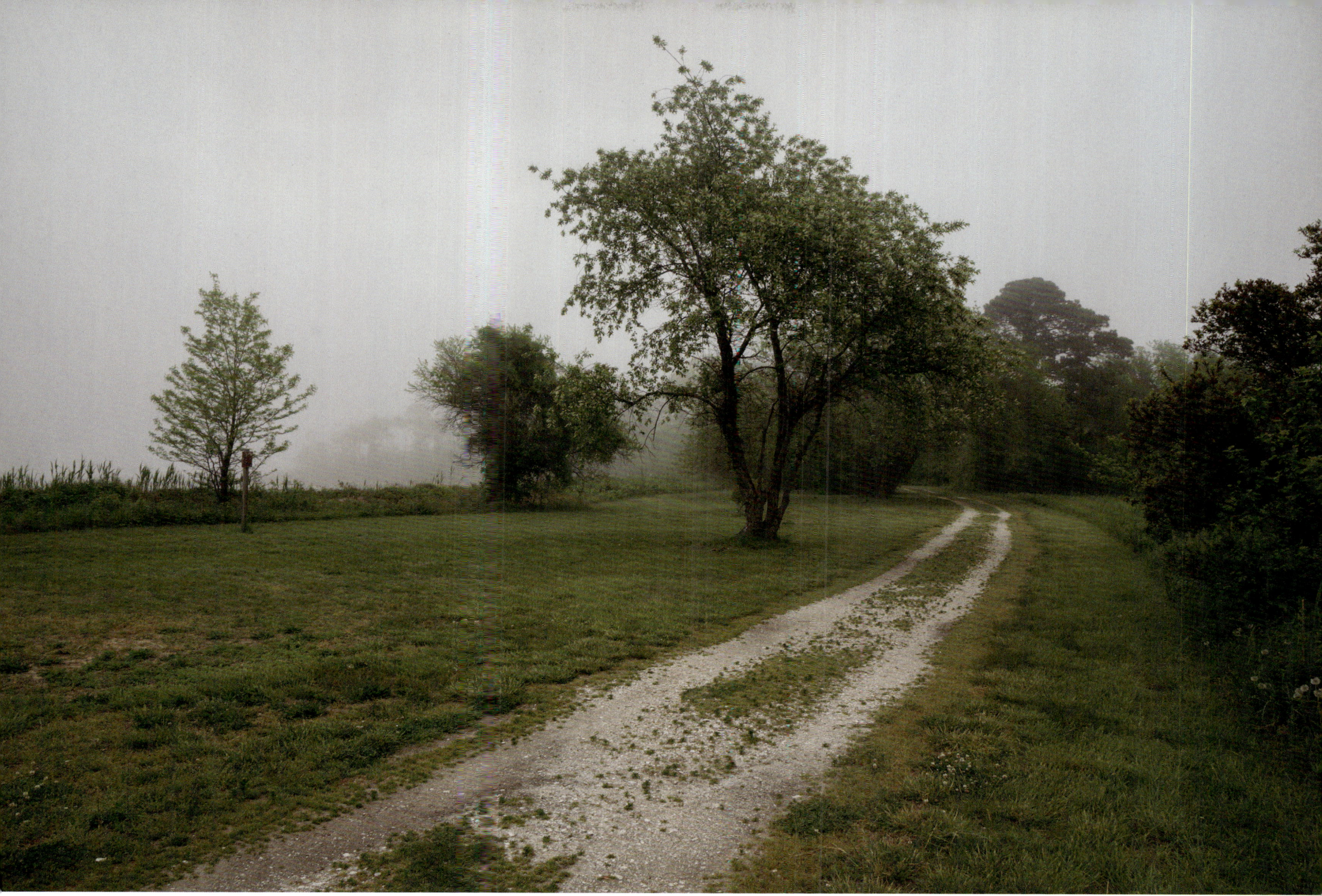

Ferry Point Park, sandwiched between the Kent Narrows and the Chester River

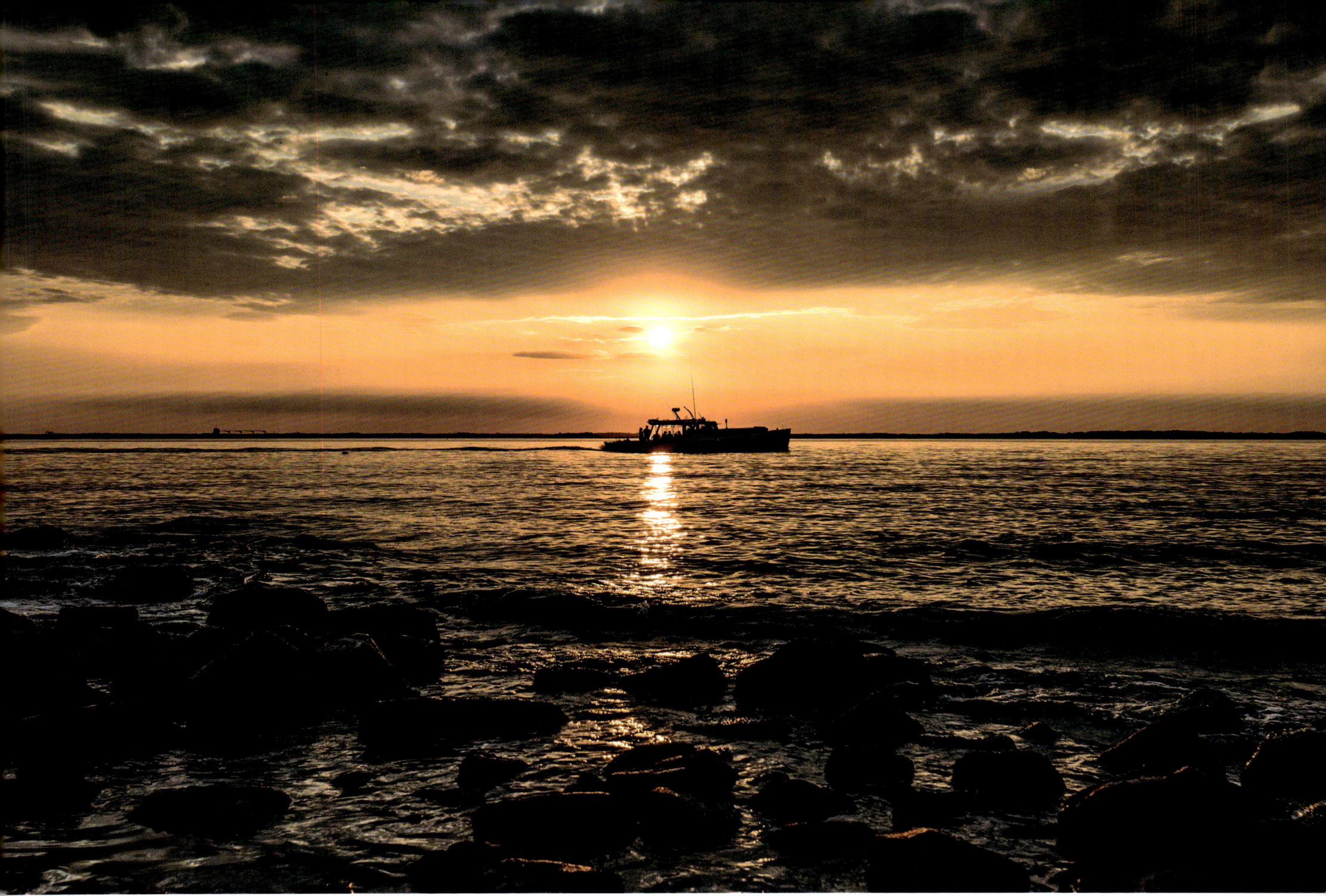

Charter boat *Breezin' Thru* breezin' by

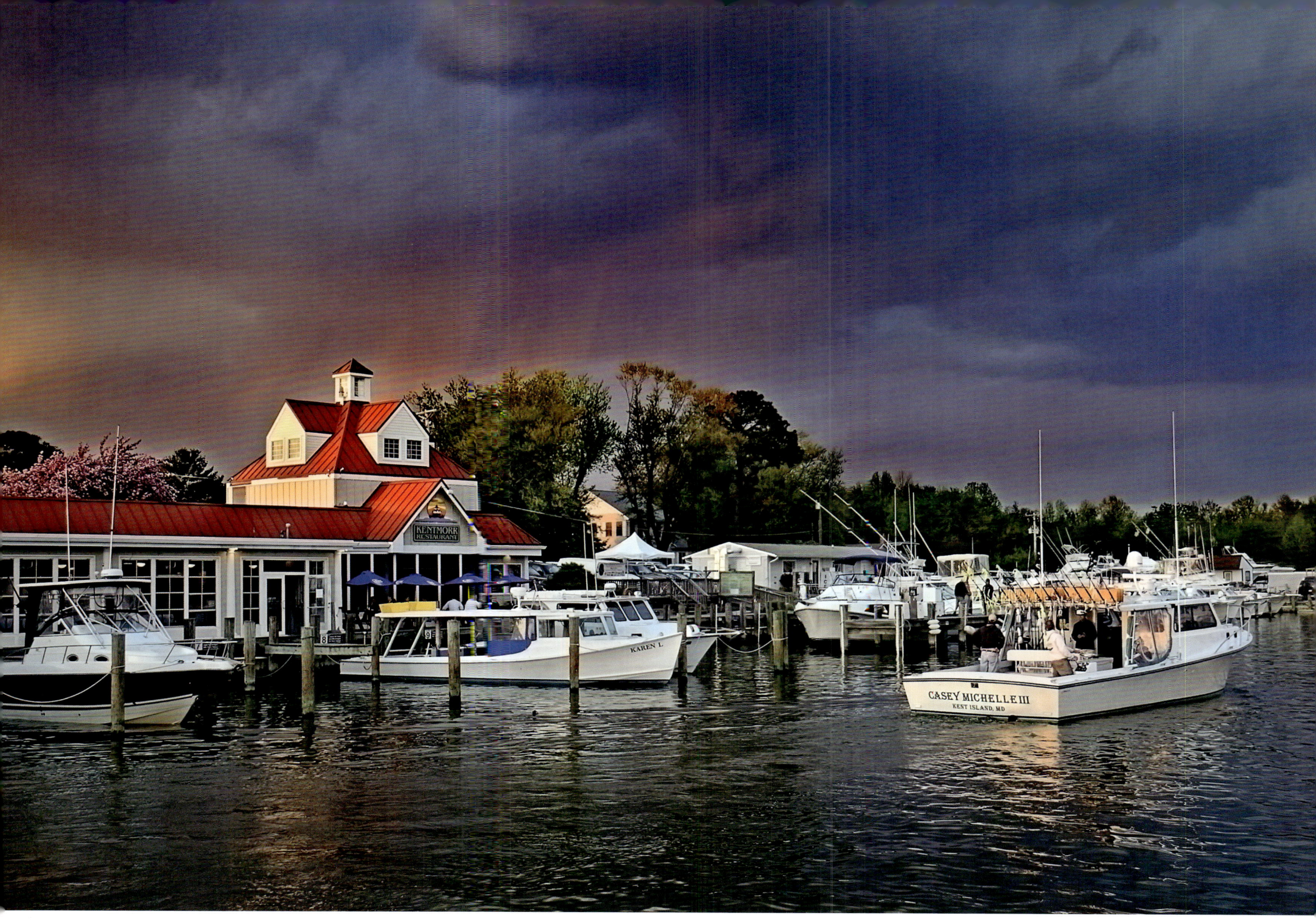

Casey Michelle III heads into Kentmorr Marina after a beautiful day of fishing in a rockfish tournament on the Chesapeake Bay in the spring of 2014.

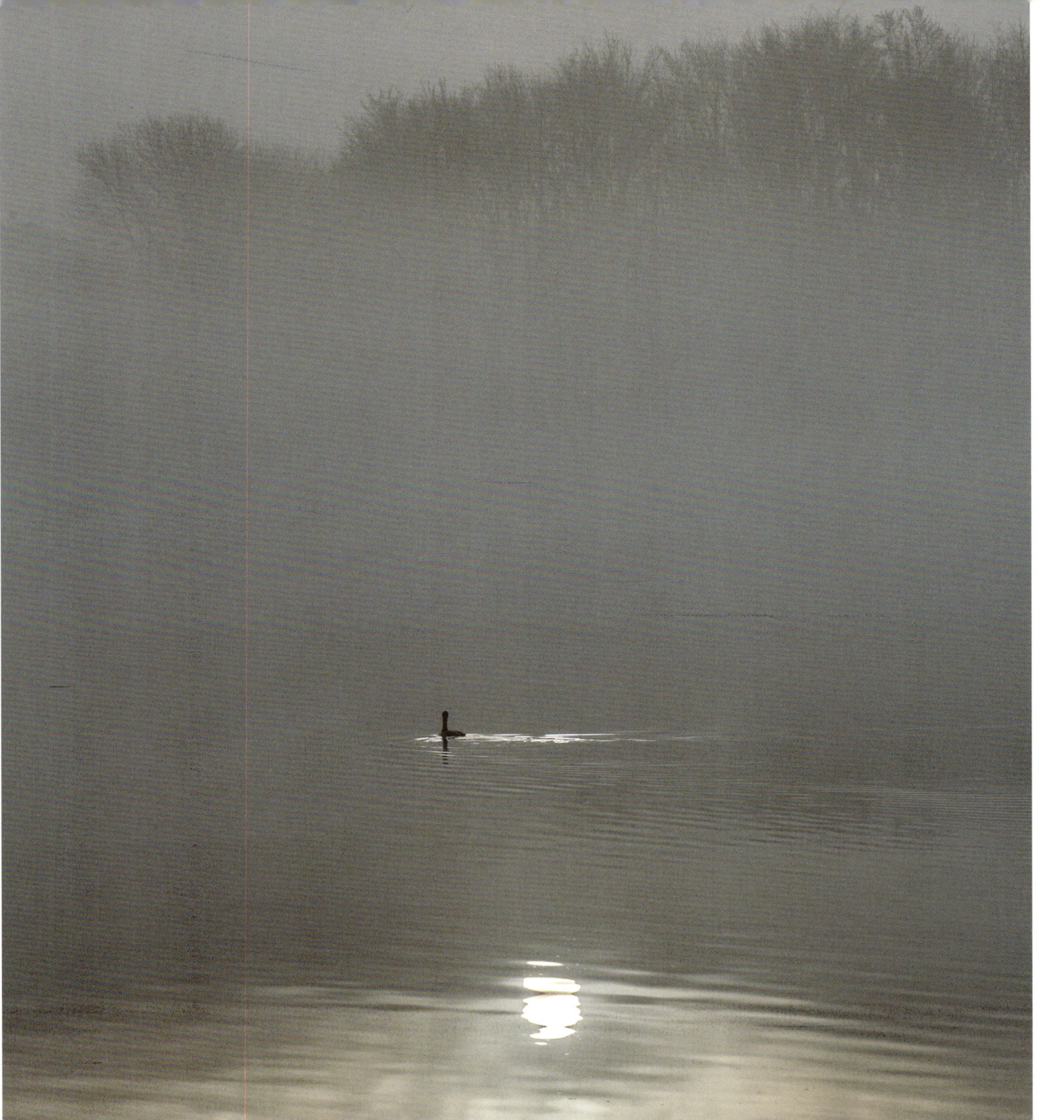

Cormorants seem to
pop up out of nowhere.

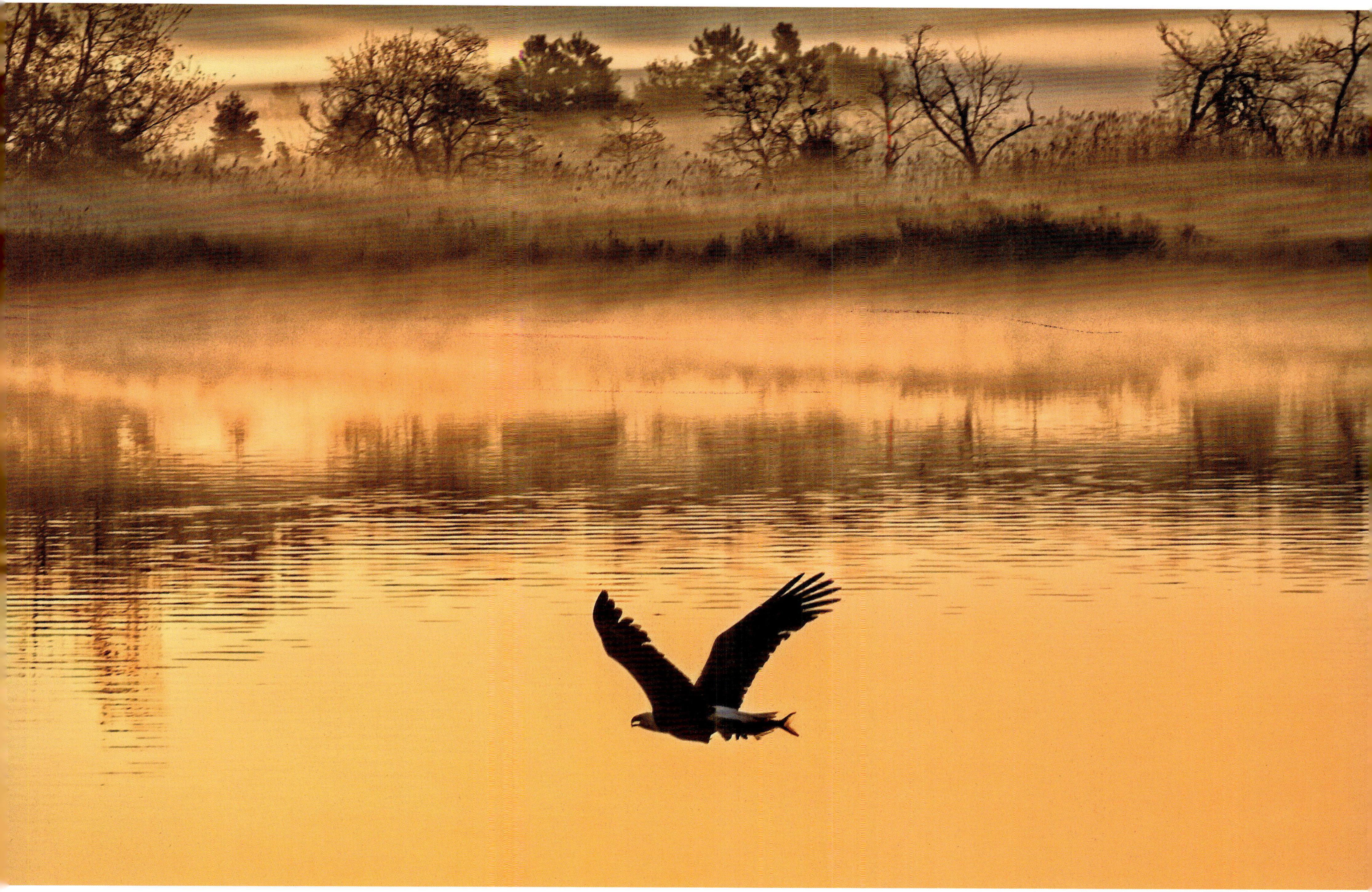

Needless to say, seeing an eagle just fly by with a fish is breathtaking.

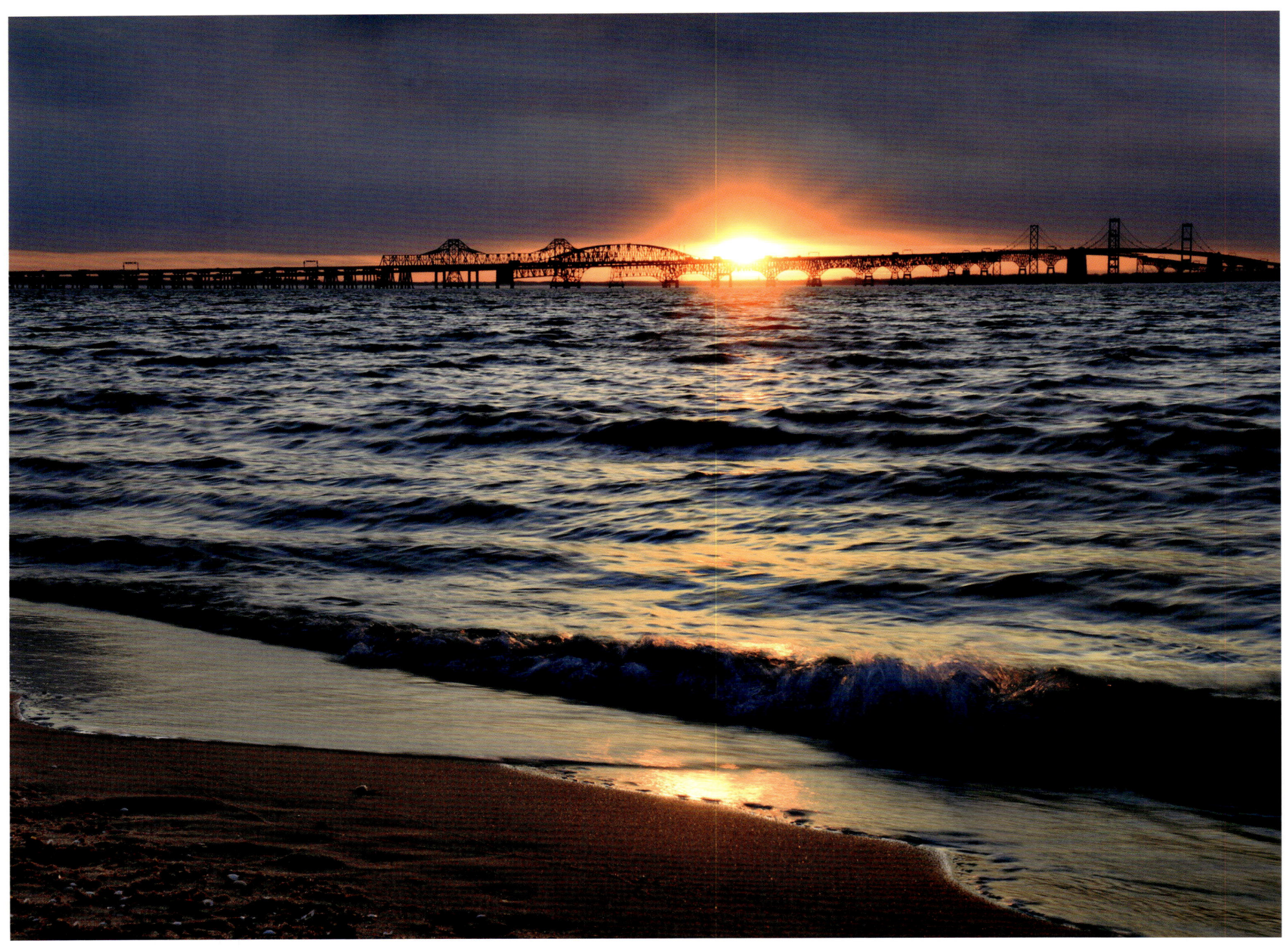

Sunset views at Terrapin Park on the northern side of the bay bridge

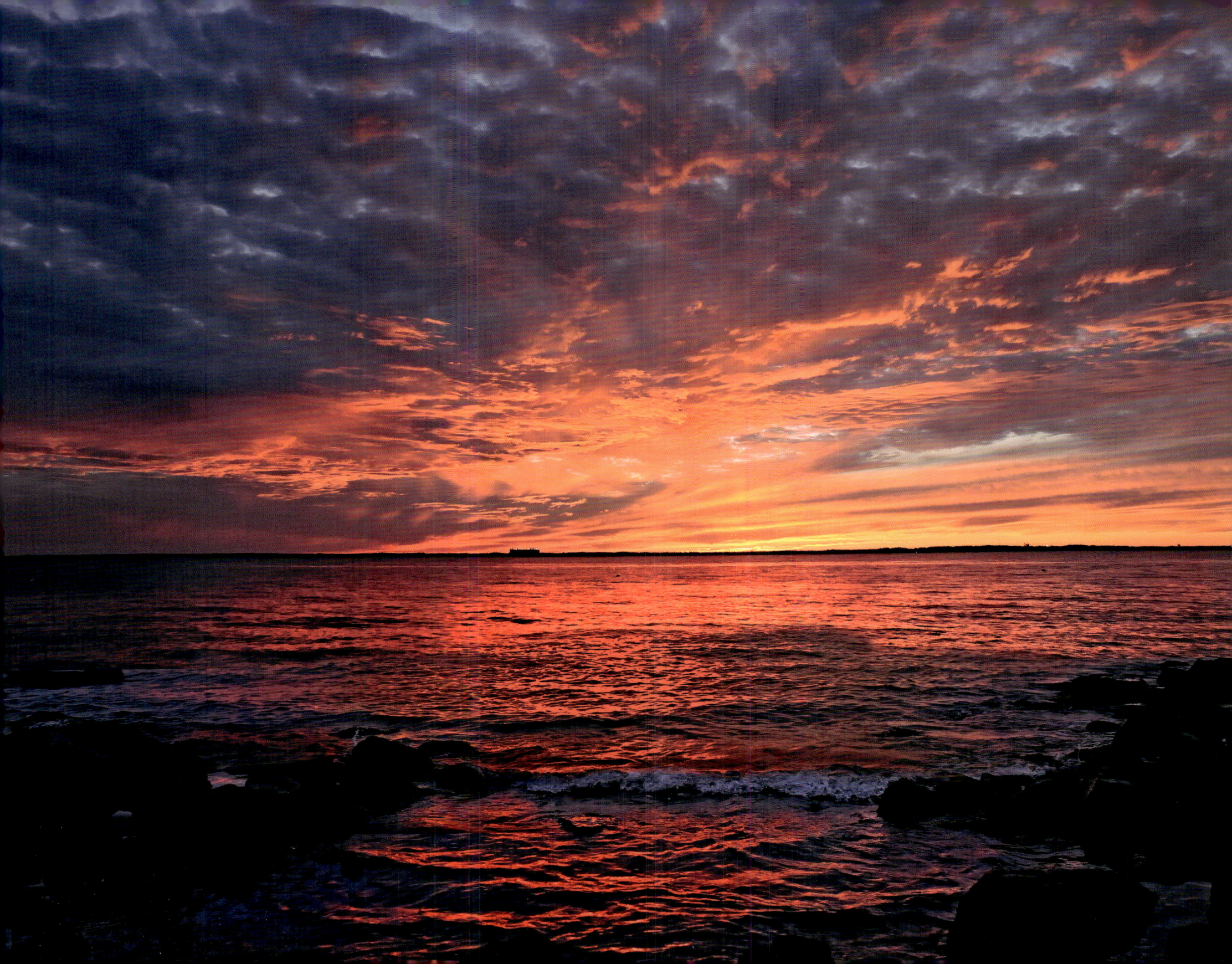

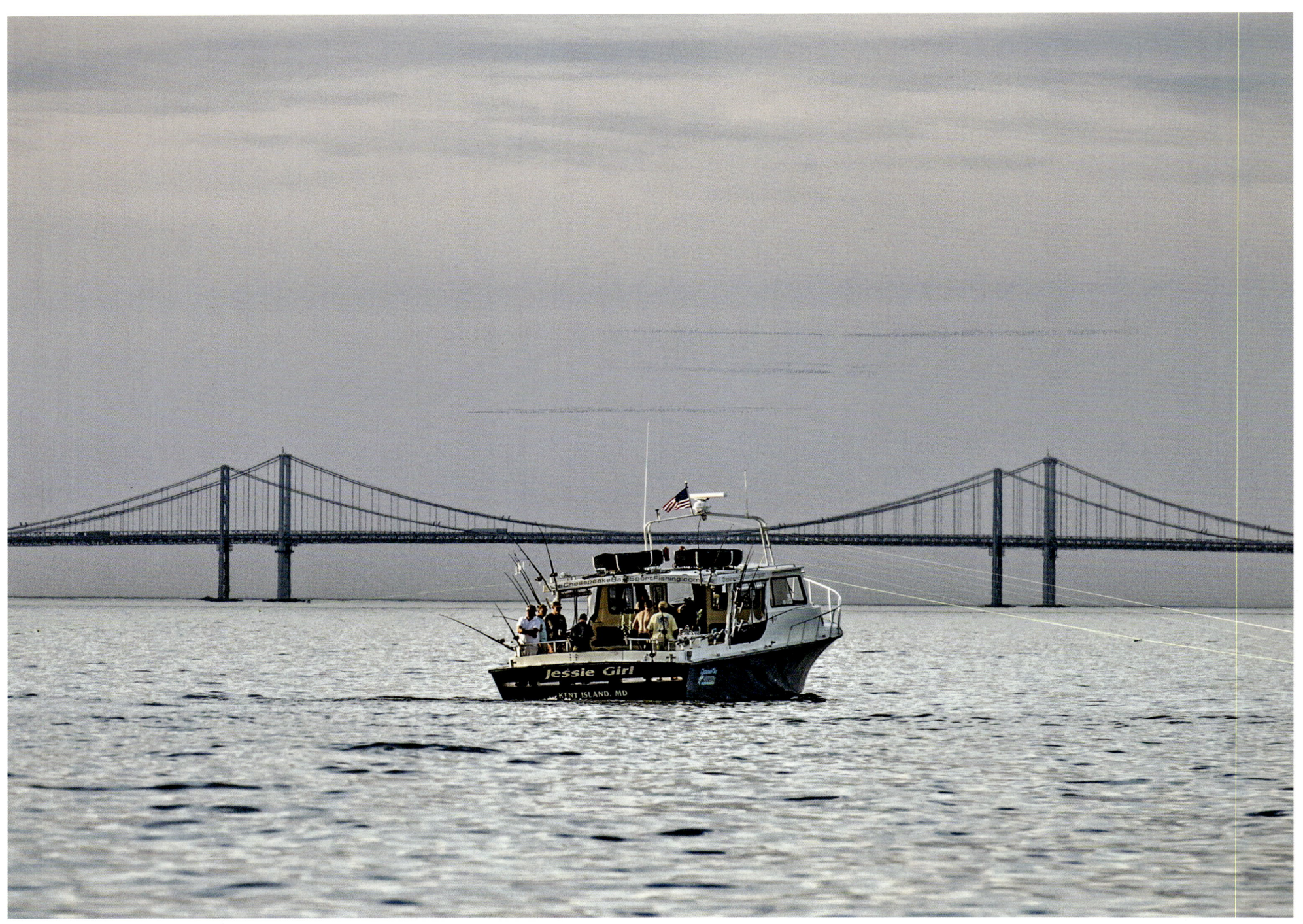

Trollin', trollin', trollin'

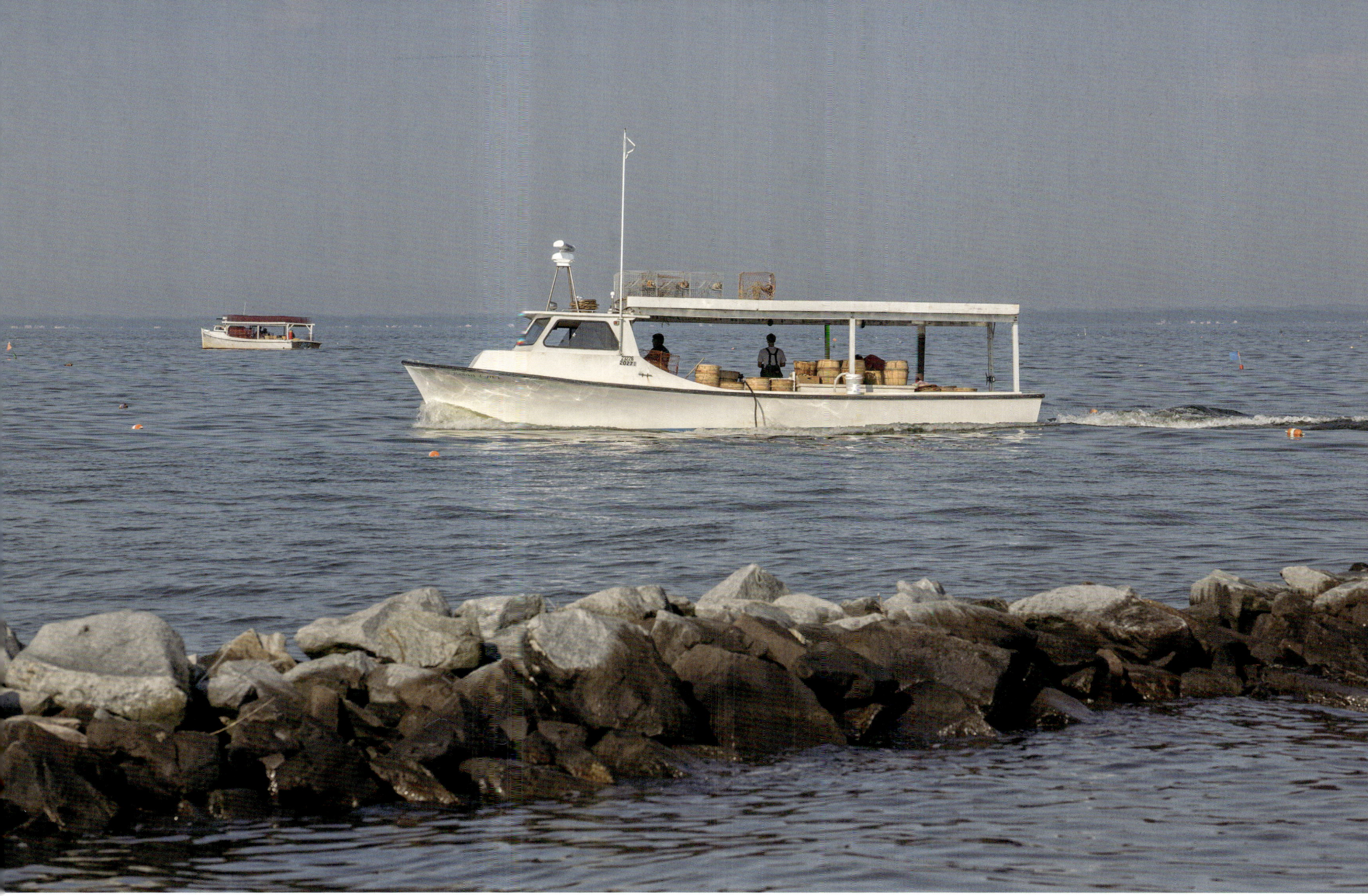

Salt life

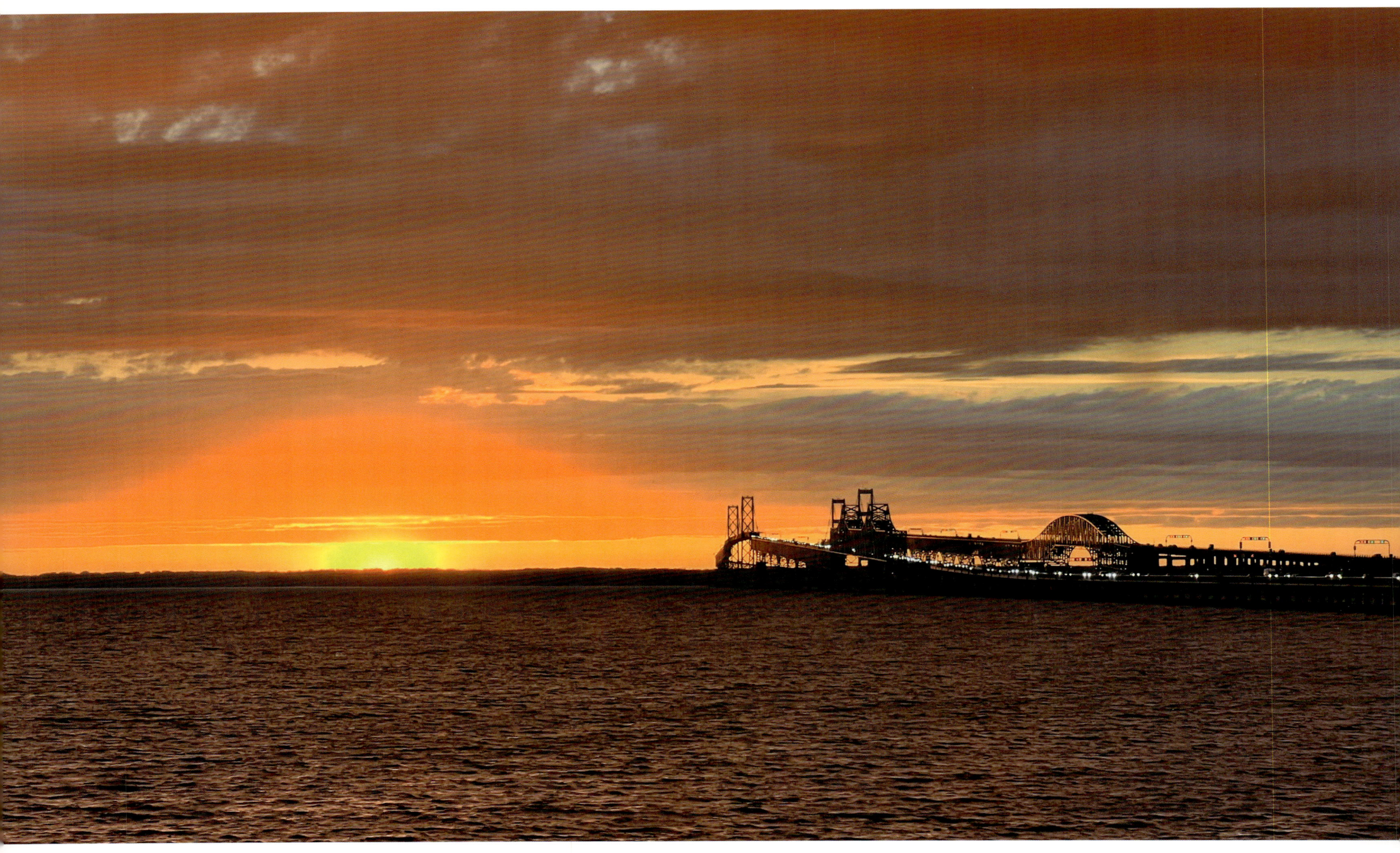

Can't beat this view from Libbey's Coastal Kitchen & Cocktails.

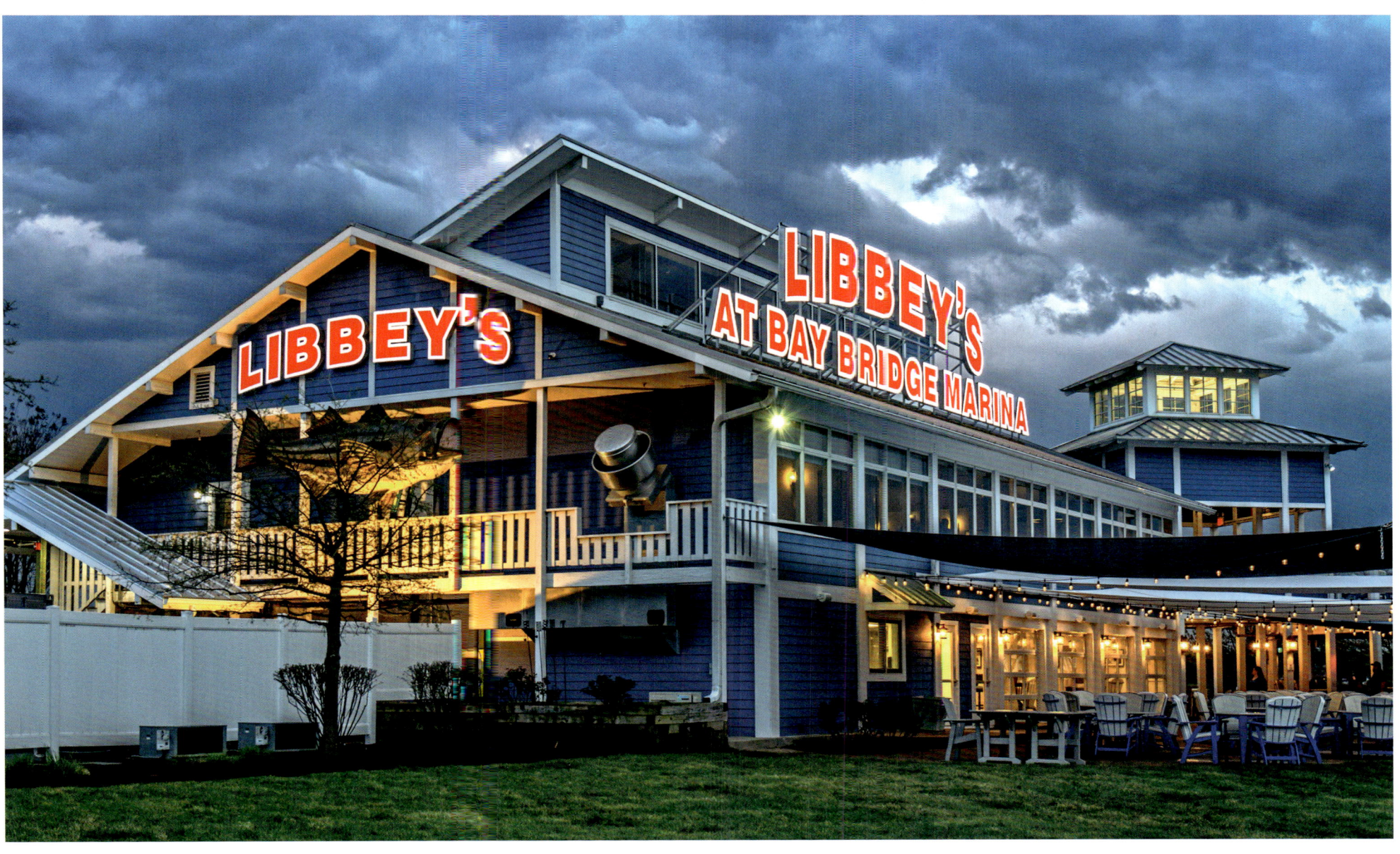

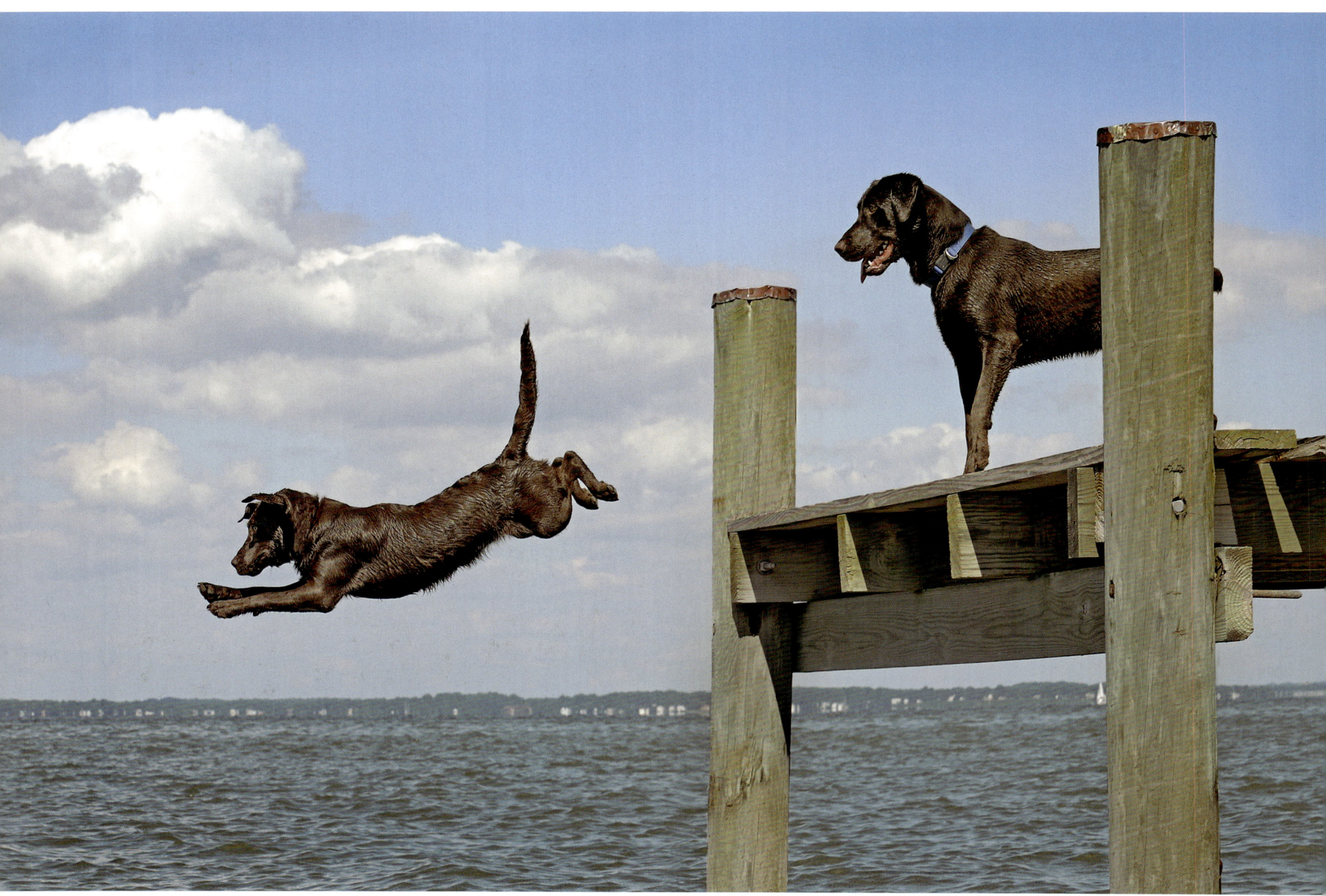

CHAPTER 3

SUMMER

Summer comes on hot! The charter fishing boats are often running seven days a week, and watermen are hauling up crab pots on regulated days. Tourist season is well underway, and waterfront restaurants are bustling.

Pleasure boats are out and about, with people enjoying fishing, crabbing, and water sports or taking a jaunt to a local waterfront restaurant. Annapolis is close enough to get to by boat easily as well. People are out in full force, enjoying their go-to water activities. You will see people kayaking, jet skiing, kiteboarding, tubing behind boats, and paddleboarding. They don't call it the land of pleasant living for nothing.

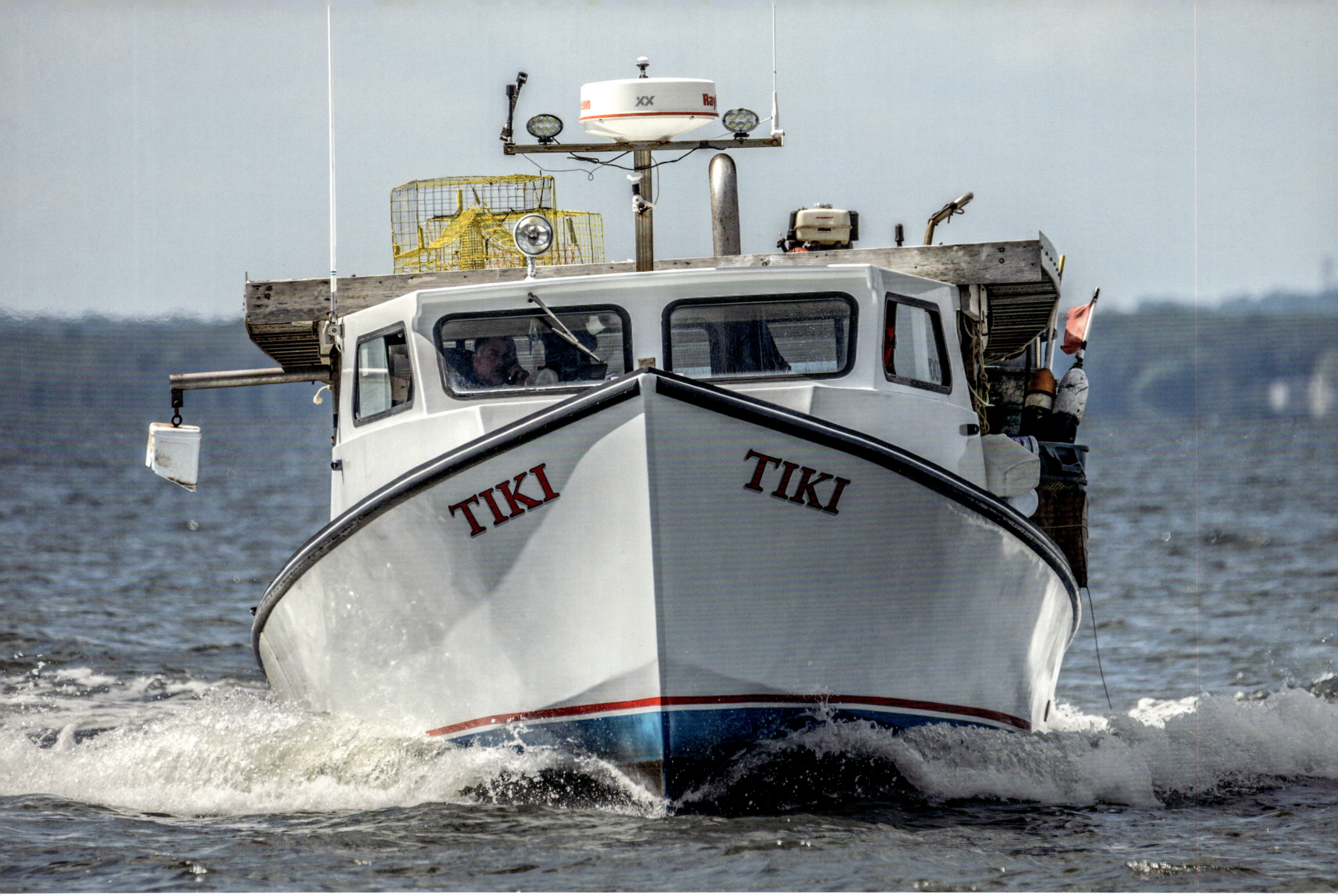

Crabbers are out before the sun comes up, and most of the time they are back to distribute the goods in early afternoon. *Tiki* heads in to Queen Anne Marina.

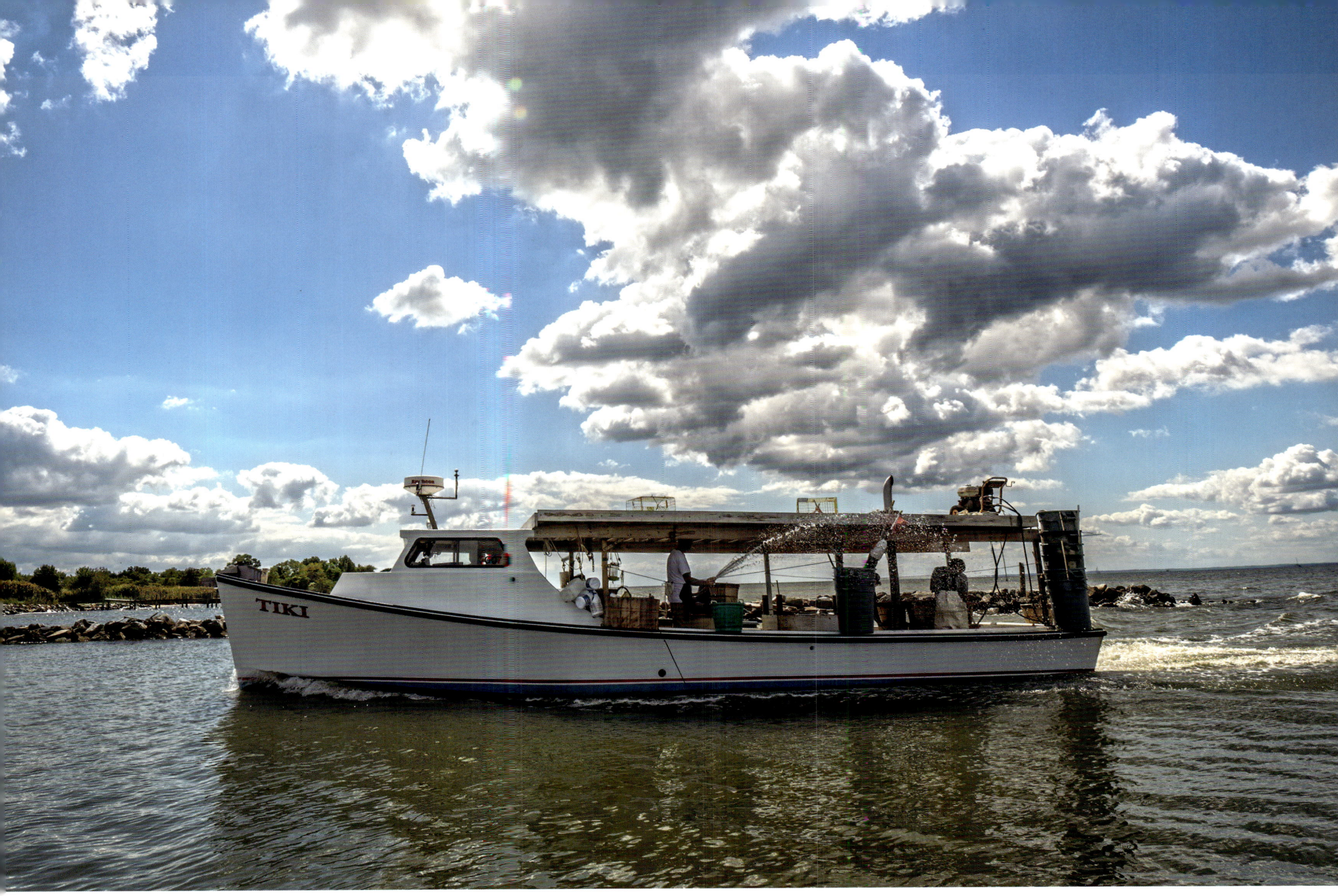

The work day isn't over yet. Cleanup is starting on the way in, and then there is prep work to do for the next day.

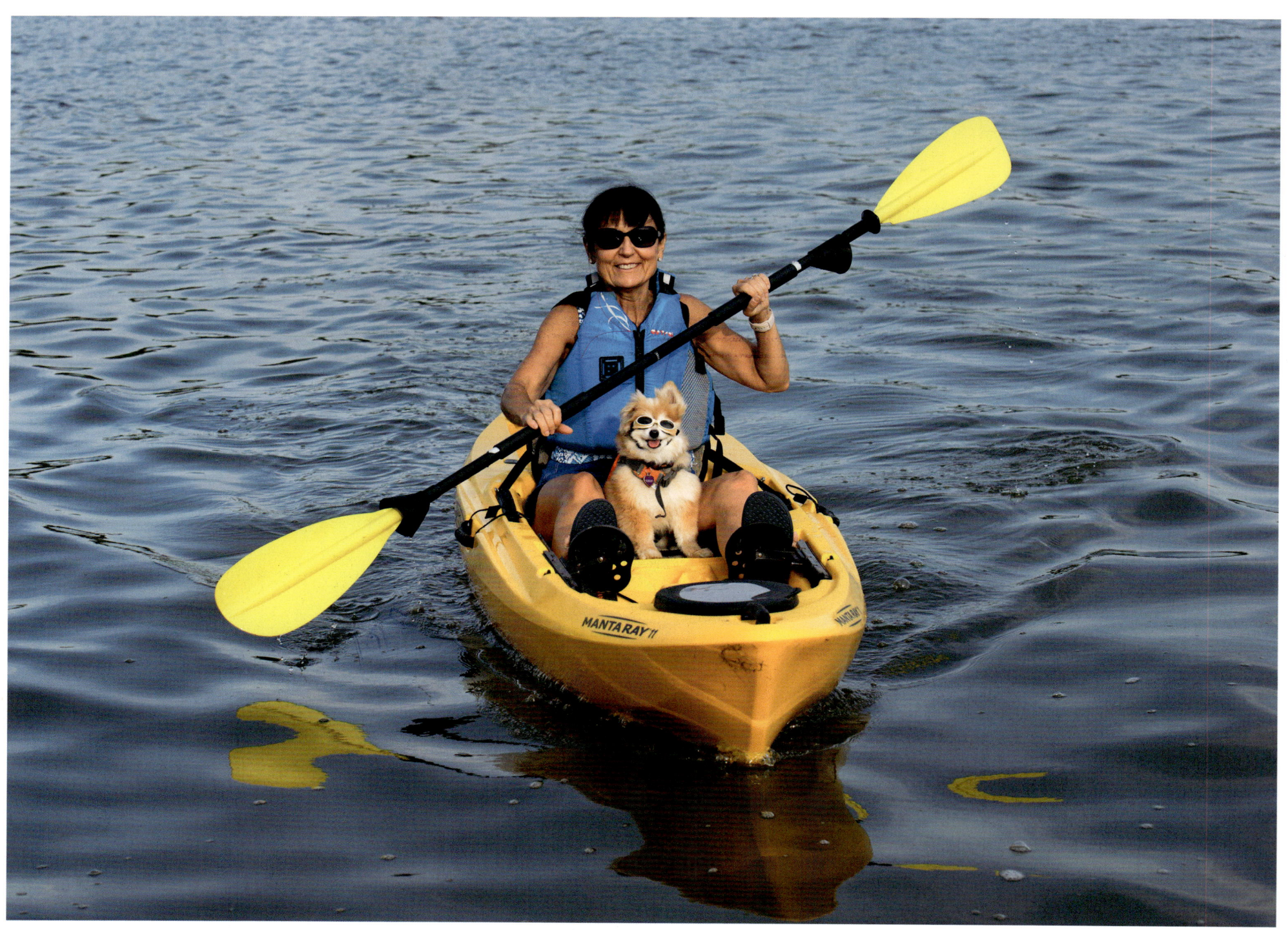

Lissie the dog loves to go paddling with her mom. She was rescued from a horrendously abusive situation with several other Pomeranians. She must have thought she died and went to heaven!

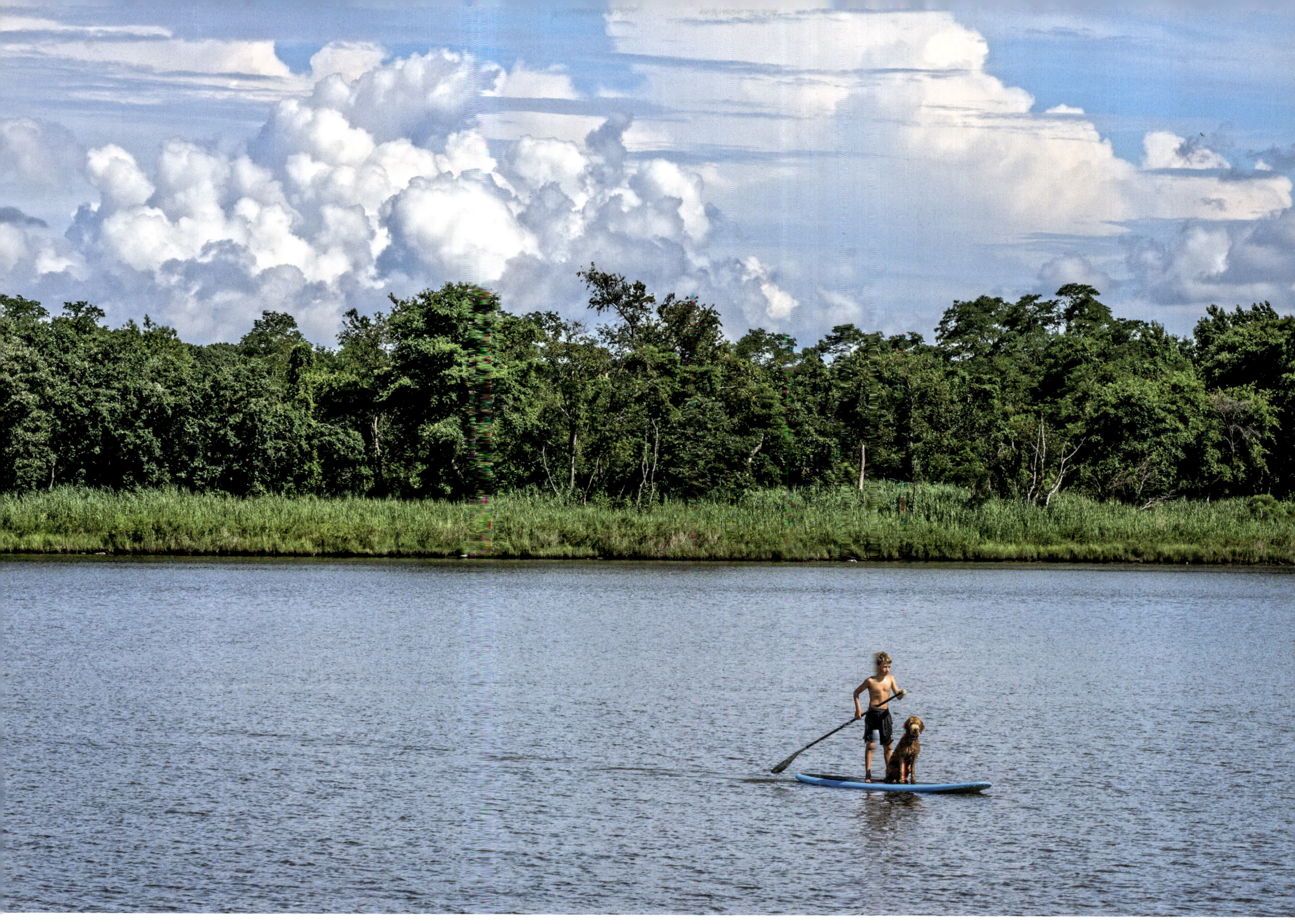

Huk also enjoys paddling with his big brother.

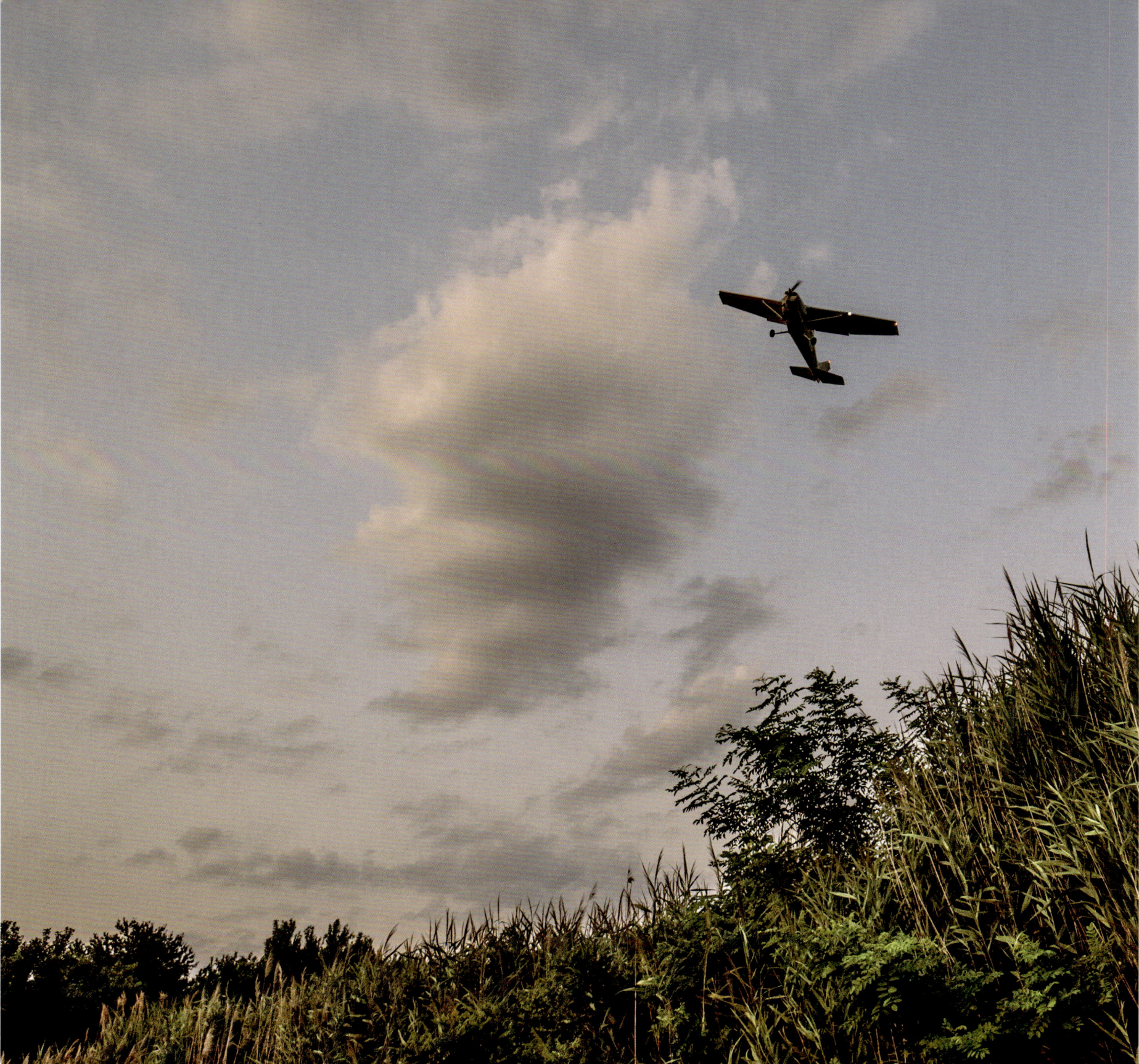

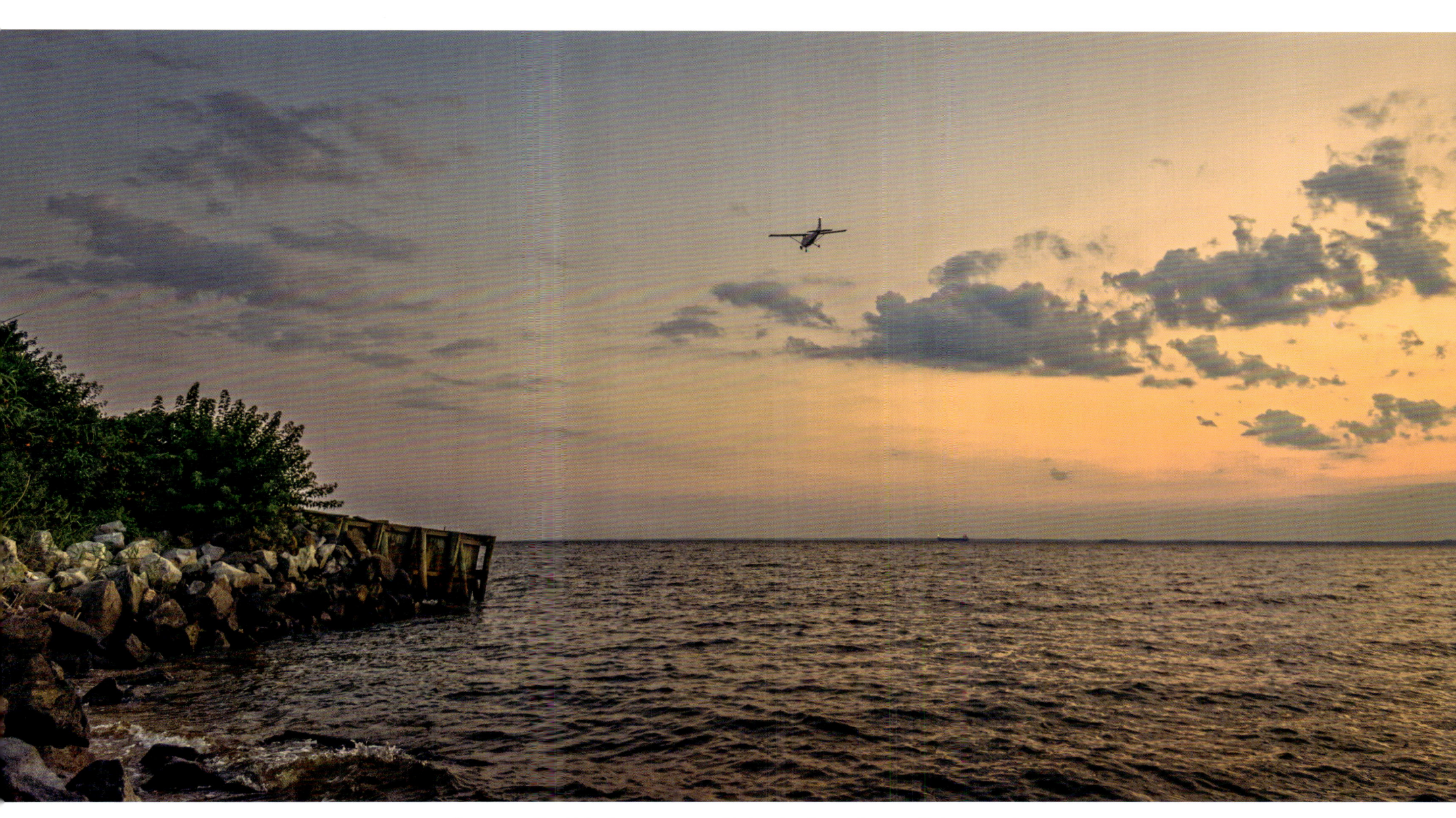

If you are a Kent Islander, you are used to hearing these planes puttering around. There's a grass runway where the planes can land and pull right into hangars attached to houses in the Kentmorr community. It's quite remarkable to see them take off from the little cliff adjacent to the shore and then to see them fly up and over the bay.

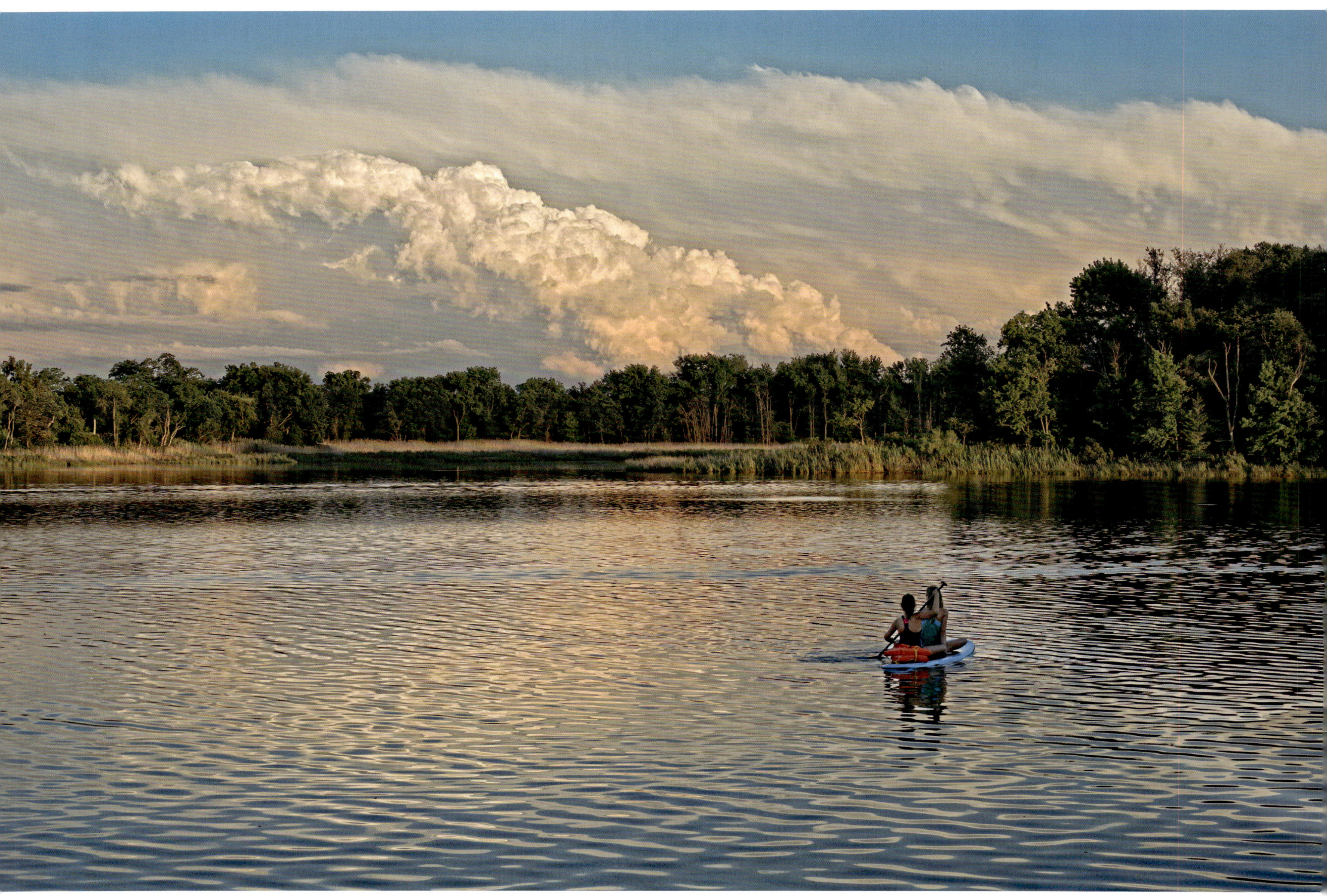

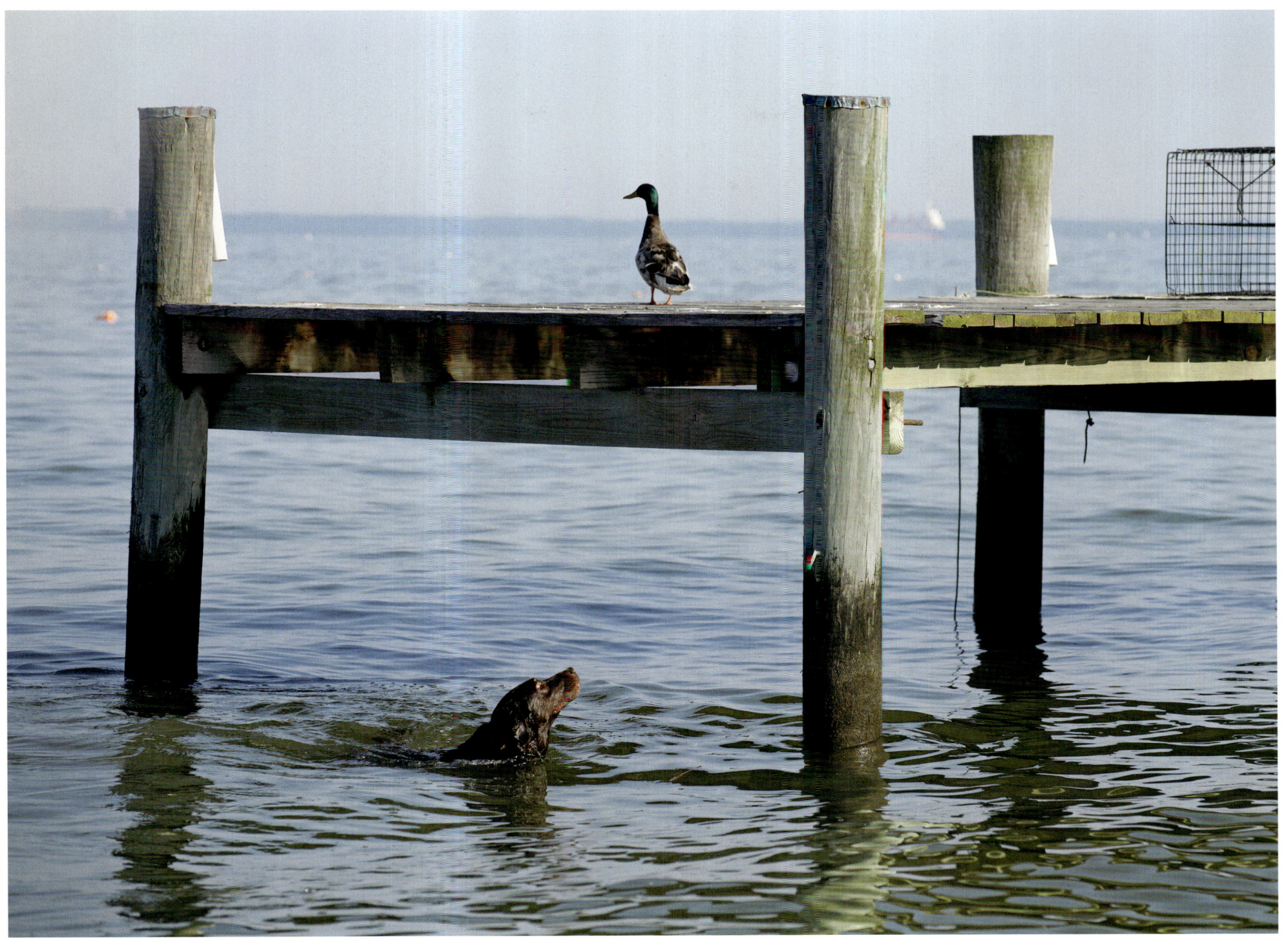

It's not duck season, but some don't care

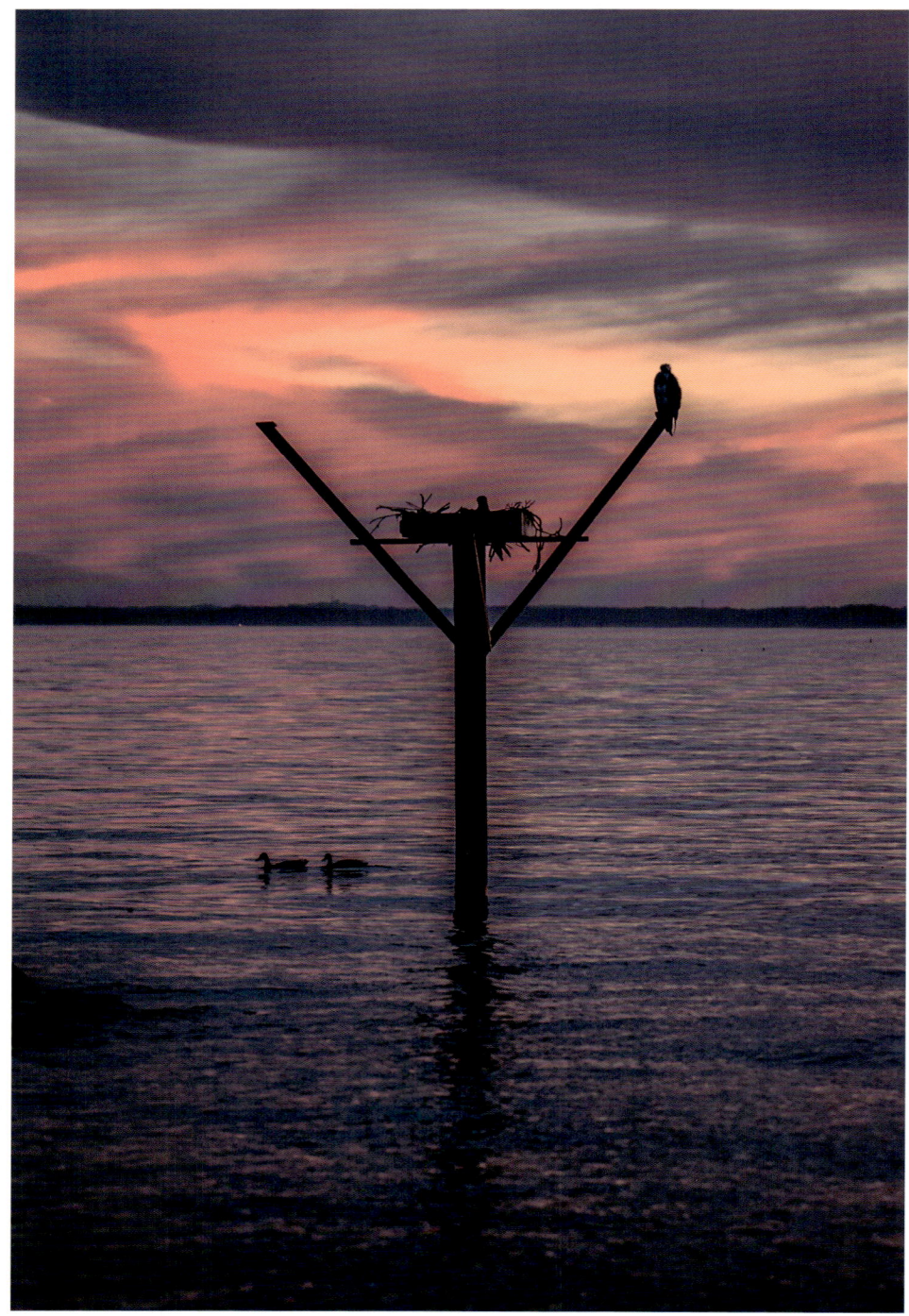
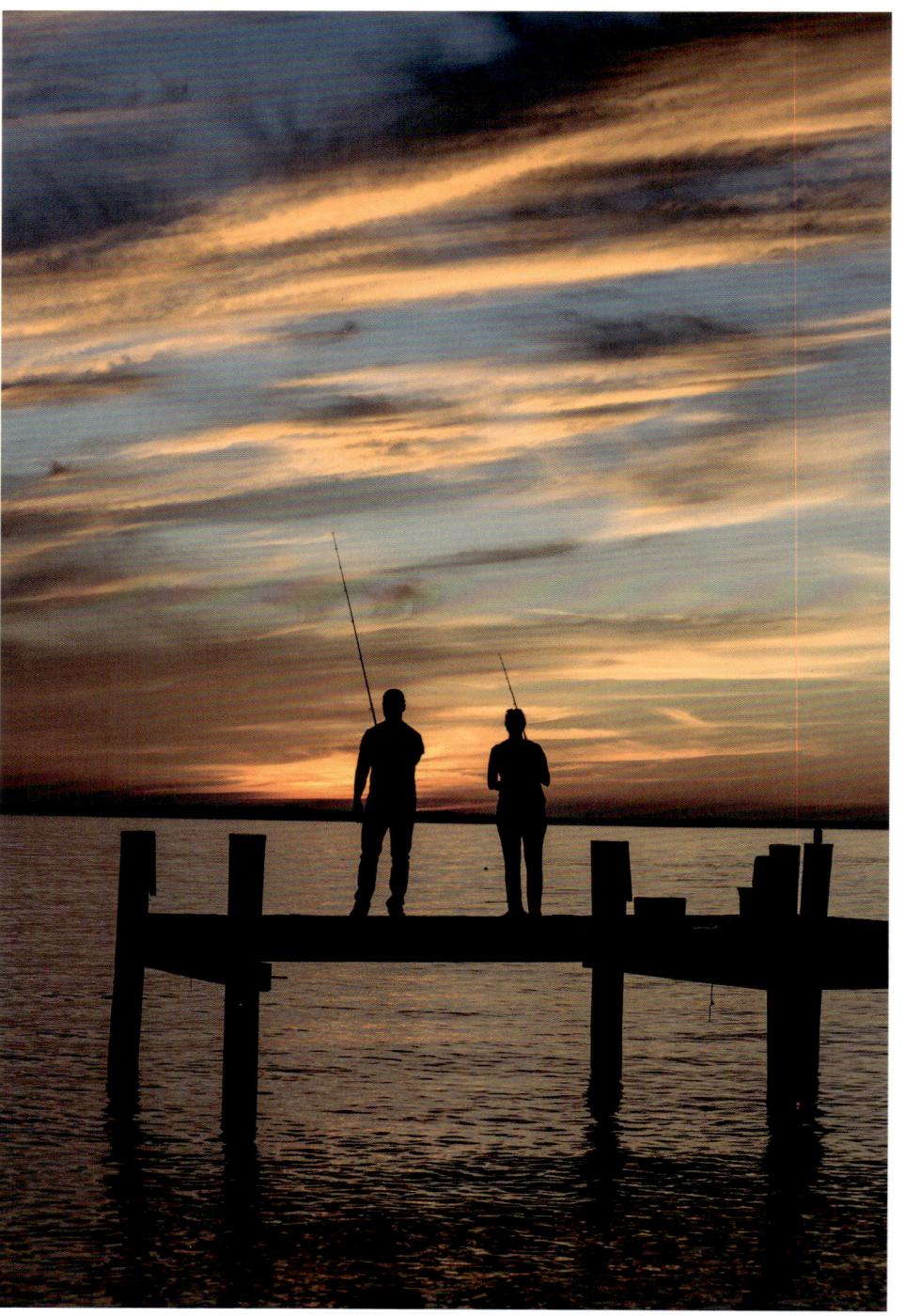

Saturday night vibes

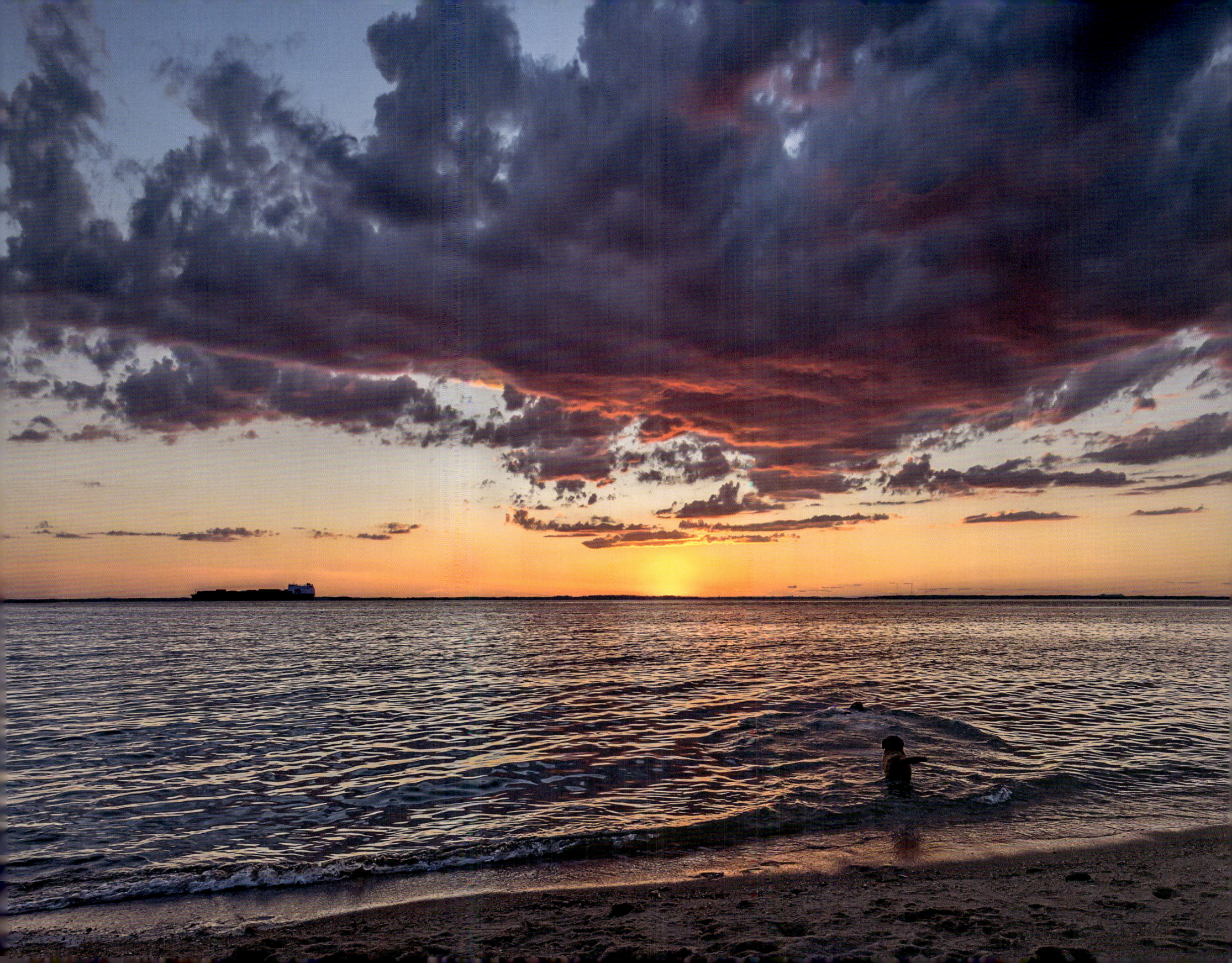

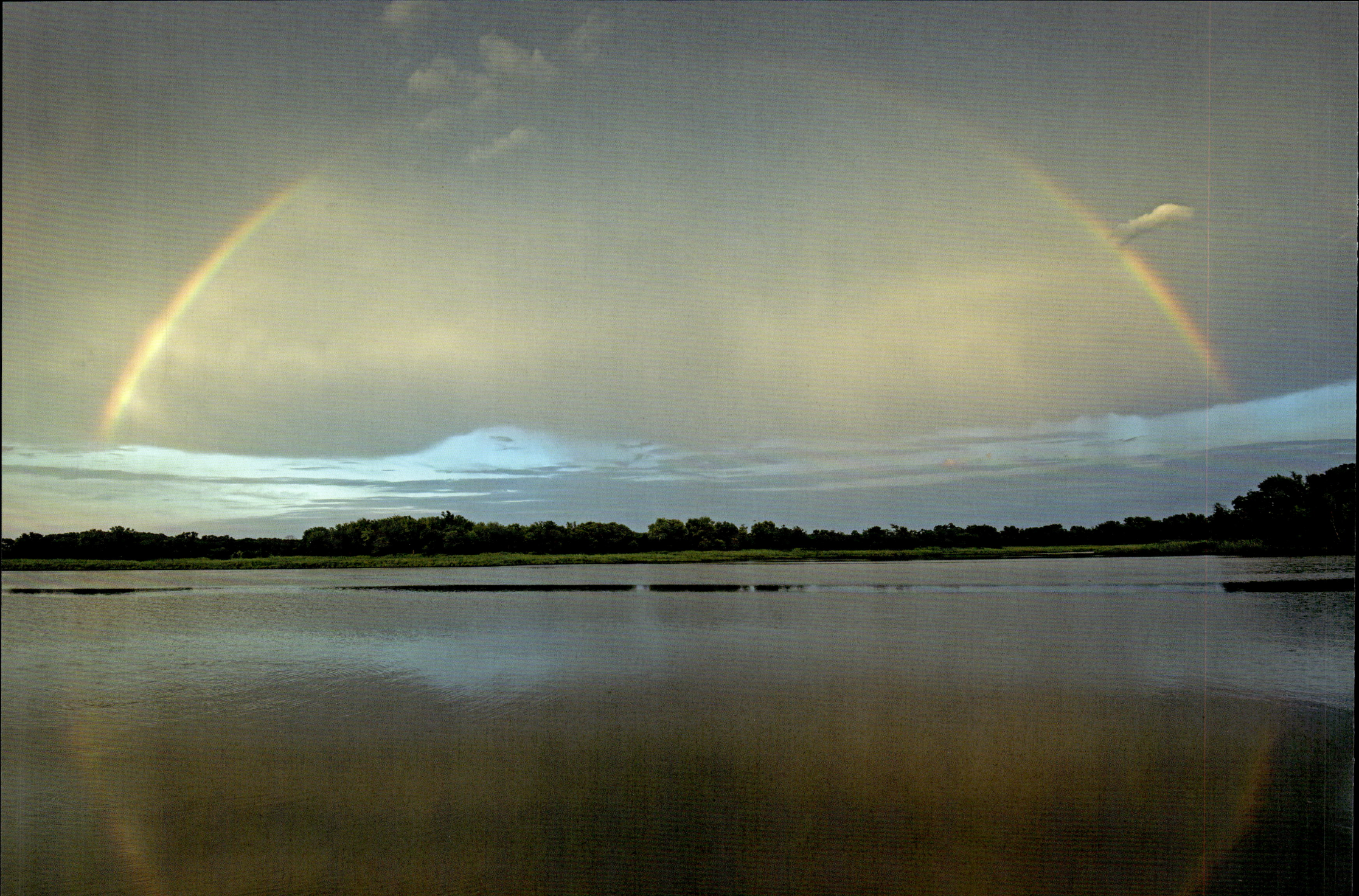

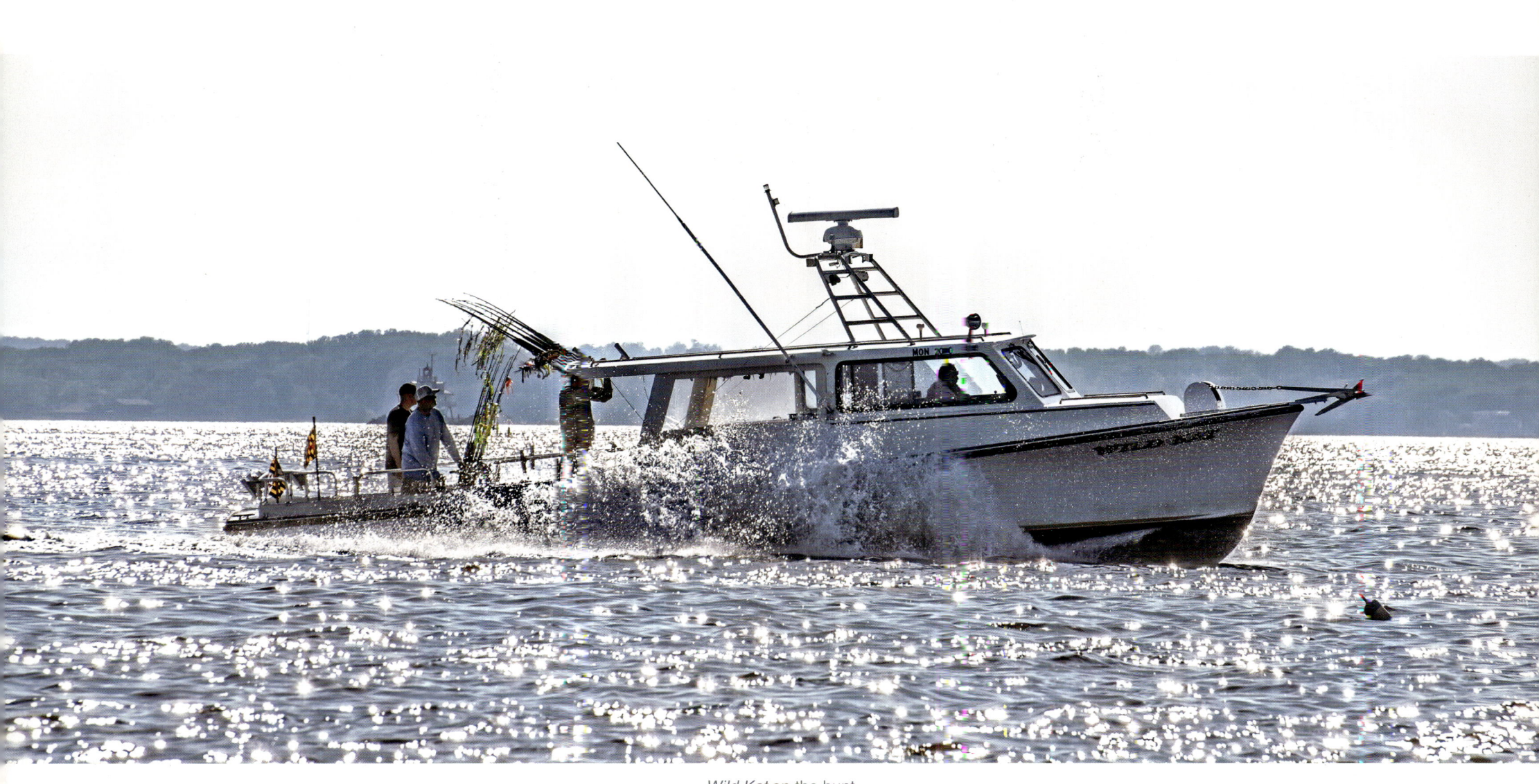

Wild Kat on the hunt

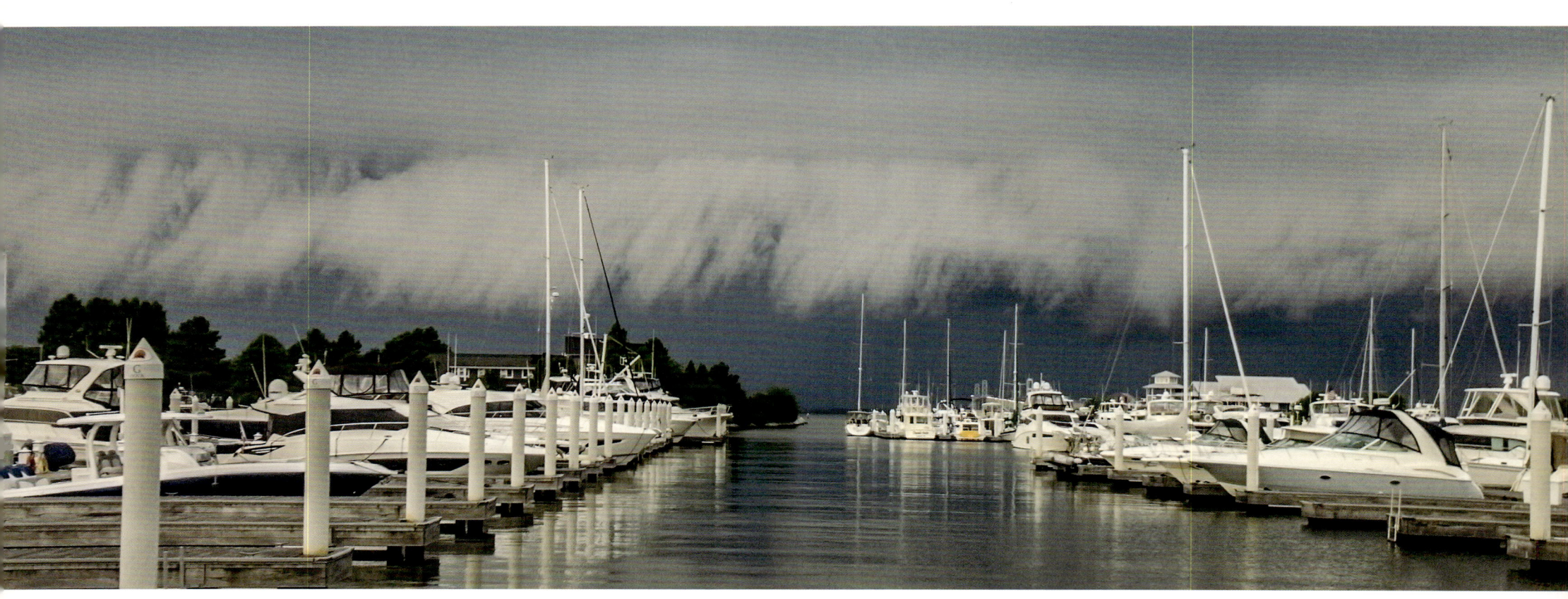

A shelf cloud o'er Bay Bridge Marina

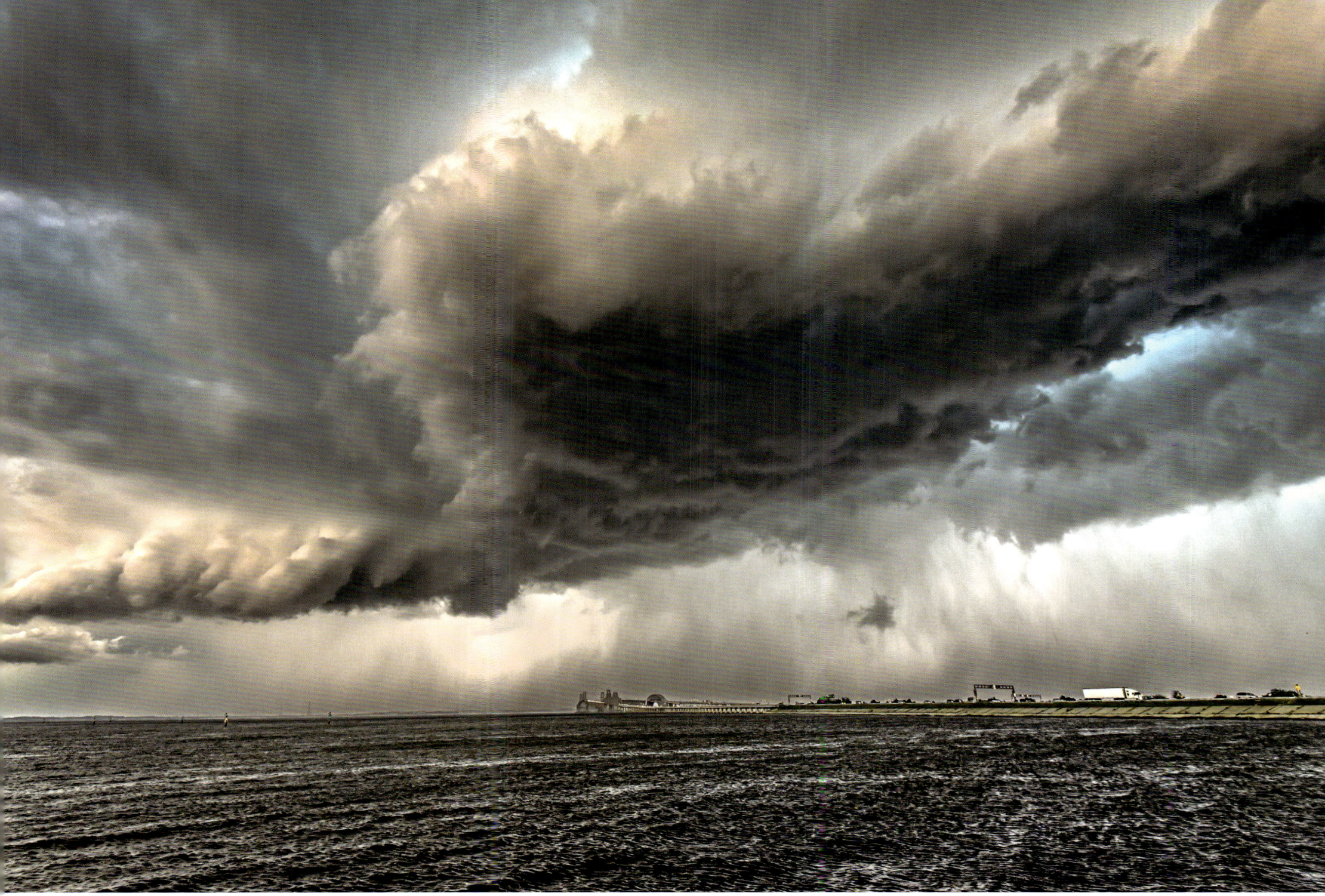

Last shot before making a run for it!

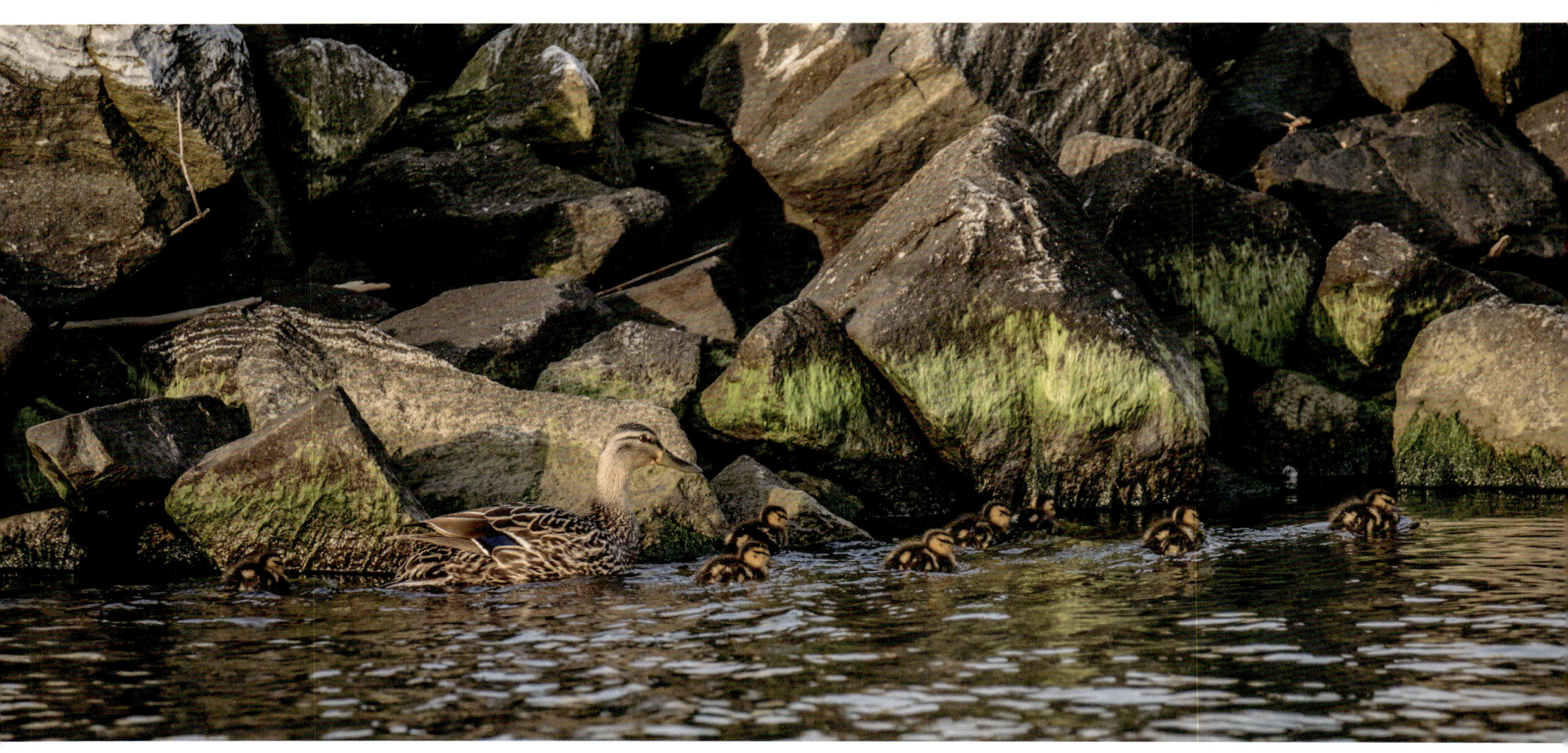

It was a fun family outing until . . .

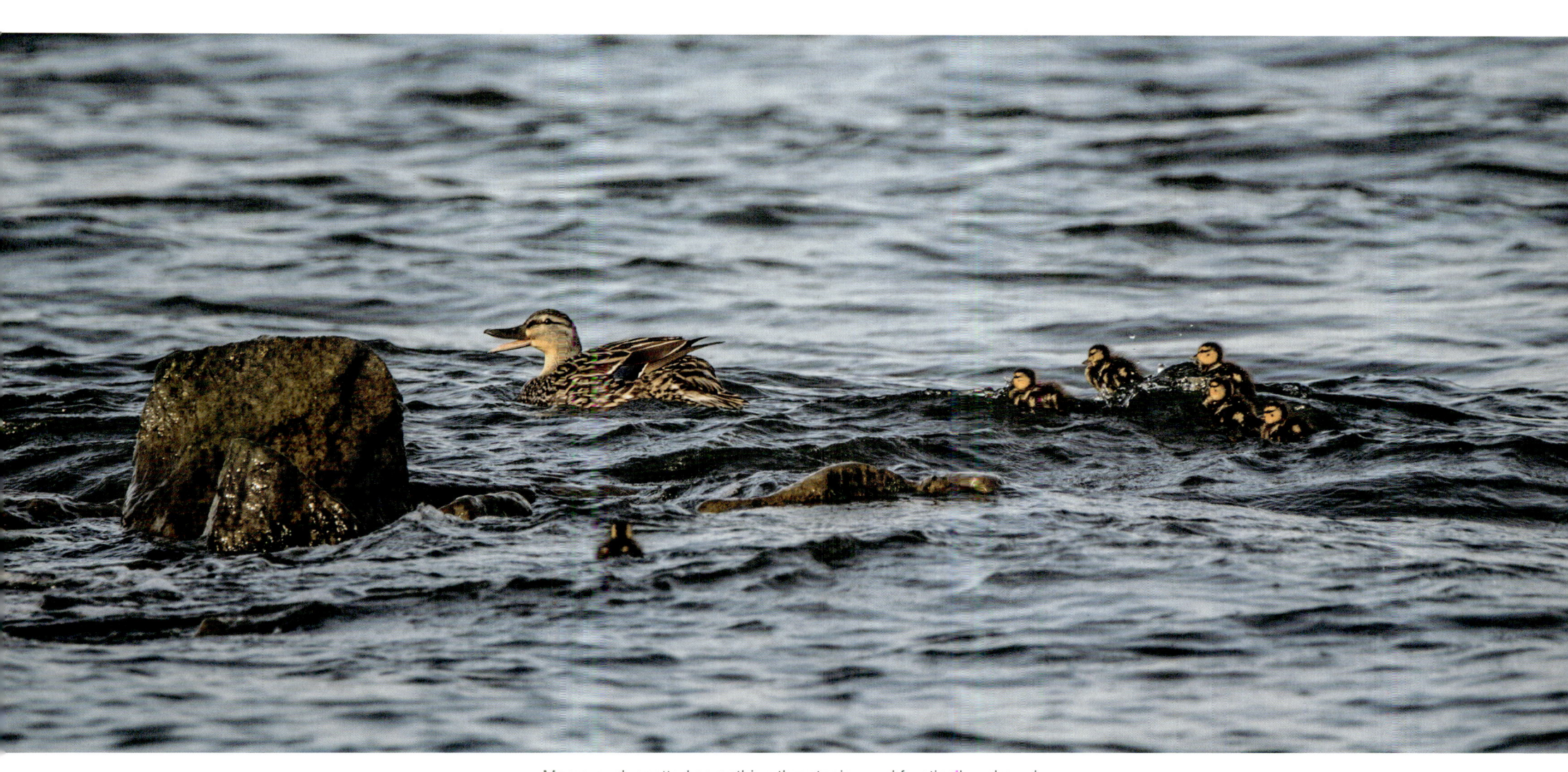

Mama Duck spotted something threatening and frantically ushered her ducklings around the jetty.

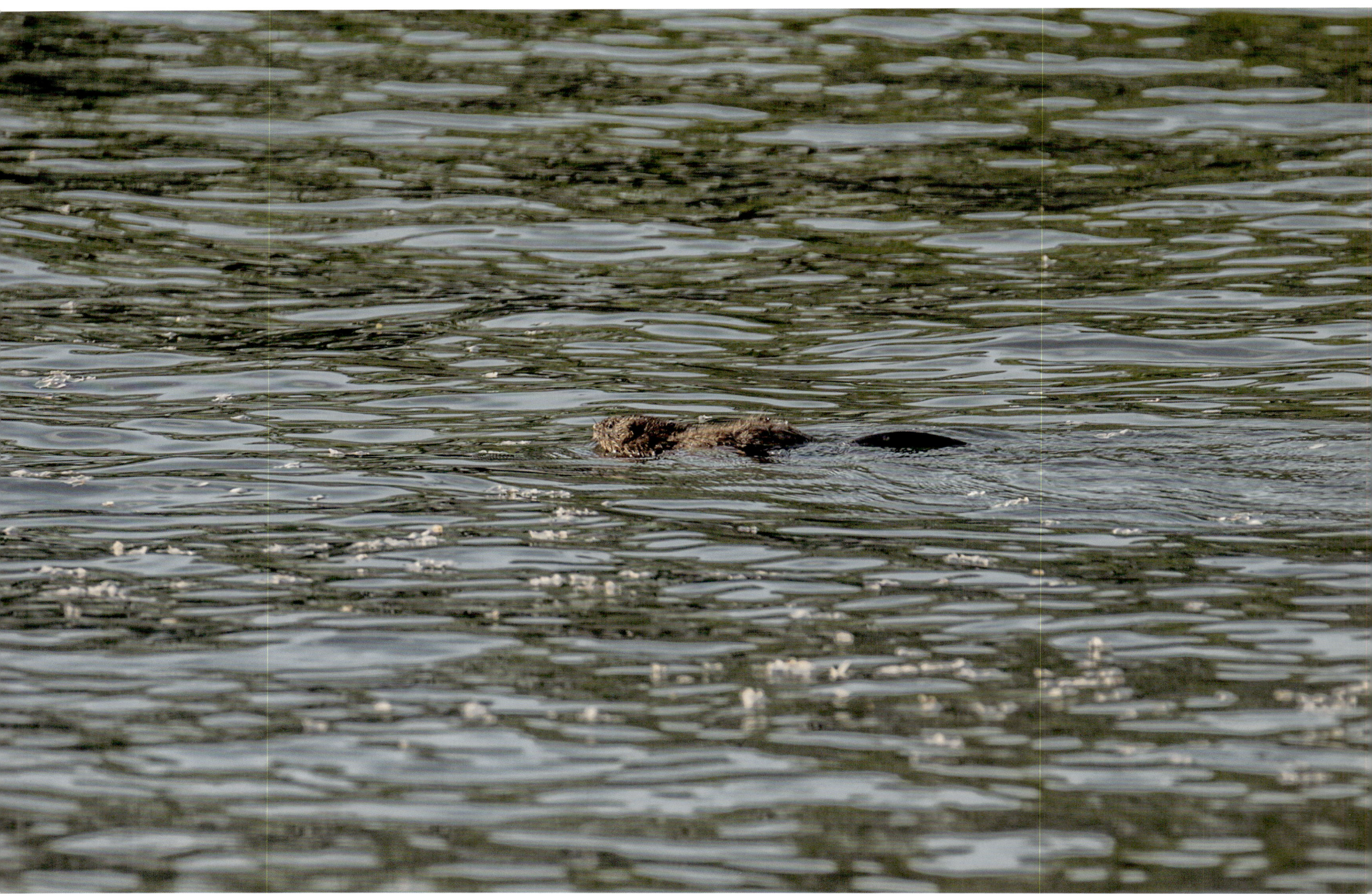

Could this guy have been nearby?

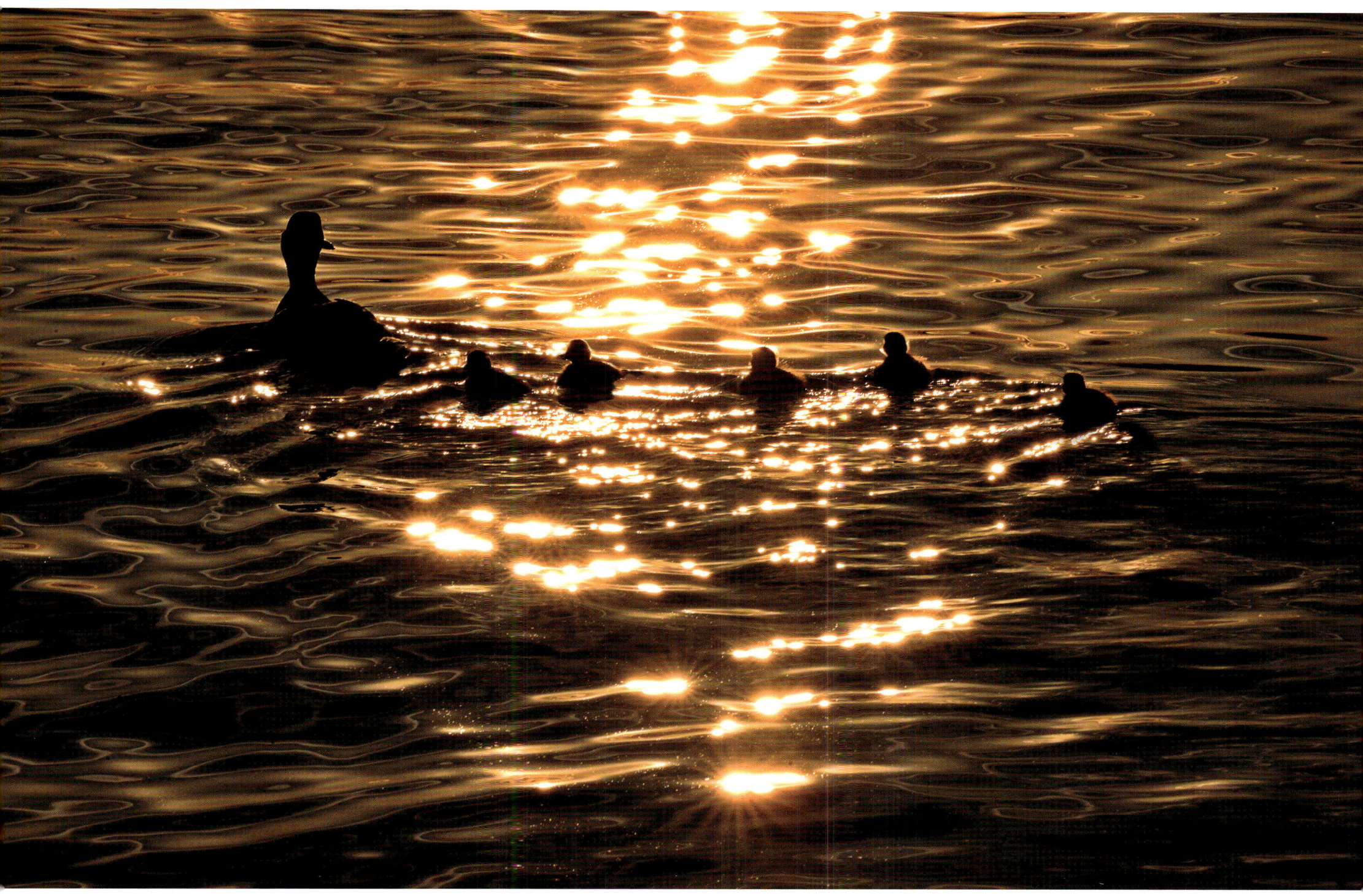

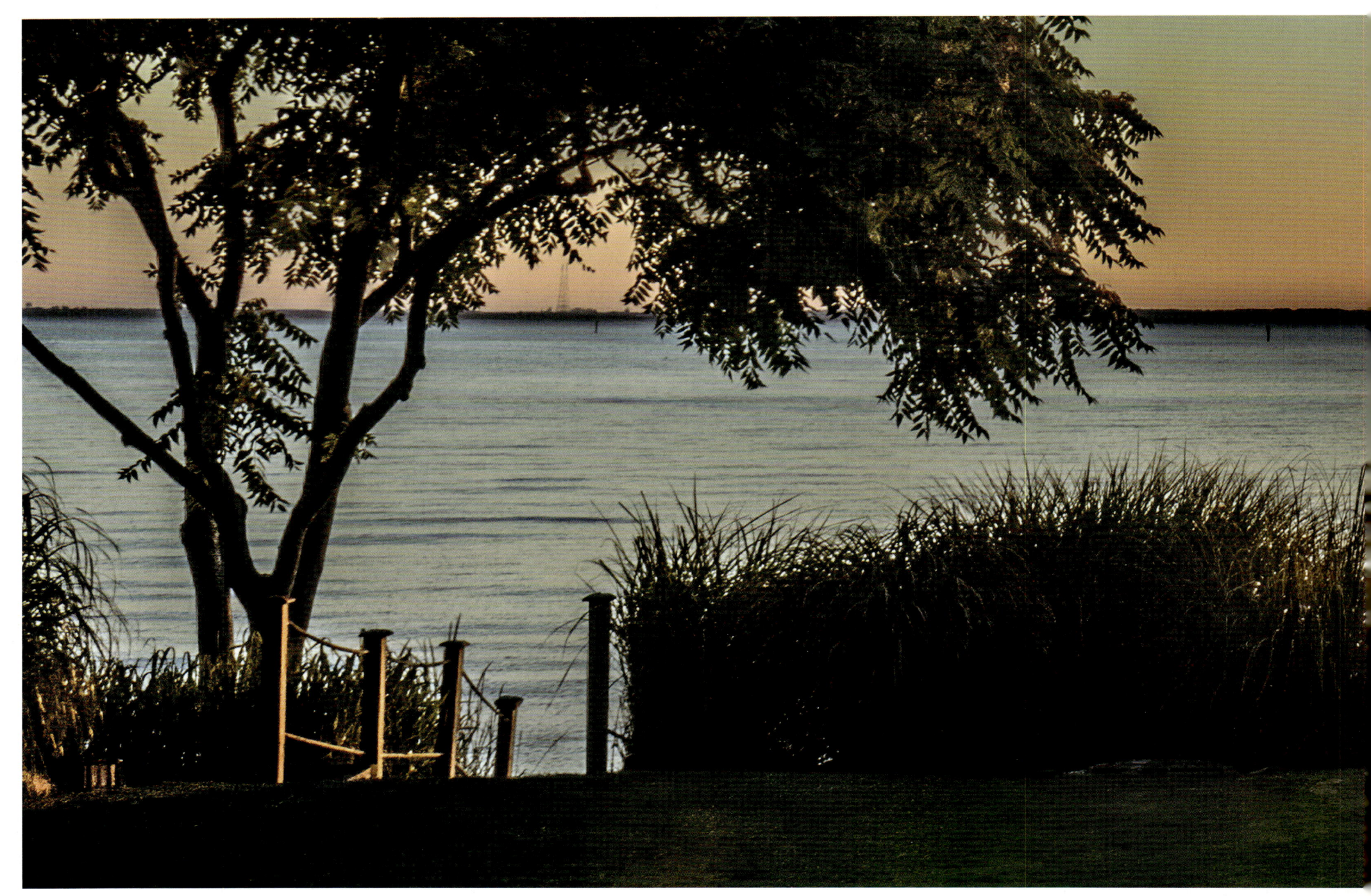

View from Chesapeake Bay Beach Club

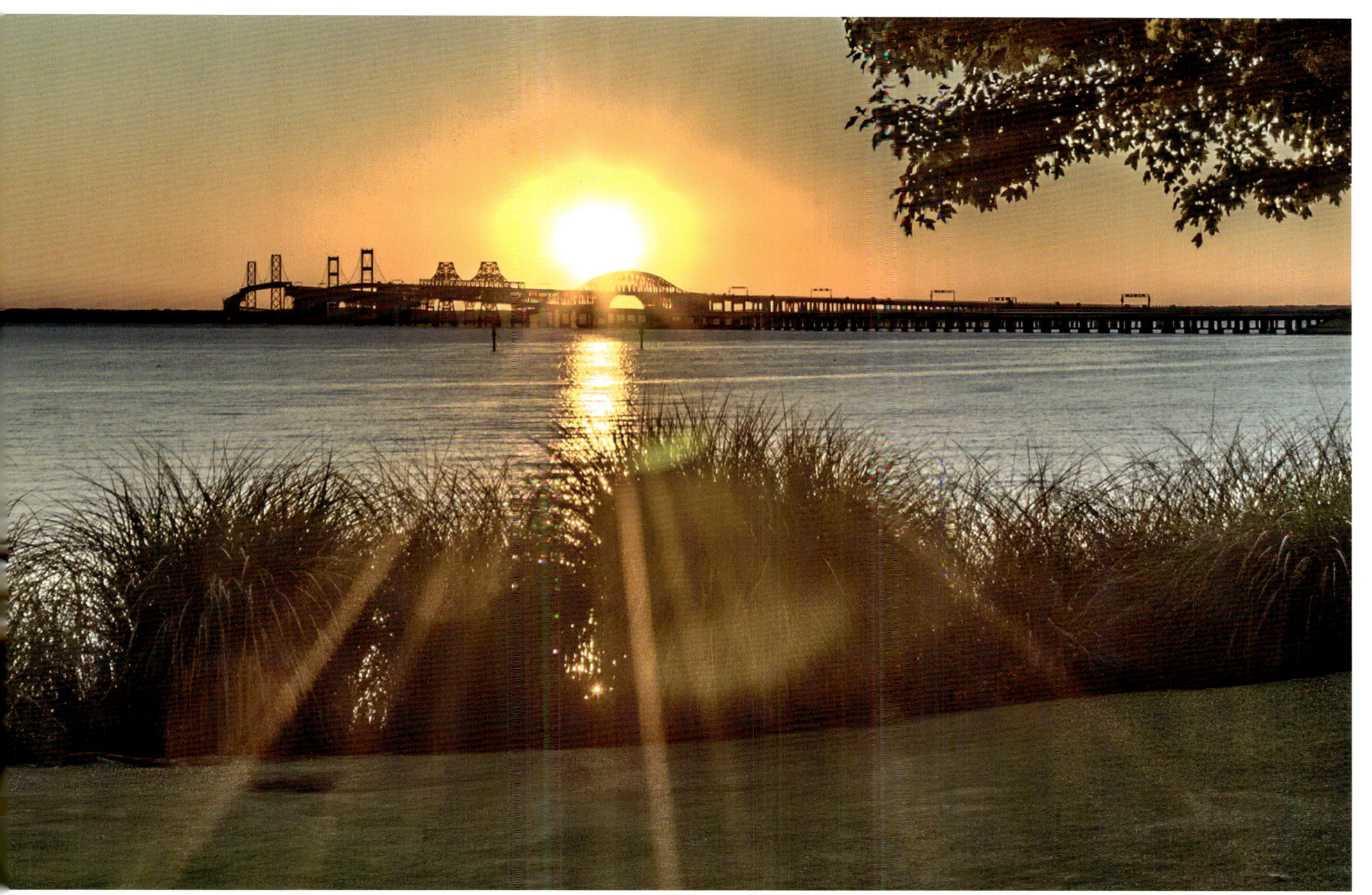

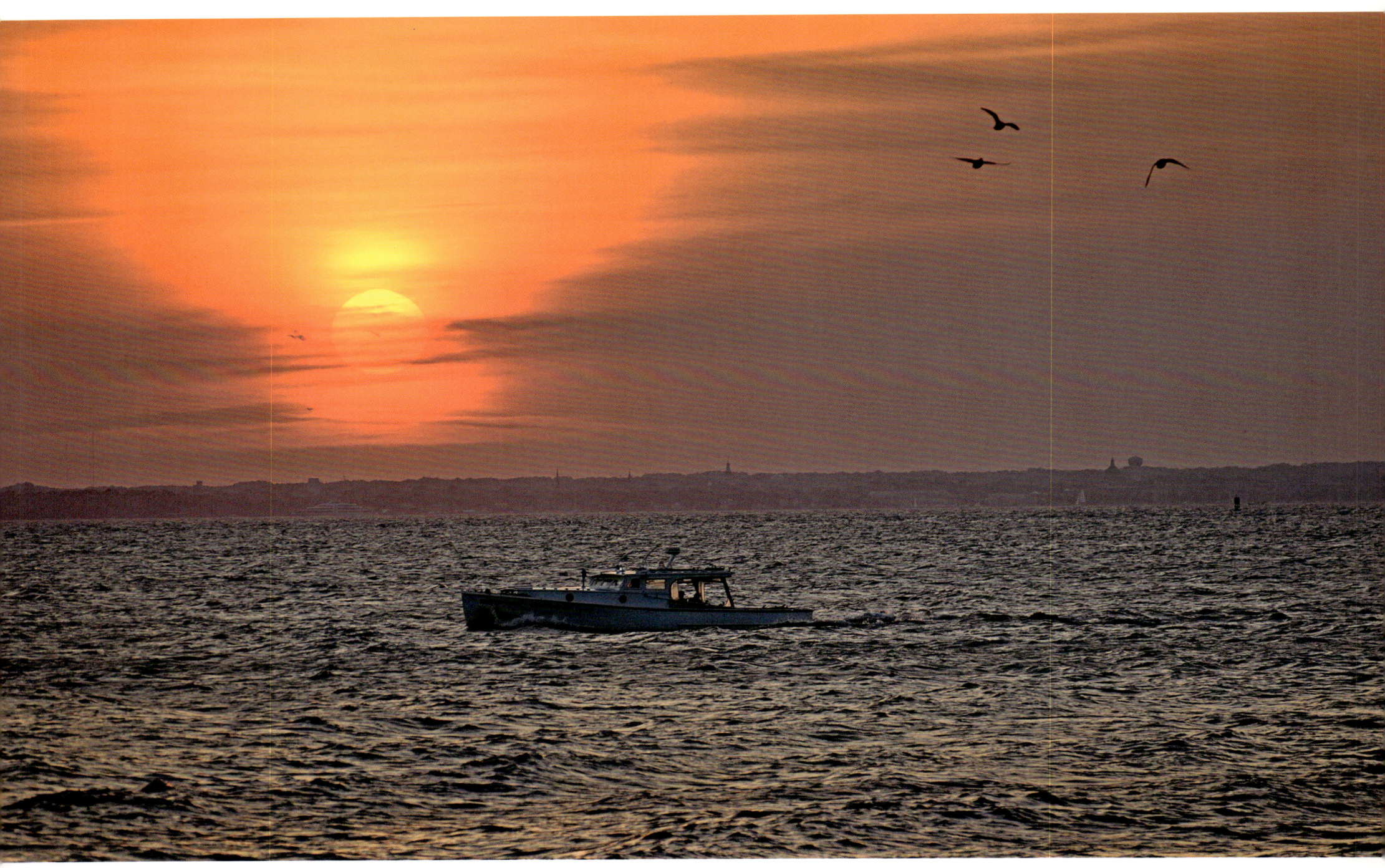

Breezin' Thru breezin' by again

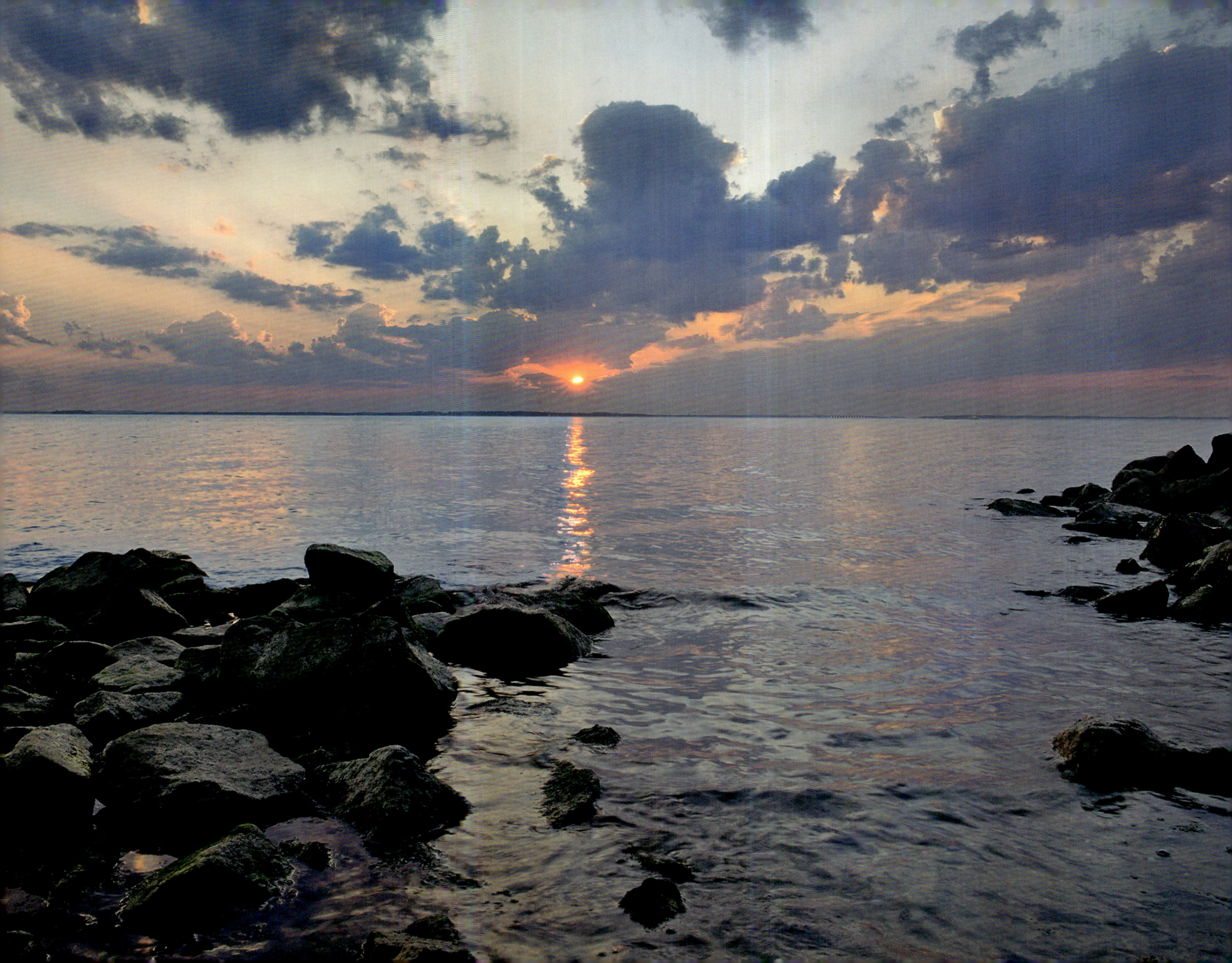

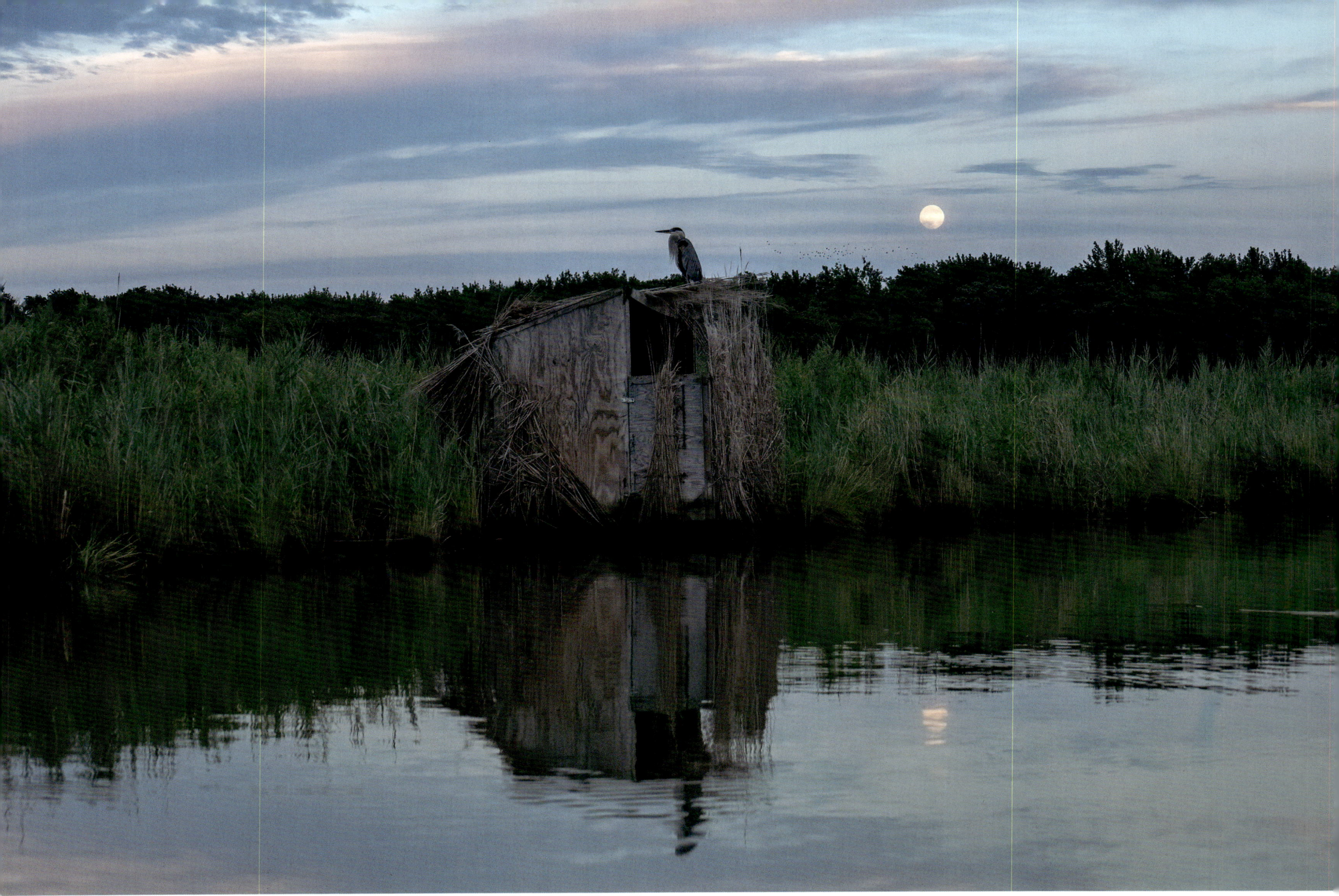

These stoic creatures will remain still for what seems like forever.

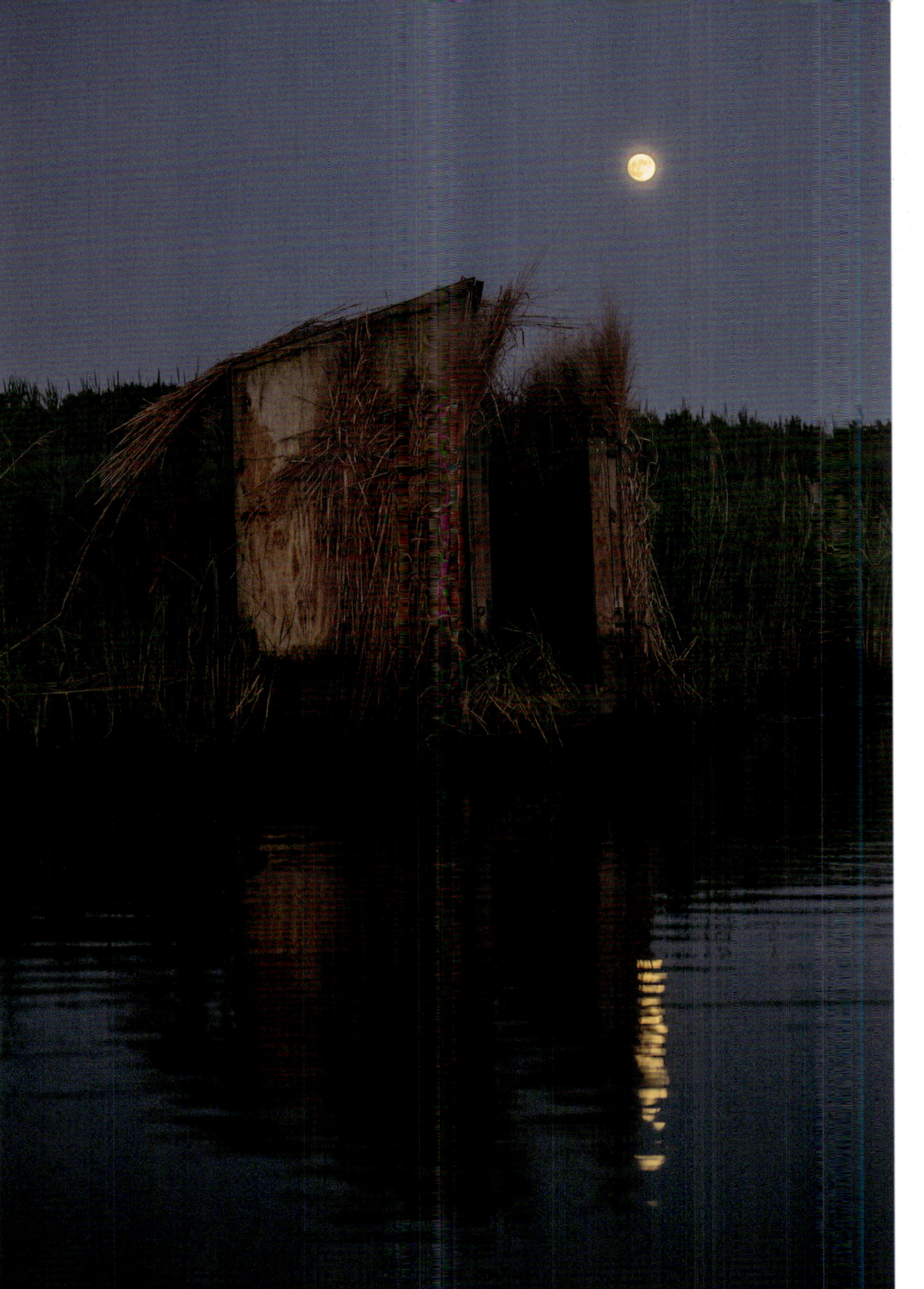

The sturgeon moon rising on Price Creek

This cormorant must have had some-thing mouthwatering because this osprey swooped down to it very quickly and proceeded to circle around several times. One must always be on the lookout.

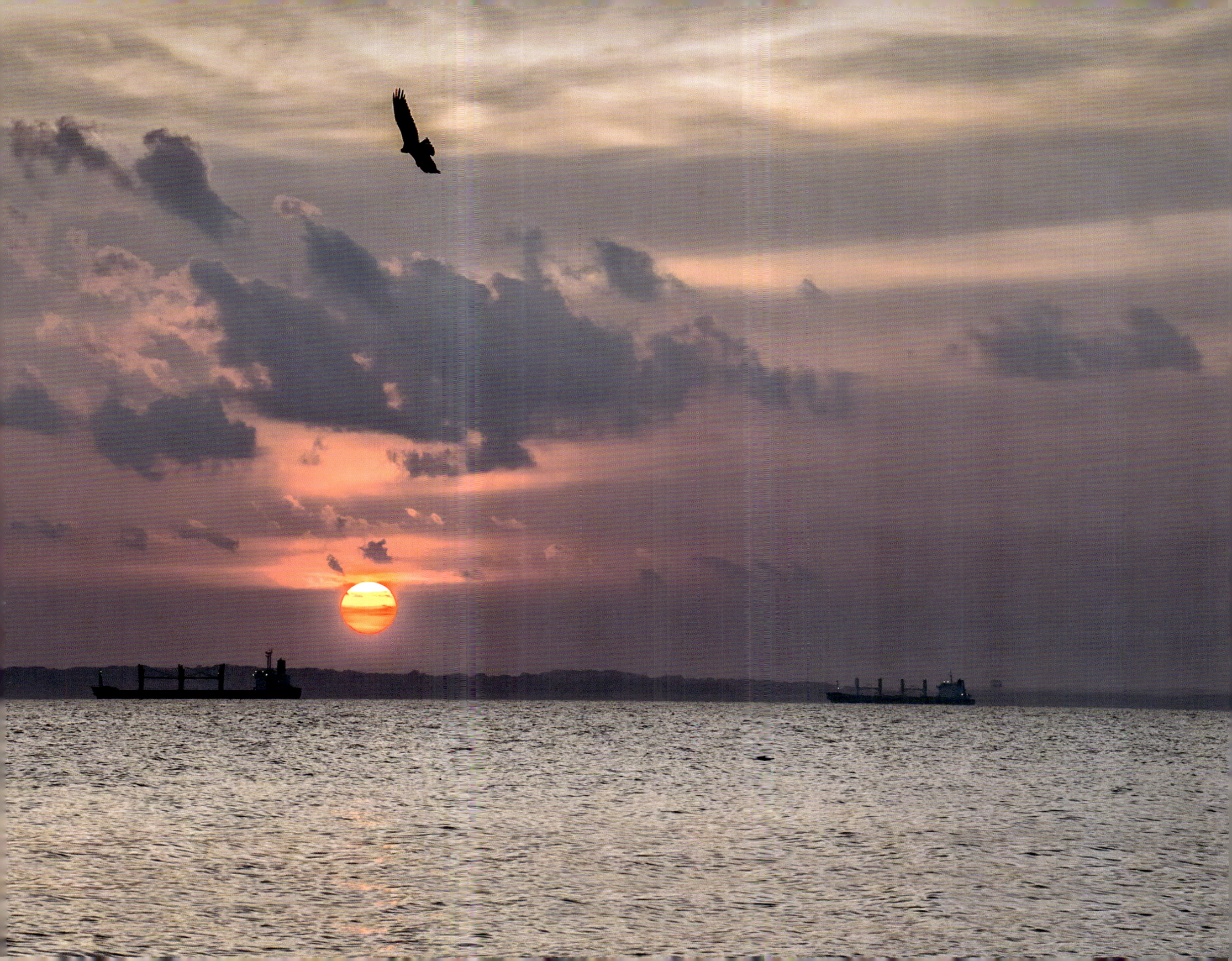

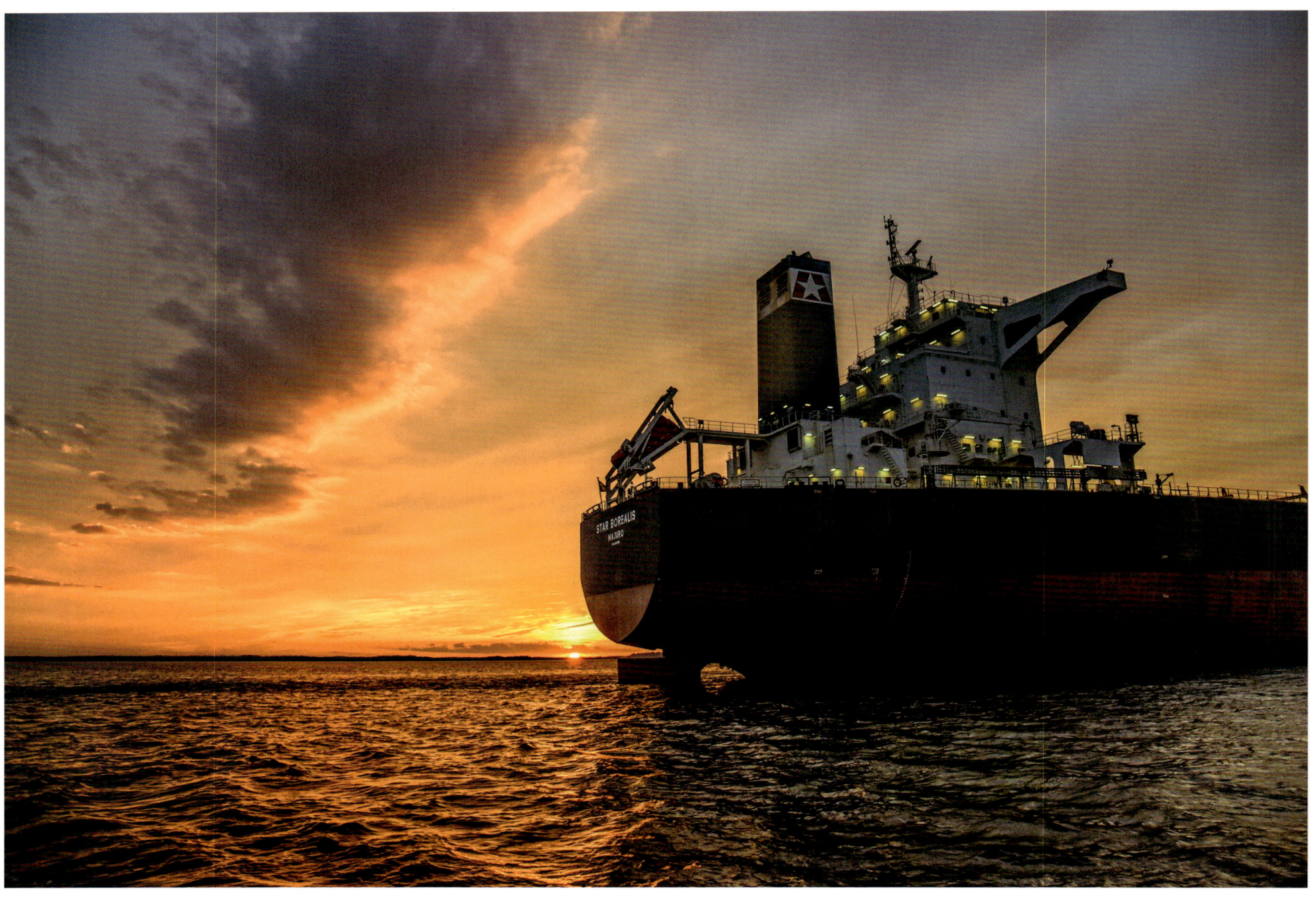

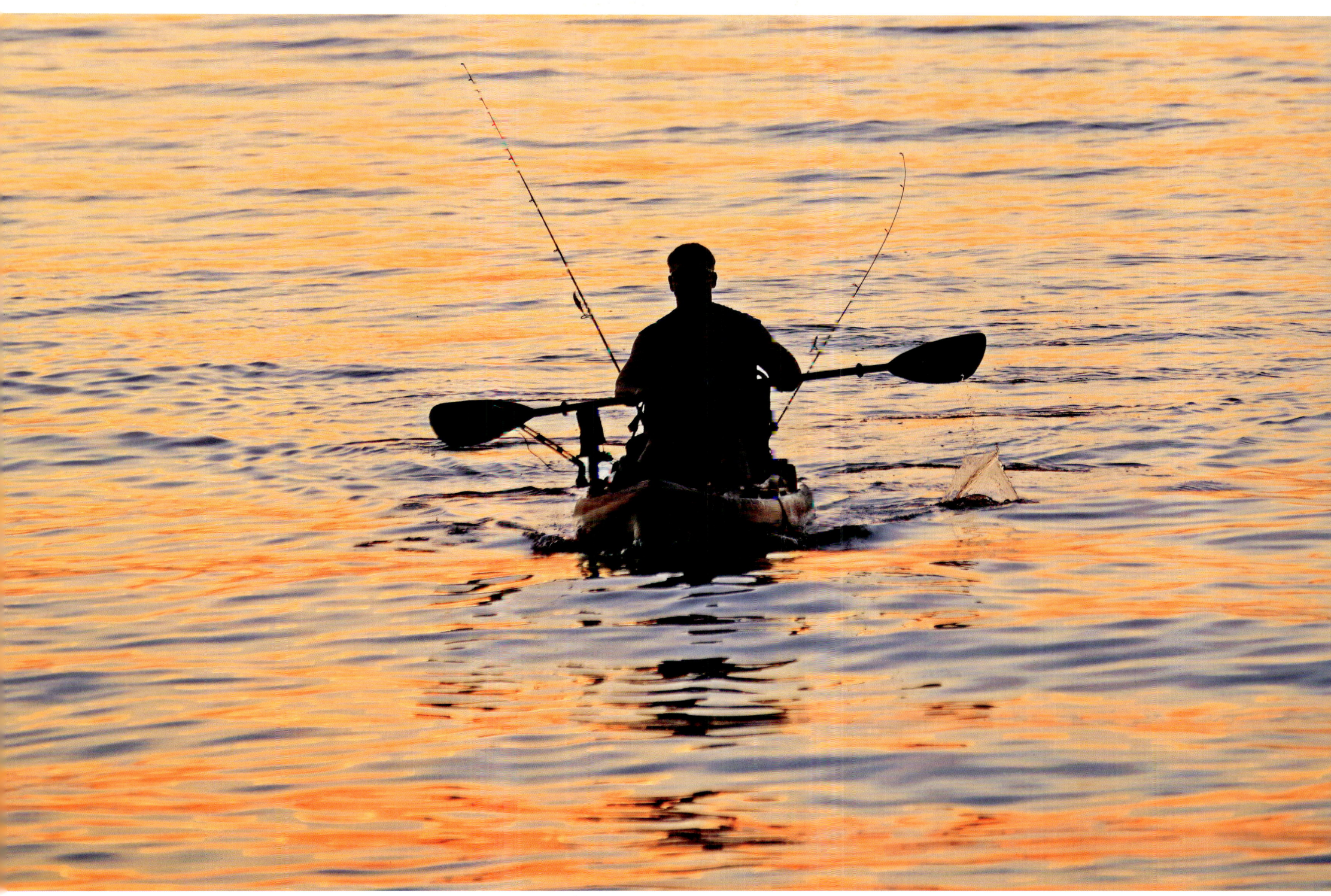

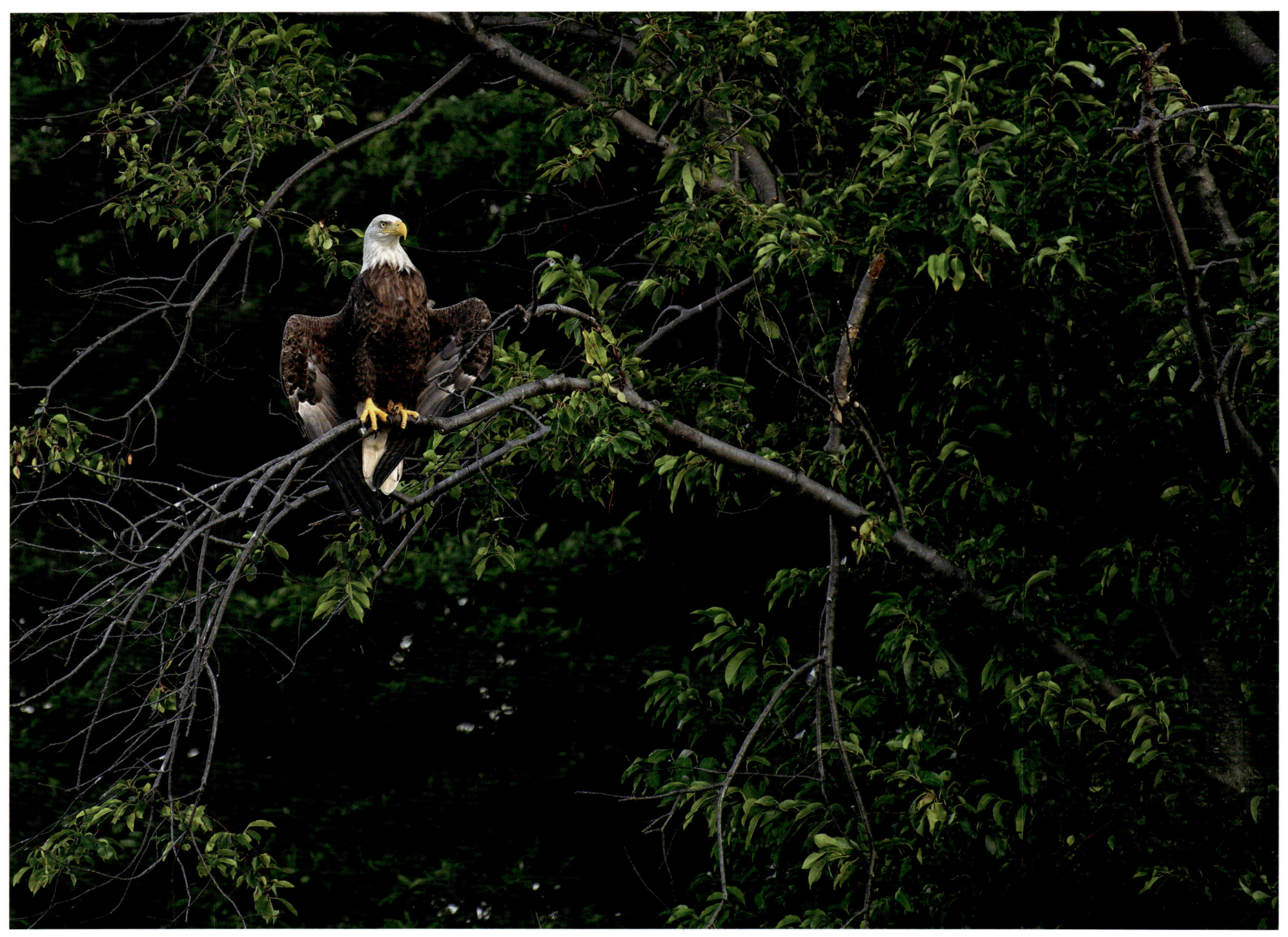

Air drying

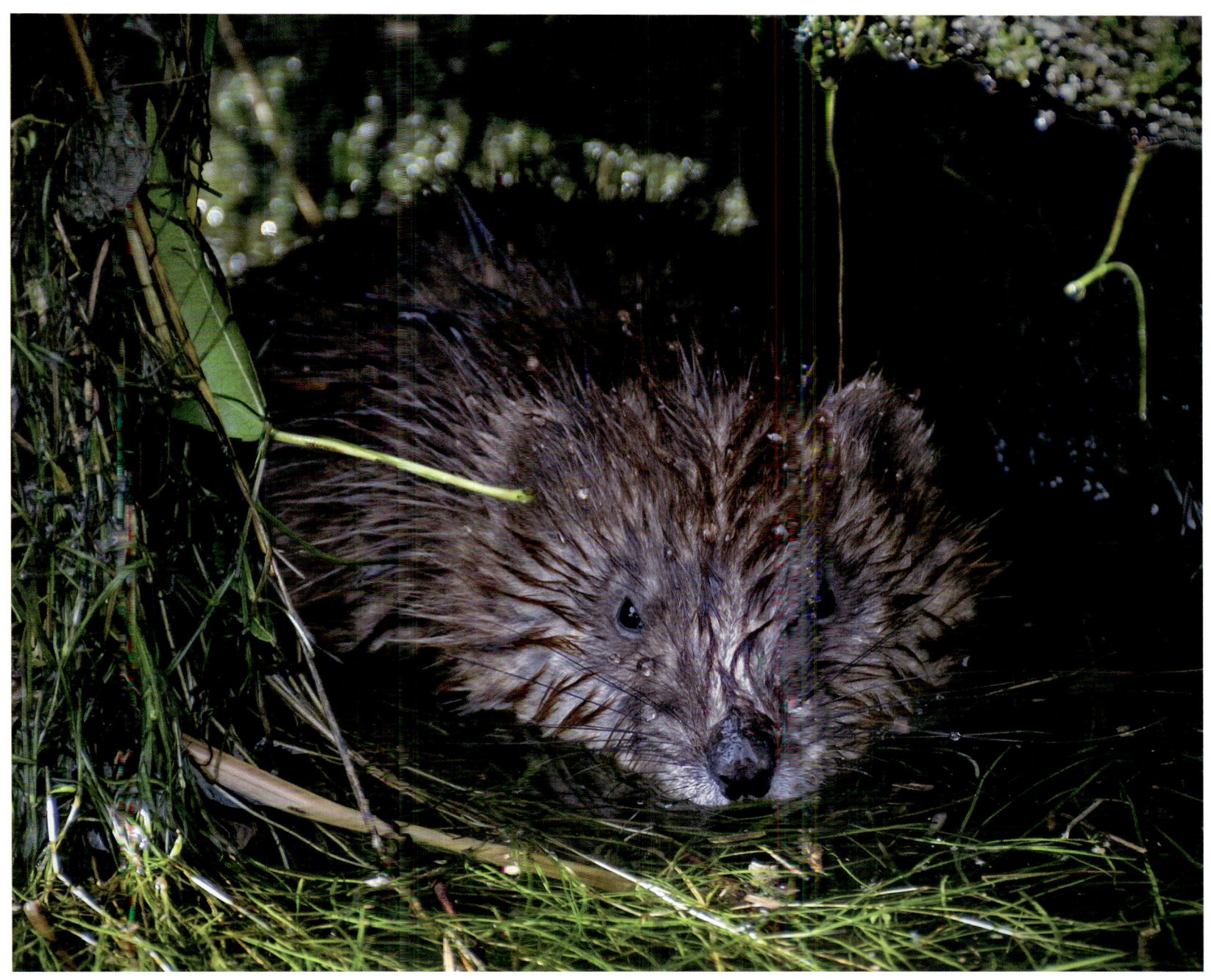

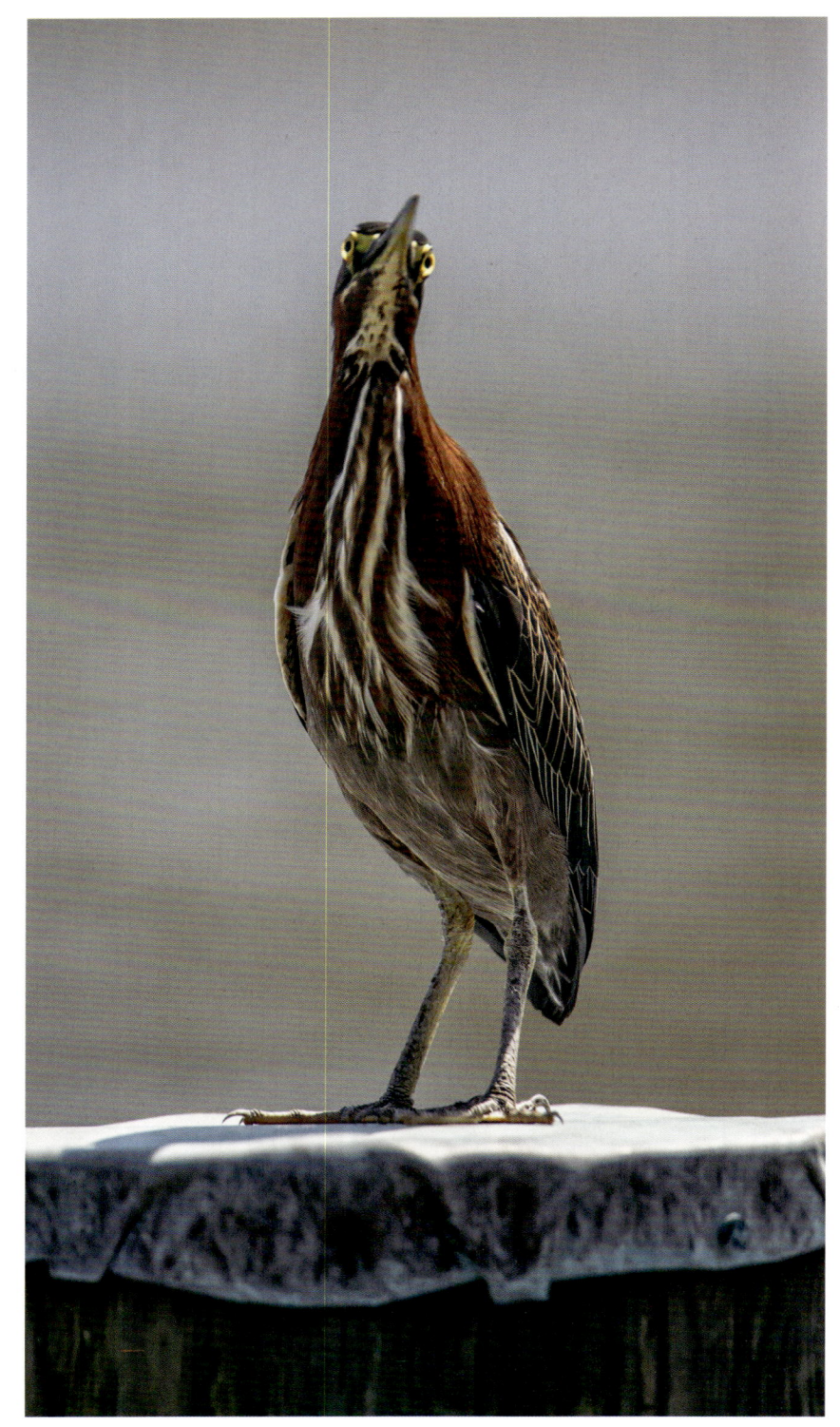

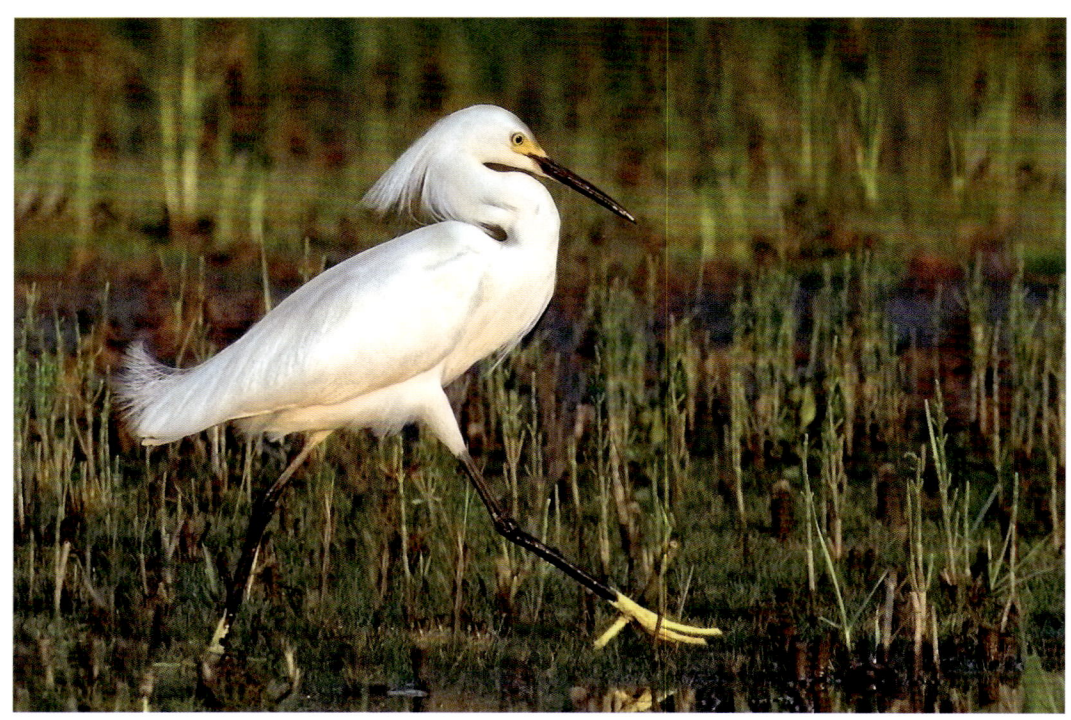

A small white egret struttin' his stuff

Here's lookin' at ya!

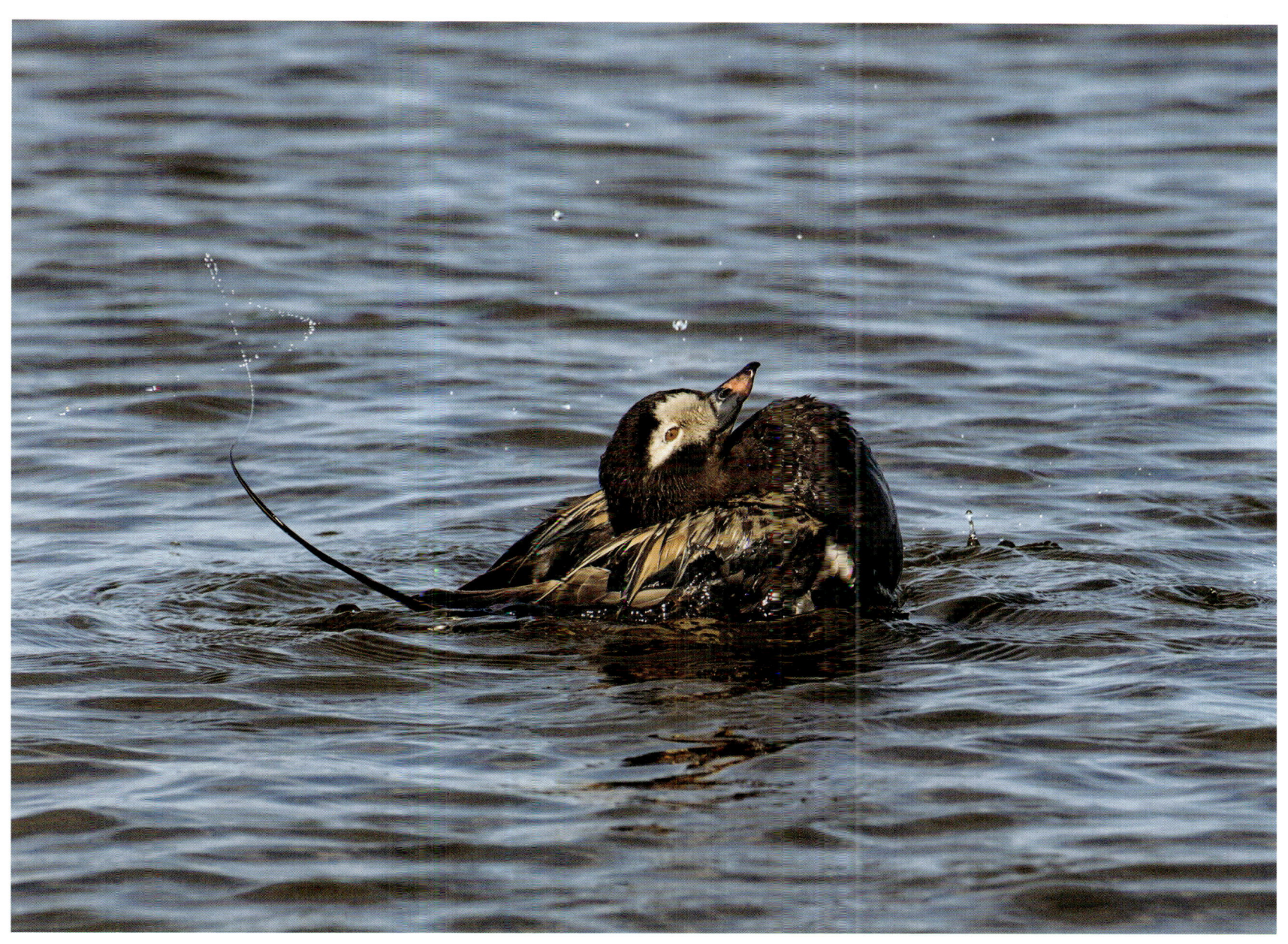

Rarely seen here: the long-tailed duck

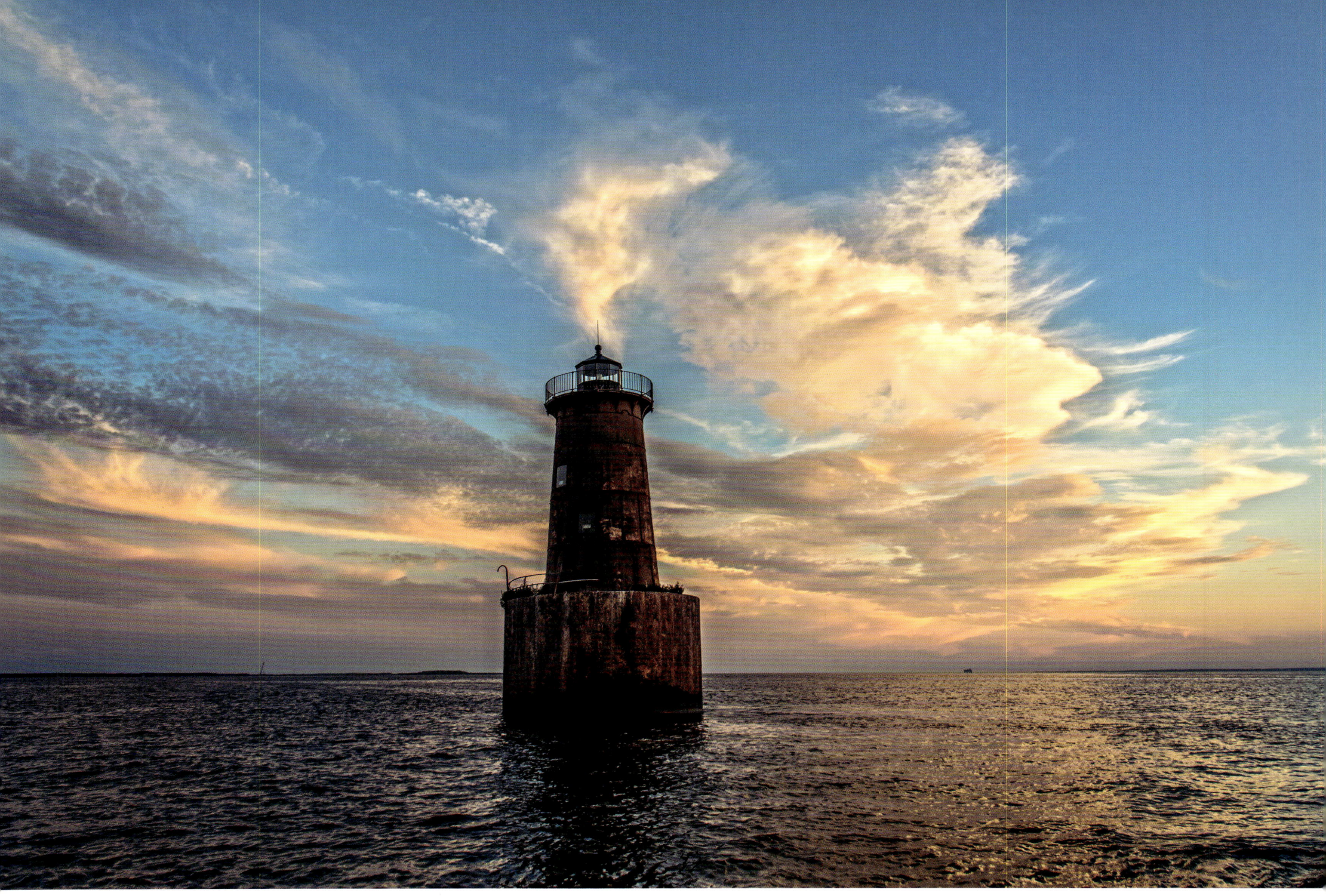

Bloody Point Bar Lighthouse at dusk

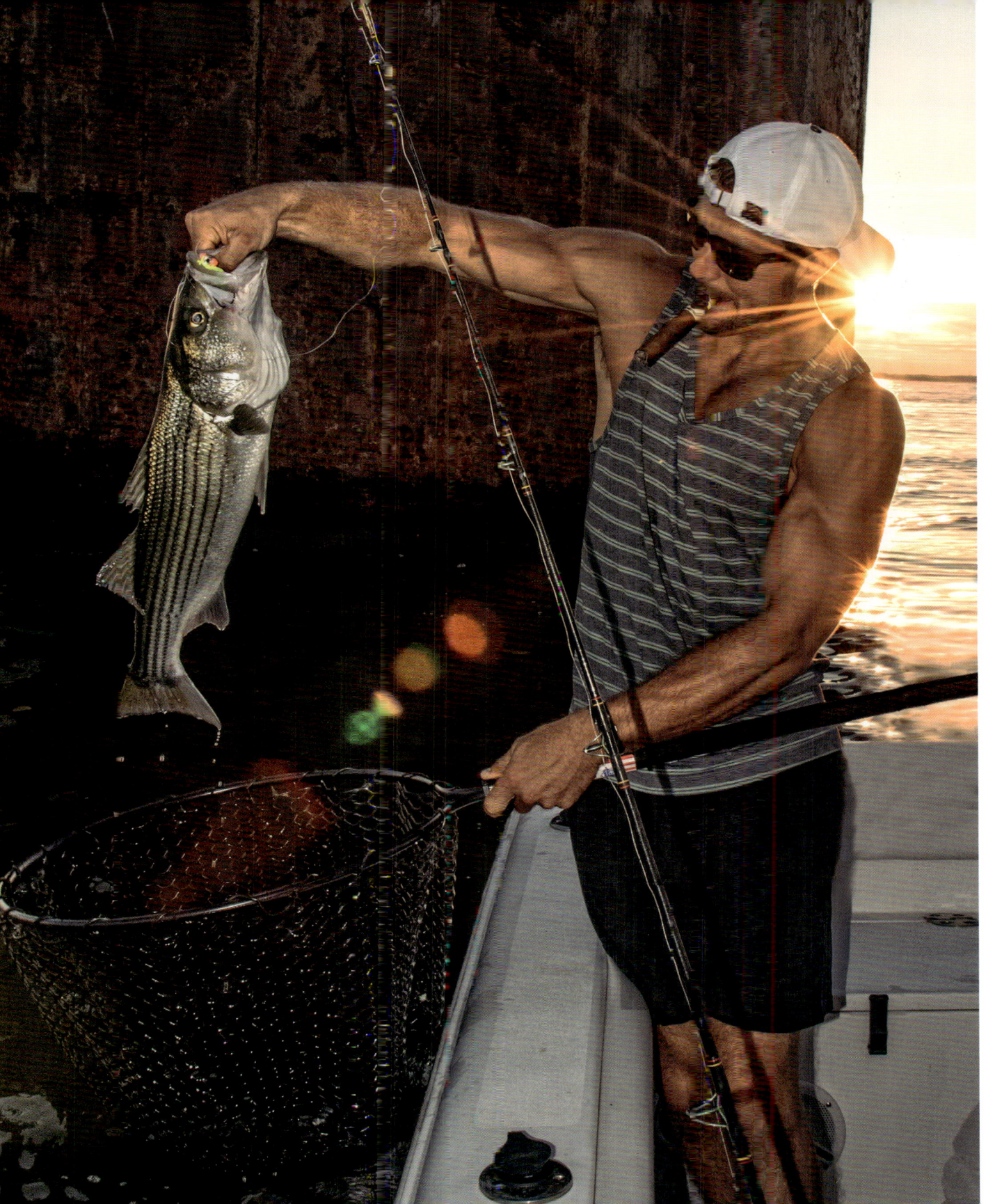

Catch of the night

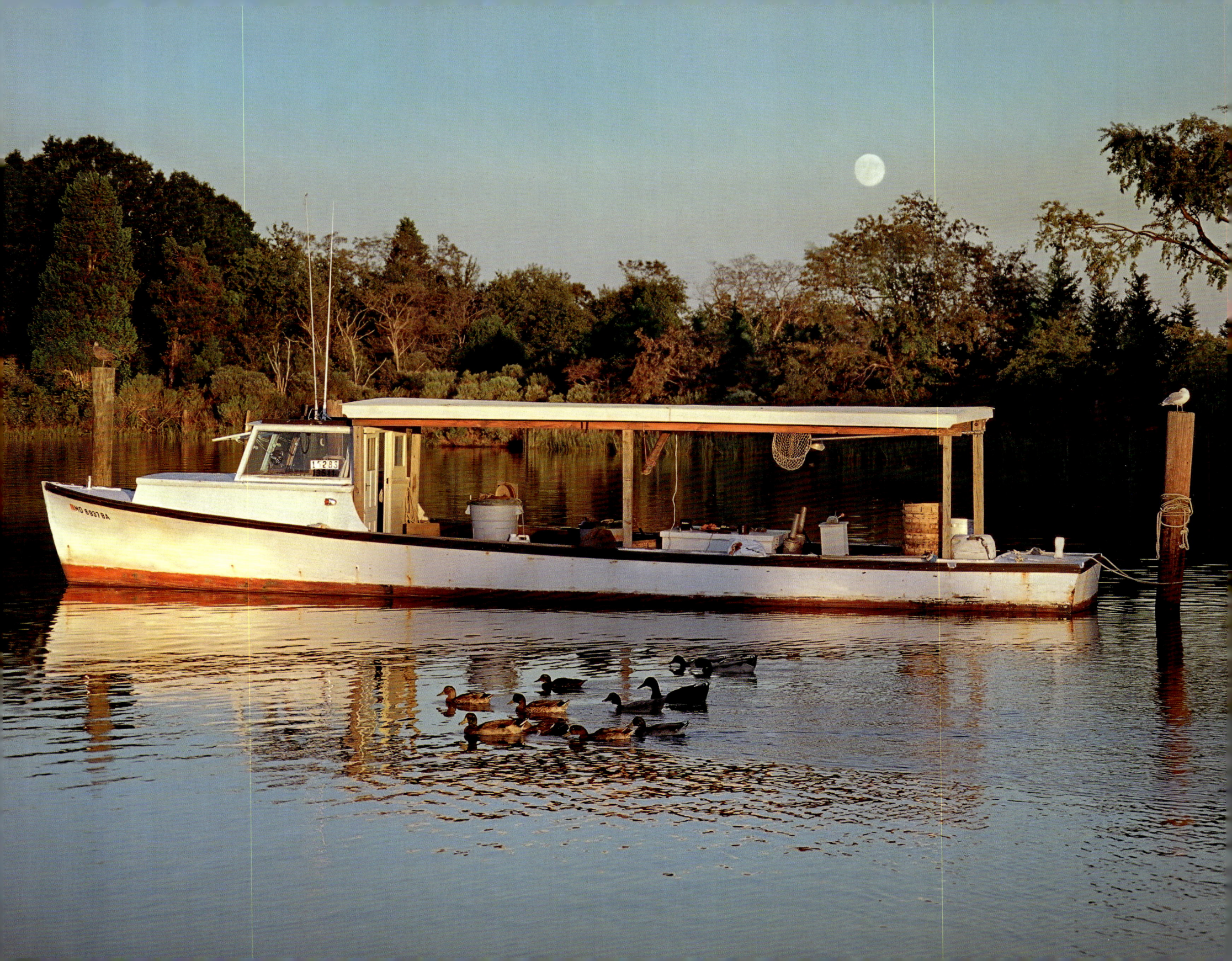

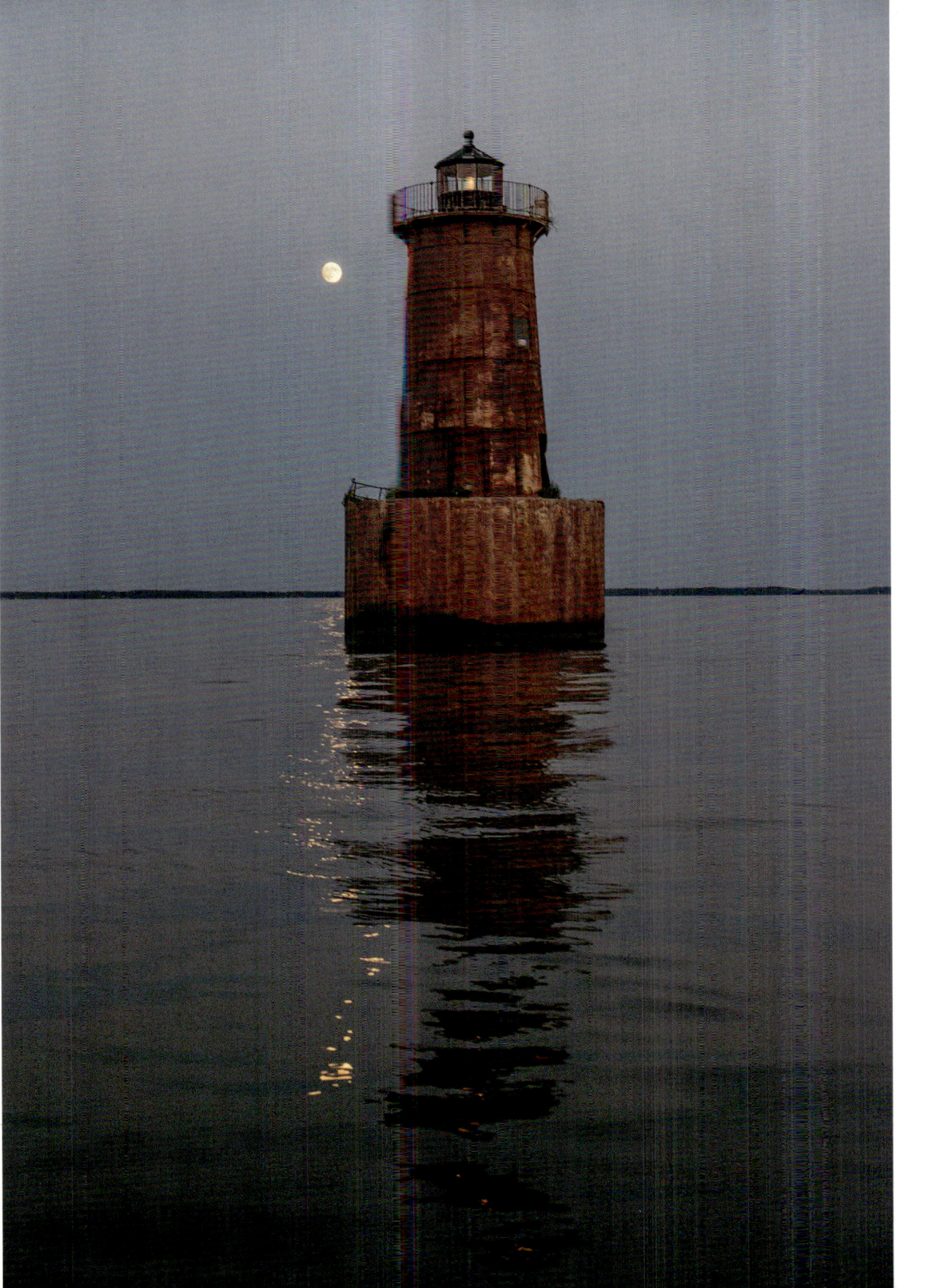

Bloody Point Bar Light moonrise

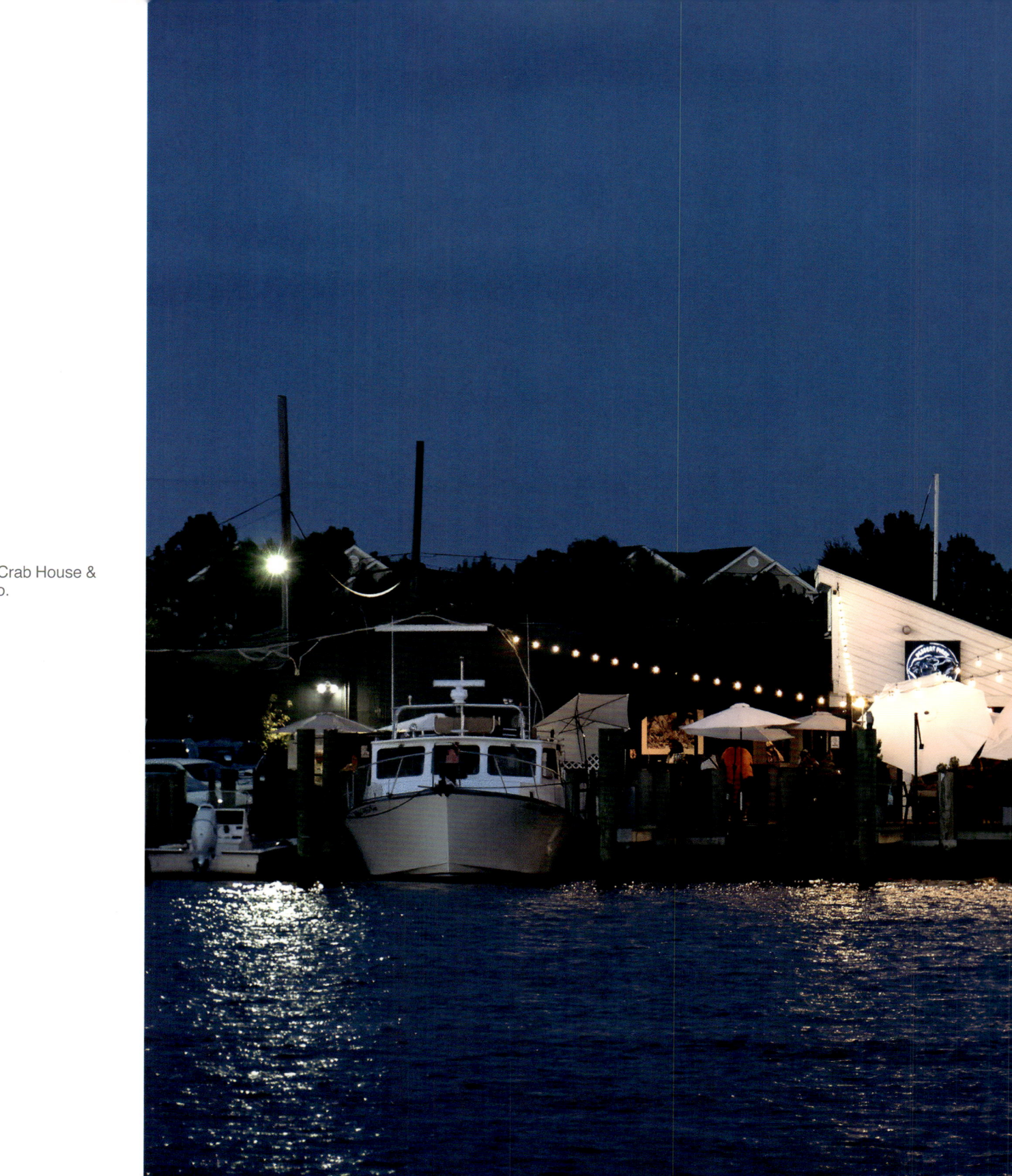

Pictured here on the east side of Kent Narrows are Harris Crab House & Seafood Restaurant, Dessert First, and Harris Seafood Co.

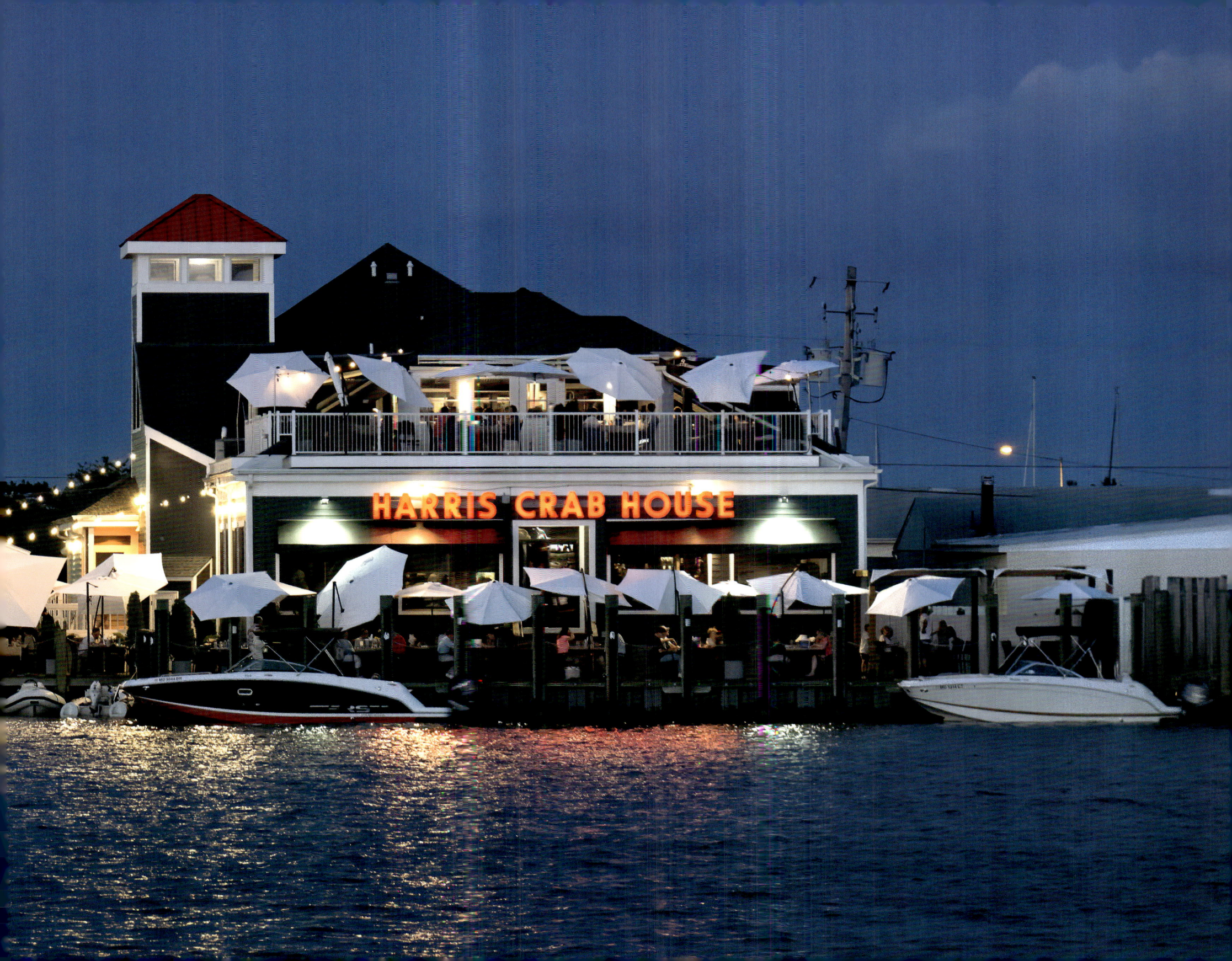

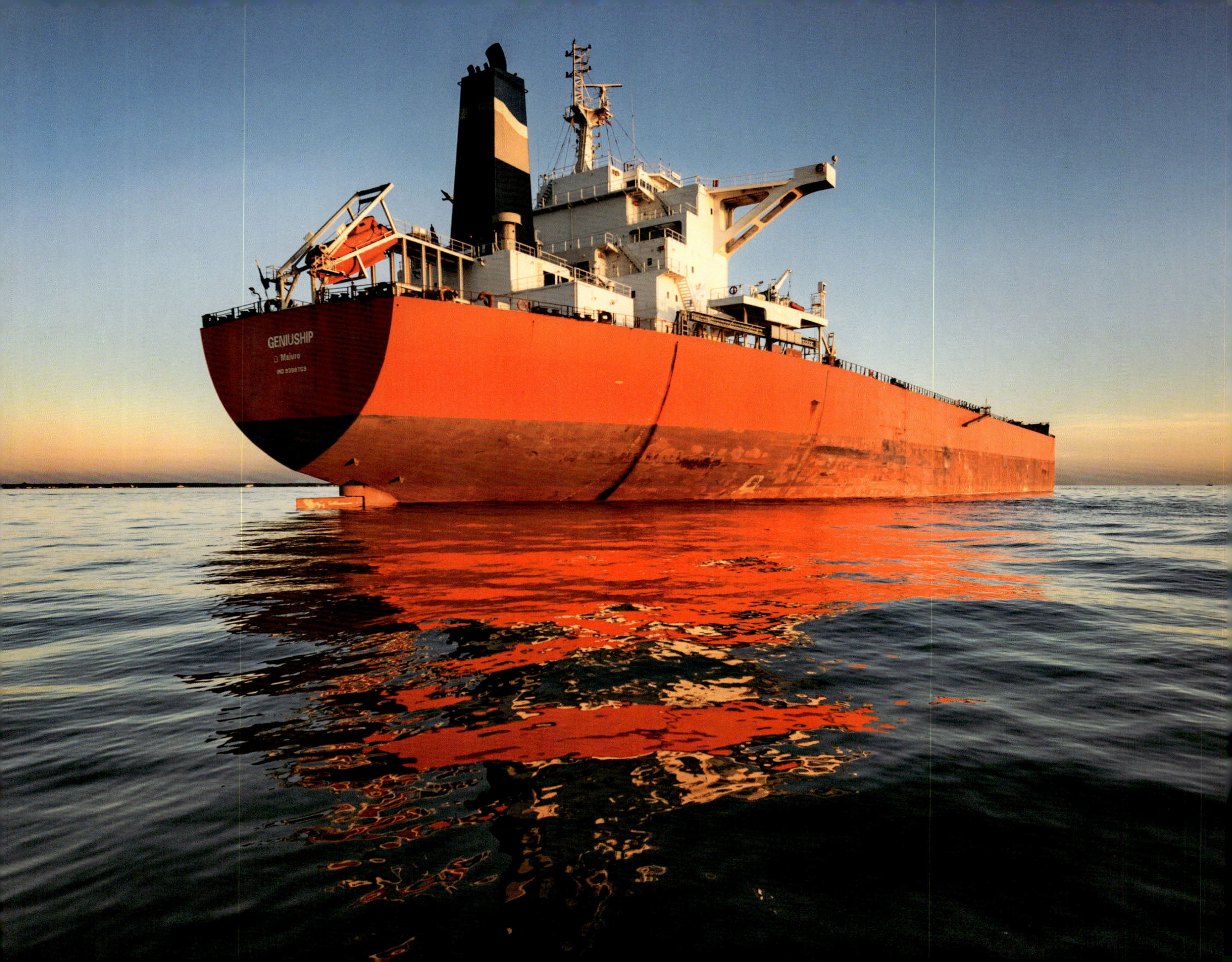

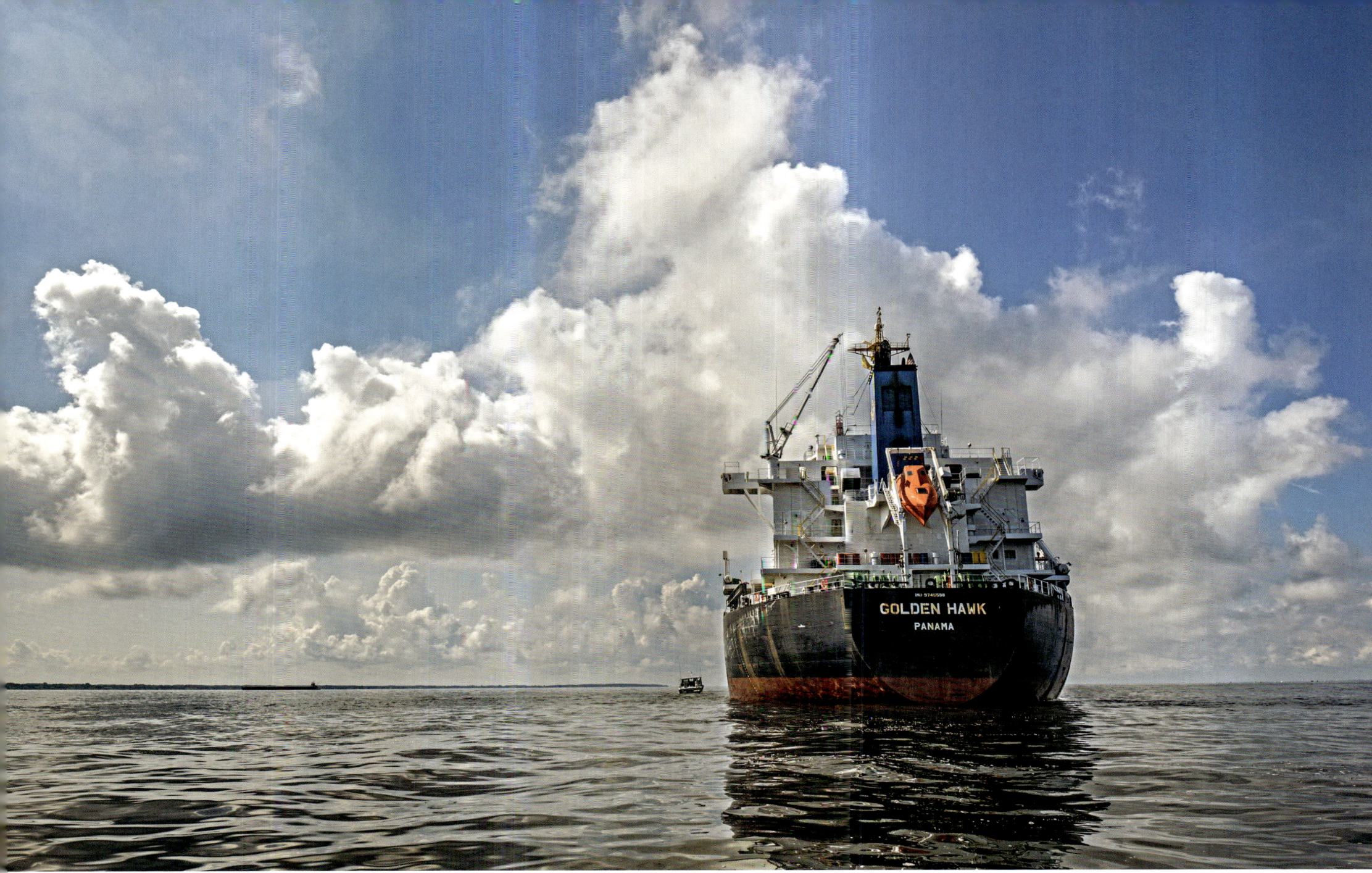

One of the largest Chesapeake Bay shipping channels runs along Kent Island.
These vessels can be seen from the shore, but up close they are an awe-inspiring sight!

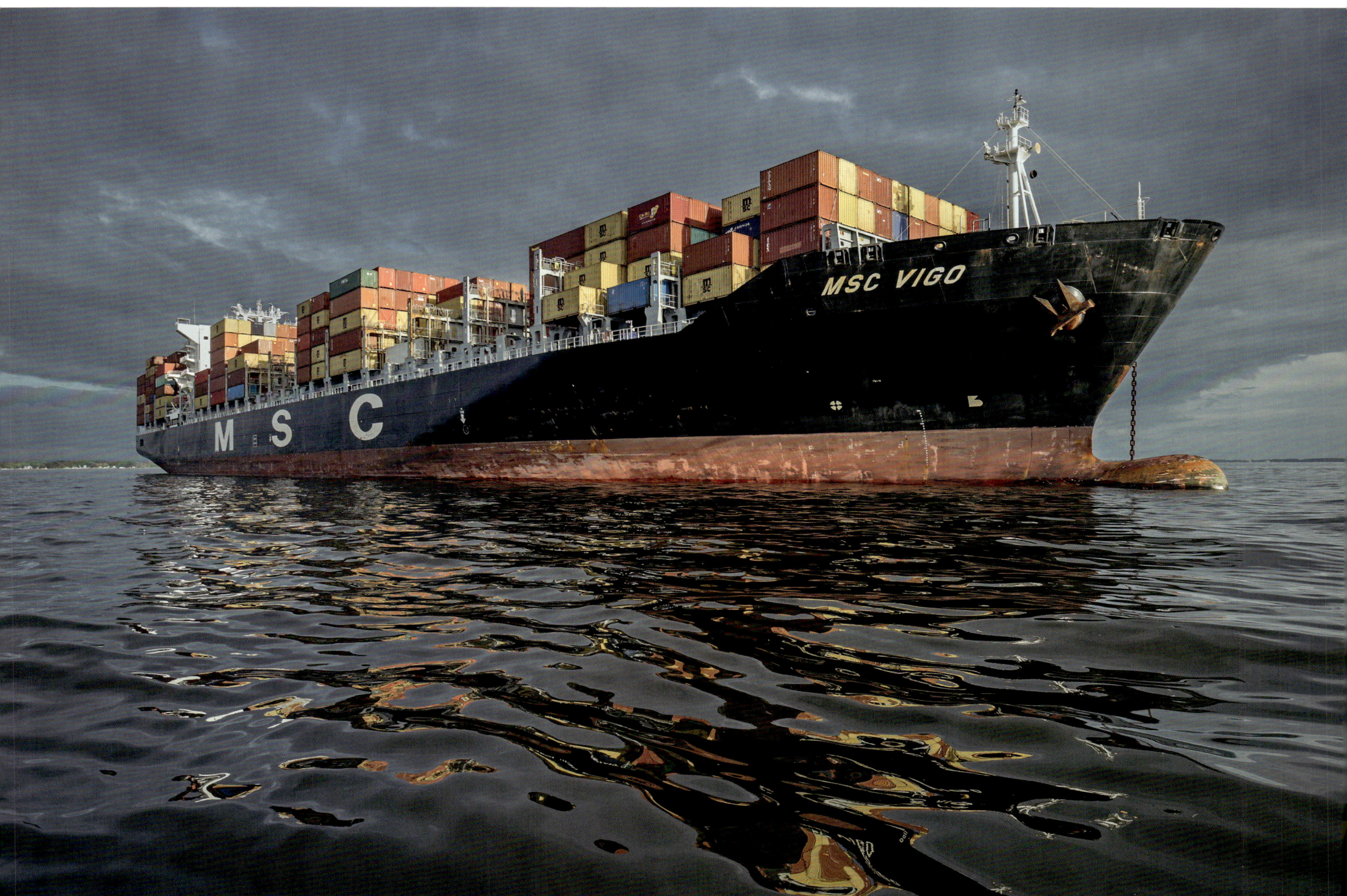

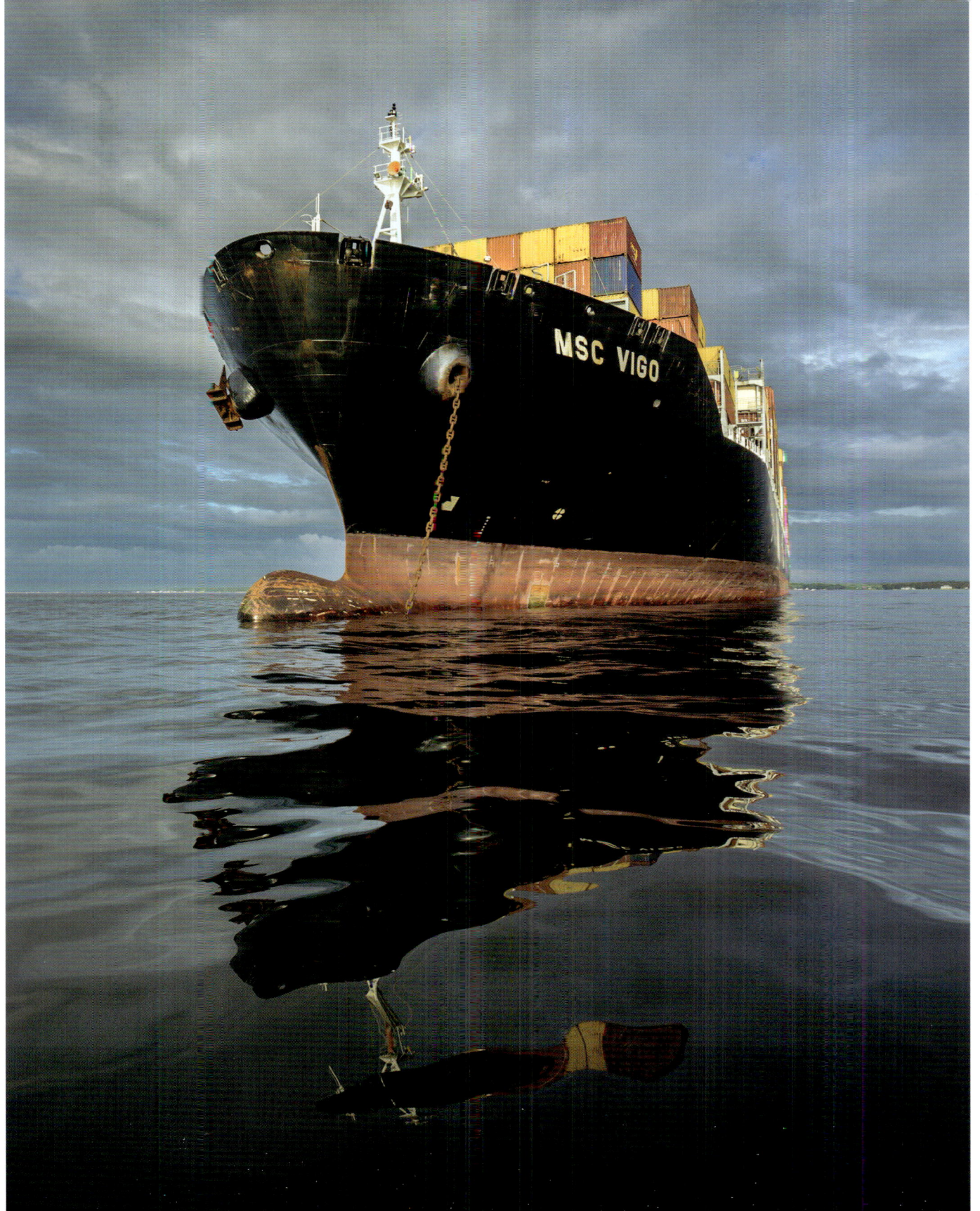

Glassy waters that create a mirror image are always a treat when shooting these vessels.

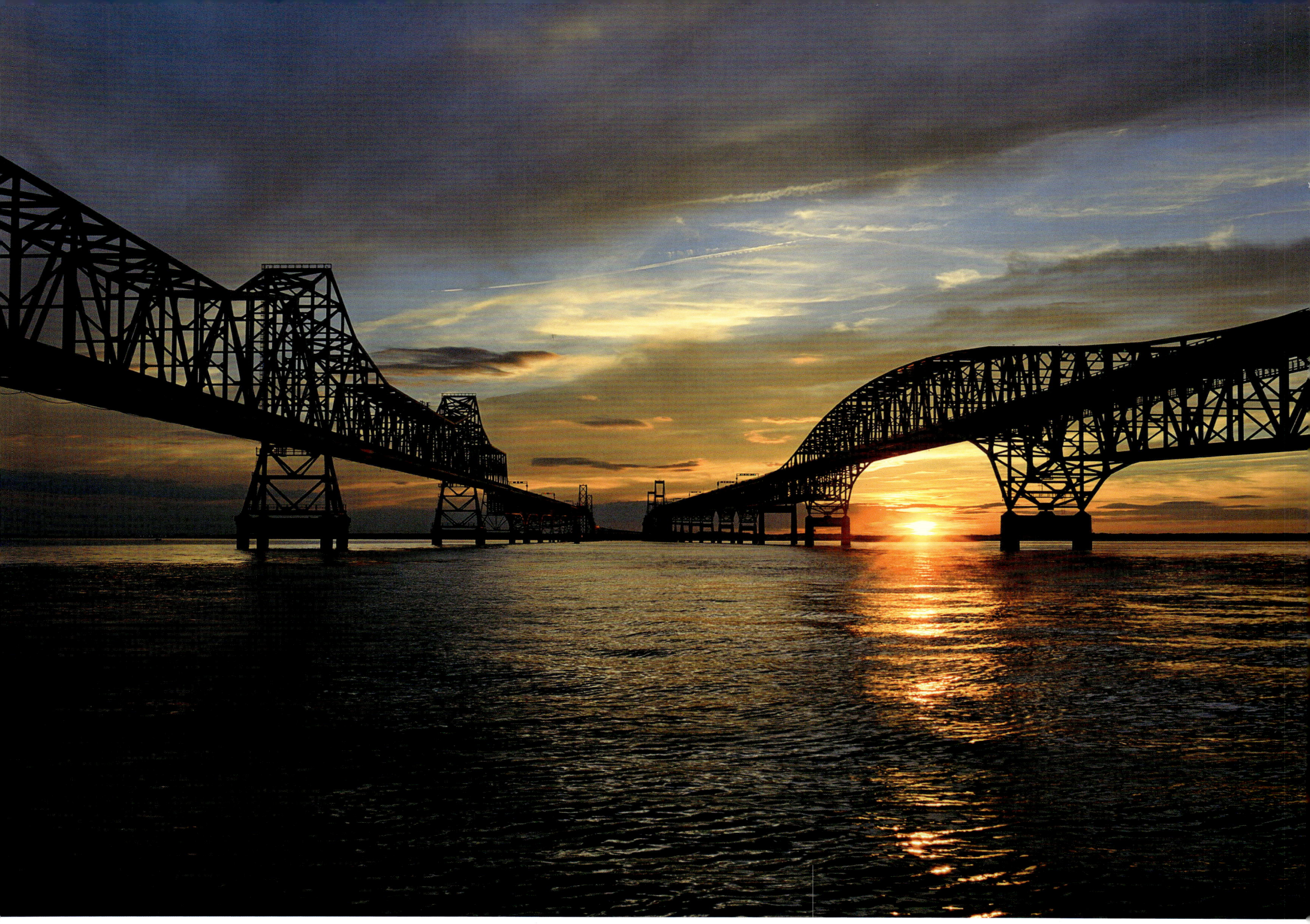

Chesapeake Bay Bridge at sunset

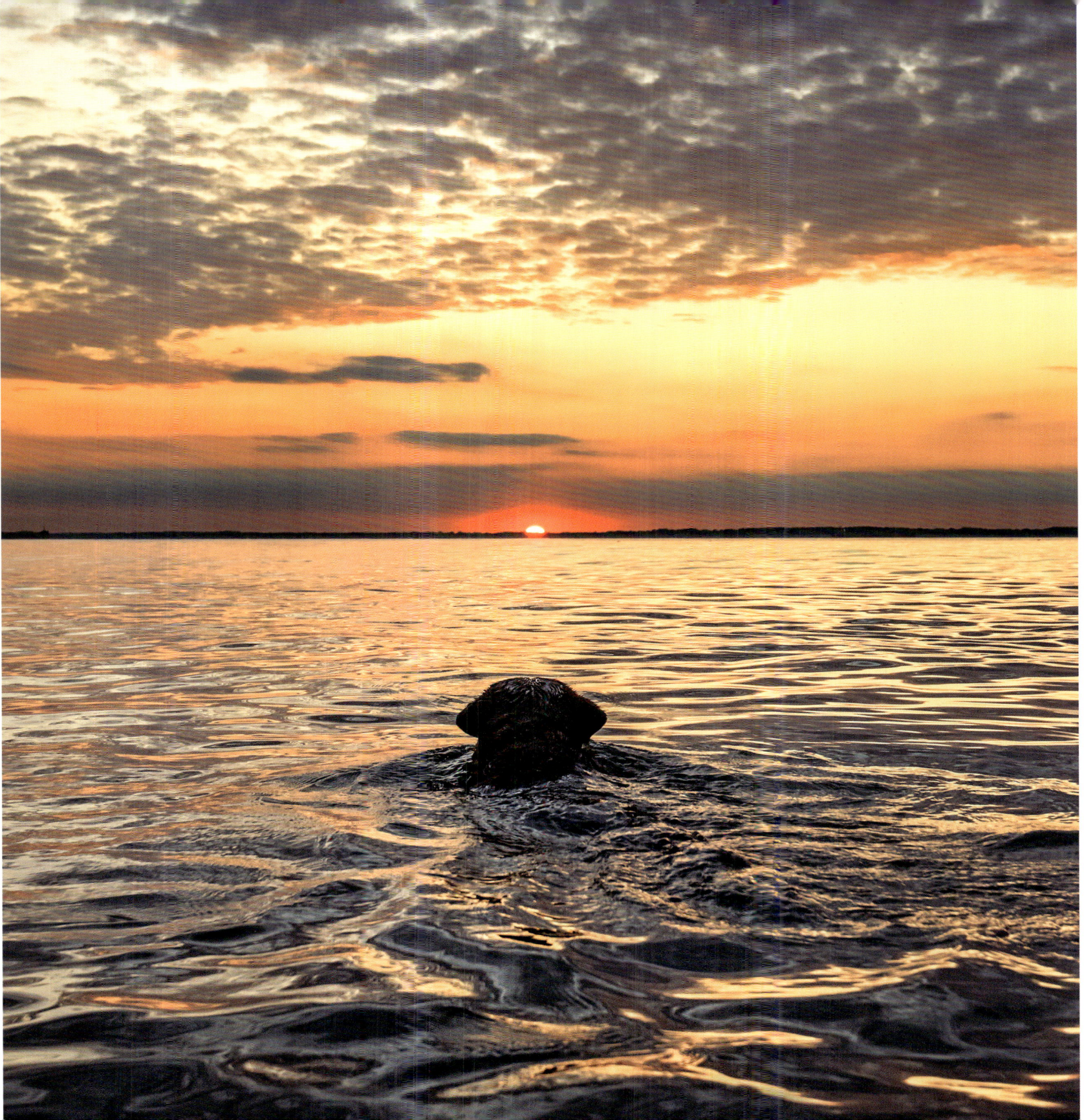

Seas the day

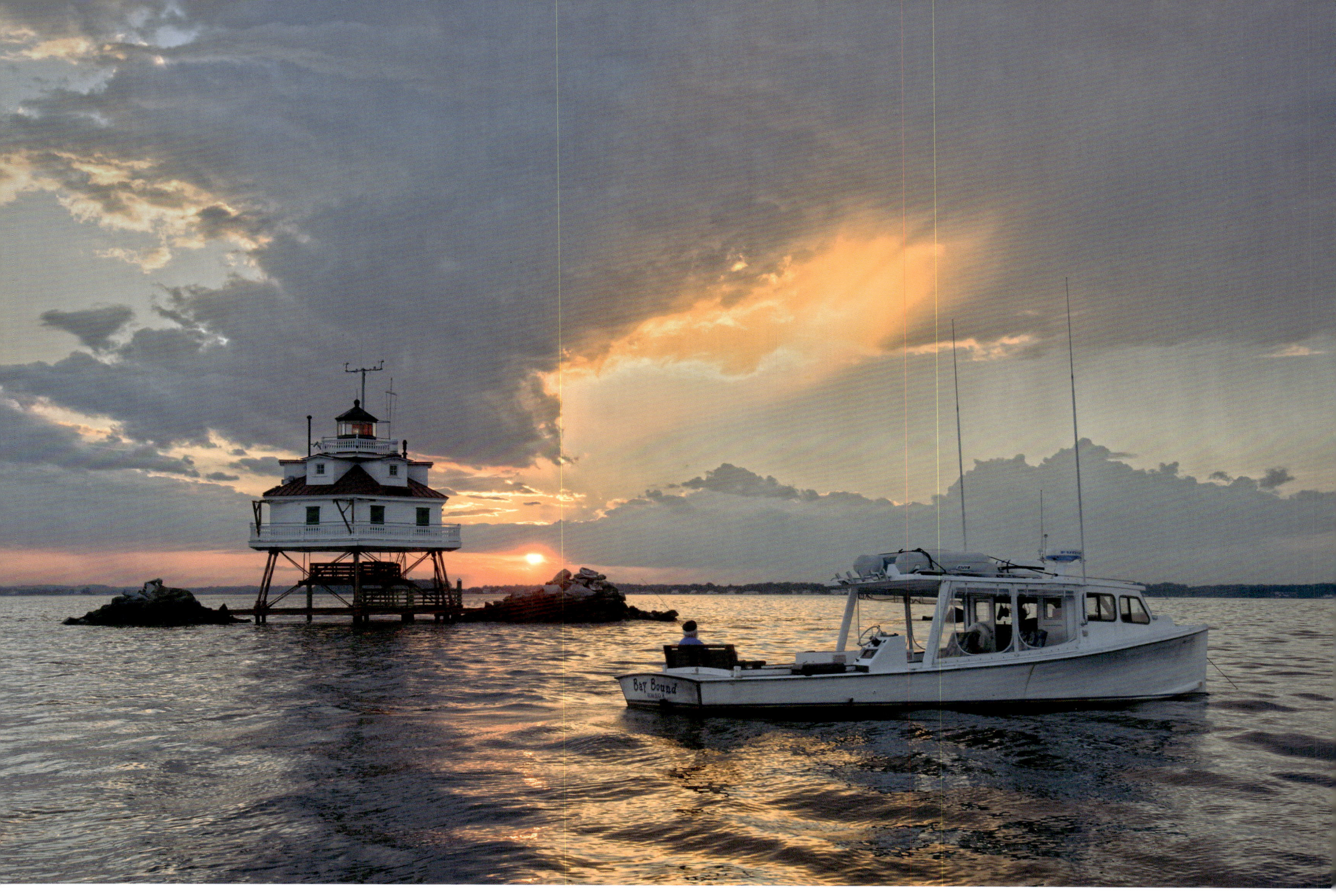

Bay Bound at Thomas Point Shoal Light

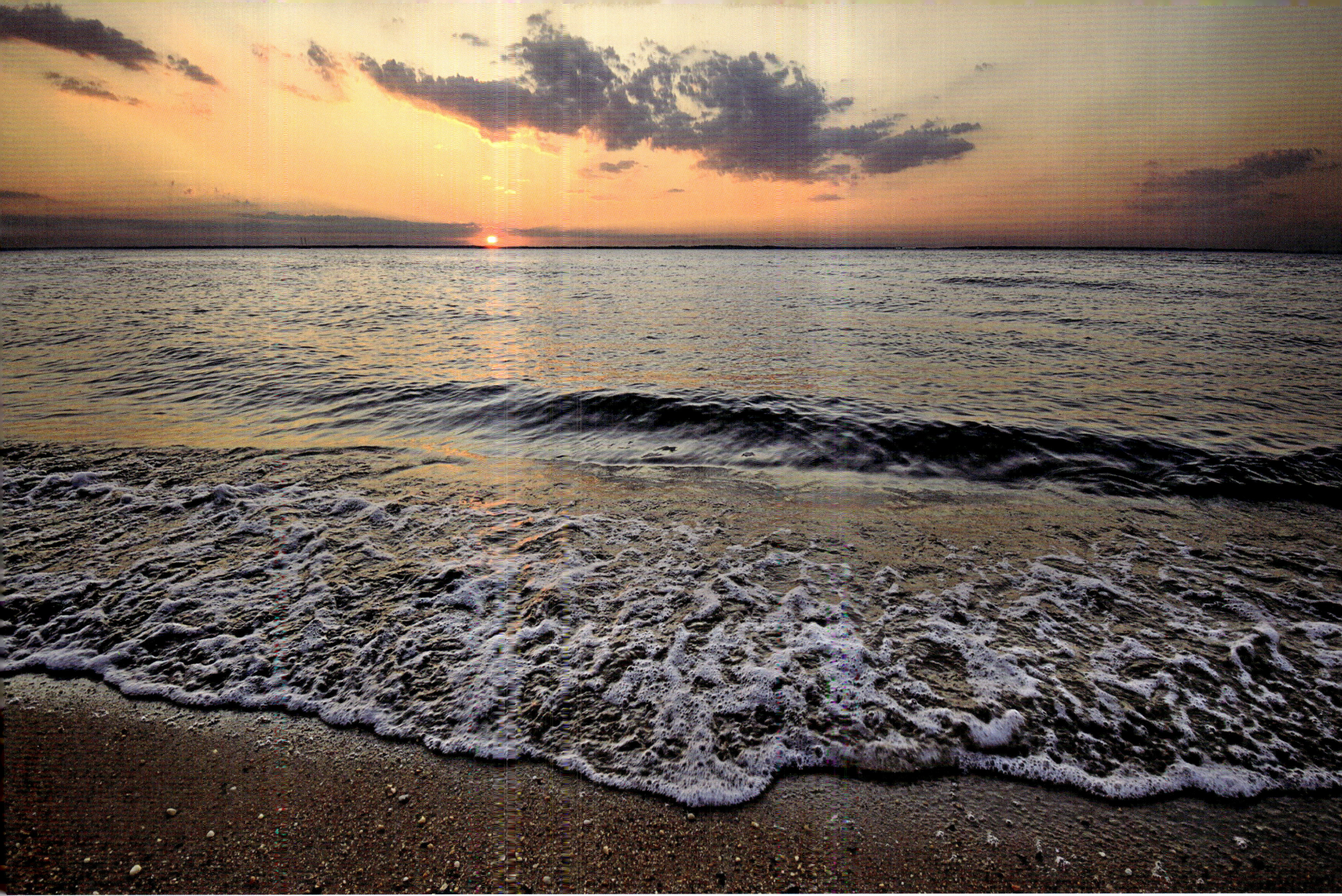

Sunset at Silver Swan Bayside

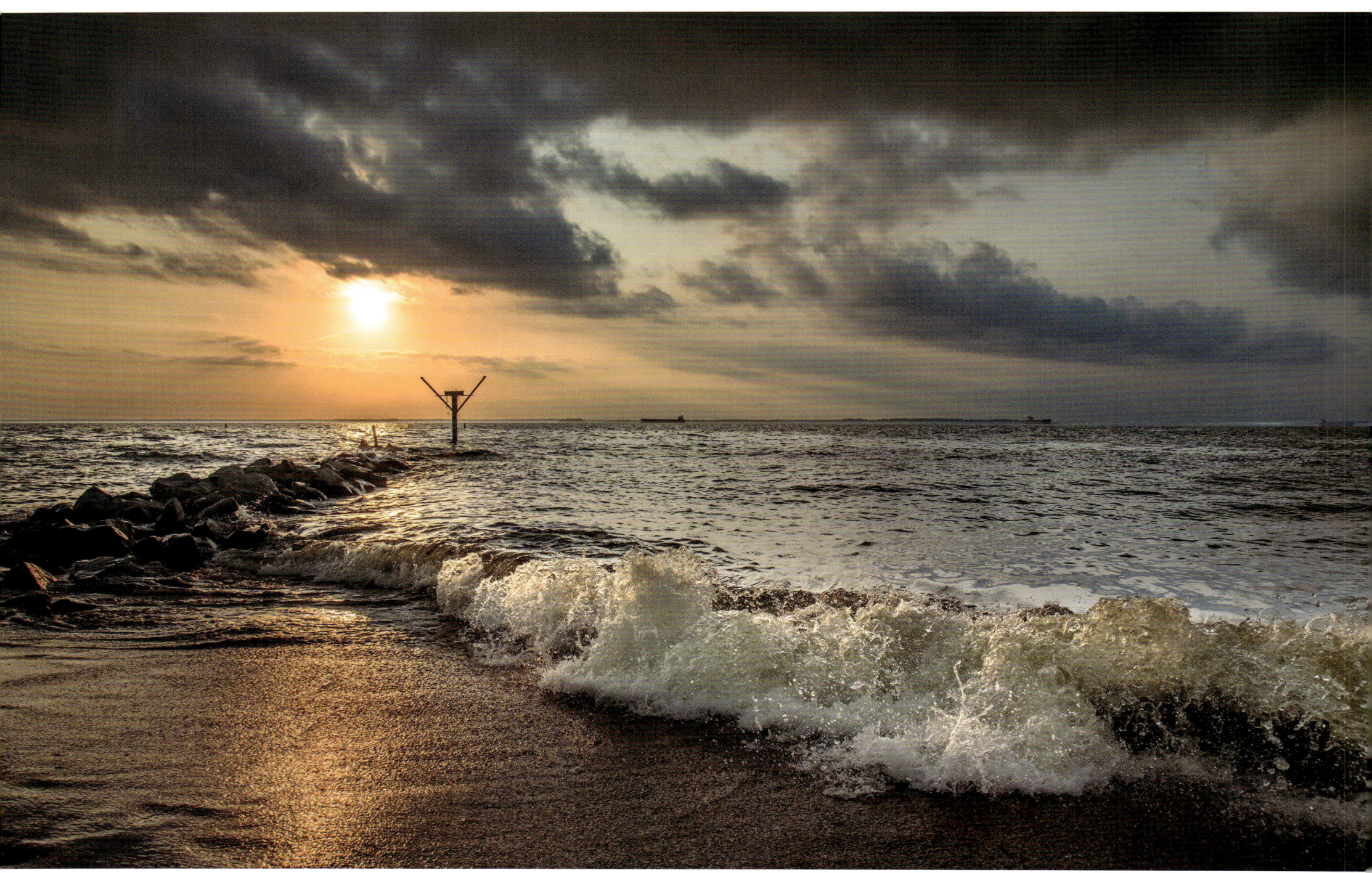

Tanker waves hitting the shore

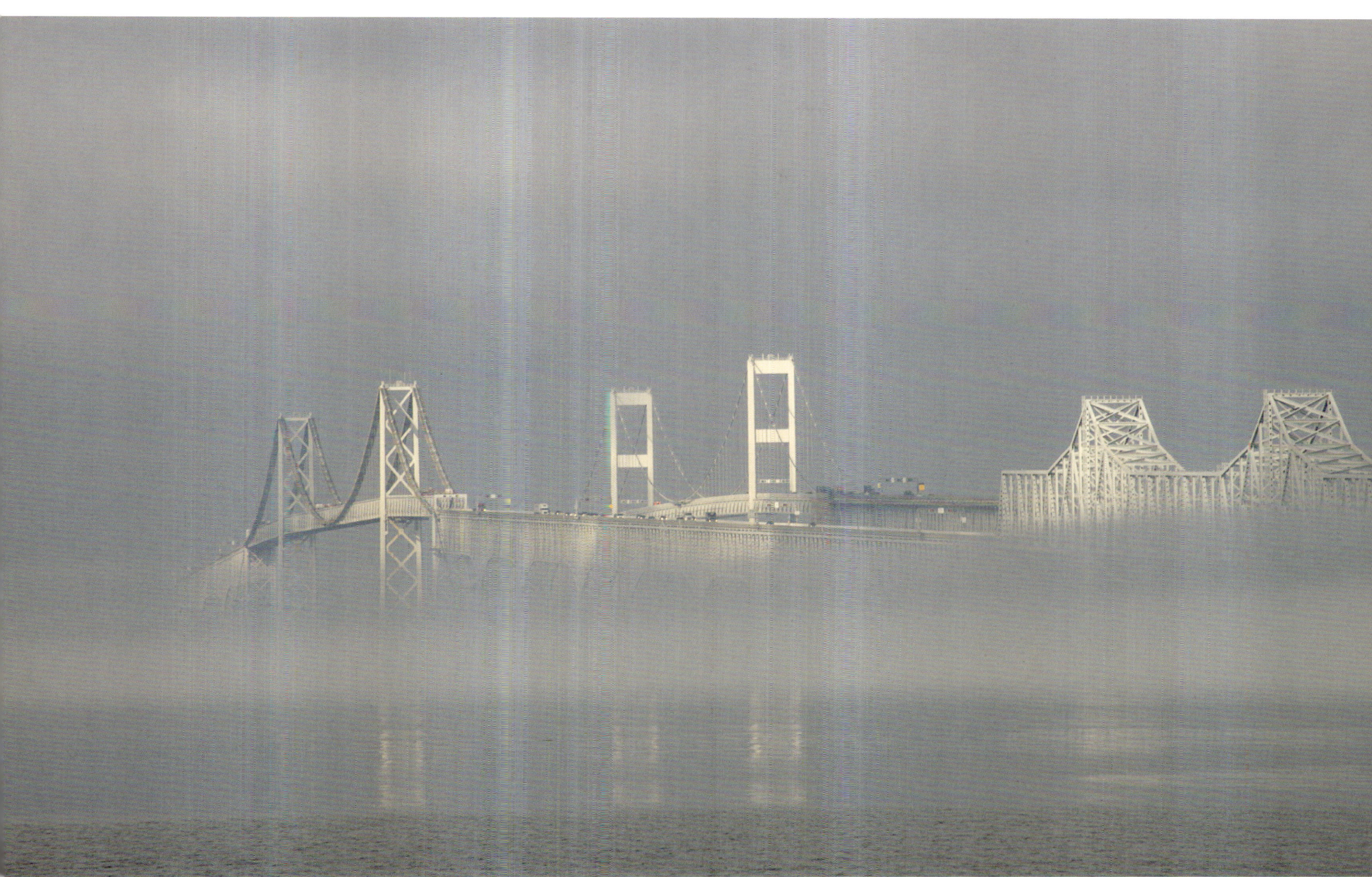

Chesapeake Bay Bridge in fog

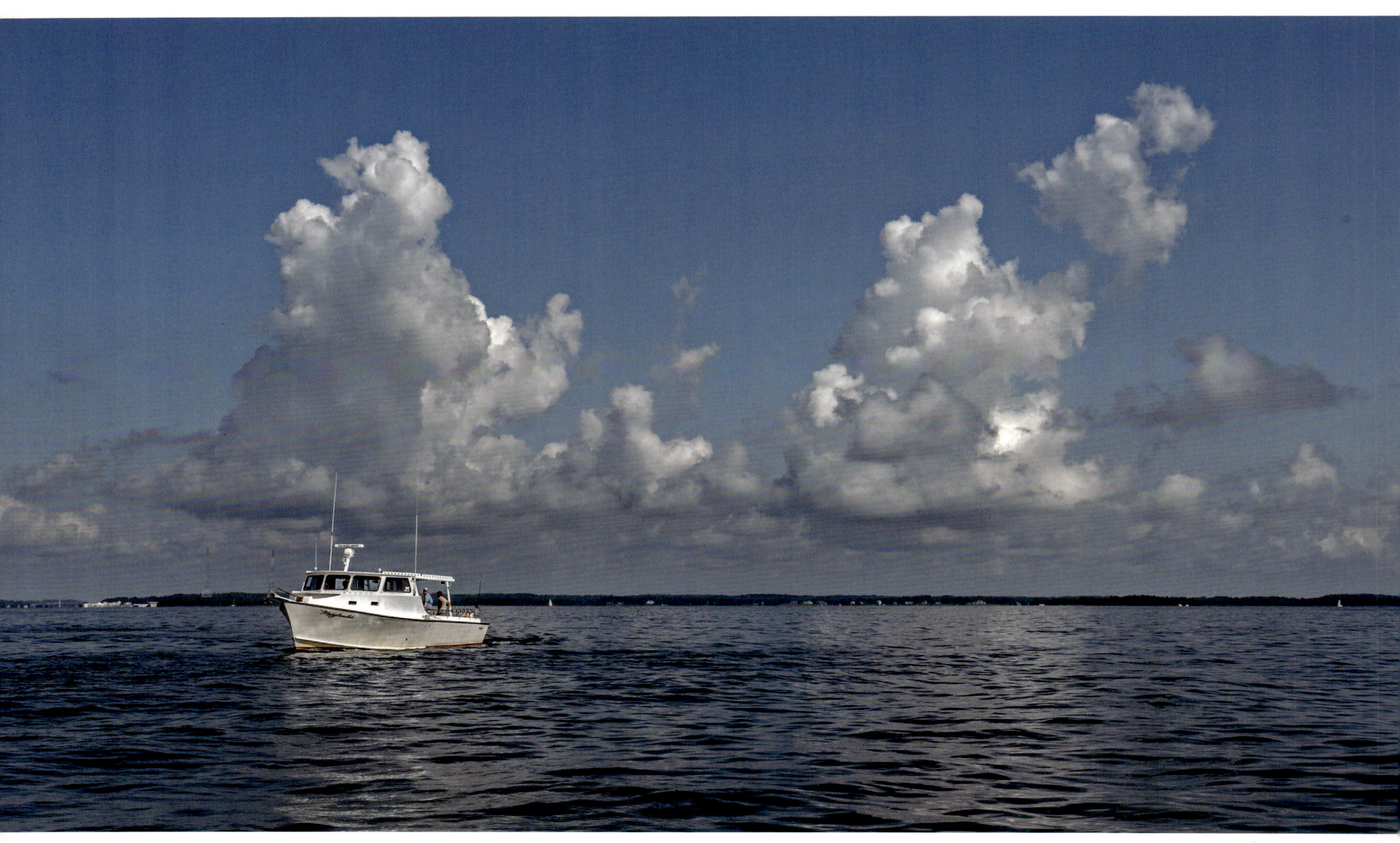

A gorgeous day for *Marylander*

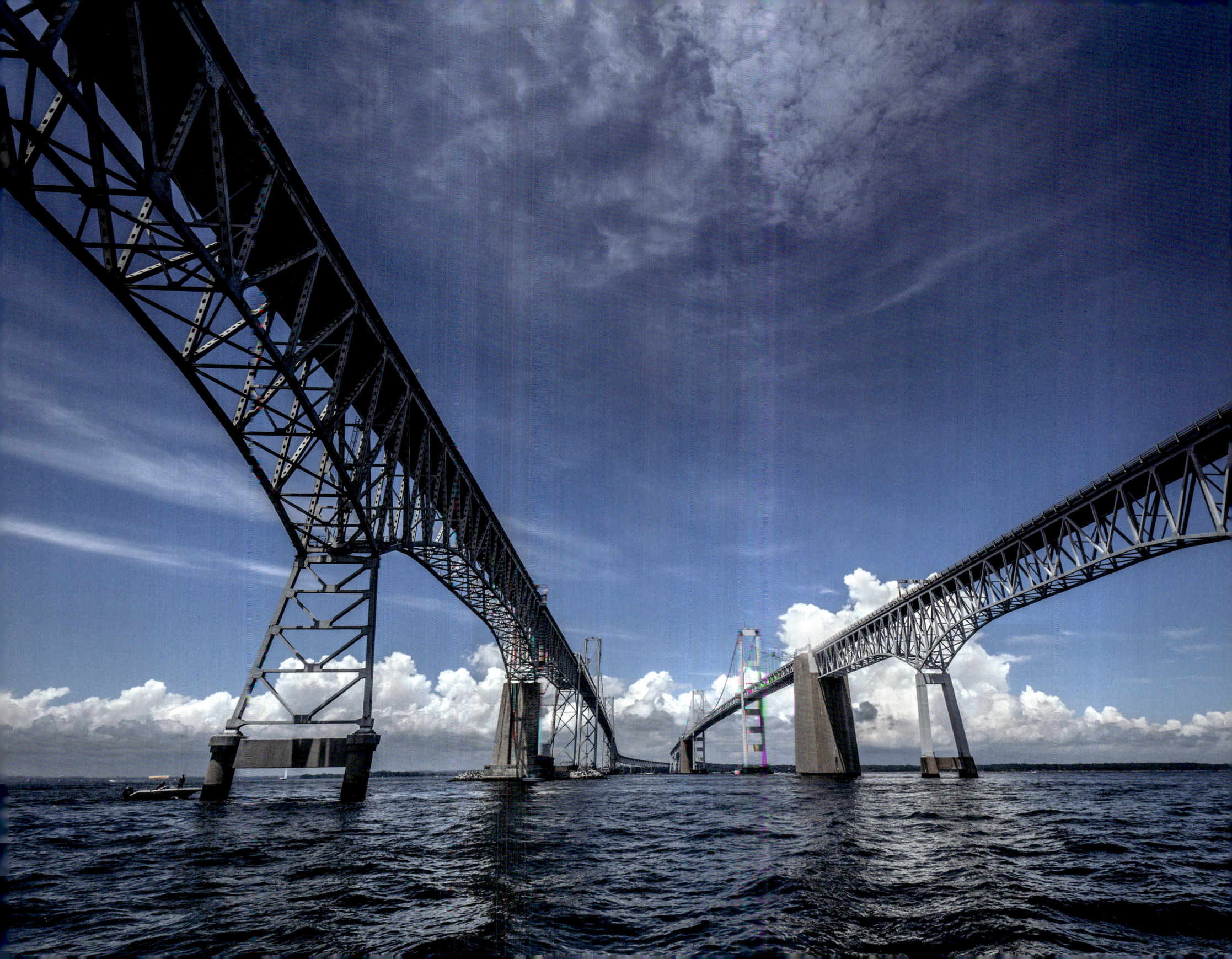

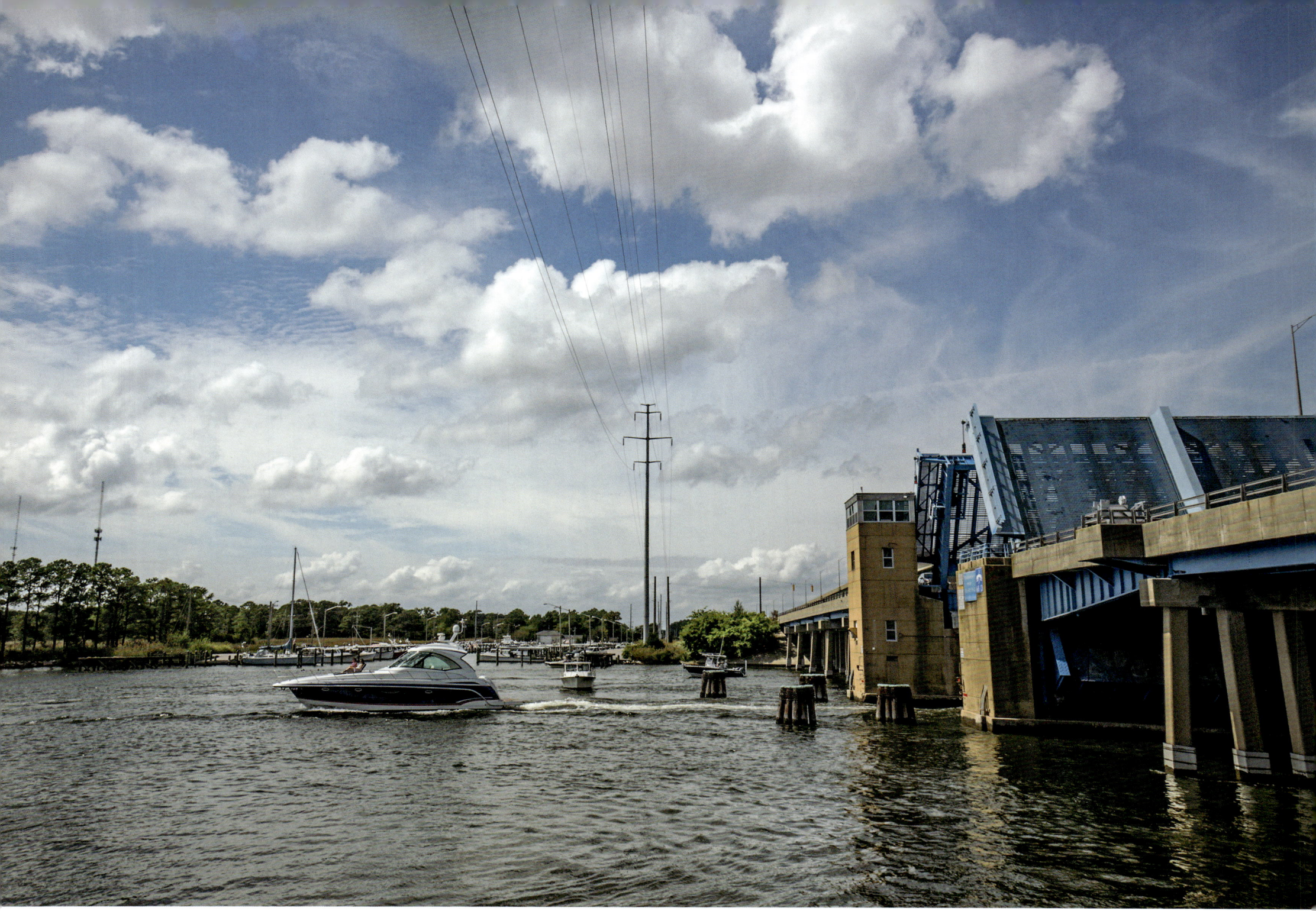

On the weekends, Kent Narrows is bustling with boats. Pictured here is the William Memorial Bridge with the Waterman's Boat Basin to the left.

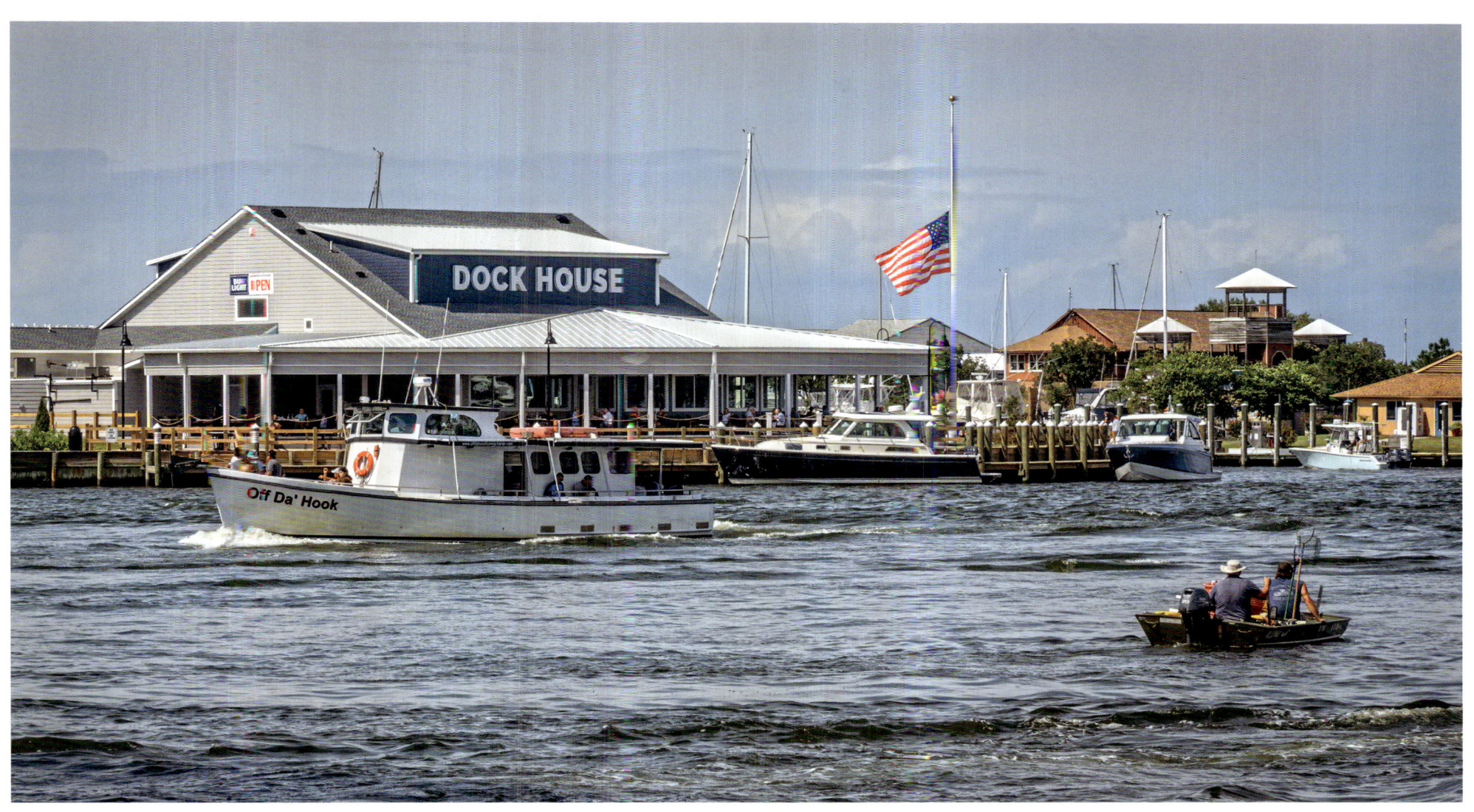

The newly opened Dock House Restaurant adds to the many waterfront restaurants that are good for boat watching. The Chesapeake Heritage & Visitor Center is seen on the right.

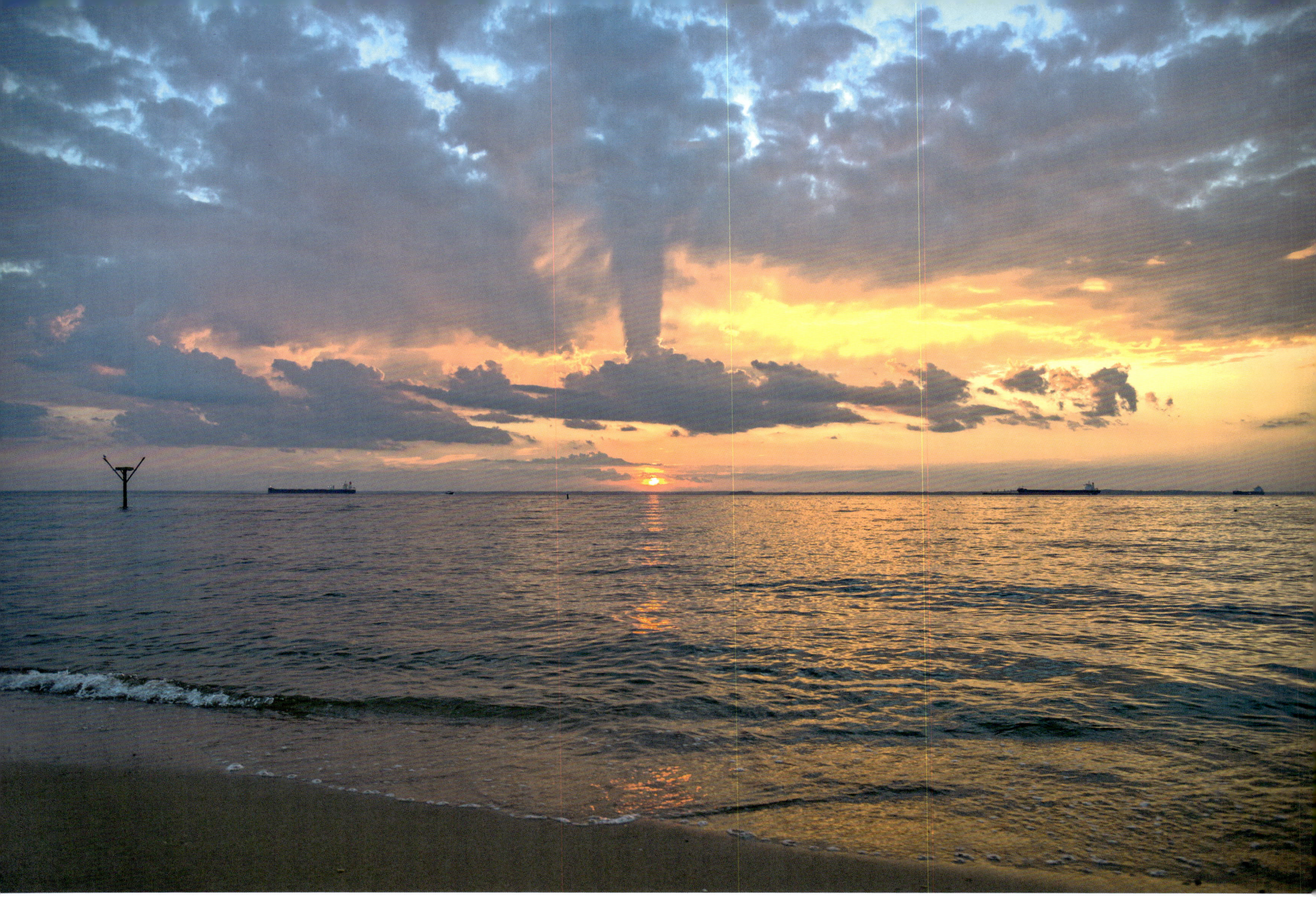

The last sunset of summer

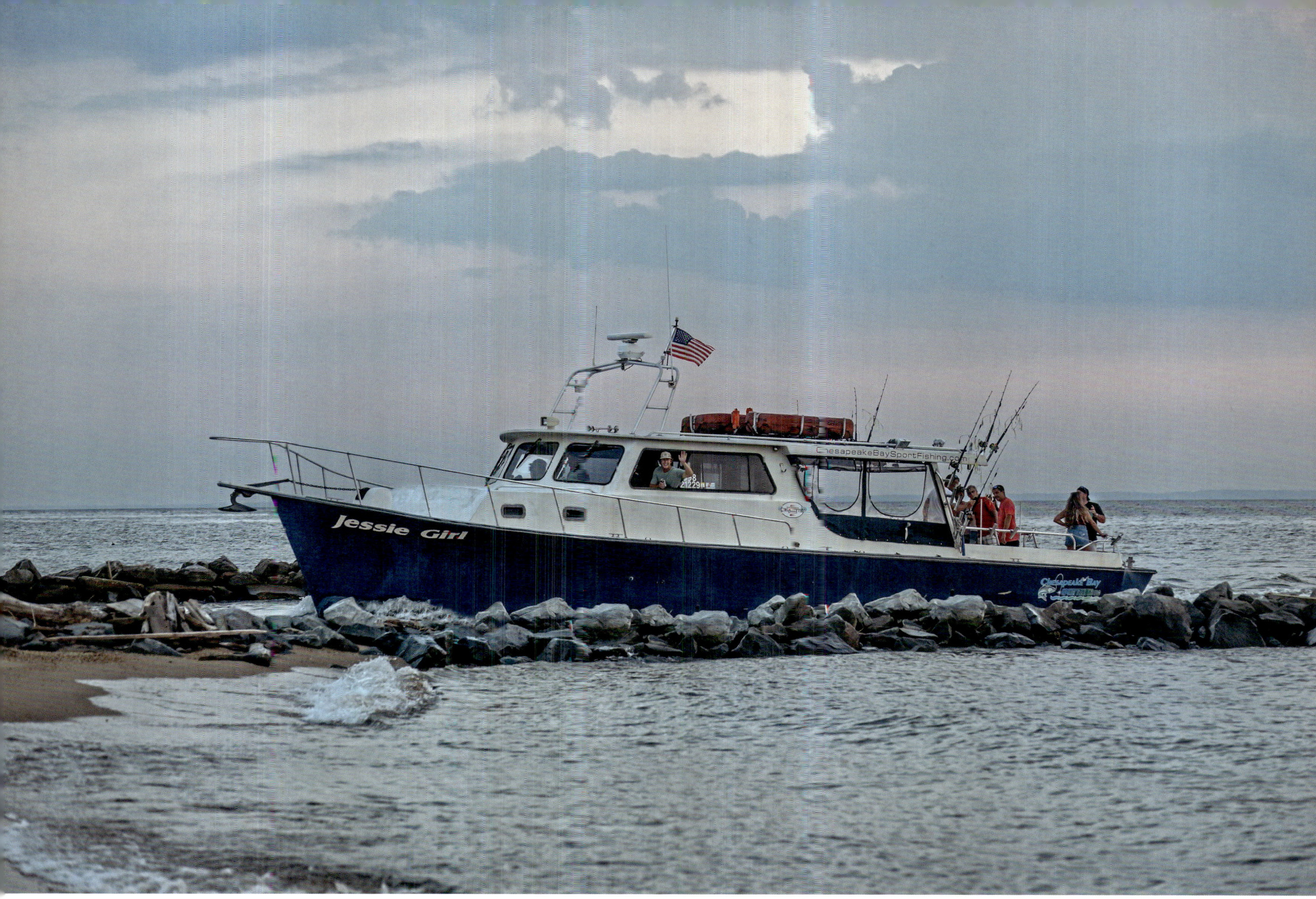

The end of a perfect summer evening on the Chesapeake with
Chesapeake Bay Sport Fishing

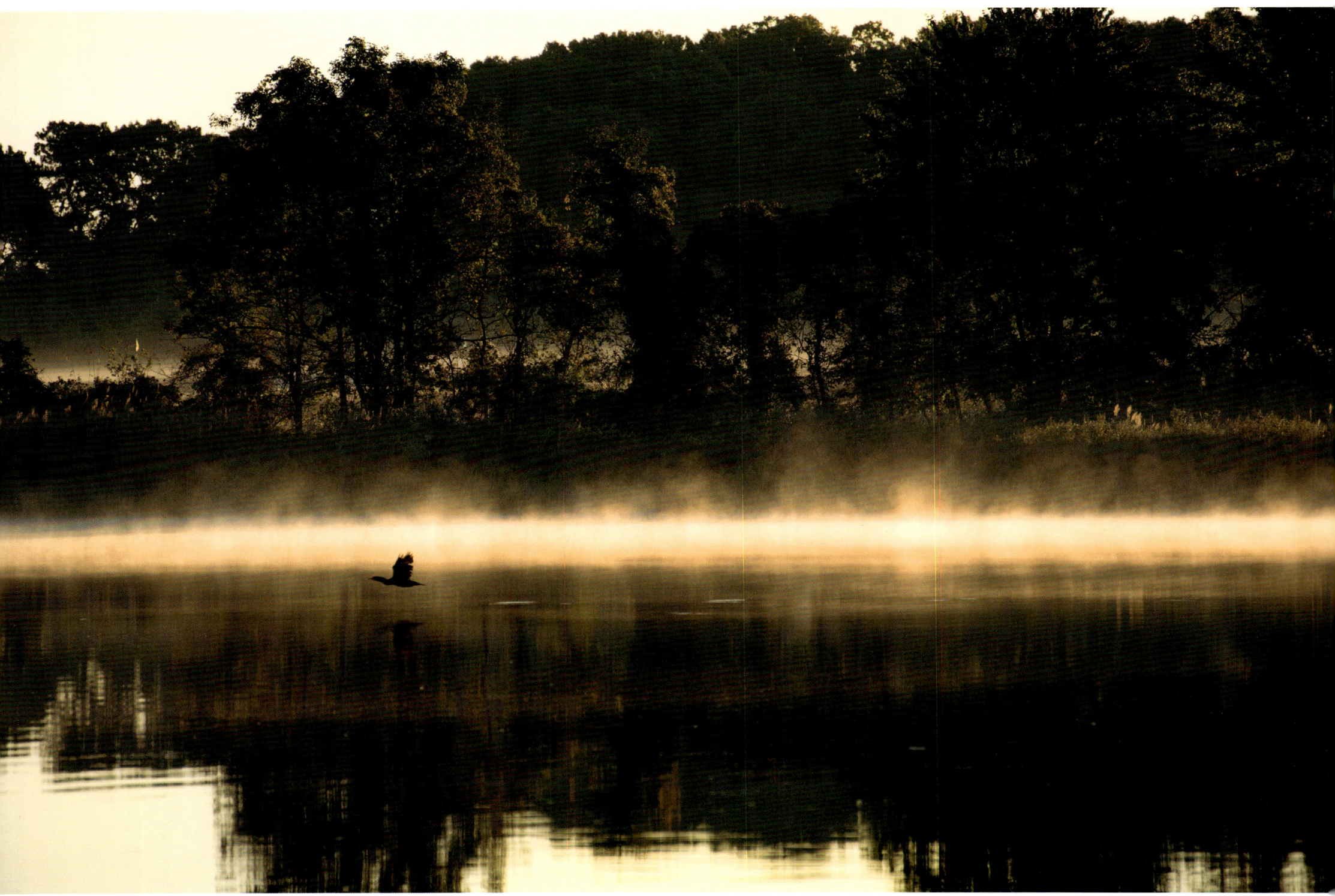

CHAPTER 4

FALL

Fall comes as a welcome relief for many, with Maryland's high humidity waning. At night, temperatures drop significantly, but quite often the sun will warm up the morning air to the point where it will create "sea smoke" just above the water's surface—giving a nice aesthetic glow to a scene.

Canadian geese return in droves. Hearing their honks from afar can be a signal that fall is upon us. The endearing osprey peeps can no longer be heard, since the osprey head south looking for warmer air. Many varieties of ducks arrive in the fall and can be seen swimming in large groups. Don't blink—they will suddenly disappear under the water's surface, only to return just seconds later. With the way they move in tandem, they almost look like synchronized swimmers.

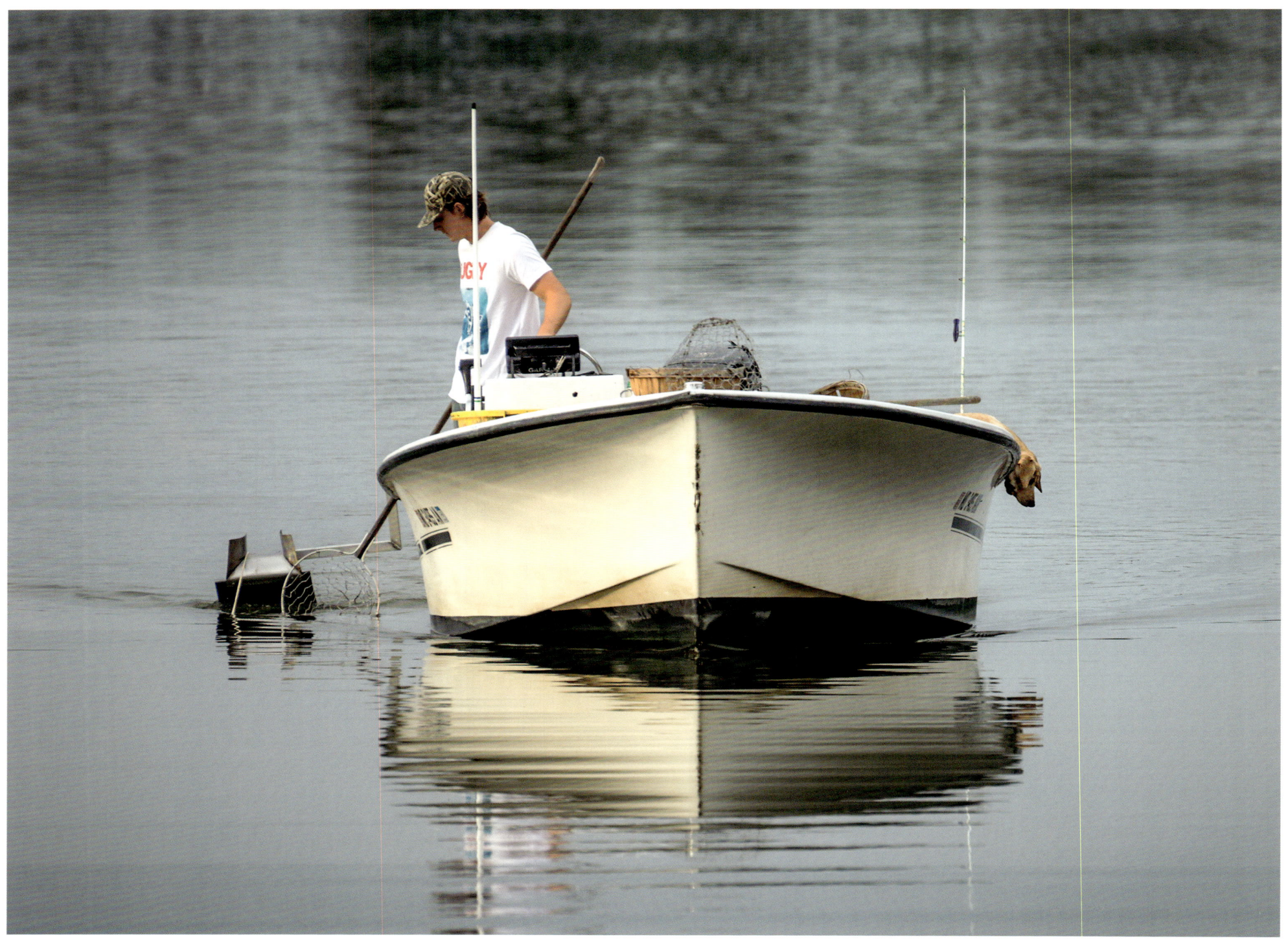

Trotlining with best mate May

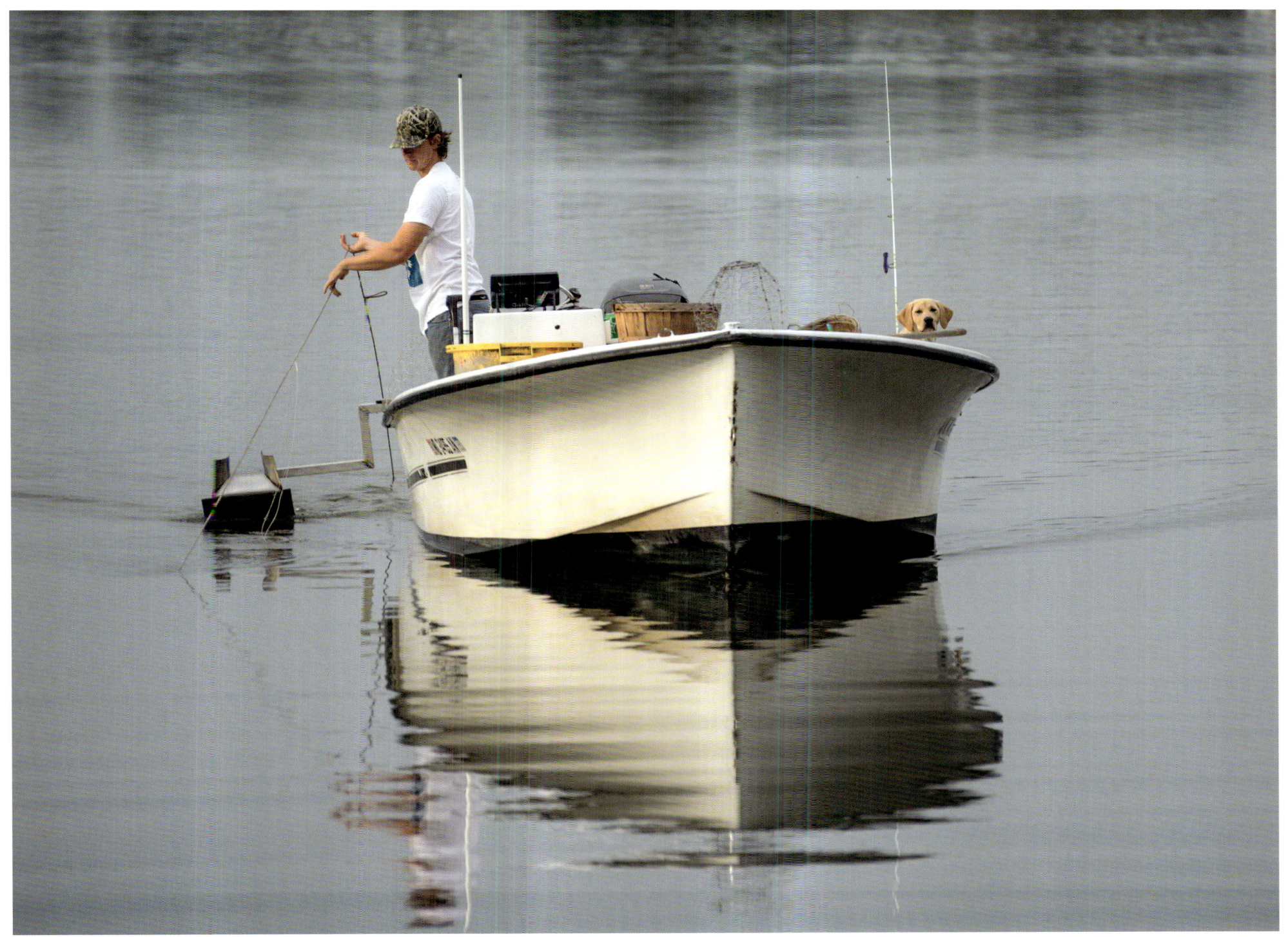

Keeping an eye out

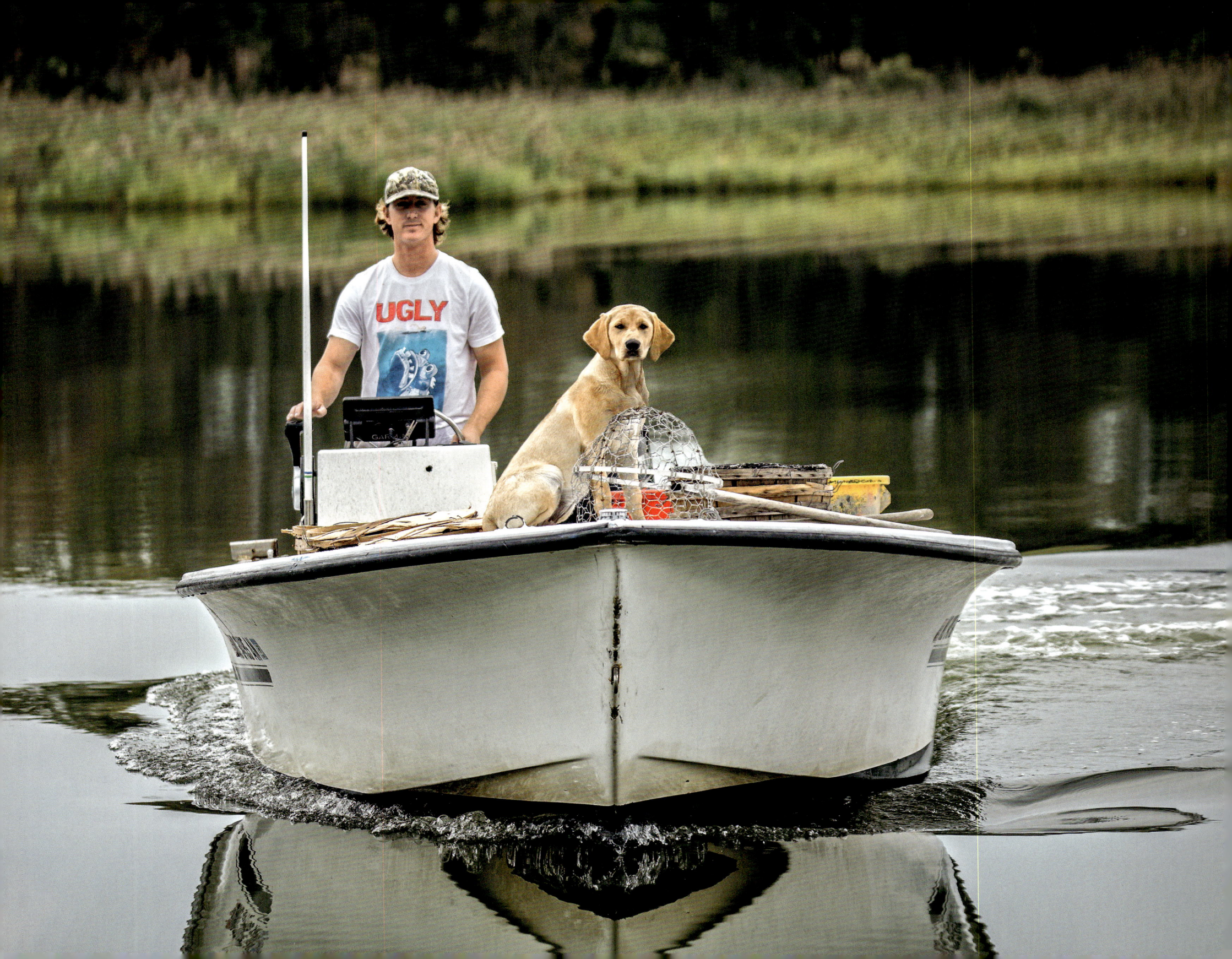

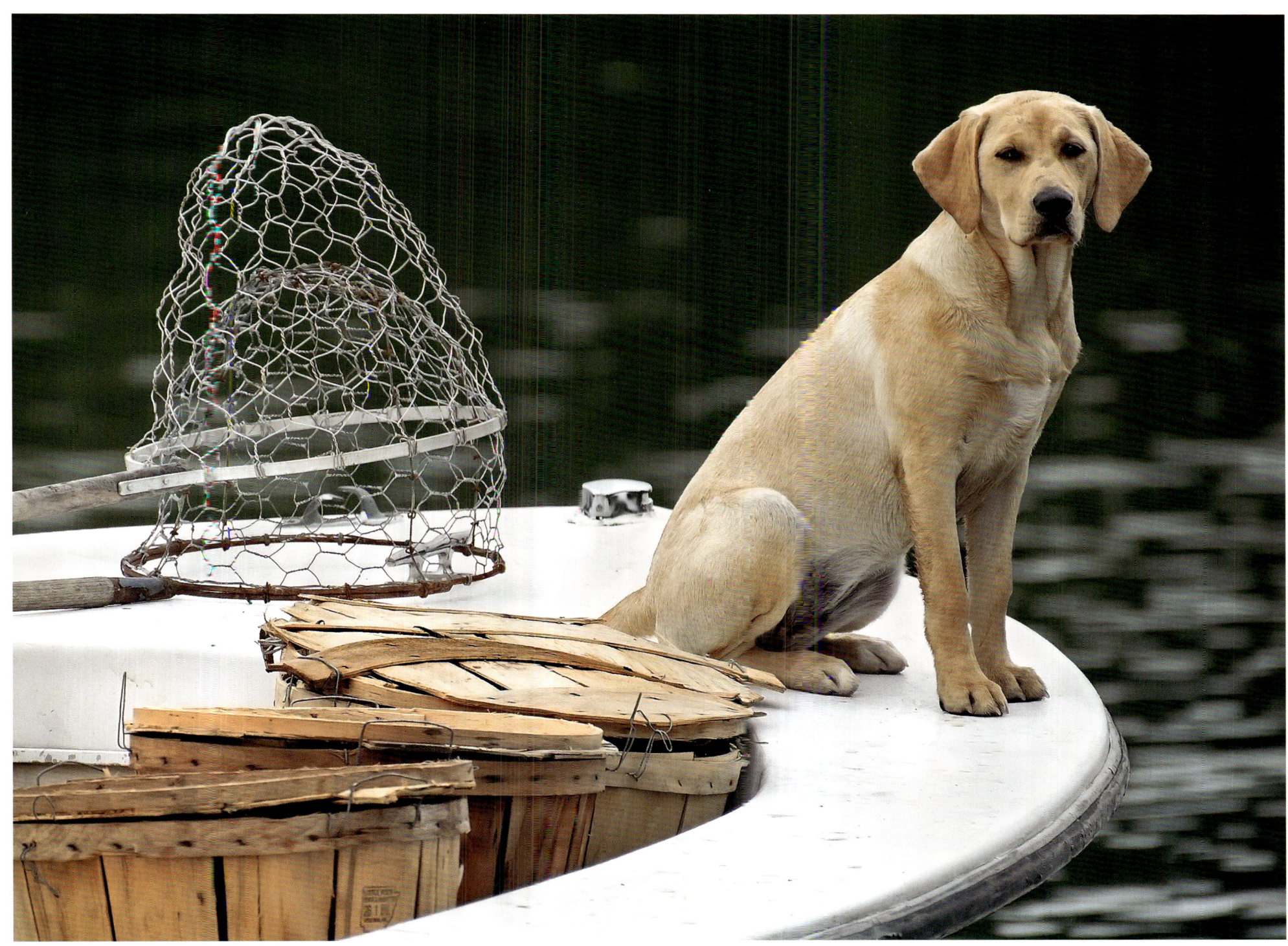

First mate May heads in with her catch.

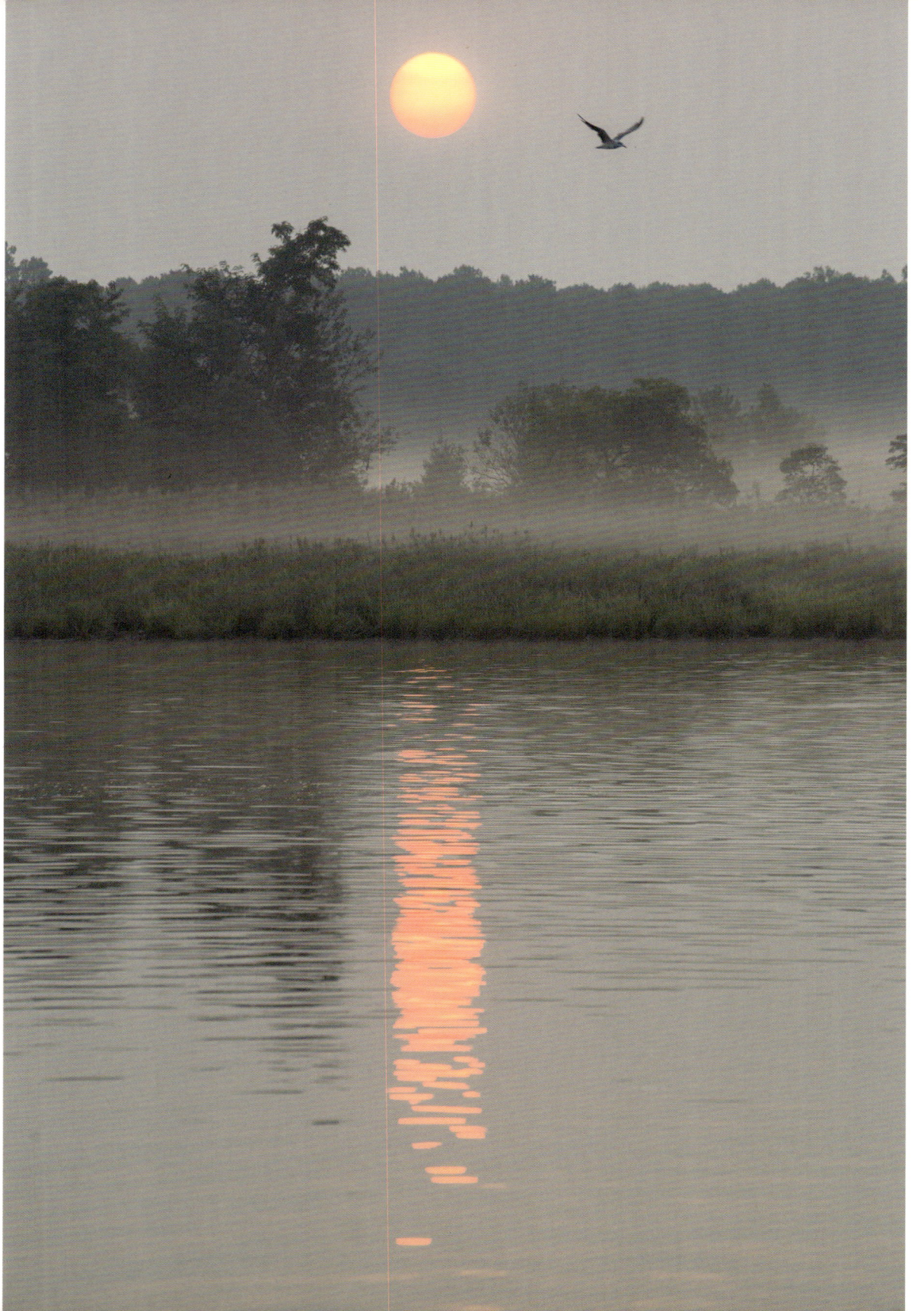

The wildfires out west were creating some unusual atmospheric effects all the way to the East Coast, making the sun appear as a perfect round ball of fire in the sky in this photograph from 2021.

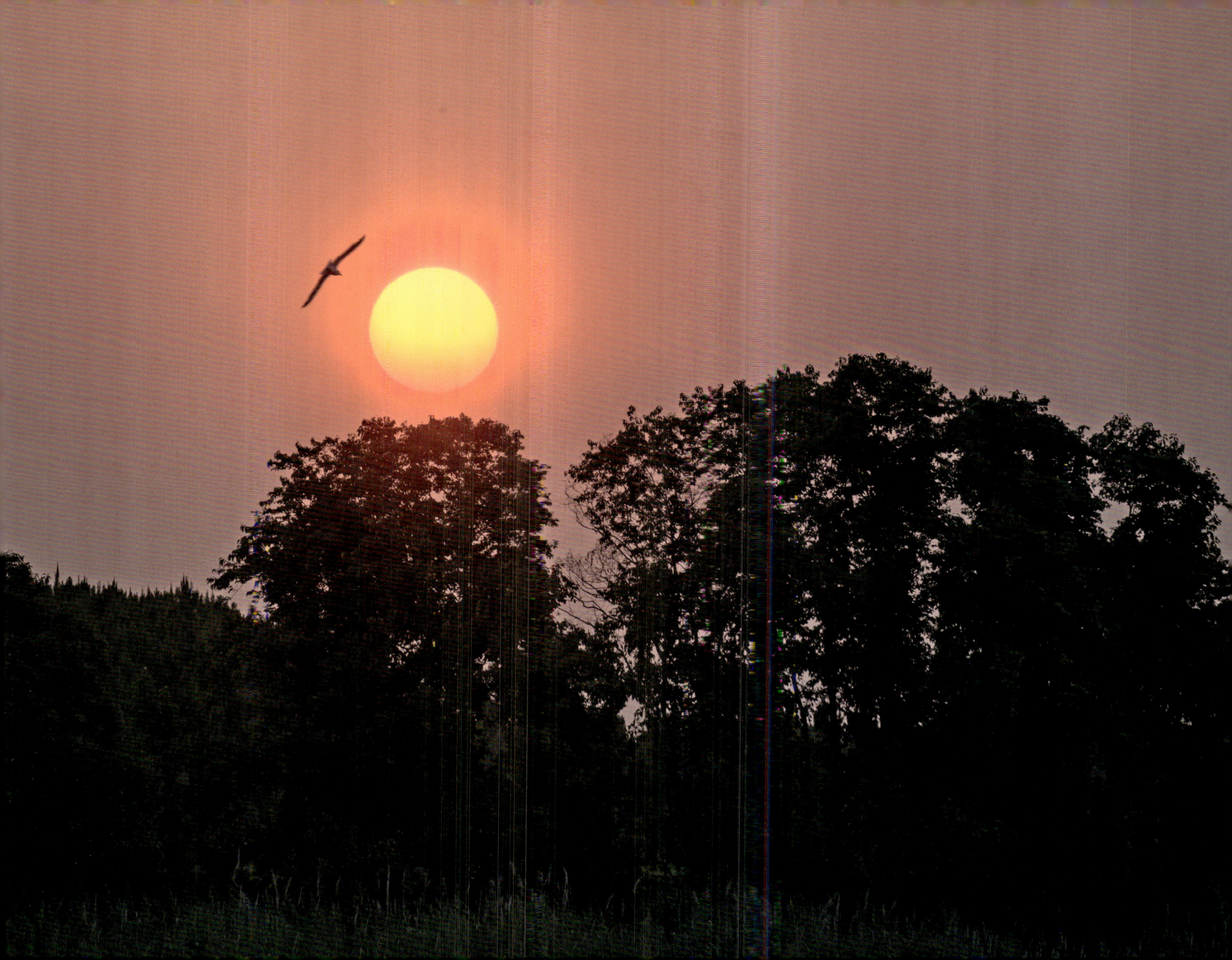

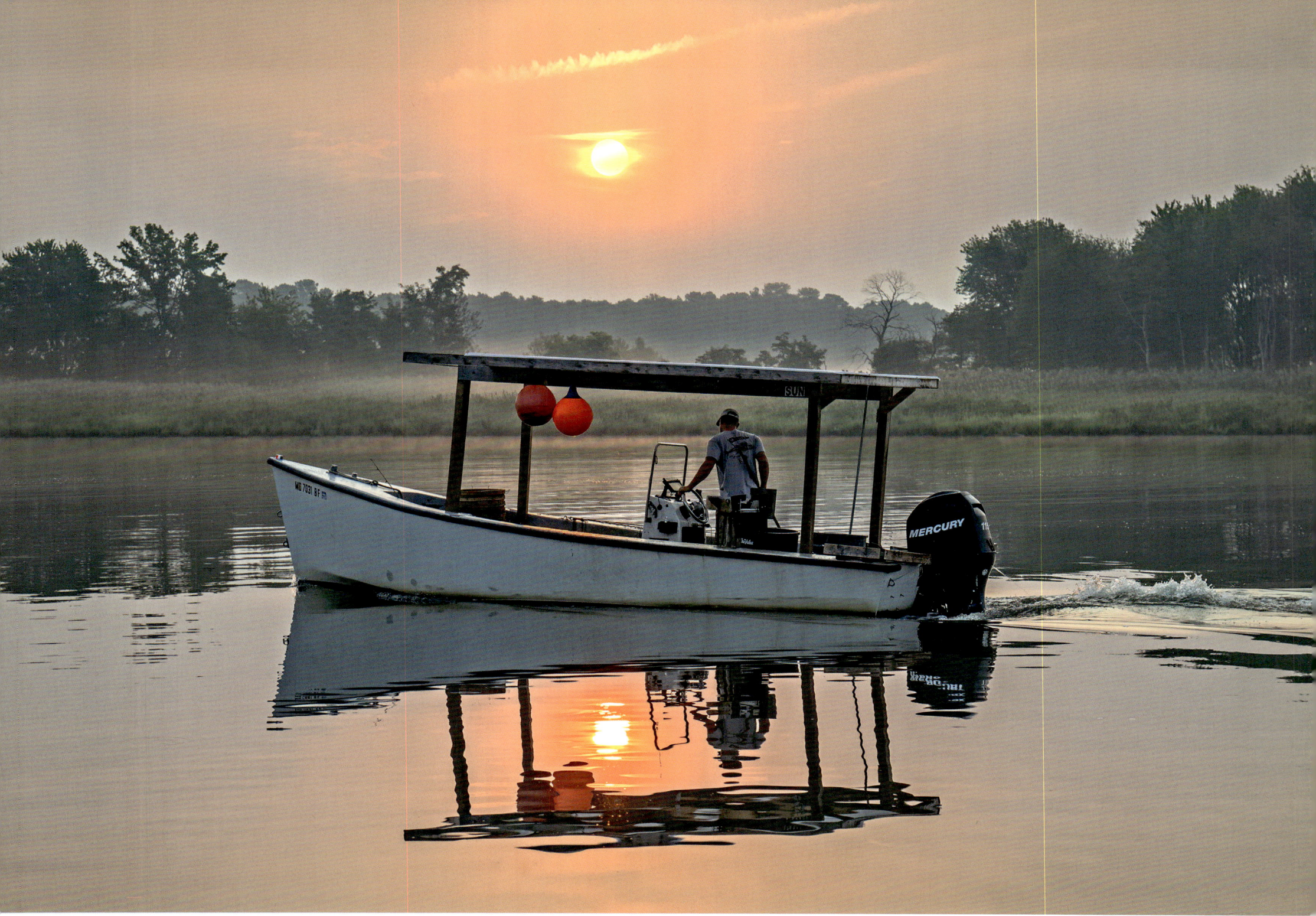

September morn

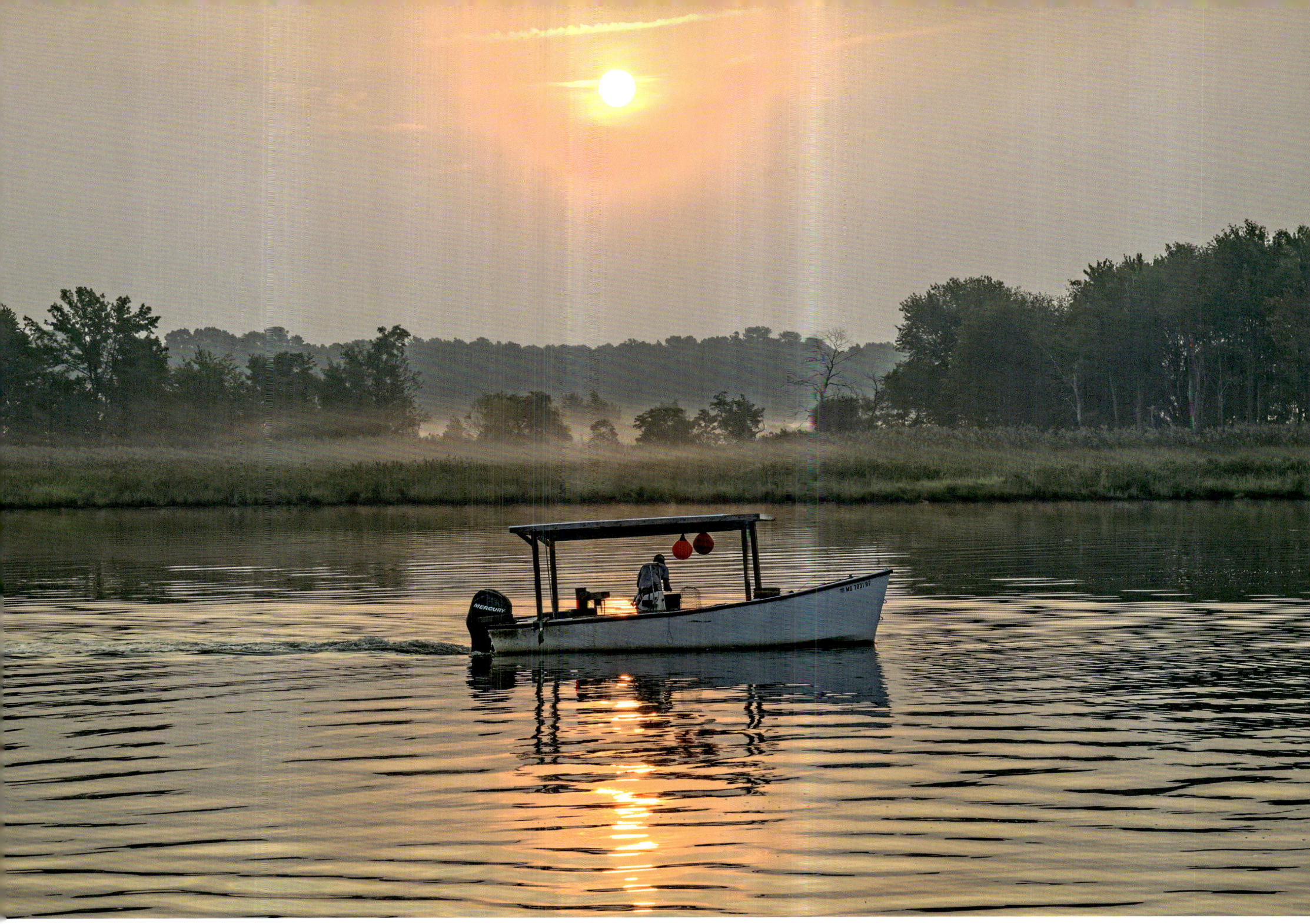

Trotlining on Price Creek

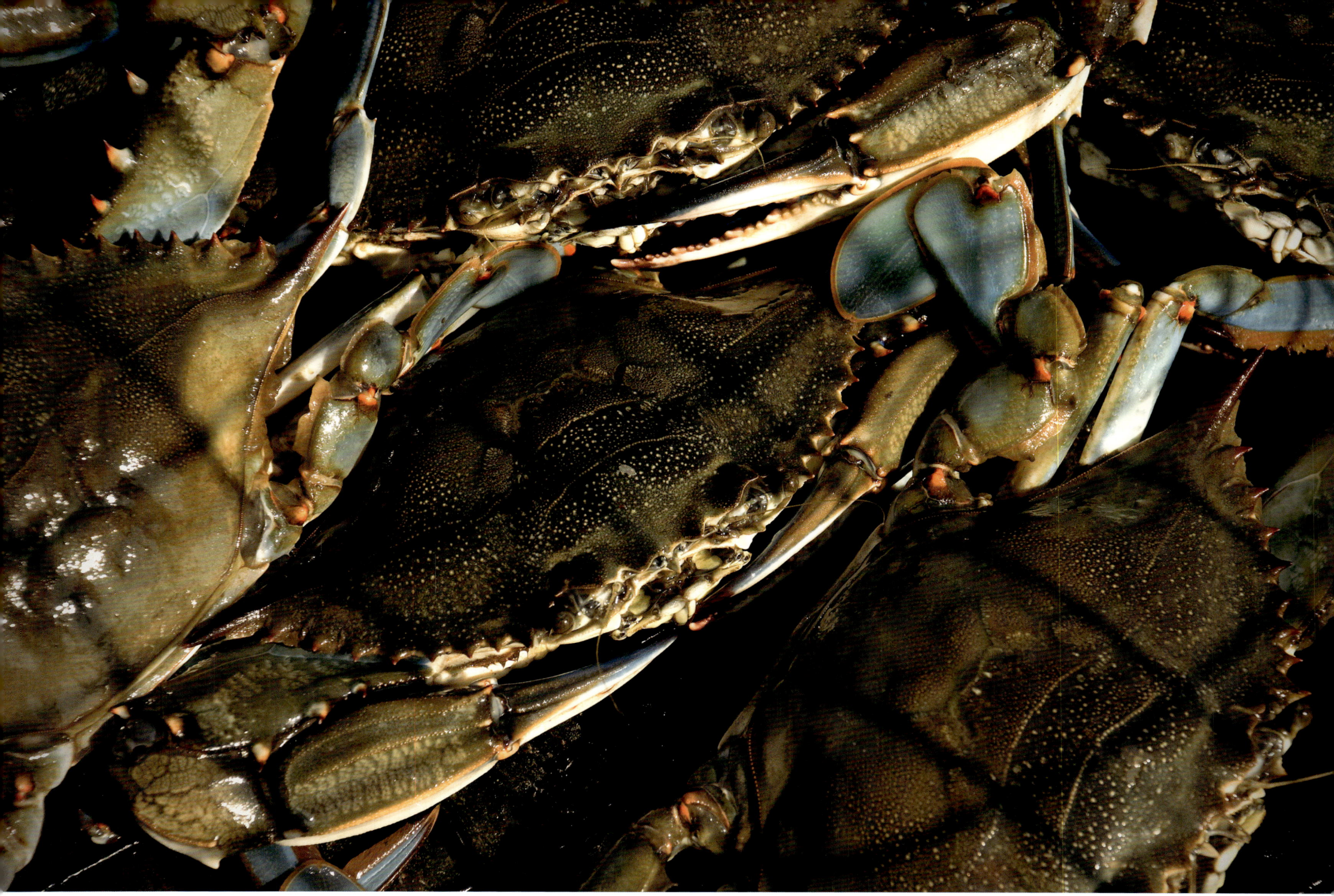

Hope that munching on that chicken neck was worth it for these "beautiful swimmers" headed for the steamer.

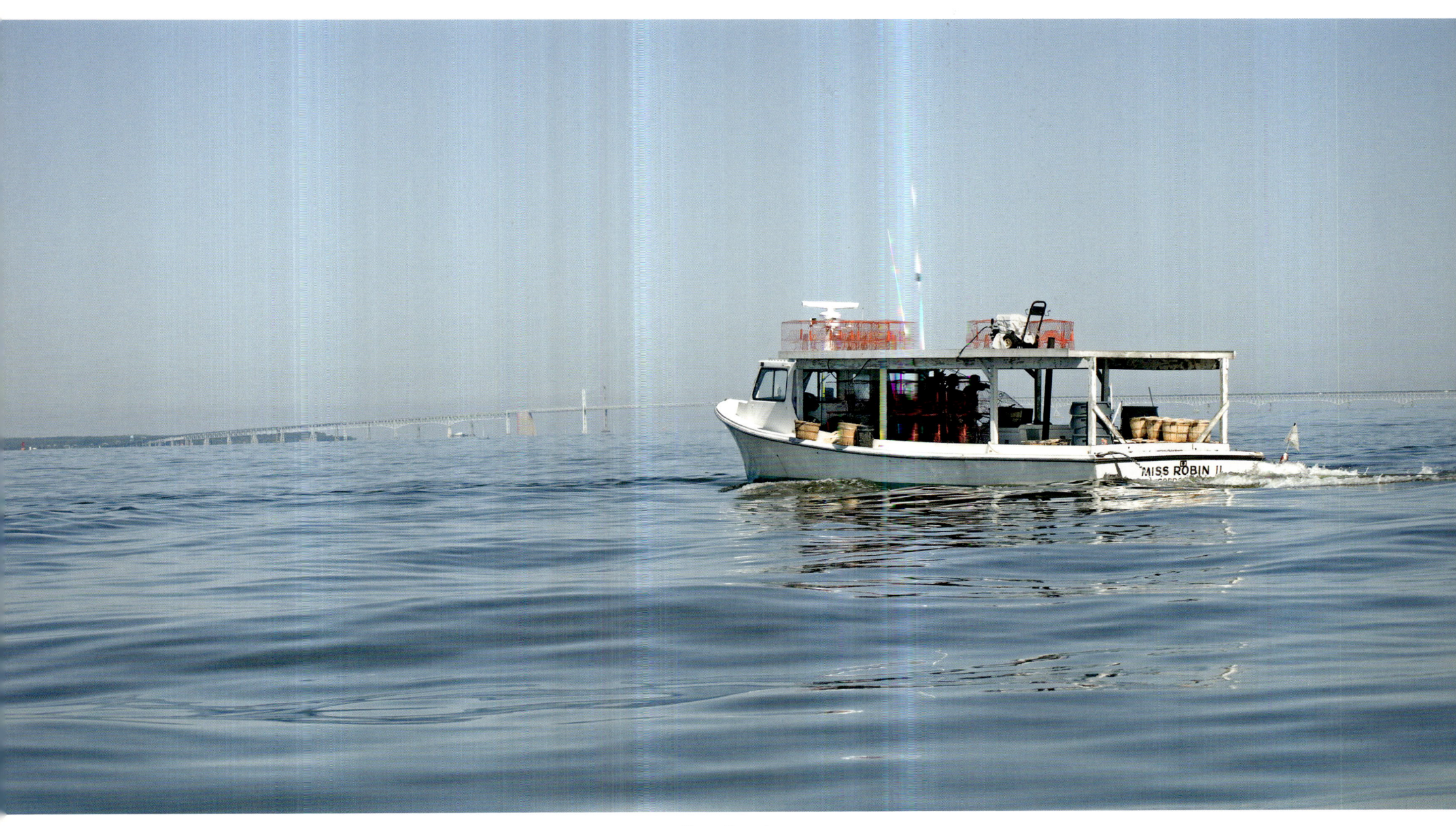

Nice office views

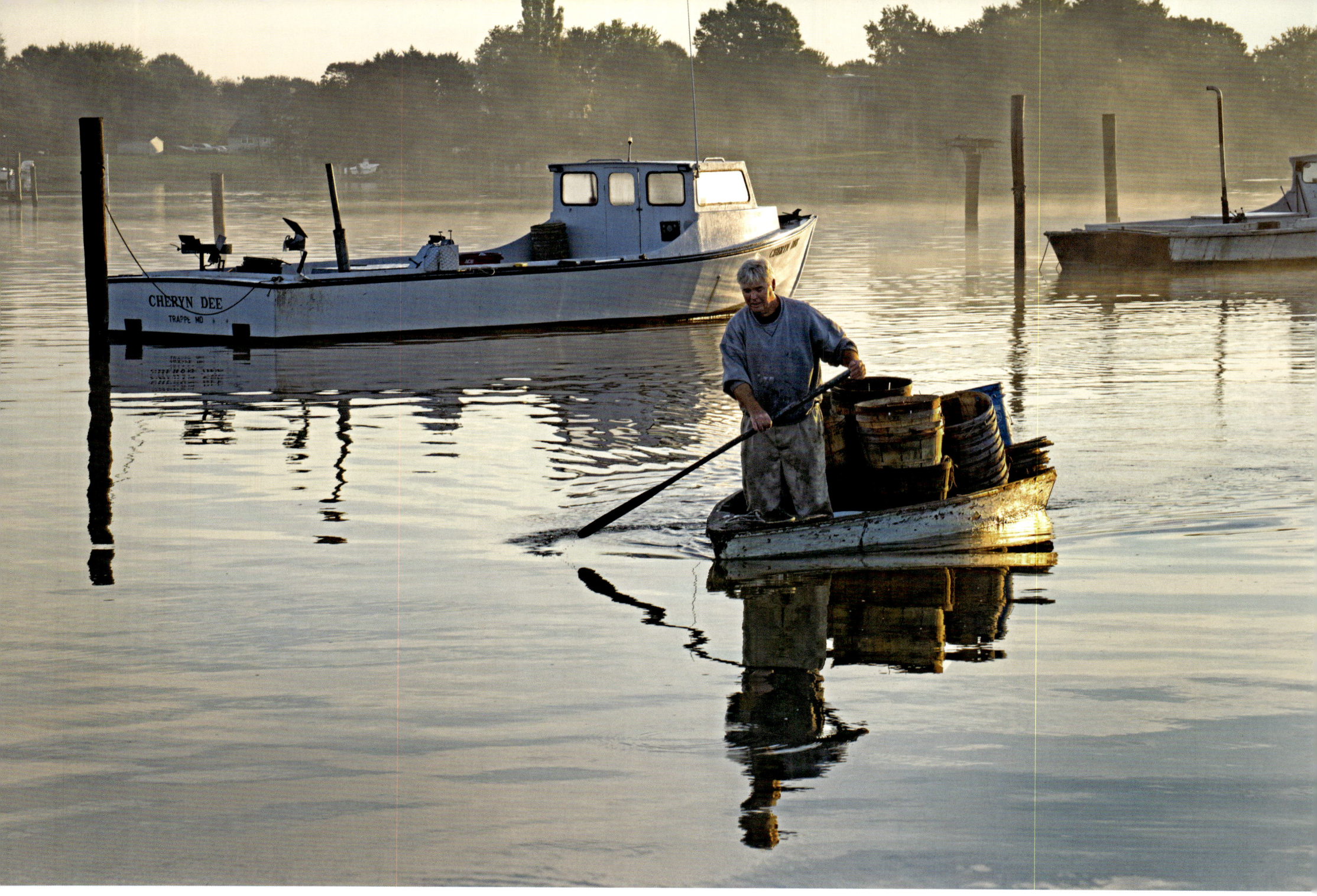

Callin' it quits

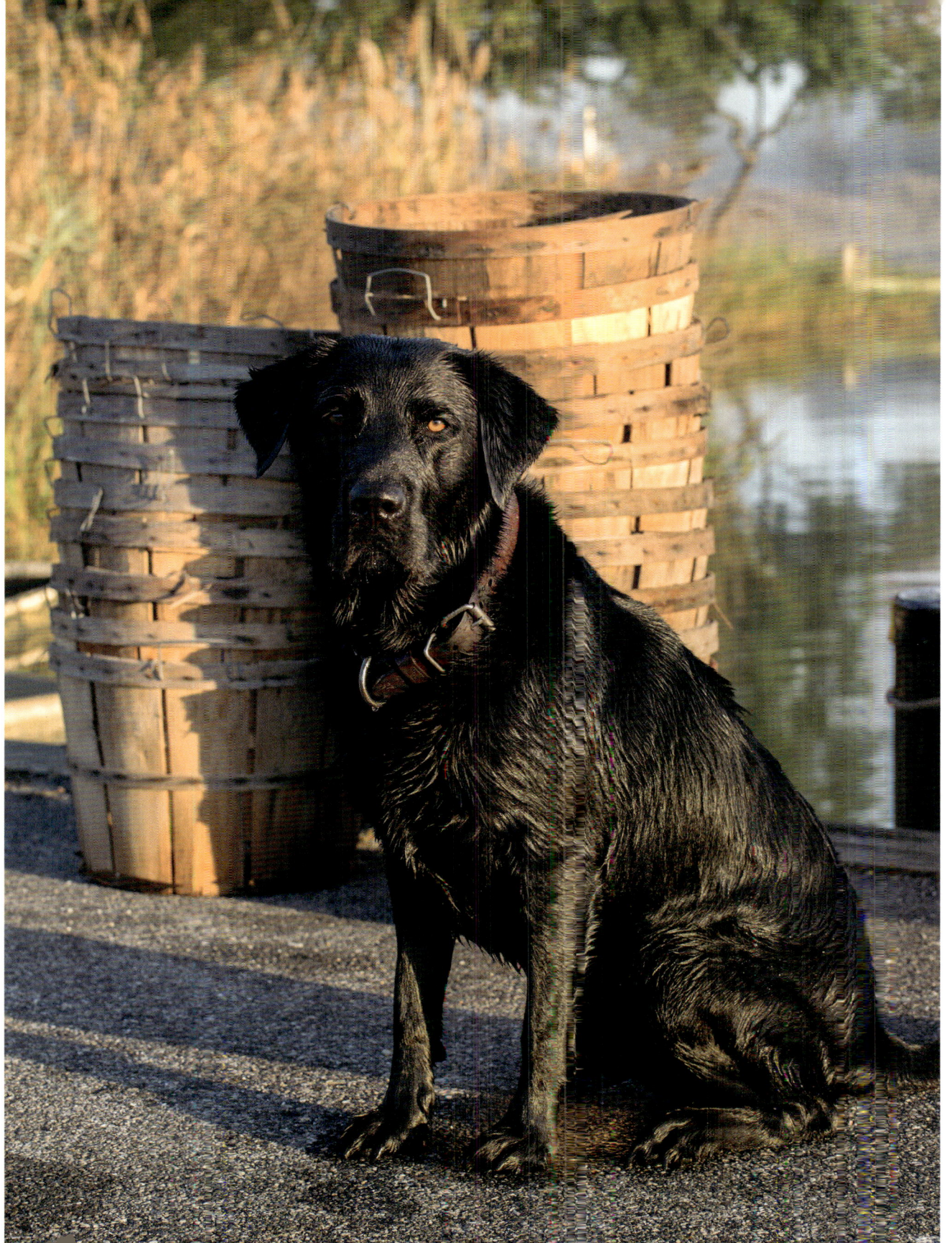

This handsome guy was kind enough to strike a pose for me at Shipping Creek Landing.

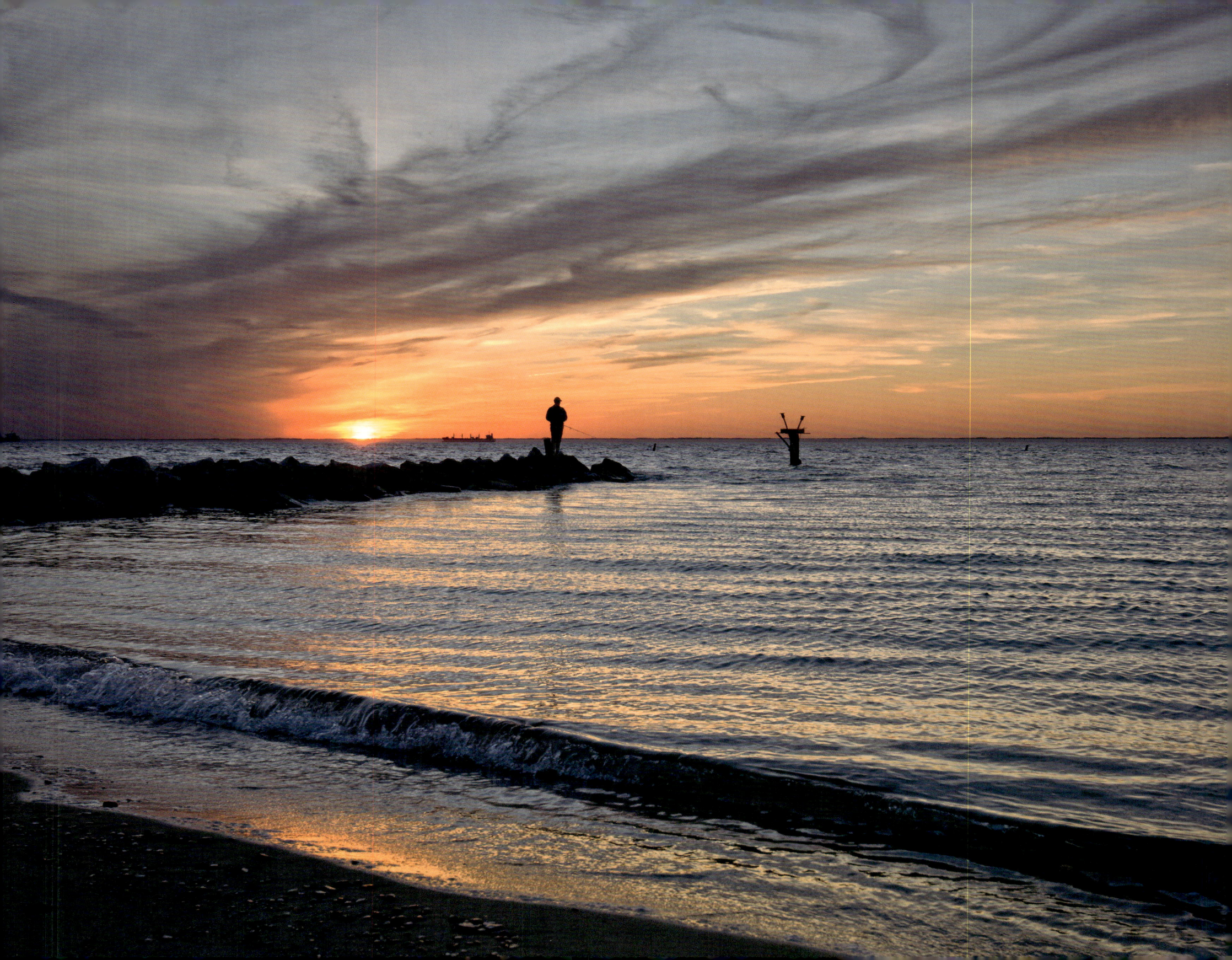

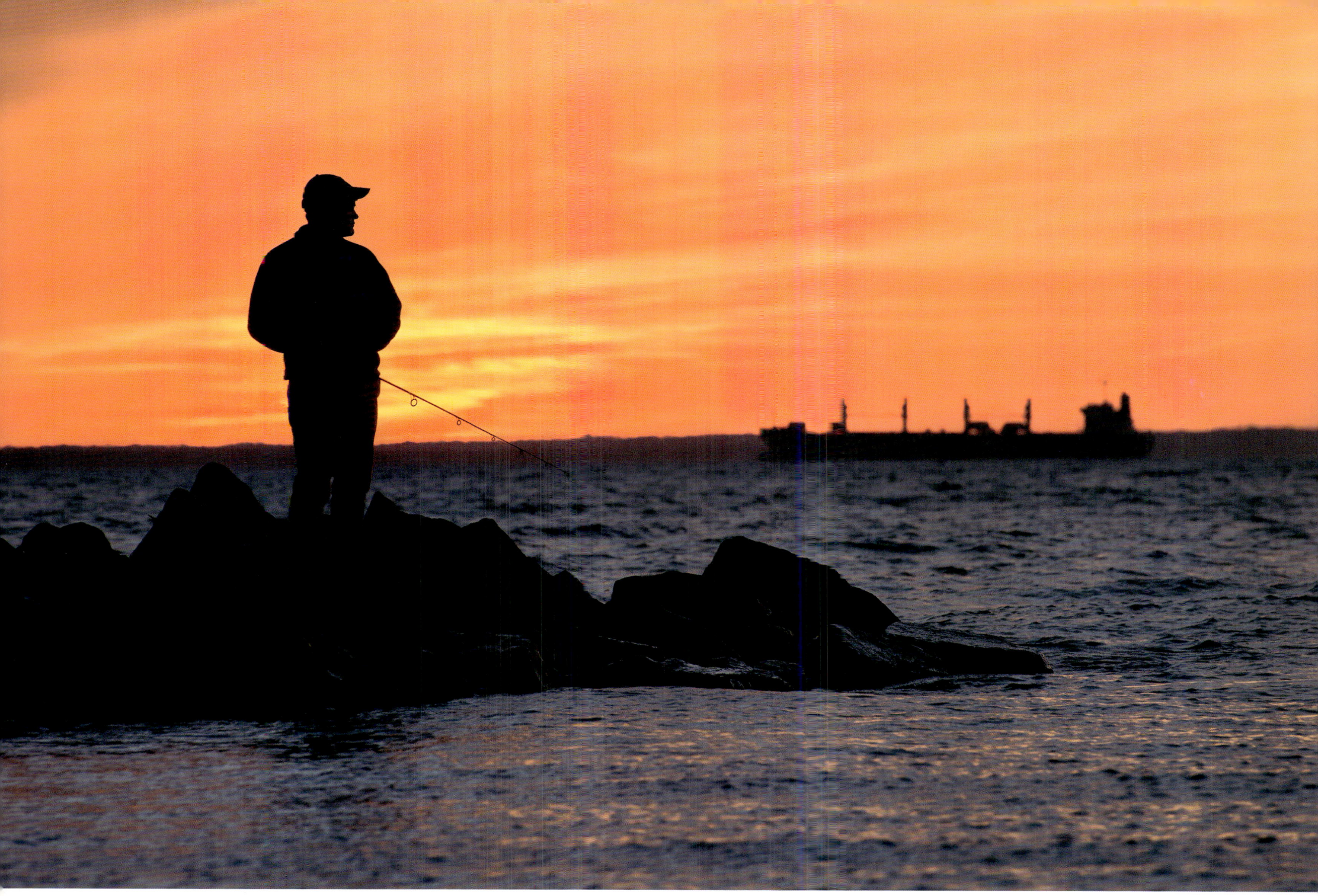

Fishing in the fall

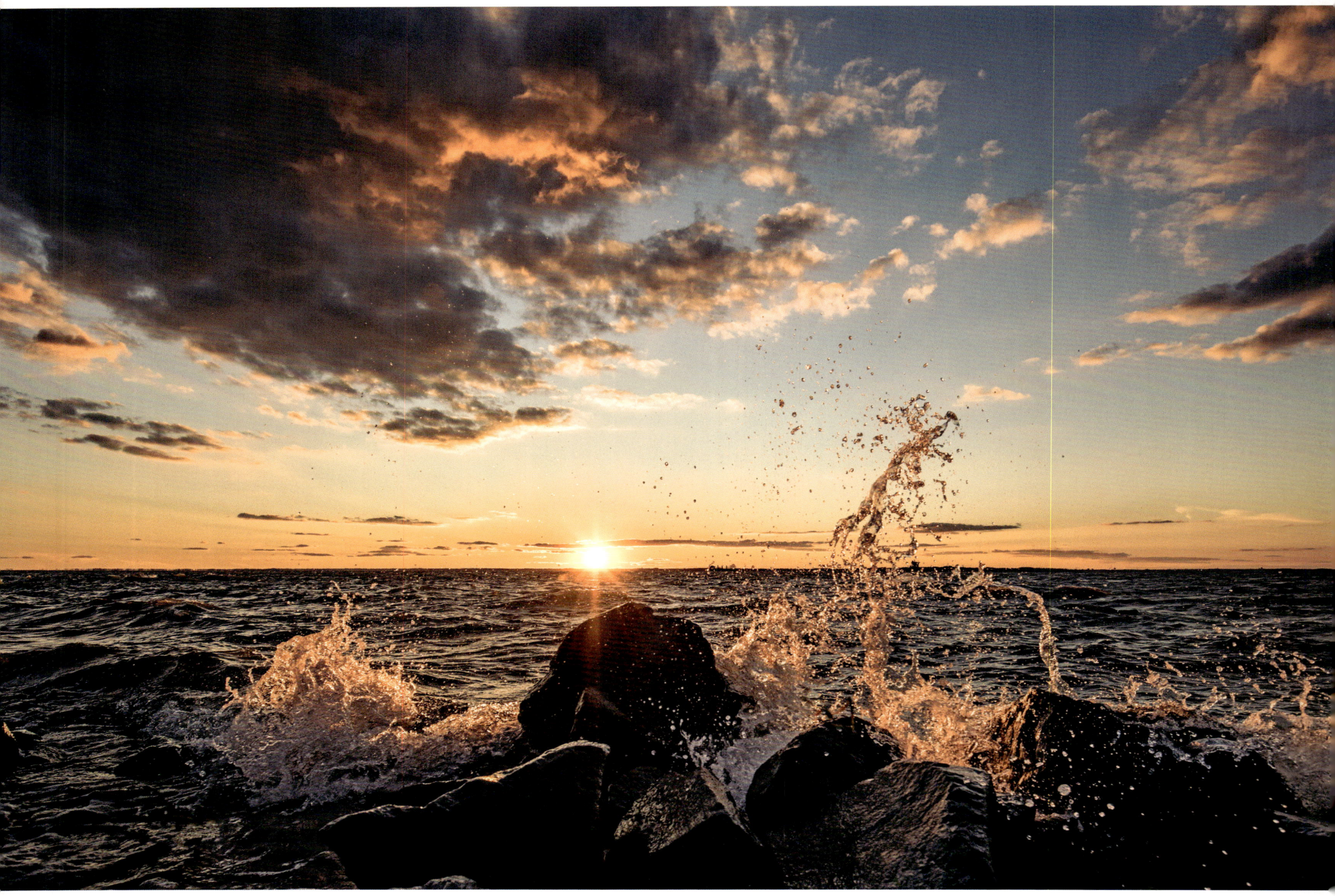

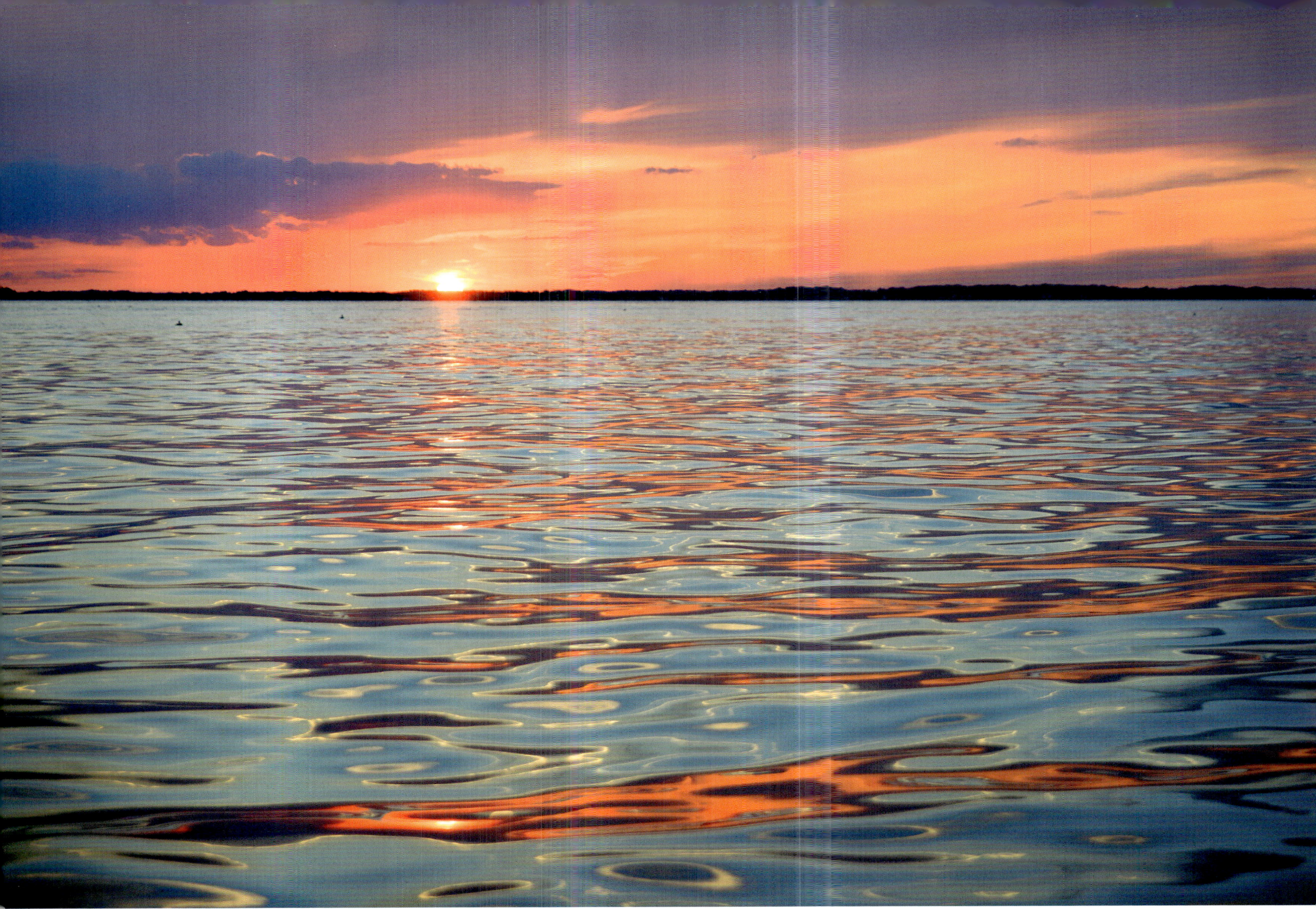

The sunsets are always glorious, whether they are illuminated in the splashing waves
upon the rocks or show the hues of the sun reflecting off the glassy water.

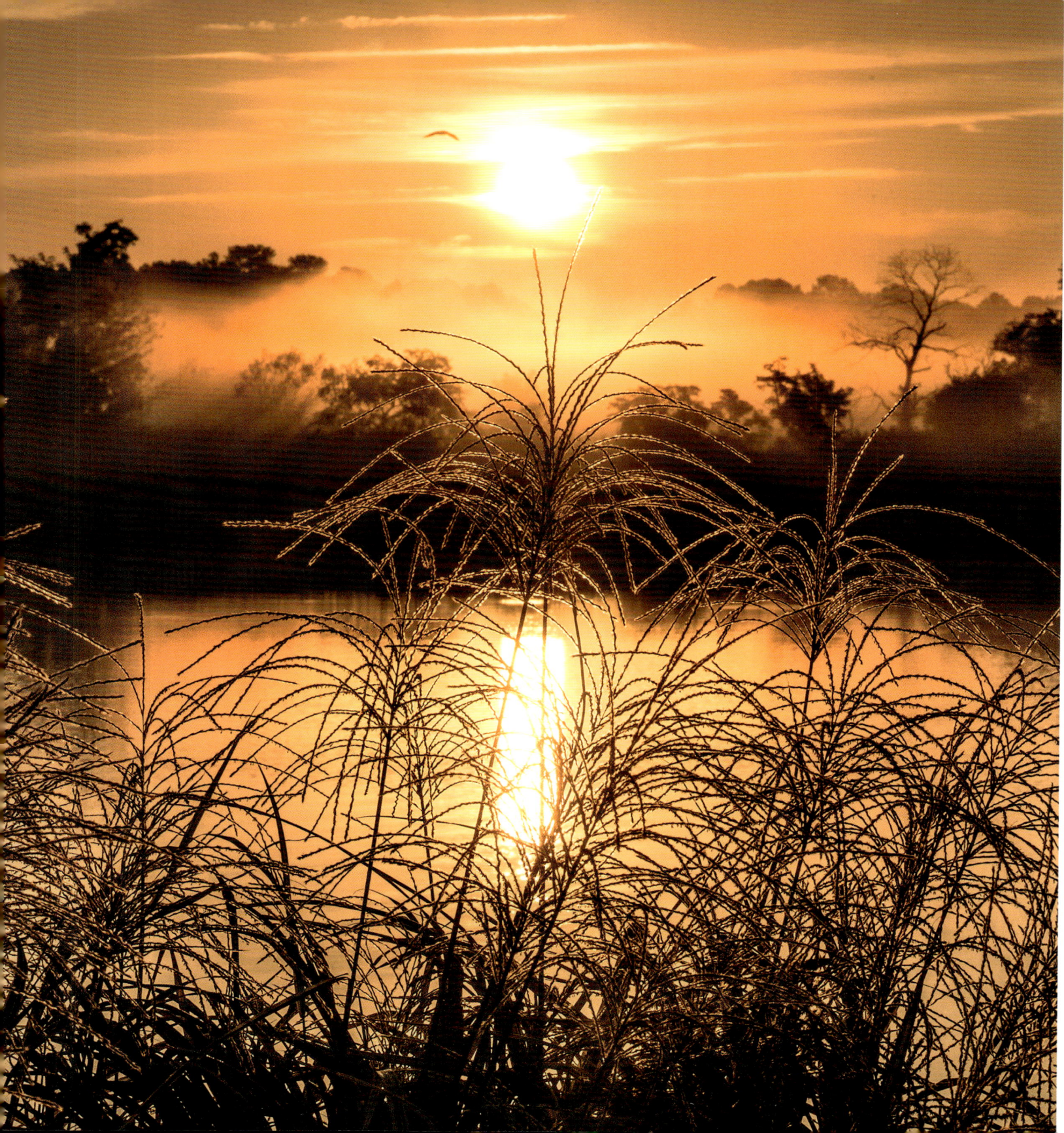

Glistening grasses on
a foggy morning

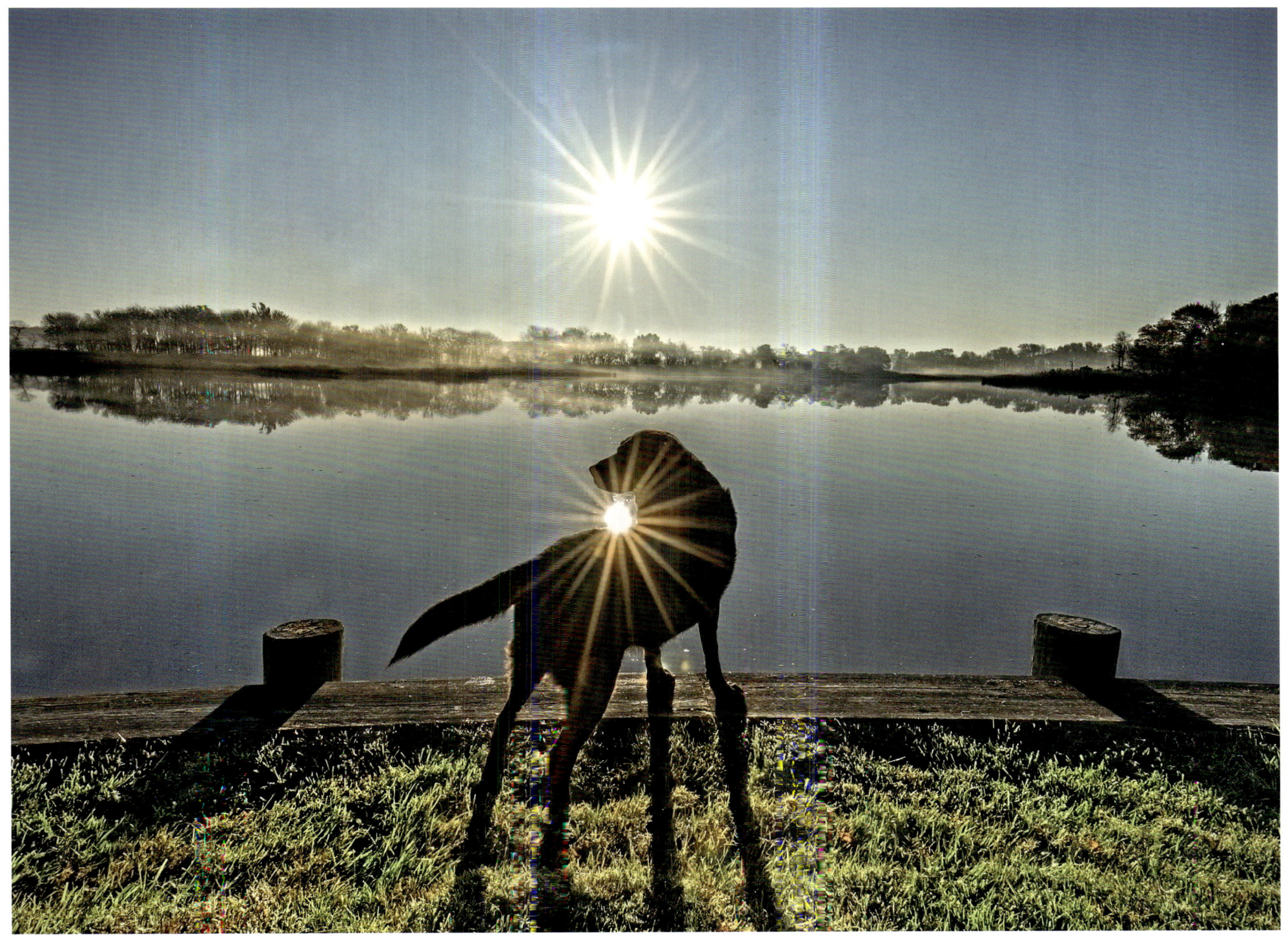

Starstruck

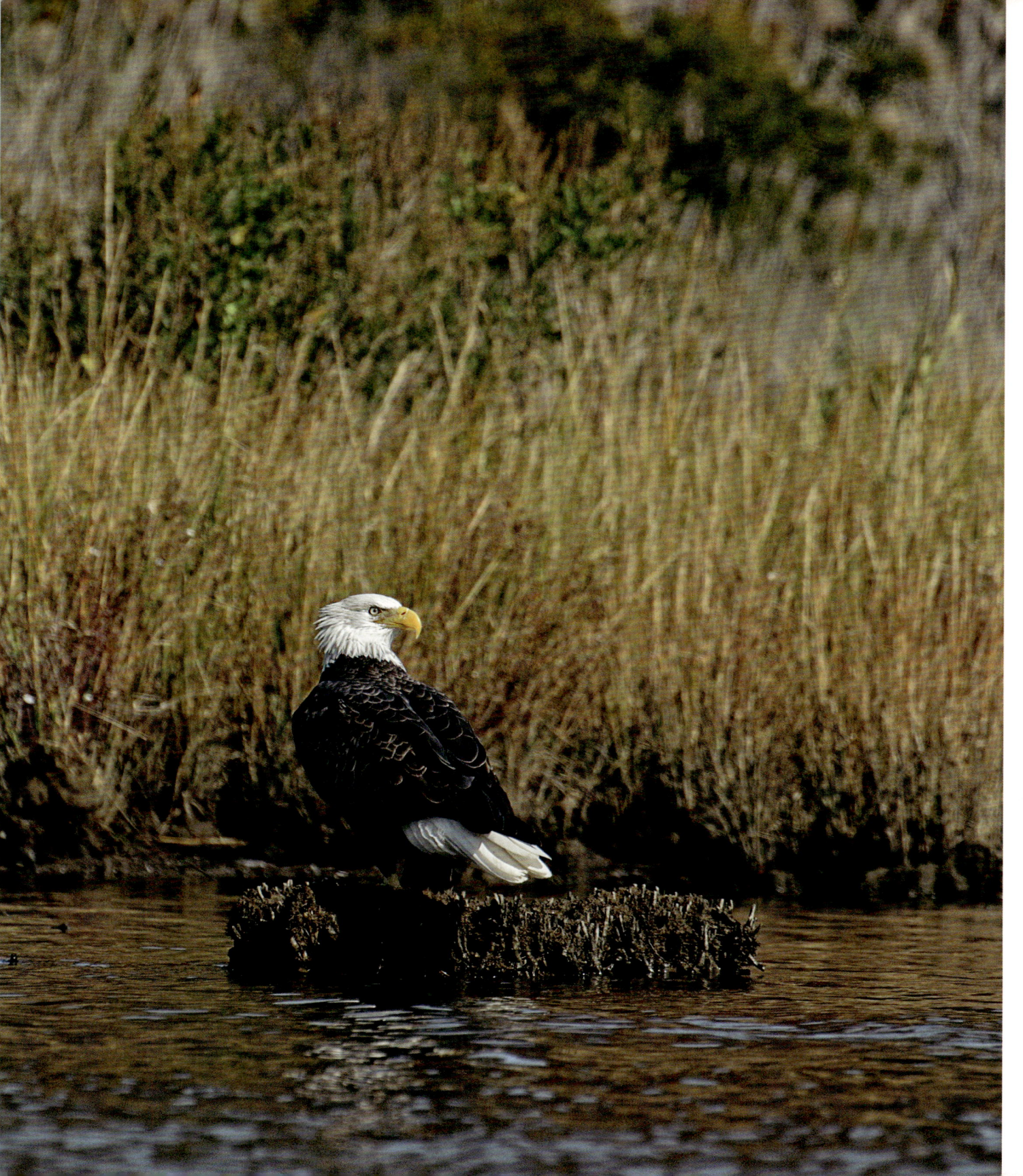

Eagle eye

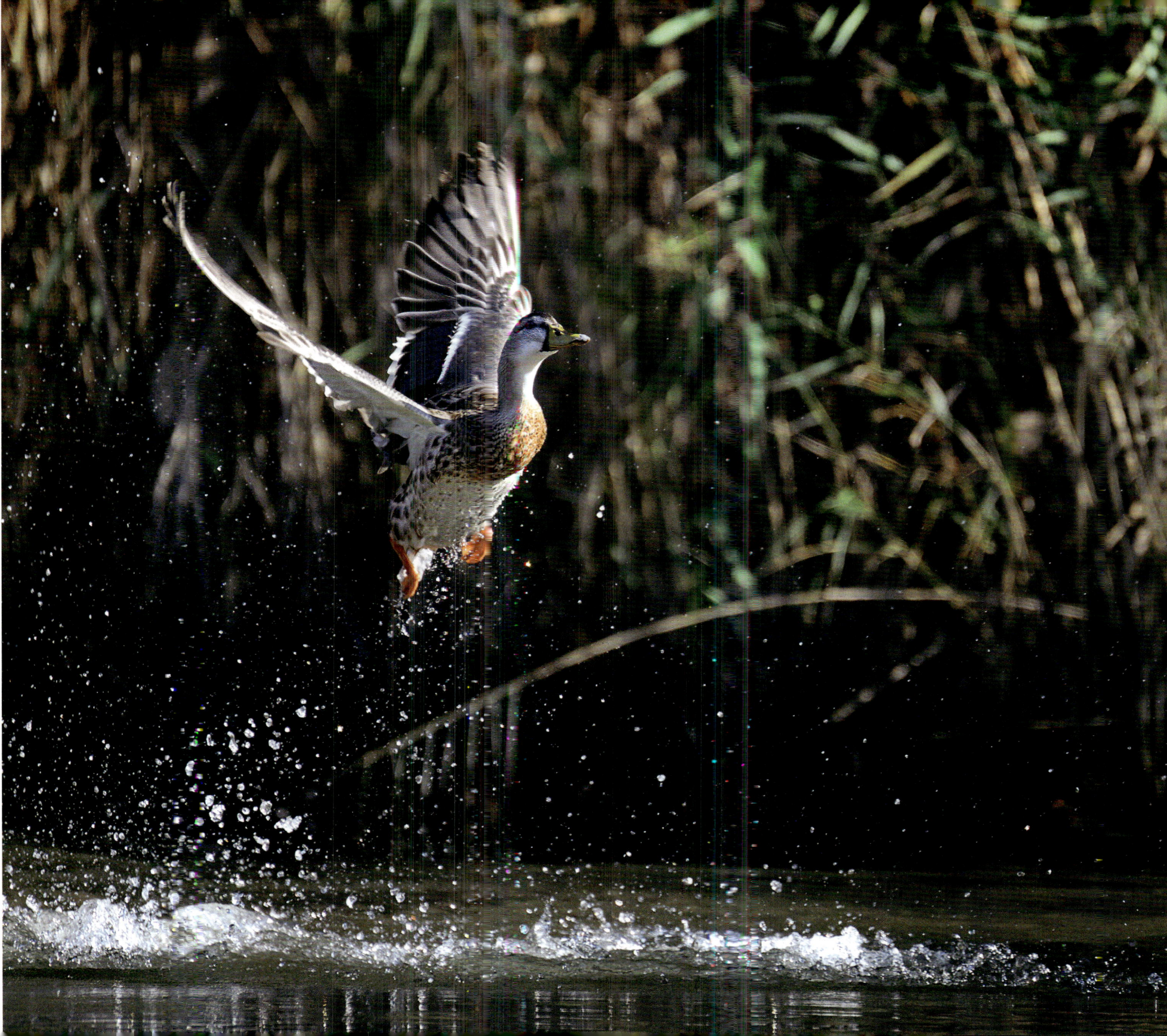

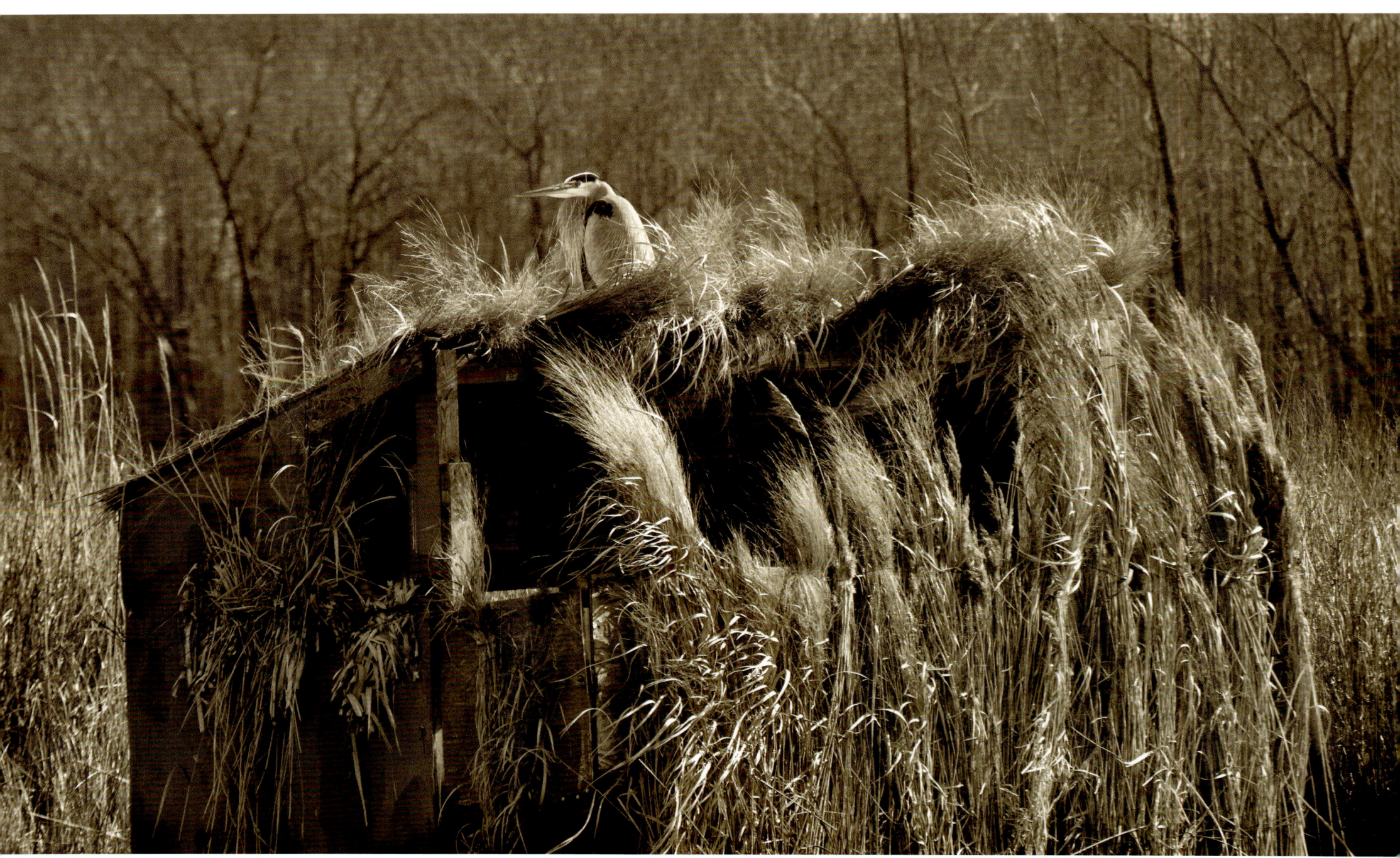

Camouflaged seemed like a fitting title for this picture.

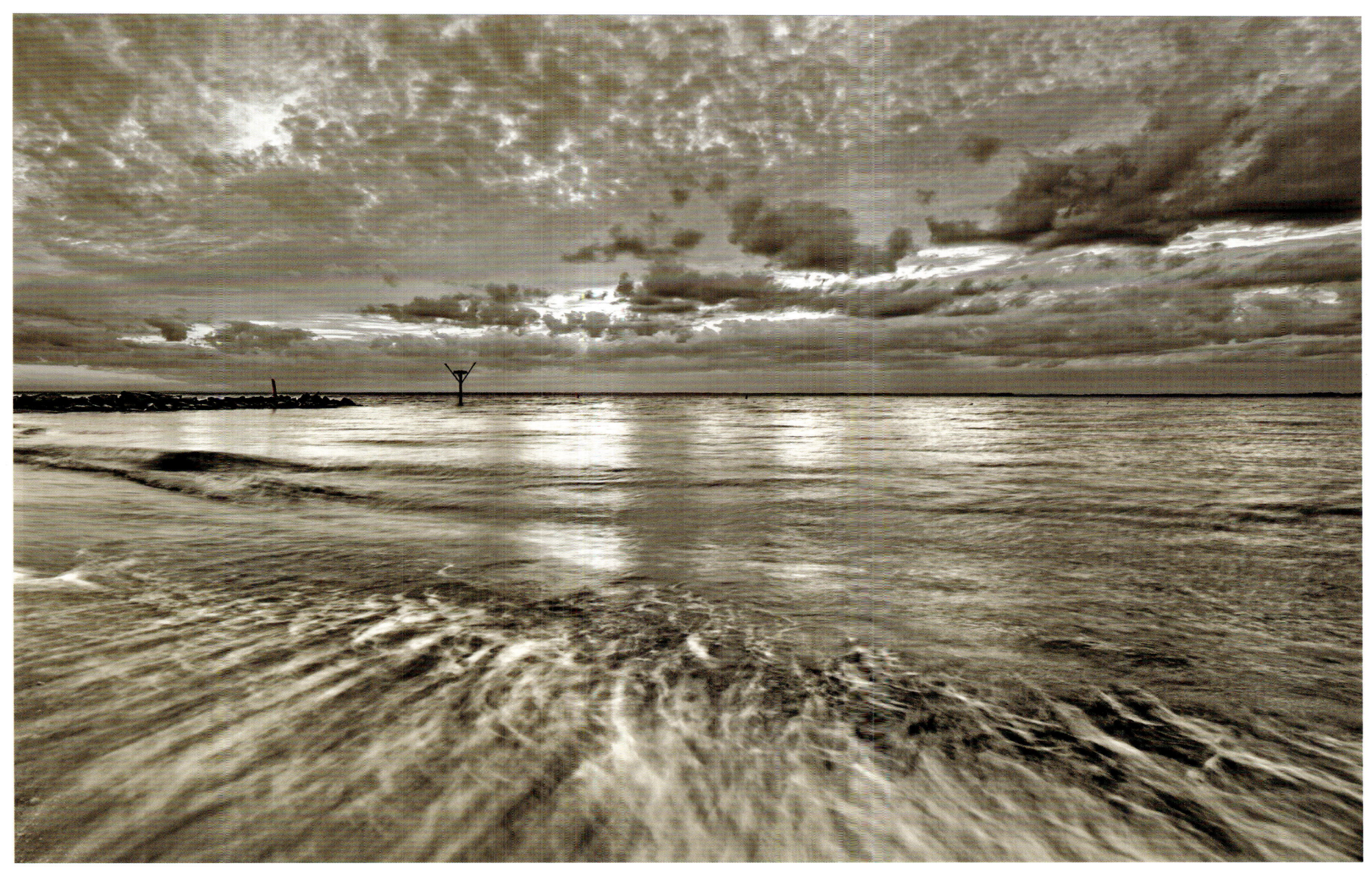

October breezes

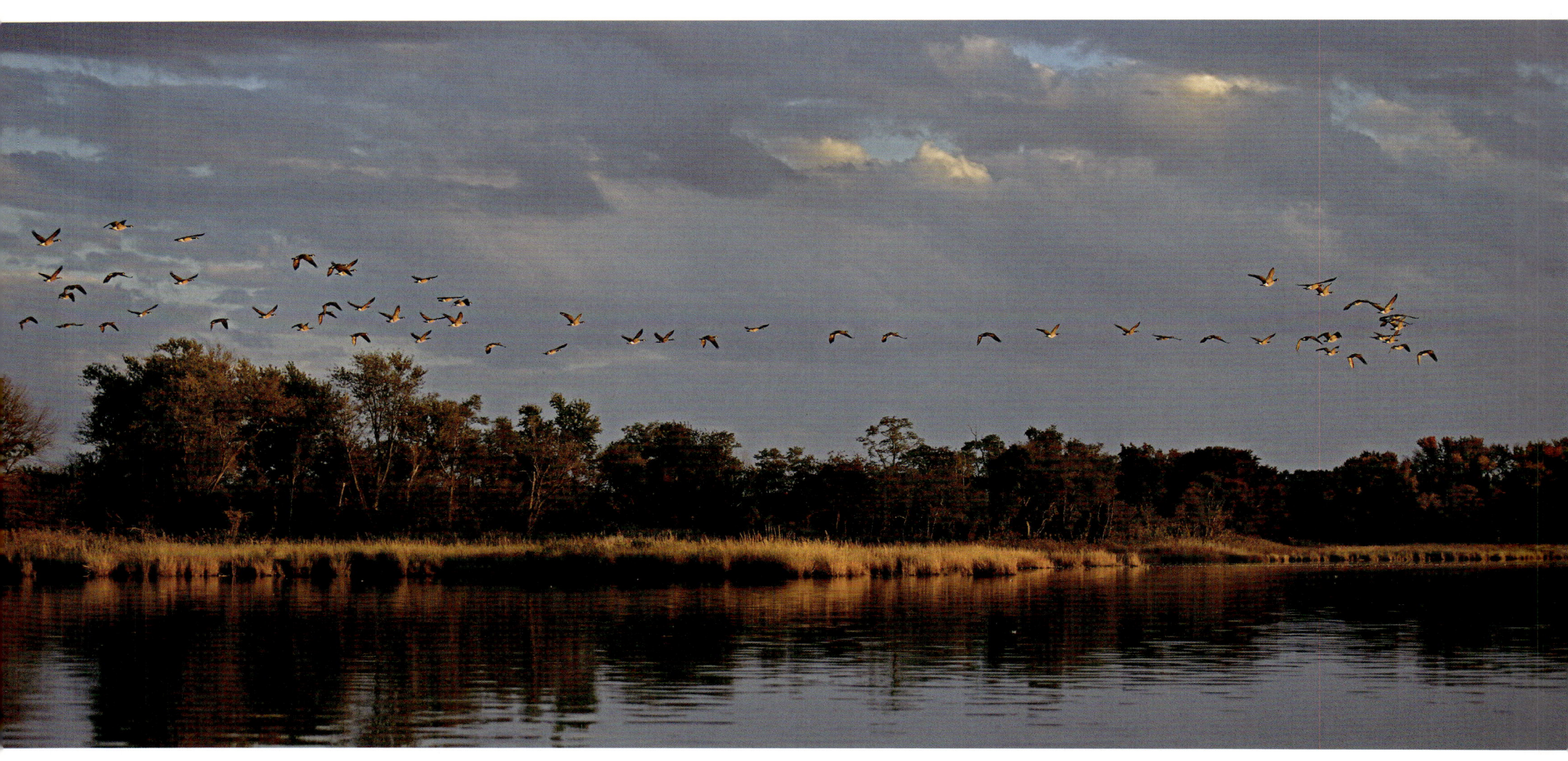

Geese in flight o'er Price Creek

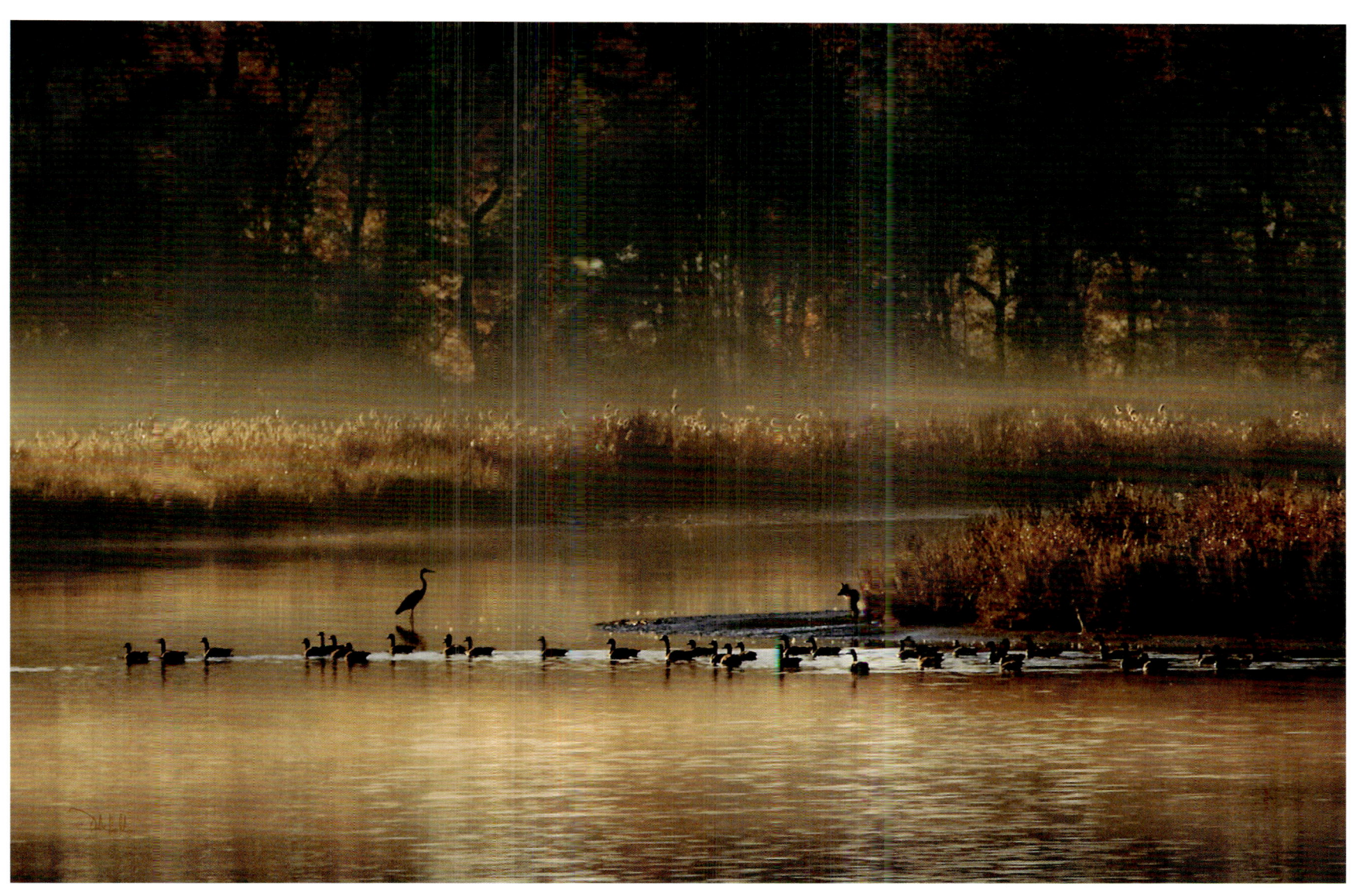

Peace on Price Creek

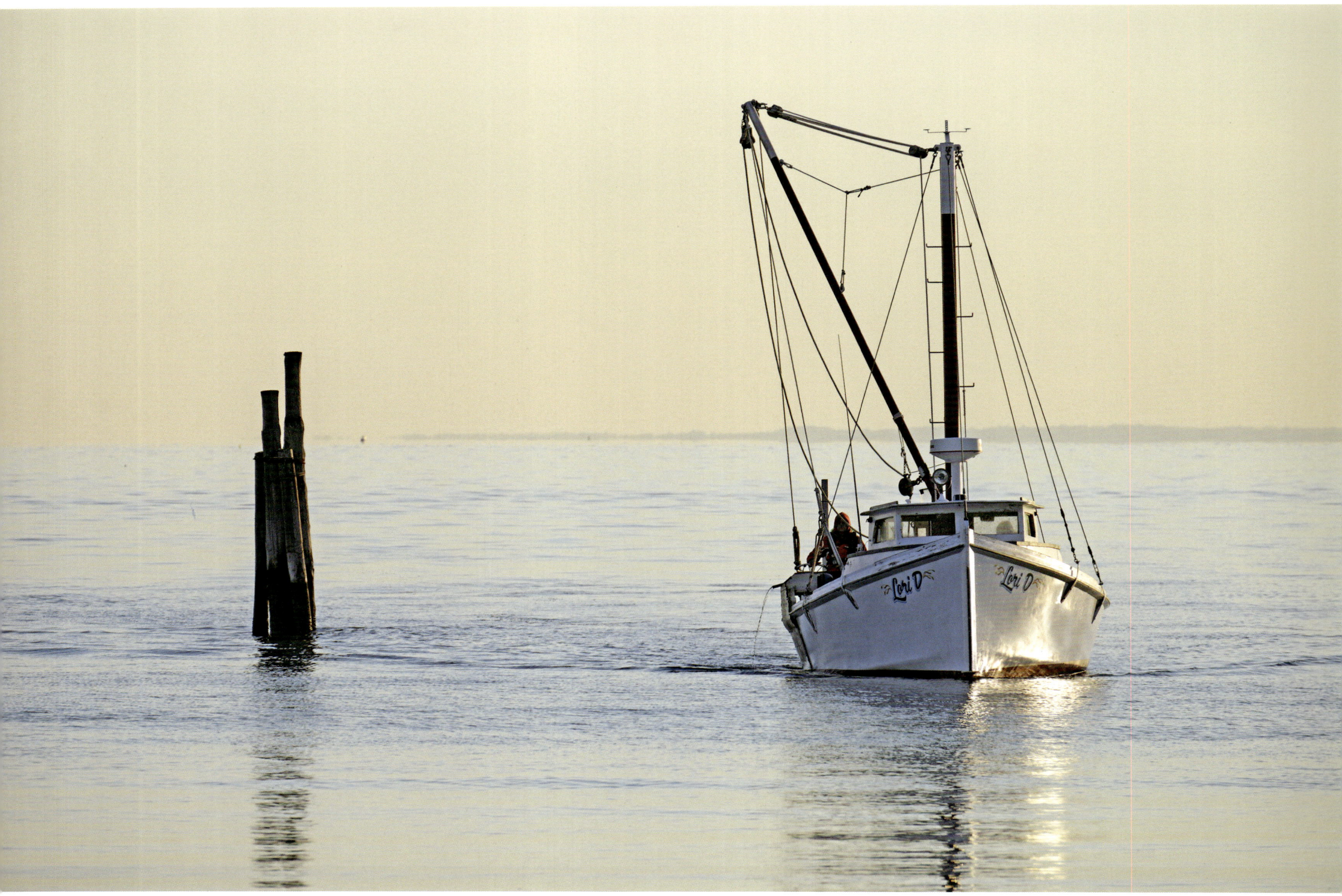

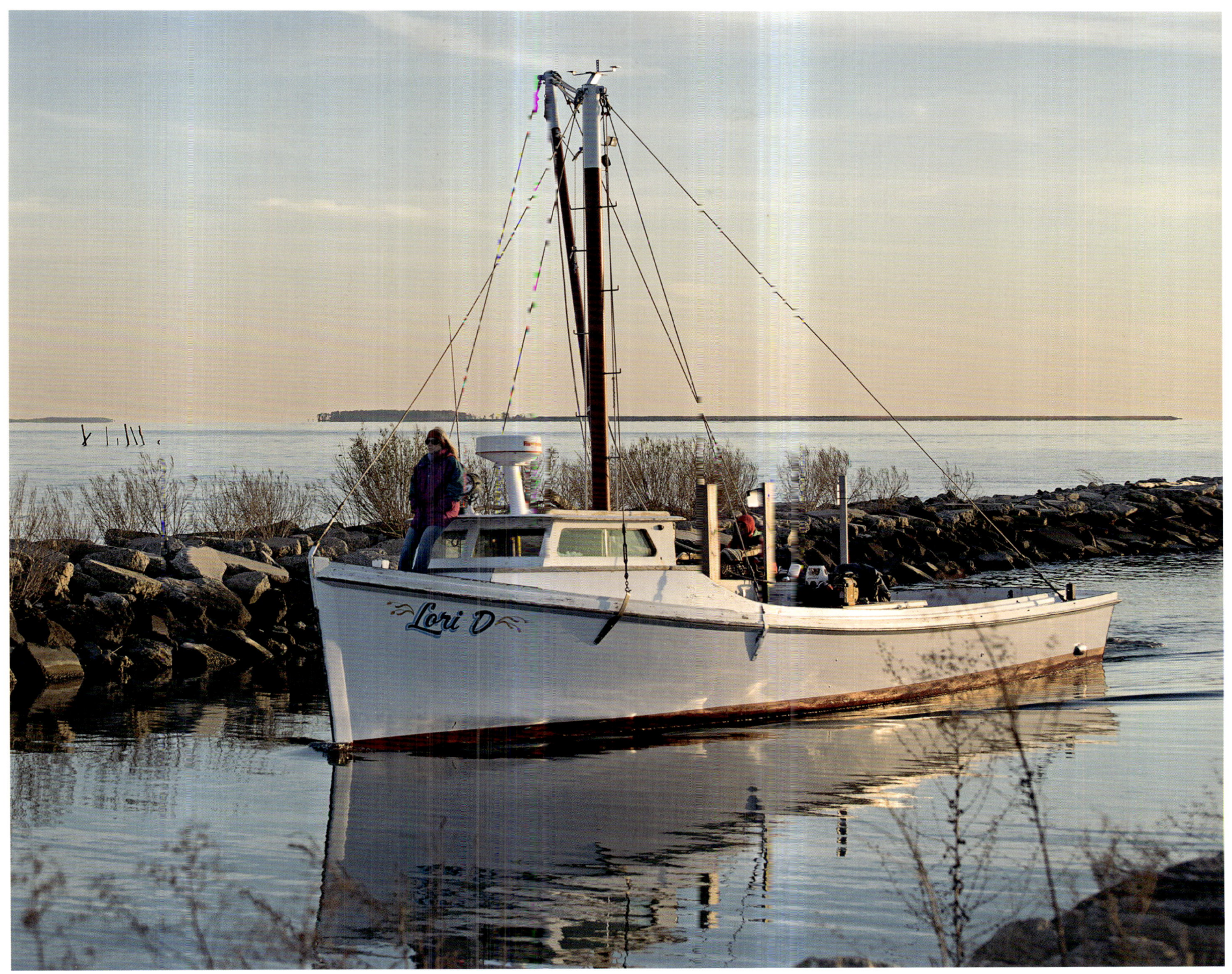

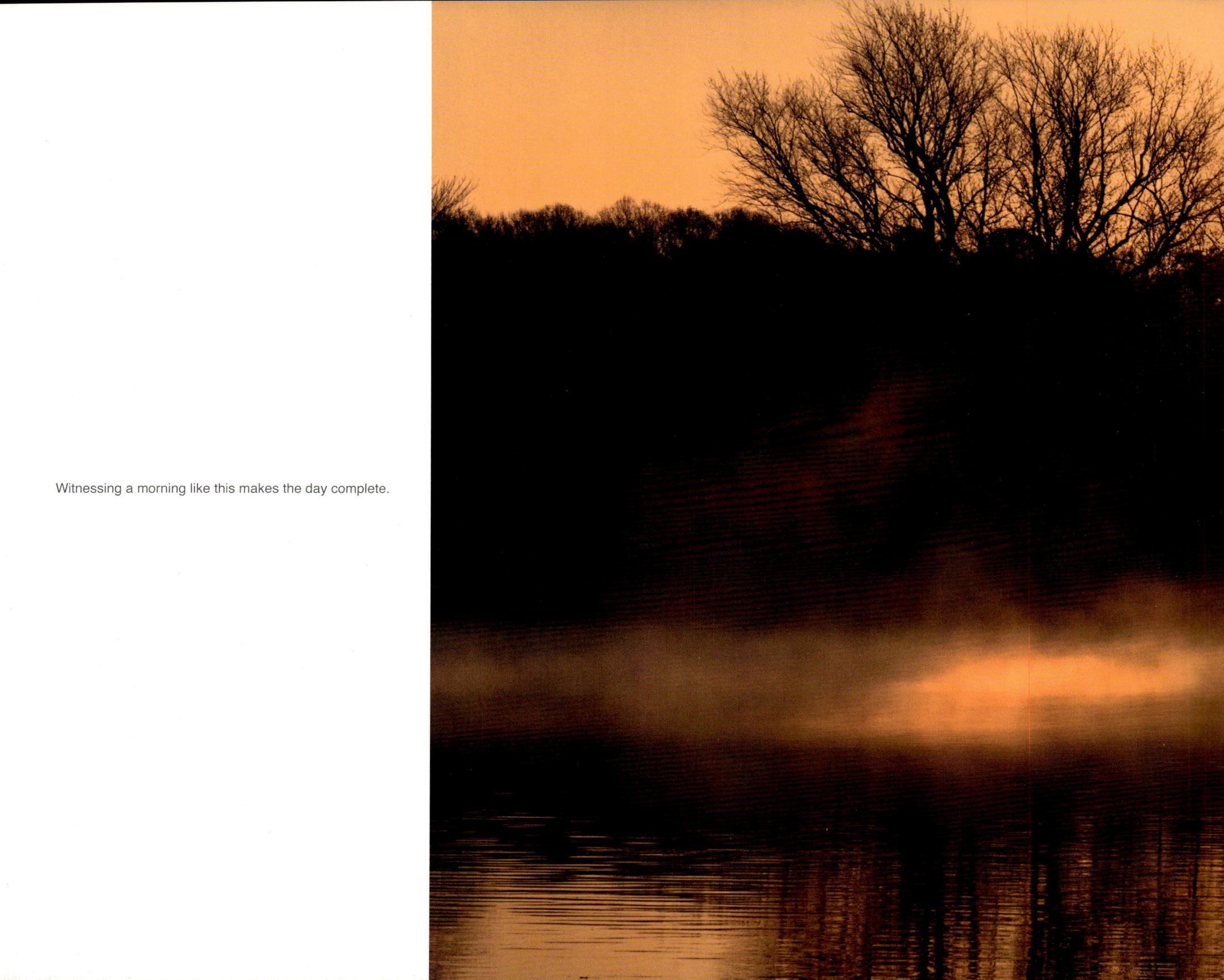

Witnessing a morning like this makes the day complete.

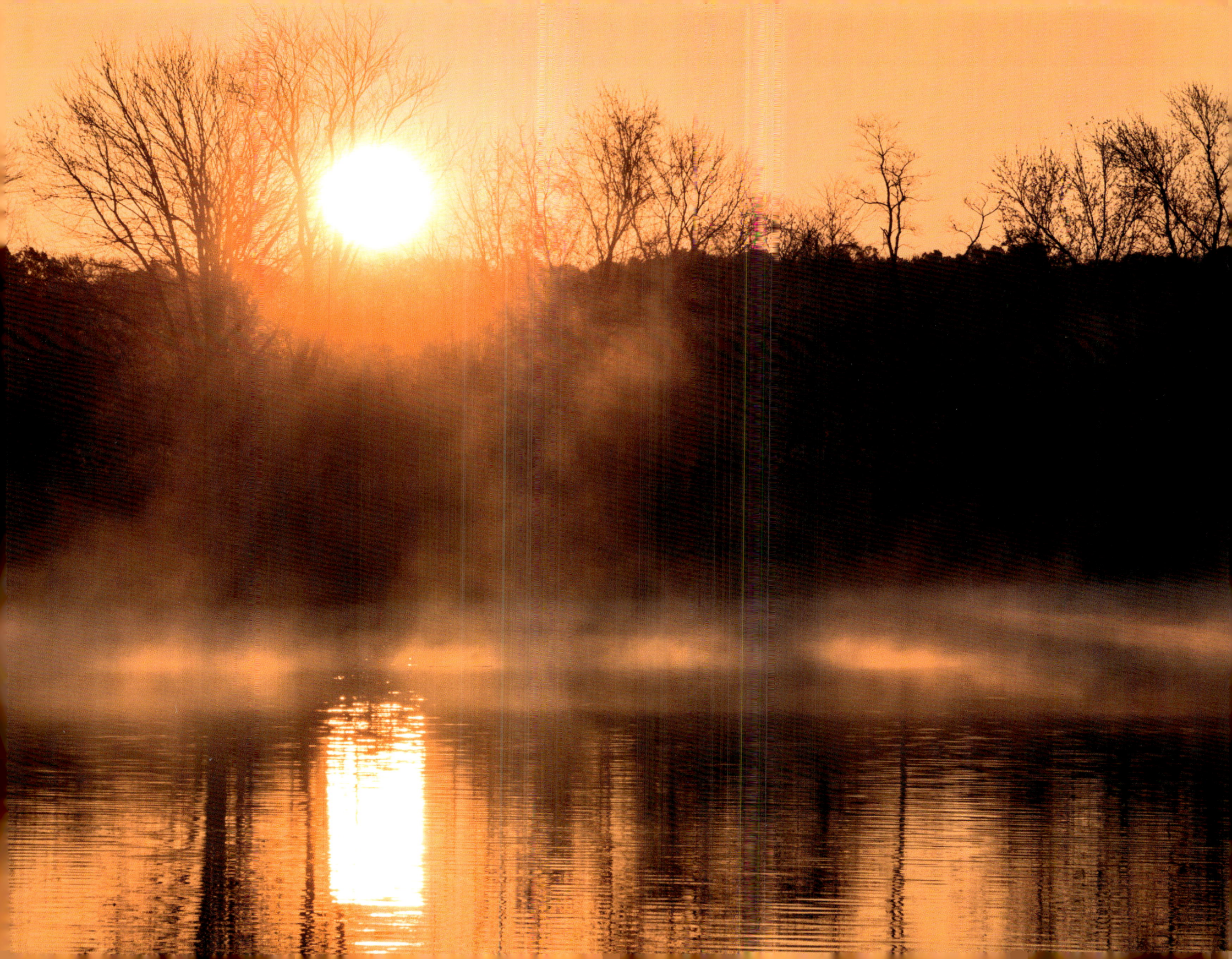

Thank you for joining me on this journey along the shores of Kent Island. It has been a labor of love for me. I hope my book has made you see and appreciate the beautiful, timeless, natural heritage that Kent Island has to offer.

ACKNOWLEDGMENTS

I'd like to thank several businesses and organizations for permission to use photographs taken in the various locations: Queen Anne County Parks and Recreation (Shipping Creek Landing: pp. 1, 33, 174, 175; Romancoke Fishing Pier: pp. 24, 25; shores of Chesapeake Heritage Center: pp. 32, 54; Watermen's Boat Basin: pp. 27, 30, 31, 63, 65; Kent Narrows Landing: p. 94; Kent Narrows East boardwalk: pp. 158, 159; Ferry Point Park: p. 95; Terrapin Nature Park: p. 100; and Matapeake Fishing Pier: pp. 17, 18); Kent Point Marina: pp. 10, 12, 13, 14, 15, 16, 17, 26, 27, 58, 59, 60, 139; Queen Anne Marina: pp. 20, 28, 34, 35, 38, 48, 69, 73, 81, 84, 85, 90, 103, 108, 109, 115, 122, 123, 124, 132, 135, 153, 154, 176, 177, 185; Kentmorr Marina: pp. 56, 67, 68, 97, 139; Chesapeake Bay Beach Club: pp. 121, 126; Bay Bridge Marina: p. 120; and Libbey's Coastal Kitchen & Cocktails: pp. 104, 105.

I'd especially like to thank Jack Broderick, president of the Kent Island Heritage Society, for his kind words and his insightful description provided in the foreword, as well as John Conley, a board member of the Kent Island Heritage Society, for his help and thoughts.

Additionally I would like to thank my editors, Cheryl Weber and Ann Charles, for their patience, knowledge, and expertise; Pete Schiffer and staff at Schiffer Publishing; and Alan James Robinson (themapguy.com), as well as Jeff McCormick and Janet McCormick (the owners of *Lady Helen*), Patrick Buckel (the waterman trotlining with his sweet Lab, May), and Dean Steele (owner of *My Destiny*) for helping me "get the shot."

SOURCES

Bishop, Doug. "Community Mourns Passing of 'a Great American,' Capt. Warren Butler." *Kent Island Bay Times*, July 16, 2021. https://www.myeasternshoremd.com/qa/community/news/community-mourns-passing-of-a-great-american-capt-warren-butler/article_51f07bcb-79b8-5449-90ae-2fc59d8f1e31.html.

"*Ever Forward*, Now Unstuck, to Resume Norfolk Port Call." *Chesapeake Bay Magazine*, April 18, 2022. https://chesapeakebaymagazine.com/video-ever-forward-now-unstuck-to-resume-norfolk-port-call/.

Ruffner, Jennifer Gayman. "History of Kent Island." Kent Island Heritage Society. https://kentislandheritagesociety.org/kent-island-history/